Question Bank for Exam Success

COMPUTER SCIENCE WITH PYTHON

Class XII CBSE (083)

by

Gurpreet Kaur

Freelance Consultant and Trainer | Teacher Tech Transformer | Edupreneur | Author | Speaker | Education Evangelist

Ashish Bhargava

Edupreneur | Author | Speaker | Education Evangelist | Ex-Employee Microsoft | Ex-Employee HCL

FIRST EDITION 2021
REPRINT 2026

ISBN: 978-93-89845-051

Distributors:

BPB PUBLICATIONS
20, Ansari Road, Darya Ganj
New Delhi-110002
Ph: 23254990 / 23254991

DECCAN AGENCIES
4-3-329, Bank Street,
Hyderabad-500195
Ph: 24756967 / 24756400

MICRO MEDIA
Shop No. 5, Mahendra Chambers,
150 DN Rd. Next to Capital Cinema,
V.T. (C.S.T.) Station, MUMBAI-400 001
Ph: 22078296 / 22078297

BPB BOOK CENTRE
376 Old Lajpat Rai Market,
Delhi-110006
Ph: 23861747

To View Complete BPB Publications Catalogue Scan the QR Code:

Published by Manish Jain for BPB Publications, 20 Ansari Road, Darya Ganj, New Delhi-110002 and Printed by him at Repro India Ltd, Mumbai

www.bpbonline.com

Dedicated to

Gurpreet Kaur dedicates this book to Her Family
Ashish Bhargava dedicates this book to His Family

About the Author(s)

Gurpreet Kaur

Freelance Consultant and Trainer | Teacher Tech Transformer | Edupreneur | Author | Speaker | Education Evangelist

She is a passionate educator, who has a vast experience of over 24 years in the field of Education and Information Technology. Her work includes teaching Computer Science, Informatics Practices, formulating and implementing the IT curriculum at all levels, training the computer science teachers. She loves integrating multiple teaching styles to intensify the range of learning for her trainees. She has authored several books in the field of Information Technology for various educational organizations like the Central Board of Secondary Education (CBSE) and the National Council for Education Research and Training (NCERT), PSS Central Institute of Vocational Education (PSSCIVE) and some private publishers. She is currently working in the field of AI, Data Analytics, Python and their use in Education.

LinkedIn Profile:

https://www.linkedin.com/in/gurpreetkaurchaudhary/

Ashish Bhargava

Edupreneur | Author | Speaker | Education Evangelist | Ex-Employee Microsoft | Ex-Employee HCL Technologies

He is passionate about learning. He has 19+ years of experience in the IT and Education sectors. He has worked with esteemed organisations like Microsoft and HCL Technologies. His area of work includes training, product development, software development, Test Automation, Performance Testing. His areas of interest are Artificial Intelligence, Machine Learning, Python, Data Analytics, Design Thinking, Algorithms and the Internet of Things. He has authored books that have been helpful for professionals and students. He is also a key contributor at computerscienceforcbse.com

Blog links:

http://computerscienceforcbse.com/

LinkedIn Profile:

https://www.linkedin.com/in/ashish-bhargava-67484218/

Acknowledgements

We would especially like to thank Mr. Manish Jain giving us the creative freedom to write this book. We would like to express our gratitude to every resource person from BPB publication who involved in the publication of this book.

This book truly reflects the collective wisdom of the numerous students and colleagues with whom we interact and learn from everyday.

We also like to express our special thanks to our families for being supportive with their unconditional love, their patience, and encouragement.

Preface

CBSE has introduced Python in the year 2014, realizing its potential. Python is the one of the fastest growing, high-level and general-purpose programming language, with an emphasis on code readability. It has various features like:

- ✓ It is a free and open source programming language
- ✓ It receives extensive support from developer community
- ✓ It has user-friendly data structures
- ✓ It is the most preferred language in the fields of scientific computation, Data Science, Statistics, Artificial Intelligence and Machine Learning
- ✓ Most of the educational institutions have adopted python as a first language

The primary goal of this book is to develop a pattern proof question bank. Pattern proof questions help the students in revising the entire syllabus, irrespective of the pattern of questions that may be asked in the examination.

This Question Bank is an essential teaching aid for teachers and helps them in setting test paper(s). It is suitable for revision, lesson tests, for teachers and students alike.

This question bank is based on the latest updated syllabus. Questions are directly linked to the marking scheme prescribed by CBSE and contain all kinds of questions -

- ★ Very short questions
- ★ Short questions
- ★ Long questions
- ★ Practical file questions
- ★ Multiple choice questions
- ★ Fill in the blanks
- ★ Match the terms
- ★ Case studies

This question bank also provides a sample project and model question paper.

Authors

Downloading the code bundle and coloured images:

Please follow the link to download the
Code Bundle and the *Coloured Images* of the book:

https://rebrand.ly/qvlu9

Errata

We take immense pride in our work at BPB Publications and follow best practices to ensure the accuracy of our content to provide with an indulging reading experience to our subscribers. Our readers are our mirrors, and we use their inputs to reflect and improve upon human errors, if any, that may have occurred during the publishing processes involved. To let us maintain the quality and help us reach out to any readers who might be having difficulties due to any unforeseen errors, please write to us at:

errata@bpbonline.com

Your support, suggestions and feedbacks are highly appreciated by the BPB Publications' Family.

BPB is searching for authors like you

If you're interested in becoming an author for BPB, please visit **www.bpbonline.com** and apply today. We have worked with thousands of developers and tech professionals, just like you, to help them share their insight with the global tech community. You can make a general application, apply for a specific hot topic that we are recruiting an author for, or submit your own idea.

The code bundle for the book is also hosted on GitHub at **https://github.com/bpbpublications/Question-Bank-for-Exam-Success-Computer-Science-with-Python-Class-XII-CBSE-083-**. In case there's an update to the code, it will be updated on the existing GitHub repository.
We also have other code bundles from our rich catalog of books and videos available at **https://github.com/bpbpublications**. Check them out!

PIRACY

If you come across any illegal copies of our works in any form on the internet, we would be grateful if you would provide us with the location address or website name. Please contact us at **business@bpbonline.com** with a link to the material.

If you are interested in becoming an author

If there is a topic that you have expertise in, and you are interested in either writing or contributing to a book, please visit **www.bpbonline.com**.

REVIEWS

Please leave a review. Once you have read and used this book, why not leave a review on the site that you purchased it from? Potential readers can then see and use your unbiased opinion to make purchase decisions, we at BPB can understand what you think about our products, and our authors can see your feedback on their book. Thank you!

For more information about BPB, please visit **www.bpbonline.com**.

Table of Contents

1 REVISION TOUR PYTHON

LEARNING OBJECTIVES

- Recall the key terms: tokens, operators and statements
- Define the syntax for: if-else if, if- elif- else, while and for loop
- Write a code to create data types like string, list, dictionary and use them to build simple programming problems
- Develop the code by using while, for loop and iterate data types like string, list, tuple and dictionary
- Outline functions and operators used with string, list and tuple

DEFINITION

- **Token:** Python breaks an instruction (statement or expression) into a sequence of lexical components these are known as tokens. Tokens include keywords, literals, identifiers, operators and punctuators.
- **Keyword:** A keyword is a reserve word that is used for special syntactic uses. The keyword carries a specific meaning for an interpreter.
- **Identifier:** The identifier represents the name of variable, function, classes, etc.
- **Variable:** A variable denotes a reserved memory location that stores a value that can be changed during the execution of the program. It allows a Python program to process data.
- **Literal:** A literal represents a constant value, string, or number that is used to build expressions and statements in a Python program.
- **Assignment operator:** An assignment operator is used to assign values to the variables.
- **Arithmetic operator:** Arithmetic operators are used to perform arithmetic operations.
- **Comparison operator:** Comparison operators are used to compare two similar data types and evaluate expression as true or false.
- **Identity operator:** Identity operators are used to check if two variables have the same memory location.
- **Logical operator:** Logical operators are used to make a decision based on a condition or multiple conditions. Each operand is considered as a condition that can be evaluated to a true or false value.
- **Membership operator:** A Membership operator is used to validate the existence of a value in a sequence, such as lists, tuples, or strings.
- **Statement:** A statement is an instruction. A Python program file is a sequence of simple and compound statements.
- **Simple statement:** A simple statement is one that contains no other statements. It is entirely within a logical line.
- **Compound statement:** Compound statement(s) contain group(s) of other (simple) statements.
- **Pass statement:** Pass statement is a null operation; no operation is performed when it runs.
- **String:** The string is a sequence that stores characters only.
- **List:** A list in Python is a data structure; it is a mutable, ordered sequence of elements. A list can be defined as a collection of values. The items in the list that are separated with comma (,) and enclosed within the square brackets [ ].
- **Tuple:** A tuple is a sequence that store elements. Once a tuple is created its elements cannot be changed. Elements in tuple are enclosed in the brackets() and are separated by comma.
- **Dictionary:** Dictionary is an unordered collection of key-value pairs. Each key and value in a Dictionary is separated by a colon ':', whereas each item (key-value) is separated by a ',' comma.

Very Short Questions and Answers 1 Mark

1. Mention the tokens in Python. Tokens in Python are:

Ans. a. Keyword b. Literals c. Identifier d. Operators e. Punctuations

2. Explain the rules to define the variables. Rules to define the variables are:

Ans.
- A variable name only consists of letters, numbers and underscores.
- Variables names must start with a letter or an underscore.

3. List a few valid variable names.

Ans. List of valid variables are:
- passwd123
- _india123
- India_123
- check
- While

Note:
- Variable names are case sensitive. For example, 'case' is not the same as 'Case'.
- A keyword cannot be used as a variable. For example, while = 0 will raise an exception.

4. List a few invalid variable names.

Ans. List of invalid variables are:
- 123passwd # Variable cannot start with numbers
- while # Keywords cannot be used as variable name
- pass@123 # Variable contains invalid character '@'

5. Differentiate between keywords and identifiers.

Ans. Keywords are the reserved words, which carry special meaning whereas, an identifier is a unique name for a variable, class and function.

6. Explain the integer literals with examples.

Ans. The integer literal is an integer value, such as 42, -1, 0, etc.

The Integer literals are of three types:

a. Decimal: ***Example:*** 10, -5, 32767

b. Octal: ***Example:*** 0o10

c. Hexadecimal: ***Example:*** 0x10 or 0X10

7. Explain the floating-point literals with examples.

Ans. The floating literal is a float or double value. ***Example:*** .14159, 3.0, -.3344, and 1000.9876.

8. Explain the imaginary literals with examples.

Ans. An imaginary literal in Python yields a complex number. A Complex number is represented as a pair of real and imaginary part. ***Example:*** 2+ 3j, 1.0j, -3 – 10j

9. Explain the string literals with examples.

Ans. The string literal is a collection of the characters enclosed in quotes (single, double, or triple). Example,

```
'hello world'
"Its time to say bye"
""" triple quoted string """
```

10. How are comments defined in the Python?

Ans. Comments in Python are defined by using '#'.

Example: #This is a comment

11. Why comments are useful?

Ans. A comment in a computer program is a readable explanation or annotation. The purpose of a comment is to make the source code easier to understand. Comments are ignored by the interpreter.

12. Explain the terms expression and operator, and how are they related?

Ans. An expression is a combination of operators and operands. The expression is evaluated to obtain the results. An operator in Python is a symbol that performs an operation on one or more operands. An operand is a literal or a variable on which an operation is performed.

13. How to create tuple?

Ans. A tuple in Python is created by placing comma-separated values in the round brackets. ***Example:***

```
_tuple = (1,3.14,"ashish","Gurpreet")
#create nested tuple
_tuple = ((1,2,3), 5,6,7)
```

14. How to create a list?

Ans. A list in Python is created by placing comma separated values in the square brackets. ***Example:***

```
_list = [1,2,5,7,-4,9,16]
_list =[1, 2.0, 2+3j, 'Python']
```

Short Questions and Answers 2/3 Marks

1. List all the built-in numeric data types in Python.

Ans. Python supports int (integers), bool (boolean a subtype of int), float (floating-point), and complex numbers. These types are defined as int, bool, float and complex class in Python.

2. List all the data types that belong to the sequence data type in Python.

Ans. Sequence are used to store multiple values in sequential order. These are strings, lists, tuples, byte arrays and range objects.

3. How does mapping data type stores the data?

Ans. A mapping type is a collection of keys and its associated values. The only built-in mapping type in Python is the dictionary. Dictionary stores key and value pairs.

4. Why is set used in Python?

Ans. A built-in set data type is an unordered collection of unique objects. It eliminates the duplicate object. The frozen set is a set that is immutable, whereas the set is mutable.

5. What are the characteristics of the mutable type?

Ans. The objects which allow the change of their content without changing their identity are called mutable objects. ***Example:*** list, dictionary, set and byte array.

6. What are the characteristics of the immutable type?

Ans. The objects which do not allow any changes to their contents or state are called immutable objects. Performing operations on them returns a new object. ***Example:*** int, complex, float, tuple, string, bytes and frozen set [immutable set].

7. Differentiate between / and // operators.

Ans. / is used to divide two integer or floats.

// is used for floor division return floor value.

The // operator and / operator both divide the numbers, but // returns an integer and / returns a float value.

Example:

```
5 / 2       = 2.5
```

```
5.0 / 2.0  = 2.5
5 // 2 = 2
5.0 // 2.0 = 2.0
```

8. Differentiate between // and % operator.

Ans. // is the floor division operator. It returns the quotient (result of division) in which the digits after the decimal point are removed.

% is the Modulus operator. It returns the remainder

Example:

```
5 // 2 = 2
5 % 2  = 1
```

9. Describe the compound assignment operator and how they are used.

Ans. The compound assignment operator consists of a binary operator and an assignment operator. They perform the operation on both operands and store the result back to the left operand.

Example:

```
x + = 1
```

Here, x is incremented by 1 and assign the result back to x.

The below table list Compound Assignment operators with examples:

Operator	Example	Equivalent Statement
`+=a`	`+= 2`	`a = a + 2`
`-=a`	`-= 2`	`a = a - 2`
`*=a`	`*= 2`	`a = a * 2`
`/=a`	`/= 2`	`a = a / 2`
`//=a`	`//= 2`	`a = a // 2`
`%=a`	`%= 2`	`a = a % 2`
`**=a`	`**= 2`	`a = a ** 2`

There are few more operators used with bitwise operator.

Example: **~= , &=, |= , ^= , >>= , <<=.**

10. Differentiate between x = x +1 and x+=1.

Ans. Both expressions are evaluated to 2; thus, they are the same.

11. Explain the simultaneous assignment with an example.

Ans. Python allows simultaneous assignment.

Syntax:

```
var_1, var_2 = value_1, value_2
```

Example: `a, b = 2, 3`

12. Define multiple assignments.

Ans. Python allows assigning a single value to several variables.

Syntax:

```
var_1 = var_2 = var_3 = 1
```

Example: `x = y = z = 1`

13. When is the 'and' operator evaluated to true?

Ans. 'and' operator evaluates true if both the operands (and conditions) are true.

14. When is the 'or' operator evaluated to true?

Ans. 'or' operator evaluates true if any operands, or conditions, or both operands are true.

15. Explain how 'not' operator works.

Ans. 'not' operator complements the operand that is not True = False and not False = True.

16. List all the bitwise operators.

Ans.

Operator	Meaning
&	Bitwise AND
|	Bitwise OR
~	Bitwise NOT
^	Bitwise XOR
>>	Bitwise right shift
<<	Bitwise left shift

17. How to check if an element exists in sequence and other data types?

Ans. Membership operator checks if an element exists in a sequence (list, string, tuple, dictionary and set).
in and **not in** are membership operators:

- **in** returns True if element is found.
- **not in** returns True if an element is not found.

Note: In the dictionary, you can check the presence of the key, not value.

18. How to verify if two objects are Identical.

Ans. Identity operators are used to check if two variables have the same memory location. The id() function returns the same value if two objects are identical.

- **is** returns **True** if both the operands are identical (refer to the same object)
- **is not** returns **True** if both the operands are not identical (do not have the same location)

19. How operator precedence and associativity help to solve an expression?

Ans. An expression contains an operator or multiple operators.
In case of multiple operators which, operator will be evaluated first. Python allows evaluating expression based on its precedence (which means the operator that has higher precedence will be evaluated first).

```
x = 1
y = 1
z = 2
res = x + y * z ** 2
```

Here, Precedence guides order, in which an expression will be evaluated.

Example:

**** has higher precedence than *, first z **2 will be evaluated:**

```
res = 1 + x + y * 2**2
res = 1 + x + y * 4 :: 2**2 = 4
```

*** has higher precedence than +, y * 4 will be evaluated before + is evaluated:**

```
res = 1 + x + 1 * 4
res = 1 + x + 4:: 1*4 =4
```

The above expression contains multiple '+' operators and they have the same precedence. When the operators have same precedence, associativity guides us to determine the order of operations.

Associativity is an order in which an expression is evaluated in case operators have the same precedence.

Associativity has two flavors:

a. left-to-right

Left-to-right associativity is where expression is evaluated from left to right.

Example:

res = 1 + x+ 4:: + has associatively from left to right, hence expression will be evaluated as follows:

```
1 + 1 + 4
= 2 + 4:: 1 + 1 = 2
= 6
```

Finally, it will evaluate to 6.

b. right-to-left

Right to Left associativity is where expression is evaluated from right to left.

Example:

2**2**3

First 2**3 is evaluated (right to left)

= 2**8 : 2**3 = 8

= 256

Note: Precedence rules are overridden by using parentheses explicitly.

20. Explain how expression 22**4 will be evaluated.**

Ans. Operator ** has associativity right to left, so first 2**4 will be evaluated. The expression is:

```
2**4 = 16
2**16 = 65536
```

21. Explain how expression 22**4 and (2**2) **4 will be evaluated.**

Ans. In the previous question 20, an expression is evaluated to 65536.

In the expression (2**2)**4, parenthesis will take precedence, so (2**2) is evaluated first, so 2**2 = 4 and then 4**4 is evaluated to 256.

```
(2**2)**4 = 256
2**2**4 = 65536
```

22. How to read string, integer and float from the console?

Ans. The input function reads input as a string. To convert input or float function, int() and float() are used respectively.

```
# Reading a string
string = input("Enter string")
# Reading integer
# Function int () # converts string to int,
```

Syntax:

```
num = int(input("Enter a number"))
#Reading float
#Function float() converts string to float
```

Syntax:

```
value = float(input("Enter a value"))
```

23. Explain the utility and usage of the print function in Python.

Ans. Print function prints object(s) to the standard output device (console) or text stream file.

Syntax:

```
print(*object, sep=' ', end='\n', file=sys.stdout, flush=False)
```

Parameter:

Argument Name	Argument Utility	Argument Status
Object	An argument to be printed on the console	It is a variable-length argument
Sep	Objects are separated by sep(separator)	The default value is ' '
End	End character is printed at the end	Optional
File	Print on stream	The default is sys.stdout (screen)
Flush	If it is true, the stream is forcibly flushed	The default value is False

Here's an example of the print() function:

```
x = 5
import sys
print("x = ", x , sep="00", end='\n' , file=sys.stdout)
x=005
```

Note: end, sep, file and flush all are keyword arguments.

24. List the different ways to create a string in Python.

Ans. String literals are represented in three ways:

a. Using single quotes, example: 'hi'

b. Using double quotes, example: "Hello"

c. Using triple quotes, example:
'"this is triple
quoted string"'

25. List the unary operators.

Ans. Unary operators are those operators that need only one operand.

List of Unary operators:

Operator	Example
+(unary)	+2
-(unary)	-2
not(logical)	Not True
~(bitwise not or one's complement)	~2 = -3

26. What are the components of a Python program?

Ans. The components of the Python program are:

a. Packages (using through the import)

b. Comments

c. Statements and Expressions

d. Functions

e. Block(s) or Suite(s)

27. Why variables are used in a program?

Ans. A variable holds a value that can be changed over the period of time. A variable in a program allows storing a value that is required to perform certain logic of a program. For example, an increment/decrement of the counter, saving the intermediate results, etc.

28. Define a block or suite.

Ans. A block or a suite is a statement or group of statements that are a part of another statement or function.

Note: All statements inside a suite or block are intended at the same level.

29. List immutable and mutable data types in Python.

Ans.

Mutable objects	Immutable objects
list, dictionary, set, byte array	int, complex, float, tuple, string, bytes, frozen set [immutable set]

30. Differentiate between implicit type conversion and explicit type conversion.

Ans.

Implicit conversion	Explicit conversion
Implicit Conversion is automatically performed by a Python interpreter. Python avoids loss of data during Implicit Type Conversion.	Explicit Conversion is known as Type casting. In this the data is converted using the predefined function by the user.

31. Give reasons why to use the immutable objects.

Ans. Immutable objects are used as:

- Immutable types are read-only data.
- As immutable types cannot change. We can pass immutable objects as function arguments without fear of modification.
- Immutable objects are thread-safe.

32. Write the syntax of if-else.

Ans. 'If block' is executed when test expression is true, otherwise else block is executed.

Syntax:

```
if test condition:
    statement(s)
else:
    statement(s)
```

33. Explain how if else works along with an example.

Ans. # Find out if a number is even and odd using if and else.

```
num = int(input("Enter a number"))
if num % 2 == 0:
        print( str(num) + " is an Even number")
else:
        print( str(num) + " is an Odd number")
```

34. Write the Syntax of if... elif... else.

Ans. ***Syntax:***

```
if test condition:
    statement(s)
elif test condition:
    statement(s)
elif test condition:
    statement(s)
else:
statement(s)
```

Note:
- if... elif... else is used to execute multiple conditions.
- elif is short for else-if.
- In "if... elif... else", there can be only one else block; however, it can have multiple elif blocks.
- if a condition is false it checks the next condition; if all conditions are exhausted else part is executed.

35. Explain how if... elif... else work with an example.

Ans.
```
# find out if an number is even, odd or zero using if… elif… else
num = int(input("Enter a number"))
if num == 0:
    print( str(num) + "is Zero not even or odd")
elif num % 2 == 0:
    print( str(num) + " is an Even number")
else:
    print( str(num) + " is an Odd number")
```

36. Explain how nested if... elif... else work with an example.

Ans. When if...elif...else or if... else statement is inside another if ... else, if...elif...else statement, this is called nested if-else.

Example:
```
    # Check if number is 0, positive or negative
num = float(input("Enter a number:"))
if (num >= 0):
    if (num == 0):
        print(str(num) +" is Zero")
    else:
        print(str(num) +" positive number")
else:
    print(str(num) +" is a negative number")
```

37. Write the syntax of a while loop.

Ans. The while loop iterates over a block of code until the test condition(expression) is true.

Syntax:
```
while test_expression:
    statement(s)
```

Note:
- The test expression is evaluated first.
- If the test expression is true, then the body of the loop is executed.
- Loop iterates until test expression is true.
- The body is indented and it ends when indentation is over.
- Python interprets 0 and None as False, rest all values are True.

38. Write a program that uses while loop to print sum of the following series.

Ans. # Program to write the sum of series of 1^2 + 2^2+ 3^2 + n^2
```
terms = int(input("Enter the number of terms: ))
cnt = 1
sum =0
while( cnt<=terms):
    sum = sum + cnt **2
    print(str(cnt) + "  ^ 2 + " ,end=")
    cnt+=1
print(' = ',end=' ')
print(sum)
```

Output:
```
Enter the number of terms: 10
1 ^ 2 + 2 ^ 2 + 3 ^ 2 + 4 ^ 2 + 5 ^ 2 + 6 ^ 2 + 7 ^ 2 + 8 ^ 2 + 9 ^ 2 + 10 ^ 2 + = 385
```

39. Differentiate between break and continue.

Ans. Break and continue, both are jump statements that alter the execution flow of a loop.

The differences between break and continue is:

Break statement	Continue statement
When break statement is encountered in a loop, it jumps out of the loop and the next statement after loop is executed.	When continue statement is encountered in a loop, control jumps to the beginning of the loop. All the statements after continue statement are skipped.

40. Write the syntax of the 'for' loop.

Ans. The for loop allows iterating over a sequence (tuple, list, string) or other iterable objects.

Syntax:

```
for element in sequence:
    statement(s)
```

Loop continues until it reaches the last element in a sequence. The body of the loop is defined by the indentation.

41. Explain how for loops iterate over a sequence.

Ans. The for loop iterates each element until all the elements of a sequence are executed.

```
sequence = [1,2,3,4,5,6,7]
# Iterate over the list
for i in sequence:
    print(i)
```

Output:

```
1
2
3
4
5
6
7
```

42. Find the output of the following Python code.

Ans.

```
for name in['Jayes','Ramya','Taruna','Suraj']:
    print (name)
    if name[0]== 'T':
        break
    else:
        print ('Finished!')
    print ('Got it')
```

Output:

```
Jayes
Finished!
Got it
Ramya
Finished!
Got it
Taruna
```

43. Find the output of the following Python code.

Ans.
```
for x in[1,2,3,4,5]:
    print(x, end=' ')
```

Output:
```
1 2 3 4 5
```

44. Find the output of the following Python code.

Ans.
```
for i in range(-500,500,100):
    print(i, end=' ')
```

Output:
```
-500 -400 -300 -200 -100 0 100 200 300 400
```

45. Find the output of the following Python code.

Ans.
```
alphabets = ["a", "e", "b", "i", "u", "d"]
for char in alphabets:
    if char not in "aeiou":
        continue
    print(char, end=' ')
```

Output:
```
a e i u
```

46. Write code that traverses a string.

Ans. For loop allows iterating the string:
```
string = "narayan"
for char in string:
    print(char, end = " ")
```

Output:
```
n a r a y a n
```

47. How to delete an element from a string.

Ans. A string is immutable; it does not allow to delete its element. Trying to delete an element will result in an error. For example, del string[0] will raise the following error:

`TypeError: 'str' object doesn't support item deletion.`

48. How to update an element of a string.

Ans. A string is immutable; it does not allow it to modify its element. Trying to modify elements results in an error. For example, `string[0] ='a' will raise the following error:`

`TypeError: 'str' object does not support item assignment.`

49. Write a program that reverse the string.

Ans. Method #1
```
string = "check"
revstring = string[::-1]
print(revstring)
```

Output:
```
kcehc
```

In the above example, slicing is used to reverse a string. Slicing has three parameters: start, stop and step. There is no value for start and stop, this means it will fetch the entire string, -1 indicates slicing from end to start thereby returns the reverse of the string.

Method #2

```
string ="check"
revstring =""

for char in string:
    revstring = char + revstring

print(revstring)
```

Output:

```
kcehc
```

The above code iterates every character in the string and joins each character at the beginning of the another string (revstring) to obtain the reversed of the string.

50. List all the operators of string datatype.

Ans. Operators of string data type are:

Operator	Description	Example
+	Concatenate two or more string	"hi" + "bye" = hi bye
*	Repeats the string n times	"hi" * 3 = hihihi
[] (Slice)	Returns a character at index	"hi"[0] = h
[:] (Range Slice)	Returns the characters between x:y	'string'[1:3] = tr
in	Returns True if x exists in string	i in 'string' = True
not in	Returns True if x does not exist in string	h not in 'string' = False

51. List all the string comparison operators.

Ans. String in Python allows comparing the string by using the comparison operator.

Operator	Example	Output	Explanation
== equals	'abc' == 'abc'	True	Compare if two strings are equal
!= not equals	'abc' = 'Abc'	True	Compare if two strings are not equal
> greater than	'a' > 'b'	False	Compare if string 1 is greater than string 2
< less than	'b' < 'a'	True	Compare if string1 is less than string 2

52. How to access the character from strings by using index and negative index?

Ans. Python allows accessing the string's element by using its index.

`string ="Pythonisfun!".`

Each character of a string has an index number which starts from 0. For example:

p	y	t	h	o	n	i	s	f	u	n	!
0	1	2	3	4	5	6	7	8	9	10	11

```
string[1]
```

Output:

```
y
```

Python allows access to characters from the end of the string using negative index number, starting at the index number -1.

p	y	t	h	o	n	i	s	f	u	n	!
-12	-11	-10	-9	-8	-7	-6	-5	-4	-3	-2	-1

```
string[-1]
```

Output:

```
!
```

53. How slicing is used to retrieve substring from a string?

Ans. Slicing allows retrieving a substring using slice operator. It has three arguments:

a. **start index:** The substring starts with start index.

b. **end index:** The substring ends with the (end index) - 1.

c. **step:** Add it to an index to retrieve the next character, if a step is not provided its default value is 1.

```
string = 'Python is fun!'
```

Example 1: Using start and stop.

```
string[0:6]
```

Output:

```
Python
```

Example 2: Using start, end and step.

```
string[0:6:1]
```

Output:

```
Python
```

Example 3: Using negative indexes.

```
string[-4:-1]
```

Output:

```
'fun'
```

Example 4: Using negative index and negative step.

```
string = 'Python is fun!'
revstr=string[-1:-16:-1]
print(revstr)
```

Output:

```
!nuf si nohtyp
```

```
string = revstr[-1:-16:-1]
print(string)
```

Output:

```
Python is fun!
```

54. What are the key features of a list?

Ans. Key features of list are:

- The list is mutable, it allows modifying and deleting its element after its creation.
- The list can store elements of different data types.
- Lists are ordered.
- The elements of a list can be accessed by their index.
- Lists are dynamic.
- Lists can be nested to an arbitrary depth.

55. How to create an empty list?

Ans. An empty list is created in two ways:

a. `_list =[]`

b. `_list = list()`

56. How to create a list from sequence?

Ans.
```
_list = list("Python")
print(list)
```

Output:
```
['p', 'y','t', 'h', 'o', 'n']
```

57. How to retrieve an element from the list?

Ans. We can retrieve an element in two ways:

a. using index

b. using slicing

```
_list = ['p', 'y','t', 'h', 'o', 'n', ' ', 'i', 's', ' ', 'f', 'u', 'n', '!']
```

An example of retrieving element using Index:

```
_list[0]
```

Output:
```
p
```

An example retrieving element using negative index:

```
_list[-1]
```

Output:
```
!
```

An example of retrieving substring using slicing:

```
_list[0:6]
```

Output:
```
['p', 'y', 't', 'h', 'o', 'n']
```

```
_list[-4:-1]
```

Output:
```
['f', 'u', 'n']
```

58. How to delete the element(s) from the list?

Ans. An element can be deleted in two ways:

a. using index

b. using slicing

```
_list = ['p', 'y', 't', 'h', 'o', 'n', ' ', 'i', 's', ' ', 'f', 'u', 'n', '!']
del _list[0]
print(_list)
```

Output:
```
['y', 't', 'h', 'o', 'n', ' ', 'i', 's', ' ', 'f', 'u', 'n', '!']
```

```
del _list[-1]
print(_list)
```

Output:
```
['y', 't', 'h', 'o', 'n', ' ', 'i', 's', ' ', 'f', 'u', 'n']
```

delete using slicing:

```
_list = ['p', 'y', 't', 'h', 'o', 'n', ' ', 'i', 's', ' ', 'f', 'u', 'n', '!']
del _list[0:6]
```

```
print(_list)
```

Output:
```
[' ', 'i', 's', ' ', 'f', 'u', 'n', '!']
```

```
_list =  ['p', 'y', 't', 'h', 'o', 'n', ' ', 'i', 's', ' ', 'f', 'u', 'n', '!']
del _list[-4:-1]
print(_list)
```

Output:
```
['p', 'y', 't', 'h', 'o', 'n', ' ', 'i', 's', ' ', '!']
```

59. How to modify the element(s) of the list?

Ans. A list can be modified in the following ways:

a. using index
b. using slicing
c. using the insert method

Modify a list using Index:
```
_list = ['p', 'y', 't', 'h', 'o', 'n', ' ', 'i', 's', ' ', 'f', 'u', 'n', '!']
_list[0]= 'p'
```

Output:
```
['P', 'y', 't', 'h', 'o', 'n', ' ', 'i', 's', ' ', 'f', 'u', 'n', '!']
```

Modify a list using Slicing:
```
_list[-4:-1] =['F','U','N']
print(_list)
```

Output:
```
['P', 'y', 't', 'h', 'o', 'n', ' ', 'i', 's', ' ', 'F', 'U', 'N', '!']
```

Modify a list using insert method:

#inserts element to the list at specified location :insert (index, element)
```
_list = ['p', 'y', 't', 'h', 'o', 'n', ' ', 'i', 's', ' ', 'f', 'u', 'n', '!']
_list.insert(13,'!!!')
print(_list)
```

Output:
```
['p', 'y', 't', 'h', 'o', 'n', ' ', 'i', 's', ' ', 'f', 'u', 'n', '!!!', '!']
```

60. How to add element in a list.

Ans. The element(s) can be added to the list by using the append() method:

The function append() add element at the end of the list for example:
```
_list = ['p', 'y', 't', 'h', 'o', 'n', ' ', 'i', 's', ' ', 'f', 'u', 'n', '!']
_list.append('!')
print(_list)
```

Output:
```
['p', 'y', 't', 'h', 'o', 'n', ' ', 'i', 's', ' ', 'f', 'u', 'n', '!', '!']
```

Add a list to another list using extend() function, for example:
```
_list = ['p', 'y', 't', 'h', 'o', 'n', ' ', 'i', 's', ' ', 'f', 'u', 'n', '!']
_listext  = ['!', '!']
```
#extend() add a list to another List:
```
_list.extend(_listext)
```

```
print(_list)
```

Output:

```
['p', 'y', 't', 'h', 'o', 'n', ' ', 'i', 's', ' ', 'f', 'u', 'n', '!', '!', '!']
```

61. How to remove element(s) from the list?

Ans. Elements in a list can be removed using clear() method

#removes all elements (Items) from a list:

```
_list = [1,2,3,4,5]
_list.clear()
print(_list)
```

Output:

```
[]
```

#remove() method removes element from the list, for example:

```
_list = [1,2,3,4,5]
```

#Remove element from the list.

```
_list.remove(3)
print(_list)
```

Output:

```
[1, 2, 4, 5]
```

To remove element at given index or last element use function pop():

Example:

```
_list = [1,2,3,4,5]
print(_list.pop())
```

Output:

```
5
```

```
print(_list)
[1, 2, 3, 4]
print(_list.pop(0))
```

Output:

```
1
```

```
print(_list)
```

Output:

```
[2, 3, 4]
```

62. How to find the index of an element in a list?

Ans. The index() is method is used to find the index of an element in a list. It returns the smallest index of element in the list.

For example

```
_list =[5,10,15,20,25]
print( _list.index(15))
```

Output:

```
2
```

63. How to find the number of occurrences of an element in a list?

Ans. The count() method returns occurrences of element in a list. For example,

```
_list = [1,2,3,2,3,4,5,6]
```

```
print(_list.count(2))  #find the occurrence of the 2
```

Output:

```
2
```

64. How to reverse a list?

Ans. The reverse() method allows to reverse a list. For example,

```
#reverses a list
_list = [1,2,3,4,5]
_list.reverse()
print(_list)
```

Output:

```
[5,4,3,2,1]
```

65. How to sort a list?

Ans. The sort() method is used to sort the elements of a list.

Example:

```
_list = [5,4,3,2,1]
_list.sort()
print(_list)
```

Output:

```
[1,2,3,4,5]
```

```
#Sort list in reverse order
_list = [1,2,3,4,5]
_list.sort(reverse=True)
print(_list)
```

Output:

```
[5,4,3,2,1]
```

66. How to make a copy of a list?

Ans. The copy() methods returns a copy of a list.

```
_list =[1,2,3,4]
_listcopy = _list.copy()
print(_listcopy)
```

Output:

```
[1,2,3,4,5]
```

67. How to find a number of elements in a list?

Ans. The len() method returns the number of elements in the list.

```
_list = [1,2,3,46,7,8,90]
len(_list)
```

Output:

```
7
```

68. How to find the element with maximum value from a list?

Ans. The max() method returns the element with maximum value.

```
_list = [1,2,3,46,7,8,90]
print(max(_list))
```

Output:
```
90
```

69. How to find the element with minimum value from a list?

Ans. The min() method returns the elements with minimum value.
```
_list = [1,2,3,46,7,8,90]
print(min(_list))
```

Output:
```
1
```

70. How to create an empty tuple?

Ans. An empty tuple can be created by using tuple() method for example
```
_tuple = tuple()
print(_tuple)
```

Output:
```
()
```

71. How to create a tuple from an existing sequence?

Ans. The tuple() method is used to create tuple by using a sequence as shown below:.
```
_tuple = tuple([1,2,3,4,5])
print(_tuple)
```

Output:
```
(1,2,3,4,5)
```

72. List all the build-in operators of tuple

Ans. List of build-in operators of tuple are:

Operator	Description	Example
+	Concatenate two or more tuple	('h', 'i') + (' ', 'b', 'y','e') = ('h', 'i', ' ', 'b', 'y', 'e')
*	Repeats the tuple n times	("hi") * 3 = ('hi', 'hi', 'hi')
[] (Slice)	Returns a character at index	("hi", "bye")[0] = hi
[:](Range Slice)	Returns the elements between start: stop	(1,2,3,4)[1:3] = (2,3)
in	Returns True if x exists in tuple	1 in (1,2,3,4) = True
not in	Returns True if x does not exist in tuple	5 not in (1,2,3,4) = True

73. How to retrieve elements from the tuple?

Ans. We can retrieve element from the tuple in two ways:

a. using index

b. using slicing

```
_tuple = ('p', 'y', 't', 'h', 'o', 'n', ' ', 'i', 's', ' ', 'f', 'u', 'n', '!')
_tuple[0]
```

Output:
```
p
```

```
_tuple[-1]
```

Output:
```
!
```

Using slicing
```
_tuple[0:6]
```

Output:

```
('p', 'y', 't', 'h', 'o', 'n')
```

```
_tuple[-4:-1]
```

Output:

```
('f', 'u', 'n')
```

74. How to join two tuples?

Ans. To join two tuples + operator is used.

Example:

```
_tuple1 = (1,2,3)
_tuple2 = (4,5,6)
_tuple = _tuple1 + _tuple2
print(_tuple)
```

Output:

```
(1,2,3,4,5,6)
```

75. How to retrieve elements from a tuple?

Ans.

```
_tuple = (1,2,3,4,5,6)
for item in _tuple:
    print(item, end=',' )
```

Output:

```
(1,2,3,4,5,6)
```

76. How to find the index of an element that exists in a tuple?

Ans.

```
_tuple =(1,2,3,4,5)
_tuple.index(4)
```

Output:

```
3
```

77. How to find the occurrence of an element that exists in a tuple?

Ans.

```
_tuple =(1,2,3,4,5,2,3,2,4,2,5,6,2)
_tuple.count(2)
```

Output:

```
5
```

78. How to delete the element(s) from tuple?

Ans. Deleting an element from tuple is not allowed since the tuple is immutable; trying to do so raises an error as shown below:

```
TypeError: 'tuple' object doesn't support item deletion
```

79. How to modify the element(s) from tuple?

Ans. Modifying element from tuple is not allowed since the tuple is immutable; trying to do so raises an error as shown below:

```
_tuple[0]=('a',)
TypeError: 'tuple' object does not support item assignment
```

80. Explain the packing in a tuple.

Ans. Tuple packing is where a set of values is placed into a new tuple. ***Example:***

```
_tuple = 1,2,3,4
```

```
print(_tuple)
```

Output:
```
(1,2,3,4)
```

81. How to unpack a tuple?

Ans. Tuple unpacking involves extracting values back from tuple into variables. Example,

```
_tuple = 1,2,3,4
a,b,c,d = _tuple
print(a,b,c,d)
```

Output:
```
1 2 3 4
```

82. How to find number of elements in a tuple?

Ans.
```
_tuple = (1,2,3,46,7,8,90)
len(_tuple)
```

Output:
```
7
```

83. How to find the element that has maximum value in a tuple?

Ans. Method max() returns the elements that has maximum value in a tuple. ***Example:***

```
_tuple = (1,2,3,46,7,8,90)
print(max(_tuple))
```

Output:
```
90
```

84. How to find the element that has minimum value in a tuple?

Ans. Method min() returns the elements that has minimum value in a tuple. ***Example:***

```
_tuple = (1,2,3,46,7,8,90)
print(min(_tuple))
```

Output:
```
1
```

85. How are list and tuple similar to each other?

Ans. List and tuple have the following similarities.

- Both are sequence data types that store items.
- Both can store heterogeneous data (different data types).
- The elements can be accessed by using index and slicing.

86. Differentiate between tuple and list?

Ans. The key difference between a tuple and a list is that lists are mutable whereas, tuples are immutable.

87. How is a dictionary created?

Ans. The dictionary can be created by using key and value pair, shown as follows:

```
_dict = {'Afghanistan':'Kabul','India':'New Delhi','UK':'London','USA':'Washington DC'}
```

88. What are the features of the dictionary?

Ans. The features of dictionary are:

- Each key-value pair is separated by a colon (:).
- The items are separated by commas.
- Items are enclosed in curly braces.

- An empty dictionary is just two curly braces {}.
- Keys in a dictionary are unique, whereas values may not be unique.
- The keys in a dictionary must be an immutable data type, whereas values in a dictionary can be of any type.

89. How to traverse a dictionary?

Ans.
```
_dict = {'Afghanistan':'Kabul' ,'India':'New Delhi',
'UK':'London','USA':'Washington DC'}
for item in _dict.items():
    print(item)
```

Output:
```
('Afghanistan', 'Kabul')
('India', 'New Delhi')
('UK', 'London')
('USA', 'Washington DC')
```

90. How to create an empty dictionary?

Ans.
```
_dict ={}
print(_dict)
```

Output:
```
{}
```

91. How to add an item to a dictionary?

Ans.
```
_dict = {}
_dict['Afghanistan']='Kabul'
_dict['India']='New Delhi'
print(_dict)
```

Output:
```
{'Afghanistan': 'Kabul', 'India': 'New Delhi'}
```

92. How to get all the items of a dictionary?

Ans.
```
_dict = {'Afghanistan':'Kabul' ,'India':'New Delhi'}
```

The function items() return a new view of the dictionary's items (key, value). The items() can be used to retrieve items(key-value pair).

```
for item in _dict.items():
    print(item)
```

Output:
```
('Afghanistan', 'Kabul')
('India', 'New Delhi')
```

93. How to retrieve all the keys from a dictionary?

Ans. keys() method is used to retrieve all the keys from the dictionary.

```
_dict = {'Afghanistan':'Kabul' ,'India':'New Delhi',
'UK':'London','USA':'Washington DC'}
for key in _dict.keys():
    print(key)
```

Output:
```
Afghanistan
India
UK
USA
```

94. How to get all the values from a dictionary?

Ans. values() method is used to retrieve all the values from a dictionary.

```
_dict = {'Afghanistan':'Kabul' ,'India':'New Delhi',
'UK':'London','USA':'Washington DC'}
for value in _dict.values():
    print(value)
```

Output:
```
Kabul
New Delhi
London
Washington DC
```

95. How to display key and value from a dictionary?

Ans. To display key and value from a dictionary:

```
_dict = {'Afghanistan':'Kabul' ,'India':'New Delhi',
    'UK':'London','USA':'Washington DC'}
for key in _dict.keys():
    print(key , _dict.get(key))
```

Output:
```
Afghanistan
Kabul India New
Delhi UK London
USA Washington DC
```

96. How to retrieve the value of a key?

Ans. The `get()` method is used to retrieve the value if key is passed as an argument.

`get(key[,d]) returns` the value of the key. If key doesn't exists, it returns (default is None).

```
_dict = {'Afghanistan':'Kabul' ,'India':'New Delhi',
'UK':'London','USA':'Washington DC'}
print(_dict.get('India'))
```

Output:
```
New Delhi
```

97. How to remove/delete an item from a dictionary?

Ans.
```
_dict = {'Afghanistan':'Kabul','India':'New Delhi',
'UK':'London','USA':'Washington DC'}
del _dict['Afghanistan']
print(_dict)
```

Output:
```
{'India': 'New Delhi', 'UK': 'London', 'USA': 'Washington DC'}
```

98. How to change the value of a key?

Ans.
```
_dict = {'Australia':'Sydney'}
```

```
_dict['Australia'] ='Canbera'
print(_dict)
```

Output:
```
{'Australia': 'Canbera'}
```

99. How to clear all the items from the dictionary?

Ans. The clear() method is used to remove all the items from the dictionary.

```
_dict = {'Afghanistan':'Kabul' ,'India':'New Delhi',
'UK':'London','USA':'Washington DC'}
_dict.clear()
print(_dict())
```

Output:
```
{}
```

100. How to remove an item from a dictionary?

Ans. pop(key[,d]) removes an item and returns its value. d is return if key is not found.

```
_dict = {'Afghanistan':'Kabul' ,'India':'New Delhi',
'UK':'London','USA':'Washington DC'}
print( _dict.pop('Afghanistan'))
```

Output:
```
Kabul
```

Note: If value is not provided and key is not found, Key Error is raised.

pop item(): It removes an arbitrary item (key, value). It raises the Key Error if dictionary is empty.

```
_dict = {'Afghanistan':'Kabul' ,'India':'New Delhi',
'UK':'London','USA':'Washington DC'}
print(_dict.popitem())
```

Output:
```
('USA', 'Washington DC')
```

101. Differentiate between pop() and pop item().

Ans. pop() removes an item where the key is specified, whereas pop item() removes an arbitrary (random) item.

102. How to merge two dictionaries?

Ans. We can use update ([dict]) method to merge two dictionary; it will overwrite the existing keys.

```
_dict1 ={1:'a',2:'e'}
_dict2 ={3:'i',4:'o',5:'u'}
_dict = _dict1.update(_dict2)
print(_dict)
```

Output:
```
{1:'a',2:'e',3:'i',4:'o',5:'u'}
```

103. How to create a copy of a dictionary?

Ans. The copy method is used to copy a dictionary, as shown below:

```
_dict ={1:'a',2:'e',3:'i',4:'o',5:'u'}
_dictcopy = _dict.copy()
print( dictcopy )
```

Output:

```
{1:'a',2:'e',3:'i',4:'o',5:'u'}
```

104. Differentiate between (10) and (10,).

Ans. (10) is string whereas (10,) is a tuple.

105. Name the methods.

1. **checks if string contains only uppercase letters**
2. **returns the length of the list**

Ans.
```
upper()
len()
```

106. What is the output of the following? **[CBSE OD 2016]**

```
Numbers= [9,18,27,36]
for num in Numbers:
    for n in range(1, num%8):
        print(n, '#',end='')
print()
```

Ans. **Output:**

```
1 #
1 #2 #
1 #2 #3 #
```

107. What is the output of the following? **[CBSE OD 2016]**

```
for name in ['Amar', 'Shweta','Parag']:
    if ( name[0] == 'S'):
        print(name)
```

Ans. **Output:**

```
Shweta
```

108. Consider a list, which print its each element thrice if its' type is integer; else it print it as shown below.

The list is:

```
lst =[41,"Drone","girraj",13, 'Zara']
414141
Drone
girraj
131313
Zara
```

Ans.
```
lst =[41,"Drone","girraj",13, 'Zara']
for ele in lst:
    if (isinstance(ele, int)):
        print( str(ele) * 3)
    else:
        print(ele)
```

Output:

```
414141
Drone
girraj
Zara
131313
```

Programming Questions and Answers 3/4 Marks

1. **Write a program to check if a year is a leap year or not.**

Ans.
```
year = int(input("Enter a year: "))

if (year % 4) == 0):
    #If year is divisible by 100 it must be divisible by 400 as well

    if (year % 100 and year % 400 ) == 0:

        print( str(year) +" is a leap year")

    else:
        print( str(year) +" is not a leap year")

else:
    print(str(year) +" is not a leap year")
```

2. **Find the output of the following programs.**

Ans. a)
```
for i in [1,2,3,4,5,6,7,8,9,10]:
    print(i, end ="\t")
```

Output:

```
1	2	3	4	5	6	7	8	9	10
```

b)
```
string = "Python is fun"
#split() functions split a string into
words words = string.split(" ")
for word in words:
    print(word)
```

Output:

```
Python
is
fun
```

c)
```
for i in  range(1,11):
    for j in range(1,6):
        print(i * j, end="\t")
    print("\n")
```

Output:

```
1   2   3   4   5
2   4   6   8   10
3   6   9   12  15
4   8   12  16  20
5   10  15  20  25
6   12  18  24  30
7   14  21  28  35
8   16  24  32  40
9   18  27  36  45
10  20  30  40  50
```

3. Write a program to add natural numbers up to n terms using while loop and for loop.

Ans.

```
# sum = 1+2+3+...+n using while
num = int(input("Enter numbers of terms: "))
# initialize sum and the counter
sum = 0
i = 1
while i <= num:
    sum = sum + i
    # increment counter
    i = i+1
# print the sum
print("The sum is", sum)
```

```
# sum = 1+2+3+...+n using for loop
num = int(input("Enter numbers of terms: "))
# initialize sum
sum = 0

for i in range(1, num+1):
    sum = sum + i


# print the sum
print("The sum is", sum)
```

4. Write a program that counts the number of digits and letters in a string.

Ans.

```
string = "room no 420"
digits=letters=0
for char in string:
    if char.isdigit():
        digits=digits+1
    elif char.isalpha():
        letters=letters+1
    else:
        pass
print("Number of Letters", letters)
print("Number of Digits", digits)
```

Output:

```
Number of Letters 6
Number of Digits 3
```

5. Write a program that converts a list of words to a string.

Ans. Example 1:

```
_list=['P', 'y', 't', 'h', 'o', 'n', ' ', 'i', 's', ' ', 'f', 'u', 'n', '!']
string = ""
```

```
for char in _list:
    string += char

print(string)
```

Output:

```
Python is fun
```

Example 2:

```
_list =['Python', 'is', 'fun!']

#using join to convert list to string
string = " ".join(_list)

print(string)
```

Output:

```
Python is fun
```

6. Write a program that counts the frequency of each letter in a string.

Ans.

```
string ="google.com"

#dictionary to store letter and its frequency

string="google.com"
freq = {}
for char in string:
    if char in freq:
    # if a letter exists in the add the frequency of letter
        freq[char] += 1
    # if a letter does exist frequency of letter is one else:
    else:
        freq[char] = 1
    #print letter and its frequency

for key, value in freq.items():
    print(key , value)
```

Output:

```
g    2
o    3
l    1
e    1
.    1
c    1
m    1
```

Multiple-Choice Questions

1. What will be output of the following?

list1=[1,2,3,4,5,6,7,8,9]
list1[::3] =[10,20,30]

a. [10, 2, 3, 20, 5, 6, 30, 8, 9]
b. [1, 2, 10, 4 5, 20, 8, 9,30]
c. Error

Ans. Option a

2. _list= [2, 33, 22, 26, 25], What is _list[-1]?

a. Error
b. []
c. 25
d. 2

Ans. Option c, -1 is the last index in the list.

3. _list = [2, 33, 22, 26, 25], What is _list[:-1]?

a. [2, 33, 22, 26]
b. [2, 33, 22, 26, 25]
c. 25
d. Error

Ans. Option a, retrieves from start to end-1.

2 FUNCTIONS

LEARNING OBJECTIVES

- Define a user-define function based on the problem statement.
- Identify the function header, parameter, argument, and body of a function
- Illustrate the scope of variables with examples

DEFINITION

- **Function:** A function is a group of statements. It is a named block design to perform some task(s). A function may accept argument(s) and it may return value(s).
- **Function header:** The name of a function and parameter list enclosed in bracket and colon at end.
- **Return statement:** A return statement returns a value to the calling script or function and terminates.
- **Scope of a variable:** A variable is created in a program which can be enclosed in a certain region. This is called scope of a variable. For example: local variables are defined and used in a function whereas global variables are used across the functions in a program and defined outside the function.

Very Short Questions and Answers — 1 Mark

1. Why functions are used?

Ans. In simple terms, a function is a named block of code that performs some task(s). This helps a program to divide the code into well-defined reusable blocks. This improves the quality of the code by making it more readable, maintainable, and reusable. Functions enable programmers to share their code. Functions may receive parameters and they may add value to the caller function. The return keyword allows returning a value.

2. Differentiate between argument and parameter.

Ans. A variable in the function definition is called a parameter. When a function is called a variable or a value is passed, this value is called as an argument.

3. Is it mandatory for functions to have parameters?

Ans. No, functions can be defined without parameters..

4. Is the return statement optional?

Ans. Yes, the return statement is optional.

5. If there is no return statement in the function, what is returned?

Ans. None

6. Differentiate between statement 'return' and statement 'return val'?

Ans. The return statement returns None to caller function whereas 'return val' returns the value of val variable.

7. Where is a docstring defined?

Ans. Python `docstring` (documentation strings) is defined in functions, classes, Python modules and methods.

A `docstring` is the first line of a function which is a short description of the function.

```
def sqr(num):
    '''Returns the square of num''' ← doc string
    return num**2
```

8. What does docstring describe?

Ans. A `docstring` is a short description of what the function or module does.

9. Differentiate between comments and a docstring.

Ans. A `docstring` describes what the function does. A comment helps to understand the code.

10. What does the function header tell?

Ans. The function header tells the name of the function and the list of parameters that are passed to the function.

11. How are the parameters and arguments related?

Ans. Parameters are defined in function header; arguments are passed in the function call. The argument is passed to the functions and saved into parameters.

12. What is the output of the following code?

```
a = 5
def func ():
    a = 10
    print(a)
```

Ans. Output:

```
10
```

13. What is the output of the following code?

```
x= 5
def func ():
    x = 25
    print(x)
```

Ans. Output:

```
25
```

14. In the following code, identify

function header,
function call,
parameter, and
function body.

```
def reverseSign(num):
    return -1 * num

reverseSign(-5)
```

Ans. Function header: `reverseSign(num):`

Function call: `reverseSign(-5)`

Parameter: `num`

Function body: `return -1 * num`

15. What is the output of the following program?

```
num = 10
```

```
def golocalscope():
    return num

print(num)
print(golocalscope())
print(num)
```

Ans. **Output:**

```
10
10
10
```

16. Differentiate between argument and parameter.

Ans. A variable in a function definition is called a parameter. When a function is called, a variable or a value that is passed is called an argument.

17. What is the output of following code?

```
var = 10
def func():
    var = 1
print(var)
func()
```

Ans. **Output:**

```
10
```

18. What is the output of the following code?

```
def func_1():
    return
print(func_1())

def func_2():
    return 5
print(func_2())
```

Ans. **Output:**

```
None
5
```

Short Questions and Answers 2/3 Marks

1. Explain how to create a function?

Ans. A function is defined using the def keyword.

Let's see the following sample:

```
def welcome(name):
    return "Welcome " + str(name)
```

A function call is a statement or an expression that passes the control and arguments to the function. Function name evaluates to its address and the parameter list in a function call is passed to the argument's list of the function.

```
print(welcome("Mr Beans"))
```

Output:

```
Welcome Mr Beans
```

2. Explain the anatomy of a function and how it is called.

Ans. A function is defined by using def keyword followed by space(s) and function name. A function accepts parameters that go in parenthesis. Parameters are separated by a comma and enclosed in brackets (), which is followed by a colon (:) and a function body.

A function body contains the statement or set of statements, it may return some value.

```
def abs_val(num):
    if(num < 0):
        return -1 * num
    else:
        return num
```

Let's see how to call a function. A function is called by using the name with the argument. We can also retrieve the value returned by a function placing a variable and equal sign before the function call, as shown below:

```
val = abs_val( -5 )
print(val)
```

Output:

```
5
```

3. What is an argument? Explain with an example.

Ans. A function performs some task(s); for which it may require some data. Arguments in function allow passing data for processing them. For example:

```
def addNum(num1 , num2):
    return num1 + num2
```

Arguments are passed to function through a function call; for example, here 2 and 3 are arguments:

```
print(addNum(2,3))
```

Output:

```
5
```

4. Why is the help() function used?

Ans. The built-in function help() displays the documentation of the module passed as an argument. It displays the **docstring** within its passed arguments definition. For example:

```
help (math)
```

In the above example, we passed the math module in the help function, it will give the following output:

```
NAME
    math
DESCRIPTION
This module is always available. It provides access to the mathematical functions defined
by the C standard.
FUNCTIONS
acos(x, /): It returns the arc cosine (measured in radians) of x.
```

It can even take function name as argument. For example:

```
help(math.sqrt())
```

The above code will list the documentation of math.sqrt() function only. It can take function name as argument. For example:

```
>>>help(math.sqrt())
```

The above code will list the documentation of math.sqrt() function only. The help built-in function sqrt in module math:

```
sqrt(x, /): It return the square root of x
```

5. Identify function header, arguments, parameters, function body and function call in the below code.

```
def SQR(x):
    return x ** 2

res = SQR(5)
```

Ans. Function header: `def  SQR(x):`

Function call: `SQR(5)`

Parameter: `x`

Function body: `return x ** 2`

6. Differentiate between local variable and global variable with an example.

Ans. The differences between a local variable and global variable are as follows:

- **Local variable:** It is a variable that is declared within a function or within a block. It is accessible within a function or block.
- **Global variable:** It is a variable that is declared above/outside all the functions. It is accessible throughout the program /file in which it is declared.

Example:

```
check = 5 #global variable

def SQR(n):
    sqrval= n * n
    return sqrval  #local variable


def CUBE(n):
    return SQR(n) * n

print("Printing Square value")
print(SQR(check))
print("Printing cube value")
print(CUBE(check))
```

Output:

```
Printing Square value
25
Printing cube value
125
```

7. Write a function that calculates the volume of a cube. Input parameter side and unit as a default parameter. The volume of a cube is side * side * side.

Ans.

```
import math

def cube_volume (side , unit="inches"):
    return str(side**3 ) + " " + unit

side =float(input("Enter the length of the side"))
print(cube_volume(side,'cms'))
```

```
side =float(input("Enter the length of the side"))
print(cube_volume(side))
```

Output:

```
Enter length of the side of the cube : 5
750.0 cms
Enter length of the side of the cube : 5
750.0 inches
```

8. Write a function that prints even numbers from the list.

Ans.

```
slist= [1, 12, 3, 4, 15, 6, 7, 18, 9, 8]

def print_even (list):
    for i in range( 0,len(list)):
        if ( list[i] % 2 == 0 ):
            print(list[i], end=", ")
print_even(slist)
```

Output:

```
12, 4, 6, 18, 8,
```

9. Write a function that prints odd numbers from the list?

Ans.

```
slist= [1, 12, 3, 4, 15, 6, 7, 18, 9, 8]

def print_odd (list):
    for i in range( 0,len(list)):
        if ( list[i] % 2 != 0 ):
            print(list[i], end=", ")
print_odd(slist)
```

Output:

```
1, 3, 15, 7, 9,
```

10. Explain the docstring in a function with an example.

Ans.

```
def my_function():
    """The function's docstring"""
```

Note: A docstring is defined in """ . . . """, should be the first line of the function.

11. How to retrieve the docstring?

Ans.

```
def my_function():
    """The function's docstring"""
```

A docstring can be retrieved in two ways:

a. Using doc attribute __doc__

   `my_function.__doc__`

b. Using the help function

   `help(my_function):`

Output:

```
>>> my_function.__doc__
"The function's docstring"
>>> help(my_function)
Help on function my_function in module __main__:

my_function()
    The function's docstring
```

12. Write a function to calculate the area of a triangle.

Ans. Arguments are base and height of a triangle. The formula used is: Area = 1/2*base*height

```
def triangle_area( base, height):
    area = .5 * base * height
    return area
height = int(input("Enter height: "))
base = int(input("Enter base: "))
print("The area of the triangle is: ")
print(triangle_area(height,base))
```

Output:

```
Enter height: 5
Enter base: 10
The area of the triangle is:
25.0
```

13. Write a function to calculate the area of a circle.

Ans. Parameter are radius and return value is area of a circle. The formula used is: area = 22/7 * r **2

```
def circle_area( radius):
    area = 22/7*(radius **2)
    return area

rad = float(input("Enter radius: "))
print(circle_area(rad))
```

Output:

```
Enter radius: 5
78.57142857142857
```

14. What is the return value of the following function?

```
def sumthree(x, y, z):
    print("The sum is: " + str (x + y + z) )

num1 = int(input("Enter number 1:"))
num2 = int(input("Enter number 2:"))
num3 = int(input("Enter number 3:"))

retval= sumthree(num1, num2, num3)
print("The return value is ")
print(retval)
```

Ans. **Output:**

```
Enter number 1 :5
Enter number 2 :10
Enter number 3 :15
The sum is: 30
The return value is
None
```

15. Find the output of the following function.

```
def sumthree(a, b, c):
    return a + b + c
    print("The sum is: ")
    print(a + b + c)

num1 = int(input("Enter number 1:"))
num2 = int(input("Enter number 2:"))
num3 = int(input("Enter number 3:"))

print("The sum of " + str(num1) + " + " + str(num2) + " + " + str(num3) + "  is
:",end= " ")
sumthree(num1,num2,num3)
```

Ans. **Output:**

```
Enter number 1 :5
Enter number 2 :10
Enter number 3 :15
The sum of 5 + 10 + 15 is :30
```

Note: Statement after return will not be executed and the sum is not printed in function.

16. Find the output of the following program.

```
num = 10

def golocalscope():

    num =50
    return num

print(num)
print(golocalscope())
print(num)
```

Ans. **Output:**

```
10
50
10
```

17. Find the output of the following program.

Ans.

```
num = 10
def golocalscope ():
```

```
        global num
        num =50

    print(num)
    print(golocalscope() )
    print(num)
```

Ans. **Output:**

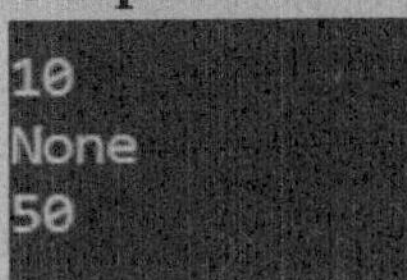

```
10
None
50
```

18. **Find out what is wrong in the below code.**

```
def Interest(principal, time, rate):
    return principal * time * rate
        print ("the interest is principal * time * rate")
```

Ans. The print function is unreachable; the return statement returns execution back to the calling statement, any statement after return statement will not be executed.

19. **Find the errors in the below code.**

```
def decrement(total, delta)
    difference = total - delta
    print (Difference)
    return (difference)
```

Ans.
- The colon (:) is missing in the function header.
- We have not defined a variable Difference.

20. **Find the errors in the below code.**

```
define cir_area(r)
    pi=3.14159
    Area = pi*r*r
    return area
```

Ans. In the above code, there are two errors:

a. The keyword def is used to define a function not 'define'.

b. The colon (:) is missing in the function header.

The correct code is:

```
def cir_area(r):
    pi=3.14159
    area = pi*r*r
    return area
```

21. **Find the errors in below code.**

```
def test1 (number, string = 'xyz'):
    test2(string)
    return number

def test2 (string)
    Return string == str(number)
```

Ans. In the above code, Return is not a keyword; instead, the return keyword should be used. Also, the colon (:) is missing in the function header.

22. What do you understand by recursion?

Ans. Recursion is a method of solving a problem where the solution can be viewed as smaller instances of the same problem. For example:

```
factorial of 5 is:
5 x factorial of 4
5 x 4 x factorial of 3 and so on
```

Recursion allows a function to call itself from within its own code.

23. Write a recursive function to add the first 'n' terms of the series: 1+ 1/2 - 1/3+1/4

Ans.

```
total = 1.0
term =-1
x= 2
def sum_series(n):
    #using global variable to retain value between multiple function calls
    global total
    global term
    global x

    if n == 1:
        return total
    else:
            # Change the sign
        term = term * -1
        total= total +( ( 1 / x ) * term )
        x+=1
    return sum_series(n-1)
print(sum_series(5))
print(sum_series(10))
print(sum_series(20))
print(sum_series(50))
```

Output:

```
1.2166666666666668
1.3412948162948166
1.2919307674894436
1.3129132029297337
```

24. Write a function that multiply all its numbers in a list.

Ans.

```
def mul_list(lst):
    mul=1
    for element in lst:
        mul*=element
    return mul

lst = [ 2,4,6,10]
print(mul_list(lst) )
```

```
print(mul_list([1,2,3,4,5]))
print(mul_list(range(1,10)))
```

Output:

```
480
120
362880
```

25. Explain the anatomy of a function and how it is called.

Ans. A function is defined using def keyword followed by space(s) and function name. A function accepts parameters that go in parenthesis. Parameters are separated by a comma and enclosed in brackets (), which is followed by a colon (:) and a function body.

A function body contains the statement or set of statements, it may return some value.

```
def abs_val(num):

    if(num < 0):
        return -1 * num
    else:
        return num
val = abs_val( -5 )
print(val)
```

26. Explain arguments with an example.

Ans. Function performs some task(s); to do so it may be required some data. Arguments in function allows to pass data for processing them. For example:

```
def addNum(num1 , num2):
    return num1 + num2
```

Arguments are passed to function when a function is called. Here 2 and 3 are arguments, for example:

```
print(addNum(2,3))
```

27. Find the output of the below code.

```
def productall( a,b,c,d):
    print( a * b * c *d)

def sumall(a,b,c,d):
    return (a + b + c + d)

resproduct = productall(1,2,3,4)
ressum = sumall(1,2,3,4)
print(resproduct, ressum)
```

Ans. Output:

```
24 10
```

28. Find the incorrect function header and state the reason.

```
def defaultargs(arg1=1, arg2=2, arg3=3,arg4):
```

Ans. The above declaration is incorrect, because of the non-default argument (arg4 is defined after default arguments arg1, arg2, arg3).

```
def defaultargs(arg1 =1, arg2=2):
```

Correct, because all the arguments are default arguments:

```
def defaultargs(arg1 =1, arg2, arg3=2)
```

Incorrect, because positional argument arg2 is defined before arg3

29. How and where the local variables are defined?

Ans. A local variable is defined inside a function block or a block.

```
total = 0
def sum(num1, num2):
    #local variable s
    s = 0
    s = num1 + num2
    return s

multiply =1

def mul(num1, num2):
    #local variable m
    m = 0
    m = num1 * num2
    return m

total = sum(2,5)
print(total)
multiply = mul(5, 2)
print(multiply)
```

Output:

```
7
10
```

30. Explain how to use global variable in function?

Ans. The global variable is declared by using the global keyword as shown in the below-defined functions:

```
def     f1():                               #1
        global val                          #2
        val = 6                             #3

def     f2():                               #4
        global val                          #5
        val = val+1                         #6
        print("printing global variable")   #7
        print(val)                          #8

def     f3():                               #10
        val = 10                            #11
        print("printing local variable")    #12
        print(val)                          #13
val = 15
f1()
f2()
f3()
```

The val is a global variable. To use the global variable in a function, add global keyword before the variable name as shown in line #2 and line#5. When function f1 is called, the value of global variable val becomes 6. The subsequent function call to f2 adds one to it and it prints its value as 7. Lastly, function f3 is called which prints the value of local var, that is 10.

Output:

```
printing global variable
7
printing local variable
10
```

31. Find the output of the following code.

```
def swaplocal(a,b):
    a,b = b,a
    print("Swapping the local variable")
    print(a,b)
x = 10
y = 20
swaplocal(x,y)
print("Values after swapping the local variable")
print(x,y)
```

Ans. Output:

```
Swapping the local variable
20 10
Values  after swapping the local variable
10 20
```

The function swap local(), swaps at local variables a and b; the value of global variable x and y remains unchanged.

32. Find the output of the following code.

```
def swapgobal():
    global x, y
    x, y = y,x
    print("Swapping the global variable")
    print(x,y)
x = 10
y = 20
swapgobal()
print("Values after swapping the global variable")
print(x,y)
```

Ans. Output:

```
Swapping the global variable
20 10
Values after swapping the global variable
20 10
```

33. Find the missing statements (statement1 and statement2) in the following code.

```
def delta(y):
    ____________ #statement1
    value = value + y
    ____________ #statement2
value =10
```

```
deltavalue = .5
delta(.5)
print(value)
```

Ans. The following are the missing statements in the above code:

- `statement1` global value
- `statement2` return value

34. What will be output of the following code?

```
def line(ch, length=10):
    print(ch * length)

ch = "*"
line(ch, 40)
```

Ans. Output:

```
>>> line('*',40)
****************************************
```

35. What will be the output of the following code?

```
def defaultargs(num1 = 10, num2 = 20):
    print(num1, num2)

defaultargs()
defaultargs(5)
defaultargs(5, 10)
```

Ans. Output:

```
>>> defaultargs()
10 20
>>> defaultargs(5)
5 20
>>> defaultargs(5, 10)
5 10
```

36. Find the output of the following code.

```
var = 10
def func():
    var = 1
    print(var)
func()
```

Ans. Output:

```
1
```

37. A program contains multiple functions is it easier to design compared to a program that does not contain any function. Discuss?

Ans. A program with multiple functions is easy to code, understand, and maintain. Long programs are difficult to understand and maintain. Debugging the code is also difficult when code in a program is long. A function enhance re-usability and it reduces redundancy (duplication of code) and makes debugging easier.

Programs have common functionality that can be placed in a function. A function can be used at multiple time without the repetition of code.

38. Explain the utility of the keyword argument.

Ans. The keyword argument is defined by placing ** before a parameter name. Keyword arguments can be passed using name and value pair, as shown in the function call.

```
def   postaladdress(username, **useraddress):
    for items in useraddress.items():
        print (items)
postaladdress("Vijay", Flatno=202, plotno=2, street="MG road", location="Bapu Nagar", pin="110001")
```

Output:

```
('Flatno', 202)
('plotno', 2)
('street', 'MG road')
('location', 'Bapu Nagar')
('pin', '110001')
```

The keyword arguments allow passing arguments without worrying about the order of the arguments.

39. Explain the default argument and its utility.

Ans. Function header with default parameters allows skipping of passing the arguments while calling the function. For example:

```
def welcome(name , title="Mr." , msg= "Welcome aboard!!!"):
    print (msg , "" ,title , "" ,name)
welcome("Ramesh Kumar")
welcome("Savita Khanna ","Mrs.")
```

Output:

```
Welcome aboard!!!  Mr.  Ramesh Kumar
Welcome aboard!!!  Mrs.  Savita Khanna
```

If we want to use the pre-defined value of an argument, we can use default values. For instance, in the above example, when we pass the name of the male, that is, Ramesh Kumar, we can omit the title and the default value is already assigned to it.

40. Can function return multiple values? If yes, how?

Ans. Function can return multiple values as shown in below code:

```
def SQR( num1, num2):
    _t = num1 * num1, num2 * num2
    return _t
print( SQR(5,10))
```

Output:

```
(25, 100)
```

41. Suggest improvements in the below code.

```
import math

def div(num1, num2):
    return math.floor(num1 / num2)
    val = num1 // num2
```

Ans. The suggested improvements are:

```
def div(num1, num2):
    return    math.floor(num1 / num2)
```

The function will return the value `math.floor(num1 / num2)` and `val = num1 // num2` statement will not execute ; hence it can be removed.

Long Questions and Answers 3 Marks

1. Write a Python function that accepts a string and returns the number of characters in uppercase and lowercase.

Ans. Let's create a dictionary to store the count of upper case and lower case characters in the dictionary:

```
_dict = {"UC":0, "LC":0}

def char_count(string):
    for char in string:
        if char.isupper():
        #increment the count of upper case
            _dict["UC"]+=1
        # increment the count of lower case
        elif char.islower():
            _dict["LC"]+=1
        # pass if character is not upper and lower case
        else:
            pass
char_count("My name is Bond!!! James Bond")
print("The number of upper case character(s): " + str(_dict.get("UC")))
print("The number of lower case character(s): " + str(_dict.get("LC")))
```

Output:

```
The number of upper case character(s) : 4
The number of upper case character(s) : 17
```

2. Write a function to check whether a number is perfect or not.

Ans. In number theory, a perfect number is a positive integer that is equal to the sum of its proper positive divisors. Equivalently, a perfect number is a number that is half the sum of all positive divisors (including itself). For example, 6 is perfect number, because 1, 2, and 3 are its proper positive divisors, and 1 + 2 + 3 = 6. Equivalently, the number 6 is equal to half the sum of all its positive divisors: (1 +2 + 3 + 6)/2 = 6. The next perfect number is 28 = 1 + 2 + 4 + 7 + 14. Other perfect numbers are 496 and 8128.

Let's write a function to find if a number is perfect or not:6

```
def perfect_number (num):
    sum = 0
    for i in range (1, num):
        if num % i == 0:
            sum += i
    return  sum == num

num = int(input("Enter a number: "))
if( perfect_number(num) == True ):
```

```
    print("The "+ str( num ) +" is a perfect number ")
else:
    print("The "+ str( num ) +" is   not a perfect number ")
```

Output:

```
Enter a number: 6
The 6 is a perfect number
Enter a number: 28
The 28 is a perfect number
Enter a number: 512
The 512 is  not a perfect number
```

3. Explain scoping rules in Python.

Ans. Scope in Python is resolved using the LEGB rule. The LEGB rule decides the order in which name spaces are to be searched for scope resolution of a variable. The scopes are listed below from highest to lowest and from narrowest to broadest:

- **L (Local):** Defined inside function or class.
- **E (Enclosed):** Defined inside enclosing function (nested function is function inside a function).
- **G (Global):** Defined outside a function; usually uppermost level.
- **B (Built-in):** Reserved names in Python's built-in modules. Let us understand it by an example below:

```
# Built-in Scope

from math  import pi
print("Build in scope")
print("Printing Built-in  variable pi(imported from math module)")
print(pi)

print("Global scope")
pi = 'Global variable pi'
print("Printing global  variable pi")
print(pi)

def func():
    pi = 'local variable pi'
    print('Local scope')
    print(pi)

    def enclosing():
        pi = 'enclosing variable pi'
        print('enclosing scope')
        print(pi)

    enclosing()

func()
```

Output:

```
Printing Built-in variable pi
3.141592653589793
Printing global variable pi
Global variable pi
enclosing variable  pi
local variable  pi
```

The following diagram illustrate the LEGB rules of scoping:

```
pi B
#Built-in pi variable math module

    pi = 'Global variable pi' G
    #global variable pi

        pi = 'enclosing variable  pi' E

            pi = 'local variable  pi' L
```

4. Write a function that converts one currency to another currency or vice versa.

Ans. In the following code, _dict contains the conversion rate. Let's see in detail:

```
_dict={"USD-INR":68.86,"INR-USD":.015, "GBP-INR":85.26,"INR-GBP":0.0117241}
def curr_converter(amt, fromcurr='INR', tocurr='USD' ):
    #create key for conversion
    key = fromcurr  + "-" + tocurr
    if( key in _dict.keys()):
        return amt * _dict.get(key)
#converting USD to  IR
print("Converting from 1 USD to IR")
print(curr_converter(1,"USD","INR"))

print("Converting from 1 INR to USD")
print(curr_converter(1,"INR","USD"))

print("Converting from 1 IR to GBP")
print(curr_converter(1,"INR","GBP"))
```

```
print("Converting from 100 INR to USD")
print(curr_converter(100))
```

Output:

```
Converting from  1 USD to IR
68.86
Converting from  1 INR to USD
0.015
Converting from  1 IR to GBP
0.0117241
Converting from 100 INR to USD
1.5
```

5. Write a function to compute the factorial of a number (a non-negative integer).

Ans. The function accepts a number and returns its factorial.

```
def fact(num):
    if(num < 0):
        print("Error ! no factorial value for negative number")
    elif(num == 0):
        return 0
    else:
        f=1
        while(num > 0):
            f*=num
            num-=1
    return f
print(fact(5))
print(fact(0))
print(fact(-2))
```

Output:

```
120
0
Error ! no factorial value for negative number
None
```

6. Find the output of the following code.

```
def printline(newline, char='*', len = 20):
    for i in range(len):
        print(char, end='')
    if(newline):
        print()
    printline(True)
    printline(True, char ='-'))
    printline( True, char='-', len =40)
    printline(False, char = '='))
```

Ans. **Output:**

```
********************
--------------------
----------------------------------------
====================
```

7. State the advantages and disadvantages of using recursion.

Ans. Advantages of using recursion:

- Reduce unnecessary calling of function.
- Recursion, in some cases, can solve problems in an easy way as compared to an iterative solution.

The disadvantages of using recursion:

- A recursive solution is difficult to trace (debug and understand).
- If the base case is not defined properly, the function will never return.
- Recursion takes a lot of stack space.
- Recursion uses more processor time.

8. Find out the correct/incorrect function calls for the following function. Explain the reason if call is incorrect.

```
def tag(name, type ="text", id="id"):
    pass
```

Function call	Result	Reason
tag()	Incorrect	Position argument is missing
tag("input")	Correct	
tag(type="button")	Incorrect	Positional argument is missing
tag(input, name="input")	Incorrect	Multiple values for keyword argument name
tag(type="checkbox", id="checkbox1")	Incorrect	Positional argument is missing

Programming Questions and Answers — 3 Marks

1. Write a program that accepts a sequence of words as input and prints the words after sorting them in alphabetical order.

Ans.

```
string = 'my name is antony'
#splits sentence into words
words = string.split(' ')
#sort the list of the words
words.sort()
#join the words into a string
print(' '.join(words))
```

Output:

```
antony is my name
```

2. Write a function that accepts a number and prints the Fibonacci series upto the number given.

Ans.

```
#function that print Fibonacci series
def Fibonacci(num):
# Simultaneous assignment
    f1,f2=0,1
    print(f1, f2, end=' ')
    while f2<num:
#simultaneous assignment f1 = f2 and f2 = f1+f2
        f1,f2 = f2,f1+f2
        print(f1, end=",")
```

Output:

```
Fibonacci(100)
0,1,1,2,3,5,8,13,21,34,55,89,
```

3. Write a function that prints the sum of the following series.

#series x + x ^2 / 2! + x ^3 / 3!+. n

Ans.

```
import math
def series(x, terms):
    sum=0
    i=1
    while i < terms:
        sum = sum + math.pow(x,i) / math.factorial(i)
        i+=1
    return sum

print(series(2,10))
```

Output:

```
6.3887125220458545
```

4. Write a program that returns the longest word from a list of words.

Ans.

```
def longestword( _list ):
    largest=""
    for word in _list:
        if( len(word) > len(largest)):
            largest = word
    return largest
#covert the string into list
lst= "this is a program to find the longest word in the sentence".split(" ")
print(longestword(lst))
```

Output:

```
sentence
```

5. Write a function that converts a list of characters into a string.

Ans.

```
def list_to_str(_list):
    return string = ''.join(_list)

lst = ['p', 'y', 't', 'h','o','n']
print(list_to_str(lst))
```

Output:

```
python
```

6. Write a function to get the frequency of each element in a list.

Ans.

```
def element_freq(_list):
    # To store elements and their occurrence
    _freq={}
    for ele in _list:
        if(ele in _freq):
            # if element exists in dictionary
```

```
            # add the frequency of an element
            _freq[ele] += 1
        else:
            _freq[ele] = 1
    return _freq

print(element_freq([1,2,4,5,6,1,2,8,3,10,5]))
```

Output:

```
{1: 2, 2: 2, 4: 1, 5: 2, 6: 1, 8: 1, 3: 1, 10: 1}
```

7. Write a program to unpack a tuple in several variables.

Ans.

```
#creating a tuple
_tuple = 1, 2, 3
print(_tuple)
```

Output:

```
(1,2,3)
```

```
num1, num2, num3 = _tuple
#unpack a tuple in variables
print(num1 + num2 + num3)
```

Output:

```
6
```

8. Write a function to convert a tuple to a string.

Ans.

```
def tuple_to_str(_tuple):
    # to convert tuple in list first and
       #use join to convert into string
    string =" ".join(list(_tuple))
    return (string)

print(tuple_to_str( ('p', 'y ', 't ', 'h ', 'o ', 'n ') ))
```

Output:

```
python
```

9. Write a program to add an item in a tuple at the beginning, end, or a given location.

Ans. The tuple is immutable and cannot be altered. To add the new tuple, the '+' operator is used; it returns a newly created tuple. Below example demonstrates to add the element in the tuple:

```
def additem(_tuple,ele,loc=0):
    # Add the element at the beginning of the tuple
    if (loc == 0):
        _tuple = (ele,) + _tuple
    # Add the element at the end of the tuple
    elif(loc == len(_tuple)):
        _tuple = _tuple + (ele,)
    else:
    # Add the element at the specified location
        _tuple = _tuple[:loc] + (ele,) + _tuple[loc:]
```

```
    return _tuple
print(additem((1,2,3,4,5,6),7,0))
print(additem((1,2,3,4,5,6),7,len((1,2,3,4,5,6)))
print(additem((1,2,3,4,5,6),7,3))
```

Output:

```
(7, 1, 2, 3, 4, 5, 6)
( 1, 2, 3, 4, 5, 6,7)
(1, 2, 3, 7, 1, 2, 3)
```

Multiple-Choice Questions

1. **Which of the following are true in Python?**
   a. Functions are reusable components of a program
   b. Modularity cannot be achieved through functions
   c. Python allows creating user-defined functions
   d. All of the above

Ans. The statement a and c are true in Python.

2. **Which keyword is used for defining a function?**
   a. Define   b. Fun   c. def   d. Function

Ans. The def keyword is used for defining a function, that is, option c.

3. **Find the output of the following program.**

```
def Hello():
    print('Welcome to Python!')
Hello()
Hello()
```

   a. Welcome to Python! Welcome to Python!
   b. 'Welcome to Python!' 'Welcome to Python!'

Ans. The output of the above program will be a.

4. **Find the output of the following program.**

```
def _func(x, y=5, z=10):
    print( 'x is ', x, ' and y is ', y, 'and z is ', z)
_ func(3, 7)
_func(25, z= 24)
_func(z = 50, x = 100)
```

   a. x is 7 and y is 3 and z is 10
      x is 25 and y is 5 and z is 24
      x is 5 and y 100 and z is 50
   b. x is 3 and y is 7 and z is 10
      x is 5 and y is 25 and z is 24
      x is 50 and y is 100 and z is 5
   c. x is 3 and y is 7 and z is 10
      x is 25 and y is 5 and z is 24
      x is 100 and y is 5 and z is 50

Ans. The output of the above program will be c.

5. Find the output of the following piece of code.

```
def gettype(posarg, **kwargs):
    print(type(kwargs))
gettype('arg1',1='a',2='b')
```

a. Tuple b. String c. Dictionary d. Error

Ans. Option c, that is, Dictionary

6. How is keyword argument specified in a function heading?

a. a double underscore followed by an identifier
b. single star followed by an identifier
c. double stars followed by an identifier
d. double underscores followed and preceded by an identifier

Ans. Option c, that is, double stars followed by an identifier.

7. A function call contains keyword arguments.

a. one b. zero c. one or more d. zero or more

Ans. Option d, that is, zero or more.

8. Find the output of the following code.

```
def chk_global():
    return total + 1

total = 0
print(chk_global())
```

a. error b. 0 c. 1 d. none of the above

Ans. Option c, that is, 1.

9. Find the output of the following code.

```
def chk_global():
    total += 1
    return total

total = 0
print(chk_global())
```

a. 1 b. 0 c. error d. none of the mentioned

Ans. Option c, that is, error. `UnboundLocalError: local variable 'total' referenced before assignment`

10. Find the output of the following program.

```
def Max(x, y):
    if x > y:
        print(x, 'is maximum')
    elif x == y:
        print(x, 'is equal to', y)
    else:
        print(y, 'is maximum')

Max(3, 4)
```

a. `3 is maximum` b. `3` c. `4 is maximum` d. `4`

Ans. The output of the above program will be c.

11. Find the output of the following program at line #7.

```
var = 50                                          #1
def func(var):                                    #2
    print('var is', var)                          #3
    var = 2                                       #4
    print('local var is changed to', var)         #5
func(var)                                         #6
print('var is now', var)                          #7
```

a. var is now 50
b. var is 2
c. local var is changed to 2
d. None of the above

Ans. The output of the above program will be a.

12. Find the output of the following program at line #3.

```
var = 50                                          #1
def func(var):                                    #2
    print(print(y,'var is', var)                  #3
    var = 2                                       #4
    print('local var is changed to', var)         #5

func(var)                                         #6
print('var is now', var)                          #7
```

a. var is now 50
b. var is 50
c. var is now 100
d. None of the above

Ans. The output of the above program will be b.

13. Find the output of the below program.

```
def printchar(char, times = 1):
    print (char * times)
    printchar( '*' , 20)
```

a. ********************
b. *
c. None

Ans. The output of the above program will be a.

14. Find the output of the following program.

```
def max(arg1, arg2):
    if arg1 > arg2:
        return arg1
    elif arg1 == arg2:
        return 'Equal'
    else:
        return arg2

print(max(12, 4))
```

a. 4
b. Equal
c. 12
d. None of the above

Ans. The output of the above program will be c.

15. What are the advantages of using functions in code?

a. It reduces redundancy of code
b. It decomposes complexity into simpler problems
c. It enhances clarity of the Python code
d. All of the above

Ans. The answer is d, All of the above

16. Name two main types of functions.

a. System function
b. Built-in and User-defined function
c. Custom function
d. User function

Ans. The answer is b, Built-in, and User-defined function.

17. Which of the following is not a build-in function?

a. abs() b. len() c. dir() d. def()

Ans. Option d is not a built-in function.

18. Where function can be defined?

a. Another function b. Class c. Module d. All of the above

Ans. Option d, that is, all of the above can be defined.

19. Conventionally function is defined inside a class called ___________?

a. Class b. Module c. lambda d. Method

Ans. Option d, that is, Method.

20. The id() function in Python is used to get ___________.

a. A unique number b. object's ID c. both a and b d. None of the above

Ans. Option b, that is, object's ID.

21. Which of the following is a mathematical function?

a. add() b. sqr() c. sqrt() d. area()

Ans. Option c, that is, sqrt().

22. Find the output of the following program.

```
def cube_num(num):
    return num **3

num = cube_num(3)

print(num)
```

a. 3 b. 9 c. 27 d. 30

Ans. Option c that is 27

23. Find the output of the following program.

```
def powerfn(arg1, arg2=2):
    power = 1
    for i in range(arg2):
        power = power * arg1
    return power

print powerfn(5)
print powerfn(3,5)
```

a. 25 27 b. 5 243 c. 25 243 d. None of the above

Ans. Option c, that is, 25 243.

24. Find the output of the following program.

```
def sumargs(*args):
    sumtotal = 0
    for arg in args:
        sumtotal += arg
```

```
        return sumtotal

    print (sumargs(1, 2, 3))
    print (sumargs(1, 2, 3, 4, 5))
```

a. 123 12345 b. 6 15 c. Error d. None of the above

Ans. Option b, that is, 6 15.

25. Find the output of the following program.

```
def f(arg1, arg2, arg3):
    return arg1 + arg2 ** arg3
f(2, 3, 2)
```

a. 18 b. 11 c. 36 d. None of the above

Ans. Option b, that is, 11.

26. Find the output of the following program.

```
def name_title(*names):
    title = 'Sir'

    for name in names:
        name = 'Sir' +" " + name
        print(name,end=' ')

    return names

name_title('viv richards', 'don bradman')
```

a. ('viv richards', 'don bradman') b. 'Sir viv richards ', 'Sir don bradman'
c. ('Sir viv richards ', 'Sir don bradman') d. a or b

Ans. Option b Sir viv richards Sir don bradman

27. The variable that is defined outside a function is referred as?

a. local variable b. global variable c. static variable d. non-local variable

Ans. Option b, that is, global variable.

28. A variable that is defined inside a function is referred as?

a. local variable b. global variable c. non-local variable d. static variable

Ans. Option a, that is, local variable.

29. Find the output of the following code.

```
val=0
def val_change(val):
    val=val+1
    return val

print (val , val_change(val))
```

a. 1 , 0 b. 0 , 1 c. No value d. Error

Ans. Option b, that is, 0, 1.

30. Find the output of the following code.

```
globala =10
globalb =20
def val_change():
```

```
    global globalb
    globala=45
    globalb=54
val_change()
print(globala, globalb)
```

a. 10 54 b. 45 54 c. 10 20 d. Error

Ans. Option a, that is, 10 54.

31. Find the output of the following code.

```
def val_change(args1 = 1, args2 = 2):
    args1 = args1 + args2
    args2 = args2 + 1
    print(args1, args2)
val_change(args2 = 1, args1 = 2)
```

a. Error b. 3 3 c. 2 3 d. 3 2

Ans. Option d, that is, 3 2.

32. Find the output of the following code.

```
def val_change(argone, *vararg):
    print(type(vararg))
val_change(1,2,3,4)
```

a. Lists b. Tuple c. Integer d. Dictionary

Ans. Option b, that is, Tuple.

Fill in the blanks

1. ________ is a variable in the declaration in function definition.

Ans. Parameter

2. ________ is the variable or actual value that gets passed to a function.

Ans. Argument

3. Keyword ________ marks the ________ of function header.

Ans. def, start

4. A function name is ________ to it.

Ans. uniquely identify

5. A Function name follows the same rules that are used to define ________ in Python.

Ans. identifiers

6. Parameters are passed ________ and they are ________.

Ans. to a function, optional.

7. A ________ is used to mark the end of ________.

Ans. colon (:), function header

8. ________ is used to describe what the function does.

Ans. A docstring "' A triple quoted string"'

9. ________ valid python ________ make a function body. Statements must have ________.

Ans. One or more, statements, same indentation level

10. An optional ________ statement returns a value from a function.

Ans. return

11. Docstrings can be accessed using __________ attribute on objects.

Ans. __doc __

12. Docstrings can be accessed by the __________ method.

Ans. help()

13. A variable defined outside all function definitions is called __________ variable

Ans. Global variable

14. A variable that is created inside a function body is a __________.

Ans. Local variable

15. __________ is the variable defined in the function definition.

Ans. Parameter

16. __________ is the variable or actual value that gets passed to a function.

Ans. Argument

17. Docstring is documentation within __________, __________, and __________.

Ans. Python modules, functions, and classes.

State whether the following statements are true or false.

1. Arguments and actual parameters or actual arguments are same.

a. True b. False

Ans. True

2. All functions should have a docstring.

a. True b. False

Ans. True

3. __doc__ attribute allows accessing docstring.

a. True b. False

Ans. True

3 RECURSIVE FUNCTIONS

LEARNING OBJECTIVES

- Break down the problem into base and recursive case in a recursive function
- Convert recursive solution to an iterative one

DEFINITION

- **Recursion:** A function that calls itself in its definition is called recursion.

Very Short Questions and Answers — 1 Marks

1. Explain recursion with an example.

Ans. Recursion is one of the problem-solving techniques in computer science, which breaks the problem into a smaller part of the same problem by calling itself in a function. A function that calls itself in its definition is called a recursive function. Let's take an example of the sum of n natural numbers using the recursion function:

```
def sum_recu(numbers):
    if ( numbers == 1):
        return 1
    #Calling itself
    else:
        return numbers + sum_recu(number-1)
```

2. Mention the steps to solve a problem by using recursion.

Ans. a. Breaking a problem into a smaller problem: Sum of n natural number (for example, n = 10) is the sum of 10 + sum of 9 natural numbers and so on.

b. Creating a base case: When a number is 1, it returns a sum of all the numbers (base case).

c. Creating recursive case: When a number is > 1, it reduces the problem by calling into itself return numbers + sum_recu (number-1).

```
def sum_recu(numbers):
    if ( numbers == 1):
        return 1
#Calling itself
    else:
        return numbers + sum_recu(number-1)
```

3. How recursion works?

Ans. Recursion solves the problem by dividing the problem into a set of smaller problems. A function calls itself and terminates when the base condition is satisfied.

4. What is the base case?

Ans. As the name suggests, it is where we get the definite solution to a problem. It is predefined and its allow to terminate the problem.

5. What is a recursive case?

Ans. A recursive case is where a problem is solved by recursively calling the function itself to solve a part of the problem of the original problem.

It is possible to have multiple base cases. ***Example:***

```
deffibo_recur(num):
    if num == 0:
        return 1
    elif num == 1:
        return 1
    else:
        return(fibo_recur(n-1) + fibo_recur(n-2))
# Get number if terms form the user
terms = int(input("Enter number of terms? "))

# check if the number of terms is valid
if terms <= 0:
    print("Please Enter a positive integer")
else:
    print("Fibonacci Series:")

for i in range(terms):
    print(fibo_recur(i))
```

6. What is a recursive function?

Ans. A recursive function calls itself to solve a problem as a smaller subset of the problem, which means that the function will call itself until some condition is met to return a result.

7. Name two cases required in a recursive function.

Ans. Two cases required in a recursive function are:

a. Base case

b. Recursive case

8. Is it necessary to have a base case in a recursive function? Why/Why not?

Ans. Yes, it is necessary to have a base condition in a recursive function. As without a base case, it will be infinitely recursive. It's a loop that runs infinitely without an exit condition.

9. What is infinite recursion? Why does it occur?

Ans. When a proper base condition is not met, the recursive function leads to infinite recursion. When a base is not properly defined, it will cause infinite recursion.

10. How can you stop/resolve an infinite recursion?

Ans. Infinite recursion can be stopped by ensuring that the base case is defined and it must return value or None.

11. Why iterative solutions are considered faster than their recursive counterparts?

Ans. Recursive functions are slower, though the difference may not be significant all the time. Recursion is more expensive (space and time) than iteration (which uses a loop).

12. If any recursive function can be easily written by using iterative code, then what is the need for recursion?

Ans. There are a few problems that are inherently easy to understand and solve by recursion. Traversing binary tree is a good example, where recursion can be used rather than a non-recursive solution.

13. Explain the base case and recursive case with examples.

Ans. Decomposing a problem into simpler or smaller instances of the same problem is a recursive case.

Example:

A factorial of number n is viewed as n! = n x (n–1)!. Factorial of n x factorial of n – 1. Finally it can be:

```
n! = n x (n-1) x (n-2) x (n-3).... x 3 x 2 x1
```

The problem is broken down into smaller or less complex ones until it can be solved without further subdivision. This is called base case.

```
n! = n x (n-1)!
n! = n x (n-1) x (n-2)!
n! = n x (n-1) x (n-2) x (n-3)!
n! = n x (n-1) x (n-2) x (n-3).... x 3!
n! = n x (n-1) x (n-2) x (n-3).... x 3 x 2 x 1
```

Here, 1! is our base case, and it equal to 1.

14. Write a recursive function for calculating factorial of a number.

Ans.

```
def _fact(num):
    # Base case: 1! = 1
    if num == 1:
        return 1
    # Recursive case: num! = num * (num-1)!
    else:
        return num * _fact(num-1)
```

15. When would you prefer recursion over iteration and vice versa?

Ans.

- **Choosing recursion:** When we have a problem statement that matches a recursive data structure. For example, a tree, where recursive is a better solution. If iterative solution leads to a complicated solution recursive solution is used.
- **Choosing iteration:** When we need faster solutions there is no constraints for time and space, we can choose iterative solutions.

16. Mention common mistakes in the recursive implementation of solutions.

Ans. There are three possible ways where a recursive implementation may go wrong:

a. The base case is missing.

b. If more than one base case is needed and all the base cases are not defined.

c. If a recursive case does not reduce the problem into a smaller sub-problem this leads to non- converge (it will not conclude).

17. Find the output of the following.

```
def fact(n):
    if n == 1:
        return 1
    else:
        return n * fact(-1)

fact(5)
```

Ans. This will lead to the following error: Recursion Error: maximum recursion depth exceeded in comparison.

Reason: fact(-1) where base case is not satisfied will lead to infinite recursion.

18. Write a code that removes the error in the above question

Ans.

```
def fact(n):
    if n == 1:
        return 1
    else:
        return n * fact(n-1)
```

Short Questions and Answers 2/3 Marks

1. Write a python function that returns the sum of all the elements of the list using recursion.

Ans. Find the sum of the all the elements of the list using recursion function:

```
lst = [1,2,3,4,5,6,7,8]
```

Recursive solution:

```
1 + [2, 3, 4, 5, 6, 7, 8]
1 + 2 + [3, 4, 5, 6, 7, 8]
1 + 2 + 3 + [4, 5, 6, 7, 8]
1 + 2 + 3 + 4 + 5 + [6, 7, 8]
1 + 2 + 3 + 4 + 5 + 6 + [7, 8]
1 + 2 + 3 + 4 + 5 + 6 + 7 + [8]
1 + 2 + 3 + 4 + 5 + 6 + 7 + 8
```

Base case: If list is empty sum is zero

Recursive case: Sum of 1st element + sum of rest of the elements

```
def sum_list(lst):
    #base case
    if(len(lst)==0):
        return 0
    else:
    #recursive case sum + first element+ sum of the remaining list
        return lst[0] + sum_list(lst[1:])

    print(sum_list(lst))
```

Output:

```
>>> lst=[1,2,3,4,5,6,7,8]
>>> print(sum_list(lst))
36
```

2. Write a function that prints the multiplication of digits of a number using recursion.

Ans. Multiplication of digits by using the recursion function:

```
def multiply_digits(num):
    #base case if all digits are exhausted number become zero returns 1
    if (num == 0):
        return 1
    else:
    #recursive case last digit   * rest of the digits
        return num%10 * multiply_digits(num//10)
print(multiply_digits(1357))
```

Output:

```
>>> print(multiply_digits(1357))
105
```

3. Find out the error in the below code.

```
def recfn(n):
    if n == 0:
```

```
        print("returning from base case ")
    else:
        recfn(n)
    n-=1
print(recfn(5))
```

Ans. The problem with the above code is that it does not terminate the recursion. Since recfn() is called before n, is decremented, and this leads to infinite recursion. The corrected function is as follows:

```
def recfn_cv(n):
    if n == 0:
        return "returning from base case"
    else:
        return recfn_cv(n-1)
```

Output:

```
>>> recfn_cv(10)
'returning from base case'
```

4. Write a Python function to calculate the GCD of two numbers.

Ans.

```
def fngcd(num1, num2):
    if(num2 == 0):
        return num1
    else:
        return fngcd(num2, num1 % num2)
```

Output:

```
>>> print(fngcd(10,15))
5
```

5. Write a function that recursively calculates the sum of below series.

$1^2 + 2^2 + 3^2 + 4^2 + 5^2 + ...$

Ans.

```
def sqrseries(n):
    if( n == 1 ):
        return 1
    else:
        return n * n + sqrseries(n-1)

print(sqrseries(10))
```

Output:

```
>>> print(sqrseries(10))
385
```

Long Questions and Answers 3/4 Marks

1. Write a function that recursively reverses a string. Explain how a recursive solution works.

Ans. Solution 1:

```
def rev_str_rec(string):
    #base case if length is 0 return the string
    if(len(string)==0):
        return string
```

```
    else:
    #recursive case add last character to string in front of the string
       return string[-1] + rev_str_rec(string[:-1])

print(rev_str_rec("narayan"))
```

Output:

```
>>> rev_str_rec('narayan')
'nayaran'
```

The above problem can be visualized as shown below:

```
n       + rev_str_rec(("naraya")
na      + rev_str_rec("naray")
nay     + rev_str_rec("nara")
naya    + rev_str_rec("nar")
nayar   + rev_str_rec("na")
nayara  + rev_str_rec("n")
nayaran
```

Solution 2:

```
def rev_recursive(string):
    #base case
    if len(string) == 0:
       return string
    else:
    #recursive case add first character to the last of the string
       return rev_recursive(string[1:]) + string[0]

a = "narayan"
print(rev_recursive(a))
```

The above problem can be visualized as shown below:

```
rev_recursive("naraya") + n
rev_recursive("naray")  + na
rev_recursive("nara")   + nay
rev_recursive("nar")    + naya
rev_recursive("na")     + nayar
rev_recursive("n")      + nayara
nayaran
```

- **Base case:** If length is equal to 0, the reversed string is printed.
- **Recursive case:** The function recursively calling the string slice expects the first one and adds the first character at the end of the sliced string.

Output:

```
>>> print(rev_recursive('narayan'))
nayaran
```

2. **Can each recursive function be represented through iteration? Give examples.**

Ans. Yes, each recursive function be represented through iteration. For example:

```
def _sumrec(num):
    if (num == 1):
```

```
        return 1
    else:
        return num + _sumrec(num-1)

# Solve it by iterative method.
def _sum(num):
    total = 0

    while( num >=1):
        total = total + num
        num = num- 1

    return total

print(_sum(10))
print(_sumrec(10))
```

Output:

```
55
55
```

Multiple-Choice Questions and Answers

1. Which of the following is a suitable definition of recursion function?

a. A function that calls itself

b. A function calls a method of class

c. A function that is called automatically

d. None of the above

Ans. Option a, that is, a function that calls itself.

2. Which of the following is not correct about recursion?

a. Recursion is faster than iterative function

b. Recursion consumes more memory than iterative function

c. Recursion functions are easy to understand

d. Recursion function can be converted to iterative functions

Ans. Option a, that is, Recursion is faster than iterative function.

3. The below code calculates the factorial of a number.

```
def fact(num):
    #base case
        if num == 0:
            return 1
#recursive case
    else:
        return __________
```

Select the correct option to fill the above line:

a. (num-1) * num

b. (num-1) * (num-2)

c. num * fact(num-1)

d. fact(num-1) * fact(num)

Ans. Option c, that is, num * fact(num-1).

4. Find the output of the following code.

```
def    check( num1, num2):
    if( num1   == 0):
        return num2
    else:
        return check( num1 -1 , num1+ num2)

print(check (4,7))
```

a. 7 b. 17 c. Infinite loop d. 13

Ans. Option b, that is, 17.

5. Find the error in the following code.

```
binNumber=[]
def bin_convert(decnumber):
    if(decnumber == 0):
        return binNumber
    else:
        digit = decnumber%2
        binNumber.append(digit)
        return bin_convert(decnumber/2)

bin_convert(7)
binNumber.reverse()
for num in binNumber:
    print(num, end="")
```

The error in the above code is:

Ans. The decnumber/2, is not an integer division and it will not convert number into float number. For example: decnumber / 2 to 3.5 and so on the number will not reduce to 0, thus it will turn out to be infinite recursion..

6. Find the output of the following code.

```
binNumber=[]
def  bin_convert(decnumber):
    if(decnumber==0):
        return binNumber
    else:
        digit=decnumber%2
        binNumber.append(digit)
        return bin_convert(decnumber//2)

bin_convert(6)
binNumber.reverse()
for num in binNumber:
    print(num,end="")
```

a. 101 b. 110 c. Infinite loop d. 3

Ans. Option b, that is, 110.

7. Find which of the following statement is false?

a. A recursive function must have a return value

b. A recursive function must have a base case

c. If the base case is not properly terminated it will become Infinite recursion

d. A recursive function can make code easier to understand

Ans. Option a, that is, A recursive function must have a return value.

8. State True or False: "iteration and recursion use the same programming approach".

Ans. False

9. Find out the outcome if the base condition is not defined in a recursive function.

a. It will be an infinite loop

b. The program will run only once

c. An error is thrown

d. The outcome will depend upon input value

Ans. Option c, that is, it will throw an error Recursion

Error: maximum recursion depth exceeded in comparison. Before it turns out to be an infinite loop, the Python interpreter will throw an error.

10. Find out which of the following options are correct.

a. Recursion allows making the code look short and clean

b. Recursion allows to break a complex task into sub-problems

c. Recursive functions take less memory

d. Recursive functions take more memory

Ans. Option a and b are correct.

11. Find out which of the following are correct.

a. A recursive function is easy to debug

b. Recursive calls take more memory than an iterative solution

c. Recursion functions take longer time than an iterative solution

d. Recursive functions may be hard to debug.

Ans. Option b, c, and d are correct.

12. Find the output of the following.

```
def f(num):
    if ( num == 0):
        return 0
    elif (num == 1):
        return 1
    else:
        return f(num-1) + f(num-2)
for n in range(0,4):
    print(f(n),end=" ")
```

a. 0 1 1 2 3

b. An exception is thrown

c. 0 1 1 2

d. 0 1 2 3

Ans. Option c will be output for the above code. The code prints the Fibonacci series.

STRING AND MATH FUNCTIONS

LEARNING OBJECTIVES

- Describe the syntax of built-in functions defined for string and math module.
- Write the simple programs using built-in functions of string data type and math module.

DEFINITION

- **String:** String, in Python, is a collection of Unicode characters. A character in Python is a string of length one. It is defined by using single, double, and triple code.
- **Math module:** The math module provides the mathematical functions defined by the C standard library.

Very Short Questions and Answers — 1 Mark

1. **How to define a string?**

Ans. Strings are defined using single quotes (' '), double quotes (" "), and triple quotes (''' ''').

Examples:

```
string='ashish'
string="Ashish"
string='''Ashish'''
```

2. **How to access the character from a string?**

Ans. Index in Square brackets is used to access character of the string.

`String = 'Python' For example, string[0] will return P.`

Slicing is used to retrieve the characters.

String[2:5] will return 'tho'

3. **Can a string be changed by using a built-in function?**

Ans. Strings are immutable; in-built function does not change its value. String methods return a new value; it does not change the original string.

4. **How to delete or modify a character in a string?**

Ans. A string is immutable; deletion or modification is not allowed.

Short Questions and Answers — 2/3 Marks

1. **Name the function that converts a string to a capitalized string.**

Ans. The capitalize() function converts the first character to the capital letter of a string.

Syntax:

```
string.capitalize()
```

- **Parameter:** It doesn't accept any parameter.
- **Return value:** The capitalize() function returns a string with the first letter in upper case and all other characters in lower case. It doesn't modify the original string.

Let's see an example:

```
string= 'python is easy to learn'
print(string.capitalize())
```

Output:

```
Python is easy to learn
```

2. Name the function that aligns the string in center, explain its syntax and how to use it.

Ans. The center() function returns the center align string.

Syntax:

```
string.center(width[, fillchar])
```

Parameter(s): It accepts two arguments:

a. **width:** The total length of a string including padded characters

b. **fillchar:** (It is optional) padding character and it's default value is space.

Example:

```
string = "python is easy to learn"
pad_string = string.center(30,'x')
print(pad_string)
```

Output:

```
xxxpython is easy to learnxxxx
```

3. Name the function that counts the occurrence of a character in a string. Explain its syntax and how to use it.

Ans. The count() function returns the number of occurrence(s) of a substring in a string.

Syntax:

```
string.count(substring, start , end )
```

Parameters: It requires a single parameter; start and end are optional parameters.

a. **Substring:** A string that is part of a string.

b. **start:** It is optional, 0 by default.

c. **end:** It is optional, len(string) by default.

The start parameter is the starting index of the substring; the end parameter is the end index of the substring.

Return value: Number of occurrences of the substring in a string.

Example:

```
string ='python is easy to learn'
string.count('ea')
```

Output:

```
2
```

Let's see another example:

```
#count the occurrence of 'ea' between index 18 and 30
string.count('ea',18,30)
```

Output:

```
1
```

4. Name the function that checks if a string starts with a specified substring. Explain its syntax and how to use it.

Ans. The startswith() function checks if a string contains a substring at the beginning of the string.

Syntax:

```
string.startswith( prefix [, start [, end ] ] )
```

Parameters: It accepts three arguments:

a. **Prefix:** string or tuple of strings to be checked.

b. **Start:** It is optional, default value is 0. The starting index where prefix is to be checked within a string.

c. **End:** It is optional. The end index till the prefix is to be checked within a string.

Return value: It returns a Boolean value, that is, True if a string starts with a prefix and False if a string does not start with a prefix.

Let's see an example:

```
string ='python is easy to learn'
string.startswith('python')
```

Output:

```
True
```

Let's see another example:

```
#startswith() with the start and the end parameters
string.startswith('easy', 10,21)
```

Output:

```
True
```

5. **Name the function that checks if a string ends with a specified substring. Explain its syntax and how to use it.**

Ans. The endswith() function checks if a string ends with a suffix.

Syntax:

```
string.endswith( suffix [, start [, end ] ] )
```

Parameters: It accepts three arguments:

1. **suffix** is a string or substring to be checked.
2. **start** it is optional, default is 0. The starting index where prefix is to be checked within a string.
3. **end** it is optional, the end index till the prefix is to be checked within a string.

Return value: It returns a Boolean value, that is, True if a string ends with a substring(suffix) and False if a string does not end with a prefix.

Let's see an example:

```
string ='python is easy to learn'
string.endswith('learn')
```

Output:

```
True
```

Let's see another example:

```
string.endswith('Learn')
```

Output:

```
False
```

Let's see one more example of ends with() with the start and the end parameters:

```
string.endswith('learn', 10,24)
```

Output:

```
True
```

6. **Name the function that finds an index of a substring in a string. Explain its syntax and how to use it.**

Ans. The find() function finds the first index of search substring in a string.

Syntax:

```
string.find(substring [, start[, end] ] )
```

Parameters: It accepts three parameters:

- **substring:** It is to be searched in a string.
- **start and end** are optional, it searches within the range string[start:end].

Return value: It returns an index of the first occurrence of the substring in a string and it returns -1 if a substring doesn't exist in the string.

Let's see an example:

```
string = 'python is easy to learn'
print("The first index of ea is " + str (string.find('ea')))
```

Output:

```
The first index of ea is 10
```

Let's see another example:

```
string = 'python is easy to learn'
print ("The index of ea is " + str (string.find('ea',13,24) ) )
```

Output:

```
The index of ea is 19.
```

Let's see one more example:

```
string = 'python is easy to learn'
string.find('Learn',13,24)
```

Output:

```
-1
```

7. Name the function that finds an index of a substring in a string from the end of the string. Explain its syntax and how to use it.

Ans. The rfind() function returns the highest index of a substring to be searched in a string.

Syntax:

```
string.rfind(substring [, start[, end] ] )
```

Parameters: It accepts:

- **substring:** It is to be searched in a string.
- **Start and end** are optional if provided with substring, searches within the range string [start:end].

Return value: It returns the index of the first occurrence of the substring from the right of the string and it returns -1 if a substring doesn't exist in the string.

Let's see an example:

```
#search substring ea in string
string = 'python is easy to learn'
print(“ The first index of ea  from right is “  + str (string.rfind('ea')))
```

Output:

```
The first index of ea from right is 19.
```

Let's see another example:

```
#search substring ea   in a string within index range 13 to 24
string = 'python is easy to learn'
print(“ The index of ea is “  + str (string.find('ea',13,24)))
```

Output:

```
The first index of ea is 19.
```

Let's see one more example:

```
#search substring Learn in string
= 'python is easy to learn'
string.rfind('Learn')
```

Output:

```
-1
```

8. **Name the function that finds an index of a substring in a string, explain its syntax and how to use it?**

Ans. The index() function returns the index of a substring in a string.

Syntax:

```
string.index( substring [, start [, end]   ]  )
```

Parameters: The index() accepts three parameters:

- **substring** is an argument whose index is to be searched with string.
- **start and end** are optional if provided, searches within range string [start: end].

Return value: It returns the first index of the substring and it raises a Value Error exception if substring is not found.

Let's see an example:

```
# find the index of substring ea in string
string='python is easy to learn'
print(" The first index of ea is "  + str (string.index('ea')))
```

Output:

```
The first index of ea is 10.
```

Let's see another example:

```
# find the index of substring 'ea' in string in index range 13 to 24
string='python is easy to learn'
print(" The index of ea is "  + str (string.find('ea',13,24)))
```

Output:

```
The first index of ea is 19.
```

Let's see one more example:

```
string='python is easy to learn'
string.index('Learn')
```

Output:

```
ValueError: substring not found.
```

9. **Name the function that finds the first index of a substring in a string from the right. Explain its syntax and how to use it.**

Ans. The rindex() function returns the highest index (first index from the right) of a substring in a string.

Syntax:

```
string.rindex(substring [, start [, end] ] )
```

It returns the index of a substring in a string from its right.

Parameters: The rindex() accepts three parameters:

- **substring,** whose index is to be searched with string.
- **start and end** are optional if provided searches within the range string [start:end].

Return value: It returns the last index of the substring and raises a ValueError exception if substring not found.

Let's see an example:

```
#search the index of the string from the right
```

```
string='python is easy to learn'
print(" The first index of ea is " + str (string.rindex('ea')))
```

Output:

```
The first index of ea is 19.
```

Let's see another example:

```
#search the index of the string from the right
string='python is easy to learn'
print(" The index of ea is " + str (string.rindex('ea',13,24)))
```

Output:

```
The first index of ea is 19.
```

Let's see one more example:

```
#search for non-existing substring
string.rindex('Learn')
```

Output:

```
ValueError: substring not found.
```

10. Name the function that checks if a string contains only alphabets. Explain its syntax and how to use it.

Ans. The isalpha() function checks if the string has alphabet (s) only.

Syntax:

`string.isalpha()`

- **Parameters:** It does not accept any parameter.
- **Return value:** It returns True if all characters are alphabets in a string, and it returns False if at least one character is not an alphabet.

Let's see an example:

```
string ="abcABC"
print(string.isalpha())
```

Output:

```
True
```

Let's see another example:

```
string ="abc@123"
print(string.isalpha())
```

Output:

```
False
```

Let's see another example:

```
string ="123abc"
print(string.isalpha())
```

Output:

```
False
```

11. Name the function that checks if a string contains an alphanumeric character(s). Explain its syntax and how to use it.

Ans. The isalnum() function checks if the string has alphanumeric (alphabet and numbers only).

Syntax:

`string.isalnum()`

- **Parameters:** It does not accept any parameter.
- **Return value:** It returns True if all characters are alphabet or digits in a string, and it returns False if at least one character is not an alphabet or a digit.

Let's see an example:

```
string ="abc123"
print(string.isalnum())
```

Output:

```
True
```

Let's see another example:

```
string ="abc@123"
print(string.isalnum())
```

Output:

```
False
```

Let's see another example:

```
string ="abc"
print(string.isalnum())
```

Output:

```
True
```

Let's see one more example:

```
string ="123"
print(string.isalnum())
```

Output:

```
True
```

12. Name the function that checks if a string contains only digits. Explain its syntax and how to use it.

Ans. The is digit() function checks if a string contains digits only.

Syntax:

```
string.isdigit()
```

- **Parameters:** It does not accept any parameters.
- **Return value:** It returns True if all the characters are digits in a string, and it returns False if at least one character is not a digit.

Let's see an example:

```
string ="9112345"
print(string.isdigit())
```

Output:

```
True
```

Let's see another example:

```
string ="login123"
print(string.isdigit())
```

Output:

```
False
```

Let's see one more example:

```
string ="123.45"
print(string.isdigit())
```

Output:
```
False
```

13. Name the function that checks if a string contains only lower case characters. Explain its syntax and how to use it.

Ans. The islower() function checks if all the alphabets in a string are in lowercase.

Syntax:

```
string.islower()
```

- **Parameters:** It does not accept any parameters.
- **Return value:** It returns True if all alphabets are in lowercase, and it returns False if a string has at least one uppercase alphabet.

Let's see an example:

```
string="lowercase"
print(string.islower())
```

Output:
```
True
```

Let's see another example:

```
string="Not in lowercase"
print( string.islower() )
```

Output:
```
False
```

14. Name the function that checks if a string contains only spaces. Explain its syntax and how to use it.

Ans. The is space() function checks for whitespace characters.

Note: The examples of whitespace characters are tabs, spaces, and a newline.

Syntax:

```
string.isspace()
```

- **Parameters:** It does not accept any parameters.
- **Return value:** It returns True if it contains all whitespace characters and returns False if it contains at least one non-whitespace character or if the string is empty.

Let's see an example:

```
string=' '
print(string.isspace())
```

Output:
```
True
```

Let's see another example:

```
string=' test '
print( string.isspace( ))
```

Output:
```
False
```

15. Name the function that checks if a string is in title case. Explain its syntax and how to use it.

Ans. The is title() function checks if a string is in title case (the first letter of each word is capital in a string).

Syntax:

```
string.istitle()
```

- **Parameters:** It does not accept parameters.

- **Return value:** It returns True if a string is a title cased string, and it returns False if a string is not a title cased string.

Let's see an example:

```
string ="Python is easy to learn"
print(string.istitle())
```

Output:

```
False
```

Let's see another example:

```
string ="Python Is Easy To Learn"
print (string.istitle() )
```

Output:

```
True
```

16. Name the function that checks if all the characters are in upper case in a string. Explain its syntax and how to use it.

Ans. The isupper() function returns true if all characters are in uppercase.

Syntax:

```
string.isupper()
```

- **Parameters:** It does not accept any parameters.
- **Return value:** It returns True if all alphabets are in uppercase and return False if a string has at least one character that is not an uppercase alphabet.

Let's see an example:

```
string="UPPERCASE"
print(string.isupper())
```

Output:

```
True
```

Let's see another example:

```
string="UpperCase"
print(string.isupper())
```

Output:

```
False
```

17. Name the function that converts a sequence to string. Explain its syntax and how to use it.

Ans. The join() function joins the element of a sequence and returns a string.

Syntax:

```
string.join(iterable)
```

- **Parameters:** It accepts iterable.
- **Return value:** It concatenates all the elements of an iterable and returns a string. Let's see an example:

```
lst = ['1','2','3']
print(''.join(lst))
```

Output:

```
123
```

Let's see another example:

```
name =('p','y','t','h','o','n')
print(''.join(name))
```

Output:
```
python
```

Let's see one more example:
```
sdlc=['Req Analysis','design','coding','testing']
print('->'.join(sdlc))
```

Output:
```
Req Analysis->design->coding->testing
```

Note: If an iterable contains a non-string value, it will raise an exception (TypeError).

18. Name the function that returns the left-justified string. Explain its syntax and how to use it.

Ans. The ljust() function returns a left-justified string.

Syntax:
```
string.ljust(width [, fillchar] )
```
Parameters: It accepts two parameters:

- **width:** It is the total width of the returned string. If width is less than the length of the string original string is returned.
- **fillchar:** It is optional and it is filled in the remaining space of the width.

Return value: It returns the left-justified string.

Let's see an example:
```
string='python'
print(string.ljust(10,'x'))
```

Output:
```
pythonxxxx
```

Note: If fillchar is not defined, it is filled with blank, otherwise,a defined character is used.

19. Name the function that returns the right-justified string. Explain its syntax and how to use it.

Ans. The rjust() function returns a right-justified string.

Syntax:
```
string.rjust(width [, fillchar] )
```
- **Parameters:** It accepts two parameters:
  width: It is the total width of the returned string. If width is less than the length of the string, the original string is returned.
  fillchar: It is optional and it is filled in the remaining space of the width.
- **Return value:** It returns the right-justified string.

Let's see an example: `string='python' print(string.rjust(10,'x'))`

Output:
```
xxxxpython
```

Note: If fillchar is not defined, it is filled with blank, otherwise, a defined character is used.

20. Name the function that toggles the case of each character in a string. Explain its syntax and how to use it.

Ans. The swapcase() function swaps the case of all the characters of a string (uppercase to lowercase and vice versa).

Syntax:
```
string.swapcase()
```
- **Parameters:** It does not accept any parameters.

➢ **Return value:** String with all the characters are swapped that is lower to upper and vice-versa.
Let's see an example:

```
string ='pYTHON'
print(string.swapcase())
```

Output:

```
Python
```

21. Name the function that removes spaces form the beginning of the string. Explain its syntax and how to use it.

Ans. The lstrip() function removes the leading characters.

Syntax:

```
string.lstrip( [chars] )
```

➢ **Parameters:** It has one parameter:

chars: It is optional. If no characters are provided, leading white spaces are removed else provided string is removed.

➢ **Return value:** It returns a string with leading characters stripped.

Let's see an example:

```
string = '    python'
print(string.lstrip())
```

Output:

```
python
```

Let's see another example:

```
string="Pypython"
string.lstrip('Py')
```

Output:

```
python
```

22. Name the function that removes the trailing spaces from a string. Explain its syntax and how to use it.

Ans. The rstrip() function removes the trailing characters.

Syntax:

```
string.rstrip( [chars] )
```

➢ **Parameters:** It accepts one parameter:

chars: It is optional. If no characters are provided, leading white spaces are removed else provided character(s) are removed.

➢ **Return value:** It returns a string with leading characters stripped (removed).

Let's see an example:

```
string = 'python '
print(string.rstrip())
```

Output:

```
python
```

Let's see another example:

```
string="pythonPy"
string.rstrip('Py')
```

Output:

```
python
```

23. Name the function that removes the leading and trailing spaces from a string. Explain its syntax and how to use it.

Ans. The strip() function removes the leading and trailing spaces.

Syntax:

```
string.strip( [chars] )
```

- **Parameters:** It accepts one parameter:
  chars: It is optional. If no characters are provided, leading white spaces are removed else character(s) are removed.
- **Return value:** It returns a string with leading characters stripped.

Let's see an example:

```
string = ' python '
print(string.strip())
```

Output:

```
python
```

Let's see another example:

```
string="PypythonPy"
string.strip('Py')
```

Output:

```
python
```

24. Name the function that replaces a substring with another substring. Explain its syntax and how to use it.

Ans. The replace() function replaces substring with another substring. It returns a copy of the string where all occurrences of a substring are replaced.

Syntax:

```
str.replace ( substring, newsubstring [, count] )
```

Parameter: It accepts three parameters:

- **Substring,** which it is to be replaced by a new substring
- **new substring,** which will replace the substring. It is optional; it tells the number of occurrences to be replaced.
- **count,** it is optional; it tells the number of occurrences to be replaced.

Return value: It returns a string where a substring is replaced with a new substring. If a substring is not found, it returns the original string.

Let's see an example:

```
#replaces all occurrences
String = "Python is EAsy to lEArn"
string.replace('EA','ea')
```

Output:

```
Python is easy to learn
```

Let's see another example:

```
#replace 1st occurrence
string="Python is EAsy to lEArn"
string.replace('EA','ea',1)
```

Output:

```
Python is easy to lEArn
```

25. Name the function that splits a string into tokens (word) based on the separator. Explain its syntax and how to use it.

Ans. The split() function splits a string to a list of substring(words). The split() method breaks up a string at the specified separator and returns a list of words(strings).

Syntax:

```
string.split( [separator [, maxsplit]] )
```

Parameters: It accepts two parameters:

- **separator** is optional. The string splits at the specified separator. If a separator is not specified, the whitespace space, newline is considered as a separator.
- **maxsplit** is optional it defines the maximum number of splits. It's default value is -1, which means there is no limit on the number of splits.

Let's see an example:

```
#split using default value
string='python is easy to learn'
wordlist= string.split()
print(wordlist)
```

Output:

```
['python', 'is', 'easy', 'to', 'learn'].
```

Let's see another example:

```
#split using space
['python', 'is', 'easy', 'to', 'learn']
wordlist = string.split(' ')
print(wordlist)
```

Output:

```
['python', 'is', 'easy', 'to', 'learn'].
```

Let's see another example:

```
#split using separator using ':'
String = 'python:is:easy:to:learn'
wordlist=string.split(':')
print(wordlist)
```

Output:

```
['python', 'is', 'easy', 'to', 'learn'].
```

Let's see one more example:

```
#split string with maxsplit=3
string='python is easy to learn'
wordlist = string.split(' ',3)
print(wordlist)
```

Output:

```
['python', 'is', 'easy', 'to learn'].
```

26. Name the function that splits a string from the right into tokens (word) based on the separator. Explain its syntax and how to use it.

Ans. The rsplit() function splits a string from the right. It works the same as split if maxsplit is not used.

Syntax:

```
string.rsplit( [separator [, maxsplit]] )
```

Parameters: It accepts two parameters:

- **Separator:** It is optional. The string splits starting from the right at the specified separator. If a separator is not specified, the whitespace (space, newline, and more) is considered as a separator.
- **maxsplit:** It is optional. It defines the maximum number of splits. It's default value is -1, which means there is no limit on the number of splits.

Let's see an example:

```
string = 'python is easy to learn'
wordlist = string.rsplit(' ',2)
print(wordlist)
```

Output:

```
['python is easy', 'to', 'learn'].
```

27. Name the function that splits a multi-line string into a list of strings. Explain its syntax and how to use it.

Ans. The splitlines() function splits a multiline string.

Syntax:

```
String.splitlines( [flag] )
```

Parameters: It accepts one parameter:

- By default line break is not included.
- It is optional if the separator is provided and True the line break is not included in items of the list.

Return value: It returns a list of lines.

Let's see an example:

```
string = '''Python is easy to learn\npython is object-oriented\npython is fun'''
lines = string.splitline(True)
for line in lines:
    print(line, end='')
```

Output:

```
Python is easy to learn
python is object-oriented
python is fun
```

28. Name the function that converts a string into title case. Explain its syntax and how to use it.

Ans. The title() function returns a string with the first letter of each word is capitalized.

Syntax:

```
string.title()
```

Parameters: The title() method doesn't take any parameters.

Return value: It returns the title case string.

Let's see an example:

```
string ="python is easy to learn"
print(string.title())
```

Output:

```
'Python Is Easy To Learn'.
```

29. Differentiate between methods index() and find().

Ans. The find() and rfind() methods find the index of the substring in a string. The difference is that find() method returns -1 if the substring is not found, whereas index() throws an exception.

30. Differentiate between methods index() and the rindex().

Ans. The index() function finds substring from left and rindex() finds string from the right of the string.

31. Differentiate between methods lstrip() and the rstrip().

Ans. The lstrip() function removes leading spaces whereas rstrip() removes trailing spaces.

32. Differentiate between methods split() and rsplit().

Ans. The split() function splits a substring from left and rsplit() splits a string from the right of the string.

33. Explain the syntax of function ceil() and how to use it with an example.

Ans. The syntax of the ceil function is:

```
ceil(val)
```

Return value: It returns an integer >= x.

Let's see an example:

```
import math
print( math.ceil(7.2) )
print( math.ceil(7.9) )
print( math.ceil(-7.9) )
print( math.ceil(7) )
```

Output:

```
8
8
-7
7
```

34. Explain the syntax of function fabs() and how to use it with an example.

Ans. The fabs() function returns an absolute value. ***Syntax:***

```
fabs(val)
```

Return value: It returns an absolute value.

Let's see an example:

```
print( math.fabs(-7.2) )
print( math.fabs(-7.0) )
```

Output:

```
7.2
7.0
```

35. Explain the syntax of function factorial() and how to use it with an example.

Ans. The factorial function returns a factorial of x.

Syntax:

```
factorial(val)
```

Return value: It returns the factorial of the number. For negative values, it raises an exception.

Let's see an example:

```
print( math.factorial(5))
```

Output:

```
120.
```

Let's see another example:

```
print( math.factorial(-5))
```

Output:

```
ValueError: factorial() not defined for negative values.
```

36. Explain the syntax of floor() function and how to use it with an example.

Ans. The floor function returns the largest integer <= x.

Syntax:

```
floor(val)
```

Return value: It returns the largest integer <= x.

Let's see an example:

```
print( math.floor(9.2))
print( math.floor(9.7))
print( math.floor(-9.7))
```

Output:

```
9
9
-10
```

37. Explain the syntax of fmod() function and how to use it with an example.

Ans. The fmod() function returns the remainder when x is divided by y.

Syntax:

```
fmod(val1, val2)
```

Return value: It returns the modulus value of val1/ val2.

Let's see an example:

```
print(math.fmod(5.0,2.0))
```

Output:

```
1.0
```

Let's see another example:

```
print(math.fmod(7.5, 2.75))
```

Output:

```
2.0
```

Let's see one more example:

```
print(math.fmod(7.0, 2.5))
```

Output:

```
2.0
```

38. Explain the syntax of fsum() function and how to use it with an example.

Ans. The fsum() function returns the sum of accurate floating-point values in an iterable.

Syntax:

```
fsum(iterable)
```

Parameter: It accepts an iterable.

➢ **Return value:** It returns the sum of values of iterable. Let's see an example:

```
# print the sum of all the numbers of a list
print( math.fsum([1.2,3.2,5.9,6.65,10.0,9.0]) )
```

Output:

```
35.95
```

Let's see another example:

```
# print the sum of all the numbers of a tuple
print( math.fsum( (1.2,3.2,5.9,6.65,10.0,9.0 )) )
```

Output:

```
35.95
```

39. Explain the syntax of modf() function and how to use it with an example.

Ans. The modf() function returns both fractional and integer parts of value (float number).

Syntax:

```
modf(val)
```

Return value: Pair (tuple) of fractional and integer part of the value.

Let's see an example:

```
math.modf(123.456)
```

Output:

```
0.45600000000000307, 123.0
```

40. Explain the syntax of trunc() function and how to use it with an example.

Ans. The trunc() function truncates the fractional part and returns an integer value.

Syntax:

```
trunc(x)
```

Return value: It truncates a fractional part from an integer and returns an integer.

Let's see an example:

```
print ( math.trunc(5.9) )
```

Output:

```
5
```

Let's see another example:

```
print(math.trunc(-5.9))
```

Output:

```
-5
```

Let's see one more example:

```
print(math.trunc(5.2))
```

Output:

```
5
```

41. Explain the syntax of exp() function and how to use it with an example.

Ans. The exp() function returns e**x. e is a numerical constant in mathematics that is equal to 2.71828.

Syntax:

```
exp(x)
```

Return value: It returns e**x.

Let's see an example:

```
print( math.exp(2))
```

Output:

```
7.38905609893065
```

Let's see another example:

```
print( math.exp(5))
```

Output:

```
148.4131591025766
```

42. Explain the syntax of log(x[, base]) function and how to use it with an example.

Ans. The logx() function returns the logarithm value, based on its base.

Syntax:

```
log(x [, base] )
```

Return value: It returns the logarithm value, based on the base (default is e).

Let's see an example:

```
print( math.log(10,10))
print( math.log(1024,2))
print( math.log(10))
```

Output:

```
1.0
10.0
2.302585092994046
```

43. Explain the syntax of log1p() function and how to use it with an example.

Ans. The log1p() function returns the natural logarithm of 1+val.

Syntax:

```
log1p(val)
```

Return value: It returns the natural logarithm of 1+val.

Let's see an example:

```
print(math.log1p(10))
```

Output:

```
2.3978952727983707
```

44. Explain the syntax of log2() function and how to use it with an example.

Ans. The log2() function returns the base 2 logarithm.

Syntax:

```
log2(val)
```

- **Return value:** It returns base-2 logarithm of val.

Let's see an example:

```
print( math.log2(1024))
```

Output:

```
10.0
```

Let's see another example:

```
print( math.log2(10))
```

Output:

```
3.321928094887362
```

45. Explain the syntax of log10() function and how to use it with an example.

Ans. The log10() function returns base10 logarithms of value.

Syntax:

```
log10(val)
```

- **Return value:** It returns base10 logarithm value of val.

Let's see an example:

```
print(math.log10(1000))
```

Output:

```
3.0
```

Let's see another example:

```
print(math.log10(500))
```

Output:

```
2.6989700043360187
```

46. Explain the syntax of pow() function and how to use it with an example.

Ans. The pow() function returns val1 raised to the power val2.

Syntax:

```
pow(val1, val2)
```

Return value: It returns val1**val2. Let's see an example:

```
print( math.pow(2.0,5.0) )
print( math.pow(4.0,.5)    )
```

Output:

```
32.0
2.0
```

47. Explain the syntax of sqrt() function and how to use it with an example.

Ans. The sqrt() function returns the square root of a value.

Syntax:

```
sqrt(x)
```

Return value: It returns the square root of value and for the negative value, it raises the ValueError. Let's see an example:

```
print(math.sqrt(5))
```

Output:

```
2.23606797749979
```

```
print(math.sqrt(25))
```

Output:

```
5.0
```

Programming Questions and Answers — 1/2 Marks

1. Find the output of the following.

```
print('123456123123'.lstrip('123'))
```

Ans. 456123123

2. Find the output of the following.

```
print('123456'.replace('23', 'xx'))
```

Ans. 1xx456

3. Find the output of the following.

```
print('1221221212112'.replace('12', 'xy'))
```

Ans. xy2xy2xyxy1xy. This replaces all occurrences of 12.

4. Find the output of the following.

```
print('1221221212112'.replace('12', 'xy',2))
```

Ans. xy2xy21212112. This replaces the first two occurrences of 12.

5. Write a program that counts the frequency of each character in a string.

Ans.

```
string="google.com"
dict = {}
keys = dict.keys()
for ch in  string:
    if ch in keys:
        dict[ch] += 1
```

```
    else:
        dict[ch] = 1
print(dict)
```

Output:

```
{'g': 2, 'o': 3, 'l': 1, 'e': 1, '.': 1, 'c': 1, 'm': 1}
```

6. Write a program that counts the frequency of each word in a string.

Ans.

```
string= "the quick brown fox jumps over the lazy dog."
wordcounts = {}
# split a sentence into words
words = string.split()
for word in words:
# if word already in dictionary add its frequency
    if word in wordcounts:
        wordcounts[word] += 1
    else:
        wordcounts[word] = 1

print( wordcounts)
```

Output:

```
{'the': 2, 'quick': 1, 'brown': 1, 'fox': 1, 'jumps': 1, 'over': 1, 'lazy': 1, 'dog.': 1}
```

7. Write a program that reverses each word of a string.

Ans.

```
string = "This is string"
# reversed() function returns reverse the string
string = reversed(string)
string =''.join(string)
print(string)
```

Output:

```
gnirts si sihT
```

8. Write a program that counts the number of vowels in a given text.

Ans.

```
vowels = "aeiouAEIOU"
vowelcount=0
string="the quick brown fox jumps over the lazy dog."
for ch in string:
    if(ch  in vowels):
        vowelcount+=1
print(" The vowel count is " , vowelcount)
```

Output:

```
The vowel count is 11.
```

9. Write a program to remove spaces from a given string.

Ans.

```
string =" This  is a  string "
string = string.replace(' ','')
print(" The string without spaces")
print(string)
```

Output:

```
The string without spaces
Thisisastring
```

10. Write a program that computes the sum of digits in a string.

Ans.

```
string="1234abcd56"
sum_digit = 0
for ch in string:
    if ch.isdigit() == True:
        digit = int(ch)
        sum_digit+= digit
    print("The sum is ", sum_digit)
```

Output:

```
The sum is 21.
```

11. Write a program that counts lowercase, uppercase, other characters, and numeric values in a given string.

Ans.

```
string="Addressis123@pin110010"
upper_cnt, lower_cnt, number_cnt, other_cnt = 0, 0, 0, 0
for ch in string:
    if ch.isupper():
        upper_cnt += 1
    elif ch.islower():
        lower_cnt += 1
    elif ch.isdigit():
        number_cnt += 1
    else:
        other_cnt += 1

print('\nUpper case characters: ',upper_cnt)
print('Lower case characters: ',lower_cnt)
print('Digit characters: ',number_cnt)
print('Other characters: ',other_cnt)
```

Output:

```
Upper case characters: 1
Lower case characters: 11
Digit characters: 9
Other characters: 1
```

12. Write a program that checks if a string is a Palindrome.

Ans. #Method 1: if string and its reverse are same, it is palindrome

```
string="nitin"
palindrome=True
if( string == string[::-1]):
    print("Palindrome")
else:
    print("Not a palindrome")
```

```
#Method 2:
#Check if characters are same from right and left side of the string

li= -1
palindrome=True

for i in range(len(string)//2):
    if(string[i]== string[li]):
        li-=1
else:
    palindrome =False
    break
print(string +" is palindrome: "+ str(palindrome))
```

Output:

```
Palindrome
nitin is palindrome:True
```

True or False

1. **State whether the following is true or false: 'abc'.islower().**

Ans. *True*

2. **State whether the following is true or false: 'z@ 1,'.islower().**

Ans. *True*

3. **State whether the following is true or false: '\t'.isspace().**

Ans. *True*

4. **State whether the following is true or false: 'HelloWorld'.istitle()).**

Ans. *False*

5. **State whether the following is true or false: print('Hello World'.istitle()).**

Ans. *True*

Multiple-Choice Questions and Answers

1. **Find out the return value of math.ceil(5.4)?**

   a. 5 b. 6.0 c. 5.0 d. 5.4

Ans. Option b, that is, 6.

2. **Find out the return value of math.floor(5.4)?**

   a. 5 b. 6 c. 4.0 d. 3.0

Ans. Option a, that is, 5

3. **Find out the return value of math.fabs(-5.4)?**

   a. -5.4 b. 5.4 c. 5 d. -5

Ans. Option b, that is, 5.4.

4. **Find out the return value of math.fact(6)?**

   a. 6 b. 720 c. error d. [1, 2, 3, 6]

Ans. Option c, that is, error.NameError, fact() is not defined in math module.

5. **Find out the return value of math.floor(0o10)?**

   a. 10 b. 8 c. 9 d. 0

Ans. Option b, that is, 8. 0o10 is octal 8 and it returns 8.

5 File Handling

Learning Objectives

- Recall the syntax of inbuilt functions for reading, writing, and updating files
- Write code to read, append, delete, and modify the content of the file by using in-built functions
- Differentiate between various file modes, functions read(), readline(), readlines(), write(), and writeline(); and text, binary files, and relative, absolute file path

Definition

- **File:** A file stores data on persistence storage devices like hard disk, USB drives, and so on. A file is a byte stream that can store text, video, music, and many more.
- **Text file:** A text file stores data in the human-readable form usually ASCII or Unicode character.
- **Binary file:** Binary files store binary data in a computer-readable format, i.e. it is only readable by computers.
- **File access mode:** File access mode allows a file to open for various operations. For example: read mode is used to view the contents of a file; and write mode is used to add, modify, or remove the content from the file. Append mode allows writing content at the end of the file.
- **Relative file path:** A relative path is a location of the file which is relative to its current directory. The relative path starts with current directory or the parent directory. Dots [a dot (.) and a double-dot (..)] are used for building paths moving up in the hierarchy.
- **Absolute file path:** An absolute path is a location of a file or a folder. An absolute path starts from the root element drive (for example, C: in windows or root directory in other systems) and goes to the end including subdirectories and filename.

Very Short Questions and Answers — 1 Mark

1. Why is a file required in programming?

Ans. The variables and data we use in a program are stored in RAM and are not available after the program's execution. To store data permanently, a file is used.

2. Mention the generic steps that are used to process a file in Python.

Ans. The generic steps that are used to process a file in Python are:

a. Open the file; it returns a file handle.

b. A file handle allows performing reading or writing on the files.

c. Close the file handle.

3. Which method is used to open a file in Python?

Ans. The built-in function open() is used to open a file. This function returns a file object that is a handle. The handle is used to read or modify the file.

4. Write the syntax of the open method of file.

Ans. *Syntax:*

```
file_object = open (file_name [, access mode][,buffering])
<file_name> It is string, that represents the path of the file including its name.
```

The access_mode open files in read, write and append mode.

Note: A filename is a relative or absolute path of the file.

5. Explain the parameter 'buffering' which is used in the open() method.

Ans. Buffering is the value for reading number of bytes from a file for buffering:

- If the value is 0, no buffering
- If the value is 1, the line buffering is performed
- If the value is > 1, then buffering will of buffer size
- If value < 0, the buffer size is default

6. What is the use of an access mode?

Ans. The access_mode is used to read, write and append the file.

7. Is access mode optional: True or False?

Ans. True, By default, it is read mode.

8. Differentiate between binary and text files.

Ans. Binary files contain a sequence of bytes. Text files only contain textual data that are ASCII or Unicode characters.

9. Define the absolute path.

Ans. The absolute path is the full path of a file, including its name. The path starts with the root directory in Linux or drive (c, d, and many more) in Windows.

10. Define the relative path.

Ans. The relative path contains a file name or a portion of the full path. It is relative to the current directory.

11. Mention the mode used to open a file for reading.

Ans. The read mode (r) is a default mode and opens a file for reading.

12. Mention the mode used to open a file for writing.

Ans. The write mode (w) opens a file for writing. It creates a new file in case the file does not exist. If the file exists, it truncates the file.

13. Mention the mode used to open a file for appending.

Ans. The append mode (a) opens a file for appending, which allows adding content at the end of the file without truncating it. If the file does not exist, a new file is created.

14. Mention the mode used to open a file for reading and updating.

Ans. The r+ mode opens a file for reading and updating.

15. Mention the mode used to open a file for writing and updating.

Ans. The w+ mode opens a file for writing and updating.

16. Mention the mode used to open a file for reading and appending.

Ans. The a+ mode opens a file for both reading and appending. If the file does not exist, it creates a new file for reading and writing.

Short Questions and Answers — 2/3 Marks

1. Differentiate between the read() and the readline() method.

Ans. The read(size) method returns the number of bytes as specified in the function. In case size is omitted, the entire content of the file is returned. Here, size is a number of bytes to be read from the file. The readline(), on the other hand, method returns a single line text from a file with a newline at the end.

2. Differentiate between readline() and readlines().

Ans. readline(): It returns a single line from a file including a newline at the end.

readlines(): It returns a list of all the lines from a file.

3. Differentiate between the write() and writeline() methods.

Ans. The write() method in Python outputs value or values on the console (screen) or a file without outputting a new line character. The writeline() method in Python adds a new line character after it outputs the values.

4. Differentiate between the writeline() and the writelines() methods.

Ans. The writeline() method in Python adds a new line character after it outputs the values to a file, whereas the writelines() method writes a sequence of strings to a file. A sequence is an iterable object of strings.

5. Where are the relative and absolute paths used?

Ans. Relative and absolute paths are used in operating systems to locate files and folders, whereas they are used to locating resources like files, images, web pages, in a website.

Long Questions and Answers — 3 Marks

1. Explain the relative path and absolute path with examples.

Ans. Data is stored in files and folders. To retrieve the data we need to traverse to the path of the file. A path is a slash-separated list of directories. For Example: the path of the file.txt is F:\Examples\Files\txtfiles\ as shown below, is the absolute path of file file.txt.

```
Examples
  Files
    binaryfiles
    txtfiles
```

Example of an absolute path

F:\Examples\files\fileexample1.py

F:\Examples\files\File.txt

Example of Relative path

If we are in examples directory the relative path of the txtfile .txt is Files\txtfile.txt or .files/txtfile. txt; here '.' represents the current directory.

Another example of a relative path is \File\ Fileexamples1.py.

Absolute path of file file.txt.

A relative path specifies the location of a directory relative to another directory or folder. Let's assume we are in the directory txtfile which has file 'File.txt'. The File.txt is relative to folder txtfile; since it is in the same folder and the relative path to file.txt from Files folder is txtfile/File.txt.

2. Mention the various ways to call the open() method.

Ans. Example 1: `_file = open('f:\\examples\\app.log', mode = 'w')`

Example 2: `_file = open('f:\\examples\\app.log', 'w')`

Example 3: `_file = open('f:\\examples\\app1.log', mode = 'w', encoding = 'utf-8')`

Example 4: Using relative path: `_file = open('app1.log', mode = 'w')`

3. How to write text for a file, explain it with an example.

Ans. Here's is the text we want to write to file.

Dream it. Wish it. Do it.

Success doesn't just find you. You have to go out and get it.

Push yourself, because no one else is going to do it for you.

Let's see an example of writing content to a file:

```
#open a file in write mode
_file = open('f:\\examples\\quotes.txt','w')
_file.write('Dream it. Wish it. Do it.\n')
_file.write('Success doesn't just find you. You have to go out and get it.\n')
_file.write('Push yourself, because no one else is going to do it for you.')
_file.close()
```

Note: Write does not add a newline, so we add it explicitly at the end of the line.

The below file is created and opened with Notepad:

Output:

quotes - Notepad

File Edit Format View Help

Dream it. Wish it. Do it.

Success doesn't just find you. You have to go out and get it.

Push yourself, because no one else is going to do it for you.

Let's see another example on how to write using the writelines() method:

```
_file = open('f:\\examples\\quotesall.txt', 'w')
_file.writelines ('Dream it. Wish it. Do it.\nSuccess doesn't just find you. You have to go out and get it.\nPush yourself because no one else is going to do it for you.')
_file.close()
```

The below file is created and opened with Notepad:

Output:

quotesall - Notepad

File Edit Format View Help

Dream it. Wish it. Do it.

Success doesn't just find you. You have to go out and get it.

Push yourself, because no one else is going to do it for you.

Let's see another example on how to write one line at a time:

```
_file = open('f:\\examples\\quotesalllines.txt','w')
textlist= ['Dream it. Wish it. Do it.\n' \
'Success doesn't just find you. You have to go out and get it.\n' \
'Push yourself, because no one else is going to do it for you.']
for line in textlist:
    #use print method to use the print line.
    print (line , file= _file)
_file.close()
```

Output:

quotesalllines - Notepad

File Edit Format View Help

Dream it. Wish it. Do it.

Success doesn't just find you. You have to go out and get it.

Push yourself, because no one else is going to do it for you.

Let's see one more example on how to read content in the file using a with keyword:

```
textlist= ['Dream it. Wish it. Do it.\n' \
'Success doesn't just find you. You have to go out and get it.\n' \
'Push yourself, because no one else is going to do it for you.']
with open('f:\\examples\\quotesalllines1.txt','w') as _file:
    for line in textlist:
        print ( line , file= _file )
```

Note: If we open a file using the keyword with it takes care to close the file once a block is over, even if errors occur.

4. **Mention the methods that allow reading content from a file.**

Ans. There are three methods for reading data from files, which are:

1. **read():** The read method returns the number of bytes from the file. If the size is omitted, then all the content is read.
   Here, the read() method returns the number of bytes from the file.
2. **readline():** It returns a line from the file including a newline character. If the size is given as an argument, bytes equal to the size will be returned.
3. **readlines():** It reads until EOF and returns a list containing all the lines.
   The hint parameter limit the number of lines returned. If the total number of bytes exceeds the specified number, no lines are returned.

5. **How to read the content of a file line by line and print it?**

Ans. Let's see an example:

```
_file = open('f:\\examples\\quotes.txt','r')
# read the line
line = _file.readline()
# keep reading one line at a time, until file is empty
while line:
    print(line,end='')
    # use realine() to read next line
    line = _file.readline()
_file.close()
```

Output:

```
Dream it. Wish it. Do it.
Success doesn't just find you. You have to go out and get it.
Push yourself, because no one else is going to do it for you.
```

Let's see an another example:

```
_file = open('f:\\examples\\quotes.txt','r')
while True:
    # read line
    line = _file.readline()
    print(line,end='')
    # check if a line is not empty
    if not line:
        break
_file.close()
```

Output:

```
Dream it. Wish it. Do it.
Success doesn't just find you. You have to go out and get it.
Push yourself, because no one else is going to do it for you.
```

Let's see an example to use readlines and iterators to print line by line:

```
_file = open('f:\\examples\\quotes.txt','r')
# return list of lines
filecontent = _file.readlines()
#iterate list to print line by line
for line in filecontent:
    print(line,end='')
_file.close()
```

Output:

```
Dream it. Wish it. Do it.
Success doesn't just find you. You have to go out and get it.
Push yourself, because no one else is going to do it for you.
```

6. Write a program that counts the number of words in a file.

Ans. wordcount = 0

```
_file = open("f:\\examples\\quotes.txt", 'r')
wordcount = 0
_lines = _file.readlines()
for line in _lines:
    #split the line into list of words
    words = line.split()
    #count the number or word in line
    wordcount += len(words)
    print("The number of words in file:")
print(wordcount)
```

Output:

```
The number of words in file:
32
```

Let's see another example:

```
_file = open("f:\\examples\\quotes.txt", 'r')
#read the entire text and split it into words
text = _file.read().split()
print("The number of words are "+ str(len(text)))
```

Output:

```
The numbers of words are 32
```

7. Write a program that counts the number of characters in a text file.

Ans.

```
chcount = 0
_file = open("f:\\examples\\quotes.txt", 'r')
ch =_file.read(1)
if ch:
```

```
        chcount+=1
    while True:
        if not ch:
            break
        else:
            chcount+=1
            ch =_file.read(1)

    print("The number of characters in file:")
    print(chcount)
    _file.close()
```

Output:

```
The number of characters in file:
148
```

8. Write a program that counts the number of vowels in a text file.

Ans.

```
vowelcount = 0
_file = open("f:\\examples\\quotes.txt", 'r')
ch =_file.read(1)

while True:
    if not ch:
        break
    else:
        if( ch in 'aeiouAEIOU' ):
            vowelcount+=1
        ch =_file.read(1)
print("The number of Vowels in file:")
print(vowelcount)
```

Output:

```
The number of Vowels in file:
48
```

9. Write a program that counts the number of word 'it' in a file.

Ans.

```
_file = open("f:\\examples\\quotes.txt", 'r')'
searchword = input("Enter the word to be searched: " )
#split the text into list of words  and count the
# occurrence of the search word using count() method
text =_file.read().split()
print("The word " + searchword +" found "+ str(text.count(searchword)) +" times.")
```

Output:

```
Enter the word to be searched: it
The word it found 1 times.
```

10. Write a program that searches a word and replaces it with another word in a text file.

Ans. Let's find and replace it with It:

```
_file = open("f:\\examples\\quotes.txt", 'r')
text =_file.read()
```

```
#read the content
searchword = input("Enter the word to be searched: ")
replaceword = input("Enter the word to be replaced: ")
#replaced the word
text = text.replace(searchword, replaceword)
_file.close()
#write the updated text
_file = open("f:\\examples\\quotesreplaced.txt", 'w')
_file.write(text)
_file.close()
# Read again after changes and print it
print("File after update")
_file = open("f:\\examples\\quotes.txt", 'r')
text =_file.read()
print(text, end='')
_file.close()
print("End of update")
```

Output:

```
Enter the word to be searched: it.
Enter the word to be replaced: IT.
File after update
Dream IT. Wish IT. Do IT.
Success doesn't just find you. You have to go out and get IT.
Push yourself, because no one else is going to do it for you.
End of update
```

11. Write a program that finds and prints the longest line in the file.

Ans. Let's assume we have the following content in quotes.txt file:

Output:

```
quotes - Notepad
File Edit Format View Help
Dream it. Wish it. Do it.
Success doesn't just find you. You have to go out and get it.
Push yourself, because no one else is going to do it for you.
```

```
_file = open("f:\\examples\\quotes.txt", 'r')
text = _file.readlines()
largestline =''
for line in text:
    if( len(line) > len(largestline)):
    largestline = line
print("The largest line is")
print(largestline)
```

Output:

```
The largest line is
Push yourself, because no one else is going to do it for you.
```

12. Write a program that finds and prints the longest word in the file.

Ans.
```
_file = open("f:\\examples\\quotes.txt", 'r')
wordlist = _file.read().split()
largestword=''
for word in wordlist:
    if( len(word)> len(largestword) ):
        largestword = word
print(''The  largest word is '')
print(largestword)
```

Output:
```
The largest word is
Yourself,
```

13. Write a program that copies the content from one text file to another file.

Ans. Let's consider the following as input file:

Output:

quotes - Notepad

File Edit Format View Help

Dream it. Wish it. Do it.

Success doesn't just find you. You have to go out and get it.

Push yourself, because no one else is going to do it for you.

```
_file = open("f:\\examples\\quotes.txt", 'r')
text = _file.read()
_file.close()
_filecopy = open("f:\\examples\\quotescopy.txt", 'w')
_filecopy.write(text)
_filecopy.close()
```

Explanation

The first step is to open a file in read mode and read its content. Then open a file in write mode and write the content to it. We will get the following output file:

Output:

quotescopy - Notepad

File Edit Format View Help

Dream it. Wish it. Do it.

Success doesn't just find you.You have to go out and get it.

Push yourself, because no one else is going to do it for you.

14. Write a program that copies the content from one text file to another file excluding the word 'it'.

Ans.
```
_file = open("f:\\examples\\quotes.txt", 'r')
lines = _file.readlines()
_file.close()
_file = open("f:\\examples\\quotes.txt", 'r')
_filecopy = open("f:\\examples\\quotesreplaced.txt", 'w')
```

```
for line in lines:
    if ( 'it' in line ):
#replace 'it'with  ''
    line= line.replace('it', '')
    _filecopy.write(line)
_file.close()
_filecopy.close()
```

Output:

quotesreplaced - Notepad

File Edit Format View Help

Dream . Wish . Do .
Success doesn't just find you. You have to go out and get .
Push yourself, because no one else is going to do for you.

15. What is the output of the following code?

Ans. The file AlbertEinstein.txt has the following text:

"Intellectuals solve problems, geniuses prevent them, weak people revenge. Strong people forgive. Intelligent people ignore. Most people say that it is the intellect which makes a great scientist. They are wrong: it is character"

```
_file = open("f:\\examples\\AlbertEinstein.txt", 'r')
text = _file.readline().split()
print(text[0])
_file.close()
```

Output:

```
Intellectuals
```

16. What is the output of the following code?

Ans. 1)
```
_file = open("f:\\examples\\AlbertEinstein.txt", 'r')
text = _file.readline(29)
print(text)
_file.close()
```

Output:

```
Intellectuals solve problems,
```

2)
```
_file = open("f:\\examples\\quotes.txt", 'r')
text = _file.read()
print(_file.read(5))
```

Output:

There will no output. The _file.read() reads all content from the file and file pointer moves to end of the file, now there is no more characters to read.

17. Write a program to display all the lines along with line numbers.

Ans.
```
import os
import sys
_file = open("f:\\examples\\quotes.txt", 'r')
count=0
```

```
for line in lines:
    count+=1
    print(count ,":",   line, file=sys.stdout)
    _file.close()
```

Output:

```
1 : Dream it. Wish it. Do it.

2 : Success doesn't just find you. You have to go out and get it.

3 : Push yourself, because no one else is going to do it for you.
```

18. Write a program that prints the last two lines form a file.

Ans.

```
_file = open("f:\\examples\\quotes.txt", 'r')
lines = _file.readlines()
print("Printing last two lines")
print(lines[-2],end='')
print(lines[-1], end='')
_file.close()
```

Output:

```
Printing last two lines
Success doesn't just find you. You have to go out and get it.
Push yourself, because no one else is going to do it for you
```

19. Write a program that searches a name that exists in a .csv file as shown below.

Ans. The file users.csv has first name, last name, password, email address, phone number, user id,

It has the following rows:

- Narayan,Sharma,1234,narayan@test.com,91-999-999-9999,101
- Mukesh,Verma,1235,mukesh@test.com,91-999-999-9998,101
- Ramesh,Kumar,3478,ramesh@test.com,91-999-999-9997,101
- Vikram,Sethi,4532,vikram@test.com,91-999-999-9996,101
- Savita,Mahajan,2343,savita@test.com,91-999-999-9995,101

Let's write a program to find a name in the file:

```
_file = open("f:\\examples\\users.csv", 'r')
name = input("\n Enter name to be searched")
lines = _file.readlines()
_file.close()
match =False
for line in lines:
    if name in line:
    match = True
    break
if(match):
    print(name + " Name found in file")
else:
    print(name + " Name is not found in file")
_file.close()
```

Output:

```
Enter name to be searched from user.csv file: Lokesh
Lokesh Name is not found in file
Enter name to be searched from user.csv file: Mukesh
Mukesh Name found in file
```

20. Write a program to delete a record from a file.

Ans. To delete a record form a file, the following steps need to be performed: .

1. Open the file that contains records in read mode.
2. Open file temp in write mode.
3. Read all lines from users.csv file.
4. Iterate each line and search the name, if it is not found, write it to a temp file.
5. Close users.csv and temp.csv.
6. Delete users.csv file.
7. Rename temp.csv to users.csv.

Let's see the code to delete a record from a file:

```
_file = open("f:\\examples\\users.csv", 'r')
_temp = open("f:\\examples\\temp.csv", 'w')
name = input("\n Enter name to be deleted: ")
lines = _file.readlines()
_file.close()
match =False
for line in lines:
   if name in line:
      pass
   else:
      _temp.write(line)
   _temp.close()
#remove
os.remove("f:\\examples\\users.csv")
os.rename("f:\\examples\\temp.csv","f:\\examples\\users.csv")
```

21. Write a program that copies a line that contains the word "Athletics" from the file sportdata. txt and copy it to the file called Atheletics.txt

Ans. Here's the data stored in file sportsdata.txt:

```
Vikas Jain Badminton national 34 51
Manish Verma Athletics international 10 18
Dinesh Agarwal TennisTable national 20 13
Anil Jain Athletics international 50 6
Mohan Prakash Athletics national 34 51
Manish Dev Athletics national 68 51
Varun Yadav TableTennis national 22 32
```

Let see the program to perform the same:

```
_file = open("f:\\examples\\Sportsdata.txt", 'r')
_temp = open("f:\\examples\\Atheletics.txt", 'w')
lines = _file.readlines()
_file.close()
for line in lines:
```

```
    if 'Atheletics' in line:
        _temp.write(line)
_temp.close()
```

Output:

```
Atheletics - Notepad
File Edit Format View Help
Manish Verma Atheletics interational 10 18
Anil Jain Atheletics international 50 6
Mohan Prakash Atheletics national 34 51
Manish Dev Atheletics national 68 51
```

Fill in the blanks

1. **The seek() method is used to set a file's __________ at the given __________.**

Ans. current position and offset

2. **__________ function is use to close a file.**

Ans. close()

3. **__________ mode opens a file for __________.**

Ans. w and writing only

4. **Opening a file in "w" mode __________ if the file already exists. If the __________ creates a __________ is created for writing.**

Ans. overwrites the file, file does not exist, and new file

5. **__________ opens a file __________.**

Ans. wb and for writing in binary format

6. **__________ opens a file for both __________.**

Ans. w+ and writing and reading

7. **__________ opens a file for __________ both in __________.**

Ans. wb+, writing and reading, and binary format

Multiple-Choice Questions and Answers

1. **Explain the meaning of the r, w, a, b, + modes**

Ans. r: reading

w: writing

a: appending

b: binary

+: updating

2. **Which of the following is the syntax of the writelines() method?**

a. `fileObject.writelines()`
b. `fileObject.writelines(sequence)`
c. `fileObject.readlines(sequence)`
d. None of the above

Ans. Option b, that is, fileObject.writelines(sequence).

3. **Which of the following is not the syntax of the readlines() method?**

a. `fileObject.readlines(size)`
b. `fileObject.readlines(sequence)`
c. `fileObject.readlines()`
d. None of the above

Ans. Option b, that is, fileObject.readlines(sequence).

4. Which of the following function is used to read all the characters from a file?

```
_file =open("filepath", 'a')
```

a. `_file.readall()` b. `_file.readcharacters()`
c. `_file.read()` d. `_file.readchar()`

Ans. Option c, that is, _file.read().

5. Which function is used to read a single line from a file?

```
_file =open("filepath", 'a')
```

a. `_file.read()` b. `_file.readlines()`
c. `_file.readline()` d. `_file.Readfullline()`

Ans. Option c, that is, _file.readline().

6. Which function is used to write all the characters to a file?

```
_file =open("filepath", 'w')
```

a. `_file.write()` b. `_file.writeall()`
c. `_file.writecharacters()` d. `_file.writechar()`

Ans. Option a, that is, _file.write().

7. Which function is used to write a list of strings in a file?

```
_file =open("filepath", 'w')
```

a. `_file.write()` b. `_file.writelines()`
c. `_file.writeline()` d. `_file.writefall()`

Ans. Option b, that is file.writelines()

8. Which of the following mode is used to open a binary file both for reading and writing?

a. `wb+` b. `w` c. `wb` d. `w+`

Ans. Option a, that is, wb+.

9. Which of the following is not a valid mode to open a file?

a. `ab` b. `r+` c. `w+` d. `rw`

Ans. Option d, that is, rw

10. Which of the following is used retrieve the file name by using file object _ofile?

a. `_ofile.name` b. `_ofile.file(name)`
c. `_ofile. name ()` d. `a and b`

Ans. Option a, that is, _ofile.name.

11. Which of the following is not a valid attribute of a file object (_file)?

a. `_file.name` b. `_file.mode`
c. `_file.closed` d. `_file.size`

Ans. Option d, that is,_file.size.

12. Which of the following is used to close a file object (_file)?

a. `close(_file)` b. `fileclose(_file)`
c. `_file.close()` d. `_file. close ()`

Ans. Option c, that is,_file.close().

13. Select the correct option to open a file for reading.

a. `_ifile = open("e:\\test.txt", "w")`
b. `_ifile = open("c:\\test.txt", "r")`
c. `_ifile = open(file = "e:\\test.txt", "r")`
d. `_ifile = open(file = "e:\\test.txt", "r+")`

Ans. Option b, that is,_ifile = open("c:\\test.txt", "r").

14. Select the correct option to open a file e:\\test.txt for writing.

a. `outfile = open("e:\\test.txt", "w+")`

b. `outfile = open("e:\\test.txt", "w")`

c. `outfile = open(file = "e:\\test.txt", "w")`

d. `outfile = open(file = "e:\\test.txt", "w+")`

Ans. Option b, that is,outfile = open("e:\\test.txt", "w").

15. Select the correct option to open a file e:\\test.txt for appending.

a. `outfile = open("e:\\test.txt", "a")`

b. `outfile = open("e:\\test.txt", "rw")`

c. `outfile = open(file = "e:\\test.txt", "a")`

d. `outfile = open(file = "e:\\test.txt", "w")`

Ans. Option a, that is,outfile = open("e:\\test.txt", "a").

16. Which of the following statements is/are true?

a. If a file does not exist and it is opened in read mode, an error occurs.

b. If a file does not exist and it is opened in write mode, a new file is created.

c. If a file exists and it is opened in write mode, the existing file will be overwritten.

d. All of the above

Ans. Option d, that is, All of the above.

17. Which of the following can be used to retrieve 2 characters from a file?

a. `_ifile.read(2)` b. `_ifile.read()`

c. `_ifile.readline()` d. `_ifile.readlines()`

Ans. Option a, that is,_ifile.read(2).

18. In the previous question, we have read 2 characters. Which of the following option is used to read the rest of the content from the file?

a. `_ifile.read(2)` b. `_ifile.read()`

c. `_ifile.readline()` d. `_ifile.readlines()`

Ans. Option b, that is, _ifile.read().

19. What is the output of the following code?

```
_file = None
for cnt in range (5):
    with open("c:\\data\\data.txt", "w") as _file:
        if cnt > 2:
            break
print(_file.closed)
```

a. Error b. True c. None d. False

Ans. Option b, that is, True.

20. Which of the following is used to read a line from a file?

a. `_ifile.readall()` b. `_ifile.read()`

c. `_ifile.readline()` d. `_ifile.readlines()`

Ans. Option c, that is,_ifile.readline().

21. Which of the following is used to read all the lines from a file?

a. `_ifile.readalllines()` b. `_ifile.read()`

c. `_ifile.readline()` d. `_ifile.readlines()`

Ans. Option d, that is,_ifile.readlines().

22. What does a readlines() method return?

a. A string
b. A list of all the lines in a file
c. A list of all the characters in a file
d. A list of integers

Ans Option b, that is, A list of all the lines in a file

23. Which one of the following is not an attribute of a file?

a. closed b. soft space c. rename d. mode

Ans. Option c, that is, rename.

Explanation: Rename is not an attribute of file; rest of the options are file attributes.

- **file.closed:** It returns true if the file is closed, otherwise it returns false.
- **file.mode:** It returns access mode with which file was opened.
- **file.name:** It returns the name of the file.
- **file.softspace:** It returns false if space explicitly required with print, otherwise, it returns true.

24. Why is the method tell() is used?

a. To know the current position of the file pointer within the file
b. To know the end position of the file pointer
c. Tells if file is opened or not
d. None of these

Ans. Option a, that is, To know the current position of the file pointer within the file.

25. What is the syntax of the rename() function?

a. `rename(current_file, new_file)`
b. `rename(new_file, current_file)`
c. `rename(()(current_file, new_file))`
d. `none of the above`

Ans. Option a, that is, rename(current_file, new_file).

26. What is the syntax for removing a file?

a. `remove(file_name)`
b. `remove(new_file, current_file,)`
c. `remove('' , file_name))`
d. `none of the above`

Ans. Option a, that is, remove(file_name).

27. Which of the following is used to get the current position within a file?

a. `_file.seek()` b. `_file.tell()` c. `_file.location` d. `_file.position`

Ans. Option b, that is,_file.tell().

28. Which is the following is used rename a _file?

a. `_file.name = 'newfilename.txt'`
b. `os.rename(_file, to_new_name)`
c. `os.rename(existing_filename, to_new_name)`
d. `os.setname(existing_filename, to_new_name)`

Ans. Option c, that is, os.rename(existing_filename, to_new_name).

29. Which of the following is used to delete a file?

a. `del (fileobject)`
b. `del fileobject`
c. `os.delete('filepath')`
d. `os.remove(filepath)`

Ans. Option d, that is,os.remove(filepath).

30. How do you change the file position to an offset value from the start?

a. `_file.seek(offset, 0)`
b. `_file.seek(offset, 1)`
c. `_file.seek(offset, 2)`
d. `none of the mentioned`

Ans. Option a, that is,_file.seek(offset, 0).

6 BINARY FILES

LEARNING OBJECTIVES

- Ability to write and read from/ to the binary file.
- Perform search, update and append operations on a binary file.

DEFINITION

- **Read mode:** Read mode allows opening file for reading.
- **Write mode:** Write mode allows opening file for writing.
- **Append mode:** Append mode allows file for appending.
- **Seek:** It allows the file pointer to move to the specified location.

Very Short Questions and Answers — 1 Mark

1. Differentiate between binary and text file in python.

Ans. A **text file** allows reading and writing the string (characters) to a file, whereas **binary file** is used to read and write the byte array.

2. Mention the method that converts string into a byte array.

Ans. The **bytearray()** method is used to convert the string into a byte array.

Example:

```
>>>string = "This is string "
>>> b= bytearray(string,'ascii')  # Here ascii is encoding
>>> type(b)
<class 'bytearray'>
```

3. Explain how the given two declarations are different from each other?

string= "Hi"

bytes= b"Hi"

Ans. The string = "Hi", is a declaration of string, whereas byte = b"Hi" is declaration for bytes, this can be validated using **type()** method.

Example:

```
>>> type(string)
<class 'str'>

>>> type(bytes)
<class 'bytes'>
```

4. Explain what is bytes() function?

Ans. The bytes() function returns a **"bytes"** object. It is an immutable sequence of integers which range from 0 to 255

Syntax:

```
bytes([input[, encoding[, errors]]])
```

Example:

```
>>> bytestr = bytes("This is string",'ascii')
>>> print(bytestr)
b'This is string'
```

5. Explain byte array?

Ans. A byte array is a mutable sequence of integers that ranges, from 0 to 255.

The **bytearray()** function manipulates its elements as the numbers range between 0-255 or one-char strings.

6. The br+ and wb+ modes are used for both reading and writing to a binary file, what is the difference between br+ and wb+?

Ans. wb+ create the file from scratch, whereas br+ does not create the file from scratch:

7. Write an algorithm to write to a binary file.

Ans. Step 1: Open a file in the write and binary mode

Step 2: Write the bytearray to the file

Step 3: Close the file

8. Write an algorithm to read from a binary file.

Ans. Step 1: Open a file in the read and binary mode

Step 2: Read byte array from the file

Step 3: Close the file

Step 4: Display the content of the file

Short Questions and Answers — 2 Marks

1. Explain the syntax and parameters of the function bytearray().

Ans. ***Syntax:***

```
bytearray([input[, encoding[, errors]]])
```

The *bytearray()* method accepts three optional parameters.

1: input (optional)

Below are the possible values parameter input

- String, encoding is required.
- byte array of integer.
- An iterable, it must be an iterable of integers ranging between 0 <= x < 256.
- Without any input value, the *bytearray()* returns an array of size 0.

2: Encoding (optional)

- Encoding is also optional. Example of encoding are: utf-8, ASCII etc. The str.encode() converts the string to byte arrays

3: Error (optional)

It can have values like strict, replace, ignore etc.

Example:

```
>>>string = 'ascii text string'
>>>bytestring = bytearray(string,'ascii')

# convert bytearray to string using decode() method
>>>print(bytestring.decode('ascii'))
```

Output:
```
'ascii text string'
```

2. Explain how to write to a binary file with an example.

Ans.
```
filepath = "F:\\files\\quotes.dat"
mode = "wb"

string="Successful and unsuccessful people do not vary greatly\
in their abilities. They vary in their desires to reach their potential \
- John Maxwell"

bytestream = bytearray(string,'ascii')

with open(filepath,mode) as _wfile:

    _wfile.write(bytestream)

print("Data is written to the filepath")

#Alternative we can write code as:
_wfile  = open(filepath,mode)
_wfile.write(bytestream)
_wfile.close()
```

Output:
```
Data is written to the filepath
```

quotes.dat
```
1 Successful and unsuccessful
  people do not vary
  greatlyin their abilities.
  They vary in their desires
  to reach their potential -
  John Maxwell
```

3. Explain how to read a binary file with an example.

Ans.
```
filepath = "F:\\files\\quotes.dat"

mode="rb"

data=""

with open(filepath,mode) as _wfile:

    data = _wfile.read()

print(data.decode('ascii'))

#The decode() method is used to convert the string into the ascii format.
```

Output:
```
Successful and unsuccessful people do not vary greatly in their abilities. They vary
in their desires to reach their potential - John Maxwell
```

4. Explain the syntax and use of the function decode()?

Ans. The syntax for *decode()* method is:

```
str.decode(encoding = 'UTF-8',errors = 'strict')
```

Parameters:

a. encoding: It tells which encoding is used. For example: uft-8 or ascii.

b. errors: It sets an error handler.

The default value for error is 'strict', which means that encoding raise a UnicodeError. Other values are 'ignore', 'replace', etc.

Return Value

It returns the decoded string.

The decode() method decodes the string by using the codec and returns encoded string. Here, codec is a function that translates the string into other formats and vice-versa.

5. Illustrate with the help of an example, how to write and read a list of integers?

Ans. ***Example:*** Write a list of integers to a binary file

```
f=open("F:\\files\\list.dat","wb")

num=[5, 10, 15, 20, 25]

arr=bytearray(num)

f.write(arr)

f.close()

#The list() function converts the byte array to list.

f=open("F:\\files\\list.dat","rb")

#Convert byte array to list

num= list(f.read())

print (num)

f.close()
```

Output:

```
[5, 10, 15, 20, 25]
```

Note: Without casting, *f.read()* return the list of bytes b'\x05\n\x0f\x14\x19'. This byte array is converted to list by using function *list()*.

6. Illustrate with the help of example how to write and read tuple of integers.

Ans. ***Example:*** Write to a Binary File

```
f=open("F:\\files\\tuple.dat","wb")

num=(5, 10, 15, 20, 25)
```

```
arr=bytearray(num)

f.write(arr)

f.close()

#The tuple() function converts the bytearray to list

f=open("F:\\files\\tuple.dat" ,"rb")

#Convert byte array to list
num= tuple(f.read())

print (num)

f.close()
```

Output:

```
(5, 10, 15, 20, 25)
```

7. **Illustrate how to append content at the end of the binary file?**

Ans. To append content at the end of binary file, open file in append mode and add the content as demonstrate in the below example.

Example: **Write to a Binary File**

```
f=open("F:\\files\\append.dat","wb")

string="Live as if you were to die tomorrow.\nLearn as if you were to live forever.\n"

f.write(bytearray(string,'ascii'))

f.close()

#Append to the binary file
f=open("F:\\files\\append.dat","ab")

newstring="-Mahatma Gandhi"

f.write(bytearray(newstring,'ascii'))

f.close()
```

Example: **Reading a Binary File**

```
f=open("F:\\files\\append.dat","rb")

string=f.read()

print (string.decode('ascii'))
```

```
f.close()
```

Output:

```
Live as if you were to die tomorrow.
Learn as if you were to live forever.
-Mahatma Gandhi
```

8. Find the size of the below file.

The text in the file is:

```
Live as if you were to die tomorrow.
Learn as if you were to live forever.
—Mahatma Gandhi
```

Ans.

```
_file = open("F\\files\\quotes.dat","rb")
_file.read()
print("The total number of characters in file " , _file.tell())
```

Note: The read() method reads all content and move the file pointer to end of file. The tell() returns the location of the file pointer that is size of file.

9. Explain the Syntax of the function seek().

Ans. seek() moves the file's current position at the offset.

Syntax:

```
fileObject.seek(offset[, whence])
```

Parameters:

a. Offset: It is a position of read or write at the file pointer within the file.

b. Whence: This is optional and defaults to 0.

0 – absolute file position.

1 – relative to the current position.

2 – relative to the file's end.

Long Questions and Answers 3/4 Marks

1. Write a function that replace a word in a binary file.

Below is the code that creates a binary file and replaces a word in it:

```
with open('F:\\files\\file.dat', 'wb') as file:
    # Write byte arrays to file
    file.write(b"This is mumbai\n")
    file.write(b"This is delhi\n")
    file.write(b"This is jaipur\n")
```

Ans.

```
# Function to update the content of binary file
def update_binfile(word, newword):
    # store each word after reading from the file
    string = b""

    # Flag variable to check if the record is found or not
    RecordFound = 0
```

```
    # Open the file in read and binary mode
    with open('F:\\files\\file.dat', 'rb+') as file:

        filepointer = 0

        # Reading file character by character
        string = file.read(1)
        data_infile = string
        # Iterate loop until end of file

        while data_infile:
            data_infile = file.read(1)
            #print(data_infile)
            # Checking if the space or new line is reached
            if data_infile == b" " or data_infile== b"\n":

                if string == word:

                    # Moving the file pointer to the read last word
                    file.seek(filepointer)

                    # Updating the content of the file
                    file.write(newword)
                    RecordFound = 1
                    break
                else:
                    # store the current position of the file pointer
                    filepointer = file.tell()
                    data_infile = string = file.read(1)
            else:
                  # Storing character until end of space or line
                  string += data_infile
                  continue

if RecordFound == 1:
    print("Record is updated")
else:
    print("Record not found")

word = input("Enter the word to be replaced: ").encode()
newword = input("\nEnter the new word: ").encode()
update_binfile(word, newword)
```

Output:
```
Enter the word to be replaced: mumbai
Enter the new word: kolkata
Record is updated

Enter the word to be replaced: japan
Enter the new word: tokoyo
Record not found
```

2. Write a function that search a word in a binary file.

Ans. Below is the code that creates a file

```
with open('F:\\files\\file.dat', 'wb') as file:
    # Write byte arrays to file
    file.write(b" This is mumbai\n")
    file.write(b" This is delhi\n")
    file.write(b" This is jaipur\n")

def Search_binfile(searchword):
    # store each word after reading
    # from the file
    string = b""

    # Flag variable to check if the record is found or not
    RecordFound = 0

    # Open the file in read and binary mode
    with open('F:\\files\\file.dat', 'rb+') as file:

        # Reading file character by character
        string = file.read(1)
        data_infile = string
        # Iterate loop until end of file
        while data_infile:
            data_infile = file.read(1)

            # Checking if the space or new line is reached
            if data_infile == b" " or data_infile == b"\n":

                if string == searchword:

                    RecordFound = 1
                    break
                else:
                    data_infile = string = file.read(1)
            else:
                # Storing character until end of space or line
                string += data_infile
                continue
```

```
    if RecordFound == 1:
        print("Record Found")
    else:
        print("Record not found")

searchword = input("\nEnter the word to be searched: ").encode()
Search_binfile(searchword)
```

Output:

```
Enter the word to be searched: mumbai
Record Found

Enter the word to be searched: japan
Record not found
```

3. Illustrate the use of functions seek() and tell() with the help of an example.

Ans. The below code demonstrate the use of the *seek()* and *tell():*

```
string = b"Your time is limited, so don't waste it living someone else's life.\nDon't be trapped by dogma\n- which is living with the results of other people's thinking.\n- Steve Jobs"
_file = open("check.txt","wb")
_file.write(string)
_file.close()

_file = open("check.txt","rb")
print("Name of the File : ",_file.name)
str=_file.read(10)
print("Position of file pointer after reading 10 characters ")
pos= _file.tell()
print("Current Position : ",pos)
#offset form the beginning of the file
pos = _file.seek(0,0)
print("Setting Pointer back to Top")
print("The current position is ", pos)
```

check - Notepad
File Edit Format View Help

```
Your time is limited, so don't waste it living someone else's life.
Don't be trapped by dogma
- which is living with the results of other people's thinking.
- Steve Jobs
```

```
_file.seek(156,0)
print("The current position is ", _file.tell())

#offset form the current position of the file
_file.seek(1,1)
```

```
print(_file.read().decode("ascii"))
_file.close()
```

Output:

```
Name of the File: check.txt
Position of file pointer after reading 10 characters
Current Position: 10
Setting Pointer back to Top
The current position is 0
The current position is 156
- Steve Jobs
```

7 PICKLE MODULE

LEARNING OBJECTIVES

- Describe the terms pickling, unpickling, serialization and de-serialization
- Explain the utility of pickle module
- Write code that uses function dump() and load()

DEFINITION

- **Pickling:** The term pickling refers to the process of converting an object stored in memory in a byte stream that can be stored on disk.
- **Unpickling:** Unpickling is where a byte stream is converted back into an object from a binary file or a byte-like object.
- **Serialization:** Serialization is converting the python object to the byte stream.
- **De-serialization:** Converting the byte-stream to the Python object is called de-serialization.

Very Short Questions and Answers — 1 Mark

1. Why serialization and de-serialization are used?

Ans. Serialization and de-serialization are used to send objects over a network. Later on, these objects can be retrieved and de-serialized back to a Python object.

2. Mention the other names of serialization?

Ans. Marshaling or flattening are other names of the serialization.

3. Is Zipping (compression) the same as serialization?

Ans. Pickling might sounds like compression to beginners. The serialization is the conversion of an object in **Random Access Memory (RAM)** to **(object on disk)**, whereas Zipping is the a process that encodes the data with lesser bits, that save space for storage and sent over the network.

4. Explain the utility of pickle?

Ans. Pickling is helpful where applications are needed to store data persistently for example secondary storage devices. The program can use it later to retrieve data by (loading) it from the disk.

It is also used to send data over an internet **(Transmission Control Protocol/Internet Protocol (TCP/IP) or a socket connection)** to access it remotely or save python objects in a database.

5. Mention when not to use the pickle?

Ans. The following are scenarios where pickle should be non-advisable :

1. When we have to use data across different programming languages.
2. When using different versions of Python itself, unpickling a file from a different version may not work properly.
3. Do not unpickle data from an untrusted source, as it could contain the malicious code inside the file that might get executed during unpickling.

Short Questions and Answers 2 Marks

1. Mention what data types can be pickled?

Ans. The following types can be pickled:

- True, False and None
- Integers, floats and complex numbers
- Strings, bytes and, byte arrays
- Lists, tuples, dictionaries, sets, containing only pickable objects
- Functions that are defined at the top level of a module (using def, not lambda)
- Built-in functions that are defined at the top level of a module
- Classes that are defined at the top level of a module

2. Mention the most commonly used methods of pickle module?

Ans. The most commonly used methods of pickle module are:

- **dump():** It writes an object to a file, the file is open in wb mode (write and binary)
- **load():** It reads a pickled object from the open file in the object file and returns the unpickled object

3. Explain how to write a file using pickle module?

Ans. Algorithm: To write an object using pickle

Step 1: import the pickle module

Step 2: open a file in write and binary mode

Step 3: use the dump method to save file as **dict.dat**

Step 4: close the file

Example 1:

```
import pickle

_dict = {1:"a",2:"b",3:"c"}

_out = open("dict.dat","wb")

pickle.dump(_dict, _out)
_out.close()
```

4. Explain how to read a file using the pickle module?

Ans. Algorithm: To read a file using pickle module

Step 1: import the pickle module

Step 2: open a file in read and binary mode

Step 3: use the load method to save file as **dict.dat**

Step 4: close the file (if not opened using 'with')

Example 2:

```
import pickle

with open('dict.dat', 'rb') as _file:
    object =pickle.load(_file)
print(object)
```

Output:

```
{1:"a",2:"b",3:"c"}
```

5. Illustrate how to pickle and unpickle an integer with an example?

Ans.
```
import pickle
data = 1
with open(F:\\files\\intdata.dat', 'wb') as _file:
    pickle.dump(data, _file)
#Read the value
with open(F:\\files\\intdata.dat', 'rb') as _file:
    _dataretrieve =pickle.load(_file )
print(_dataretrieve)
```

Output:
```
1
```

6. Illustrate how to pickle and unpickle a float with an example?

Ans.
```
data = 1.0
with open(F:\\files\\floatdata.dat', 'wb') as _file:
    pickle.dump(data, _file)
#Unpicking the float data
with open(F:\\files\\floatdata.dat', 'rb') as _file:
    _dataretrieve =pickle.load(_file )

print(_dataretrieve)
```

Output:
```
1.0
```

7. Illustrate how to pickle and unpickle a tuple with an example?

Ans.
```
tuple = (1,2,3,4)
with open(F:\\files\\tupledata.dat', 'wb') as _file:
    pickle.dump(tuple, _file)
#unpickling the tuple
with open(F:\\files\\tupledata.dat', 'rb') as _file:
    _dataretrieve =pickle.load(_file )
print(_dataretrieve)
```

Output:
```
(1,2,3,4)
```

8. Illustrate how to pickle and unpickle list with an example?

Ans.
```
list = [10,20,30,40]
with open(F:\\files\\listdata.dat', 'wb') as _file:
    pickle.dump(list, _file)
#Unpickling the list
with open(F:\\files\\listdata.dat', 'rb') as _file:
    _dataretrieve =pickle.load(_file )
print(_dataretrieve)
```

Output:
```
[1,2,3,4]
```

9. Illustrate how to pickle and unpickle dictionary with an example?

Ans.
```
dictionary = {1:'a',2:'b',3:'c'}
```

```
with open(F:\\files\\dictionarydata.dat', 'wb') as _file:
    pickle.dump(dictionary,_file)
# Unpickling the dictionary
with open(F:\\files\\dictionarydata.dat', 'rb') as _file:
    _dataretrieve = pickle.load(_file )
print(_dataretrieve)
```

Output:

```
{1:'a',2:'b',3:'c'}
```

10. Illustrate how to pickle and unpickle a string with an example?

Ans.

```
string ="this is test string"
with open(F:\\files\\stringdata.dat', 'wb') as _file:
    pickle.dump(string,_file)
# Unpickling the string

with open(F:\\files\\stringdata.dat', 'rb') as _file:
    _dataretrieve =pickle.load(_file )
print(_dataretrieve)
```

Output:

```
"this is test string"
```

Long Questions and Answers — 3/4 Marks

1. Illustrate how to pickle and unpickle multiple records with an example?

Ans.

```
import pickle
# database
employeedb = {}

def storeData():
    # initializing data to be stored in db
    employee1 = {'name' : 'Sankar Mahadev','desigantion' : \
'SE-II', 'pay-bracket' : 'C'}
    employee2 = {'name' : 'Vishnu Pathak', 'desigantion' : '\
Architect-I', 'pay-bracket' : 'E'}
    employee3 = {'name' : 'Ganesh Shankar','desigantion' : '\
Evangalist', 'pay-bracket' : 'D'}

    employeedb['20111234'] = employee1
    employeedb['20112345'] = employee2
    employeedb['20122356'] = employee3

    dbfile = open(F:\\files\\employee.dbf', 'ab')

    pickle.dump(employeedb, dbfile)
    dbfile.close()

def loadData():
```

```
        # for loading open file in binary mode
        dbfile = open(F:\\files\\employee.dbf', 'rb')
        empdb = pickle.load(dbfile)

        for keys in empdb:
            print(keys, '=>', empdb[keys])
            print()

        dbfile.close()

    storeData()
    loadData()
```

Output:

```
20111234 => {'name': 'Sankar Mahadev', 'desigantion': 'SE-II', 'pay-bracket': 'C'}
20112345 => {'name': 'Vishnu Pathak', 'desigantion': 'Architect-I', 'pay-bracket': 'E'}
20122356 => {'name': 'Ganesh Shankar', 'desigantion': 'Evangalist', 'pay-bracket': 'D'}
```

Multiple-Choice Questions and Answers

1. What is the correct code of writing an integer to file?

x = 1

a. with open('datafile.txt', 'wb') as _file:
    pickle.dump(x, _file)

b. with open('datafile.txt', 'rb') as _file:
    pickle.dump(x,_file)

c. with open('datafile.txt', 'rb+') as _file:
    pickle.dump(x,_file)

d. with open('datafile.txt', 'wb') as _file:
    pickle.dump(_file)

Ans. a.

2. What is the correct code to read an integer from a file?

a. with open('datafile.txt', 'rb') as _file:
    pickle.load(val, _file)

b. with open('datafile.txt', 'wb') as _file:
    pickle.load(val,_file)

c. with open('datafile.txt', 'wb') as _file:
    val = pickle.load(file)

d. with open('datafile.txt', 'rb') as _file:
    val = pickle.load(_file)

Ans. d.

8 CSV MODULE

LEARNING OBJECTIVES

- Read the CSV File with *reader()* and *DictReader()* methods
- Write header to a CSV file
- Write row and multiple row using *writerow()* and *writerows() function in a CSV file*
- Iterate rows returned by the reader and the DictReader functions

DEFINITION

- **CSV:** A text file that stores the data in tabular format where values are separated by comma.
- **Delimiter:** A separator that separates the fields of a CSV file.

Very Short Questions and Answers — 1 Mark

1. Define a CSV file?

Ans. CSV stands for **C**omma **S**eparated **V**alues. It is plain text file, which stores data in tabular format, such as a spreadsheet or database. Each row is treated as a data record. Each record consists of one or more fields, these fields are separated by commas.

2. Mention the most common use of the CSV file.

Ans. The most common uses of the CSV files are:

- CSV files are used to store data in tabular format.
- CSV file format is mainly used for Data Visualization.

3. Mention the advantage of using the CSV file.

Ans. The CSV file is platform independent as it can be used in Window, Mac or Linux etc. The CSV files are parsed by multiple languages.

4. Explain the difference between text file and CSV file.

Ans.

CSV file	Text file
The values in CSV files are comma separated.	The values in text files are plain text.
The extension of the CSV file is .CSV.	The extension of the text file is .txt.

Note: All CSV files are text file but, all text files are not CSV file.

Short Questions and Answers — 2 Marks

1. Write a pseudo code that writes rows to a CSV file.

Ans. Pseudo code that writes rows to the CSV file:

Step 1: Import the CSV module.

Step 2: Open CSV file in write mode and create a file object.

Step 3: Pass the file object to the CSV.writer (), it returns a writer class object.

Step 4: The writer's writerow() function writes a row to the CSV file

Step 5: Close the file object.

2. Illustrate a CSV file with an example.

Ans. ***Example:***

Fname, Lname, Department, DOB ← **Header**

gupinder, kaur, Accounting, 02/12/1990

Erica, Smith, IT, 02/12/1995 } **Rows**

Manish, Dev, administration, 03/12/1997

This file has four fields:

Fname(first Name),

Lname(Last Name),

Department,

DOB(Date of Birth)

It has 3 rows and a header, the first rows is also called a **header.**

Here ',' is a **file separator.**

3. Define field separator and what is the most commonly used separator?

Ans. The field separator is also known as **delimiters** that separates the fields of a record. Apart from comma, semicolon(:), colon(:), space( ), tab are commonly used separators.

4. Illustrate how to add rows in a CSV file with an example?

Ans.
```
import CSV

_file =open('F:\\files\\employee1.CSV', mode='w',newline='')

with _file:
    employee_writer = CSV.writer(_file, delimiter=',', quotechar='"')
    employee_writer.writerow(['Vijay Shankar', 'Accounting', 'November'])
    employee_writer.writerow(['Kiran Kumar', 'IT', 'March'])
```

Output:

F:\Files\employee1.csv - Notepad++

File Edit Search View Encoding Language Settings Tools Macro Run Plugins Window ?

copyfile.py | csvdb1.py | csvdb2.py | employee1.csv

```
1 Vijay Shankar,Accounting,November
2 Kiran Kumar,IT,March
```

5. How to write tuple(s) to the CSV file?

Ans. Writing tuple to the CSV tuple is simple, tuple(s) can be written to CSV file after converting it to the list. For example:

```
import CSV

_file =open('F:\\files\\employee1.CSV', mode='w',newline='')
employee1 = ('Vijay Shankar', 'Accounting', 'November')
employee2 = ('Kiran Kumar', 'IT', 'March')

with _file:
```

```
    _writer = CSV.writer(_file, delimiter=',', quotechar='"')
    _writer.writerow(list(employee1))
    _writer.writerow(list(employee2))
```

Output:

F:\Files\employee1.csv - Notepad++

```
Vijay Shankar,Accounting,November
Kiran Kumar,IT,March
```

6. How to write multiple rows to the CSV file?

Ans. The Writerows() function accepts a list of lists and write all the rows at once.

```
import CSV
with open('F:\\file\\employee2.CSV', mode='w', newline='') as _file:
    _writer = CSV.writer(_file, delimiter='|', quotechar='"')
    _writer.writerows(
    [
        ['Vijay Shankar', 'Accounting', 'November'] ,
        ['Kiran Kumar', 'IT', 'March']
]
)
```

Output:

F:\Files\employee2.csv - Notepad++

```
Vijay Shankar|Accounting|November
Kiran Kumar|IT|March
```

7. How to write a dictionary to a CSV file?

Ans. The DictWriter() function is used to write the dictionary to the CSV file. For example:

```
import CSV
with open('F:\\files\\names.CSV',mode='w',newline='') as _f :
    #Creating header for the file

    fnames = ['first_name', 'last_name']

    writer = CSV.DictWriter(_f, fieldnames=fnames)

    writer.writeheader()

    writer.writerow({'first_name' : 'Khaniya', 'last_name': 'Kumar'})
    writer.writerow({'first_name' : 'Zoya', 'last_name': 'Khan'})
    writer.writerow({'first_name' : 'Julia', 'last_name': 'Roberts'})
```

Output:

```
F:\Files\names.csv - Notepad++
first_name,last_name
Khaniya,Kumar
Zoya,Khan
Julia,Roberts
```

7. How to write multiple dictionaries by using function *writerows()* to the CSV file?

Ans.
```
import CSV
with open('F:\\files\\students.CSV',mode='w',newline='') as _f :

   fnames =['Id','Name','Course','Location','Block']

   writer = CSV.DictWriter(_f, fieldnames=fnames)
   writer.writeheader()

   writer.writerows([
      {'Id': '0021', 'Name': 'Vijay', 'Course': 'C++', 'Location': 'CV Raman
      Hall', 'Block':'A'},
      {'Id': '0101', 'Name': 'John', 'Course': 'Android', 'Location': 'Vivekanand
      Hall', 'Block': 'C'},
      {'Id': '0102', 'Name': 'Arun', 'Course': 'Python','Location': 'Albert
      Eisten Hall', 'Block':'A'},
      {'Id': '0010', 'Name': 'Shaun', 'Course': 'C', 'Location': 'Mahatma Ghandi
      Hall', 'Block': 'B'}
      ])
```

Output:

```
F:\Files\students.csv - Notepad++
Id,Name,Course,Location,Block
0021,Vijay,C++,CV Raman Hall,A
0101,John,Android,Vivekanand Hall,C
0102,Arun,Python,Albert Eisten Hall,A
0010,Shaun,C,Mahatma Ghandi Hall,B
```

8. How to create a tab separated file?

Ans. To create the tab separated file, the TAB {'\t'} is used as a separator. For example:

```
import CSV
_file =open('F:\\files\\employeetab.CSV', mode='w',newline='')
```

```
with _file:
    _writer = CSV.writer(_file, delimiter='\t', quotechar='"')
    _writer.writerow(['Vijay Shankar', 'Accounting', 'November'])
    _writer.writerow(['Kiran Kumar', 'IT', 'March'])
```

Output:

F:\Files\employeetab.csv - Notepad++

File Edit Search View Encoding Language Settings Tools Macro Run Plugins Window ?

copyfile.py csvexamples.py employeetab.csv

```
1 Vijay Shankar	Accounting	November
2 Kiran Kumar	IT	March
```

9. How to read a CSV file?

Ans. The *reader()* method of the CSV module is used to fetch all the rows from a CSV file for example

```
import CSV

_file =open('F:\\files\\employee1.CSV', mode='r')

with _file:
    _reader = CSV.reader(_file)
    for row in _reader:
        # Print each row at a time
        print(row)
```

Output:

```
['Vijay Shankar', 'Accounting', 'November']
['Kiran Kumar', 'IT', 'March']
```

10. Explain how to read a CSV file with delimiter "|"?

F:\Files\employee2.csv - Notepad++

File Edit Search View Encoding Language Settings Tools Macro Run Plugins Window ?

copyfile.py csvexamples.py employeetab.csv employee2.csv

```
1 Vijay Shankar|Accounting|November
2 Kiran Kumar|IT|March
```

Ans. import CSV

```
_file = open("F:\\files\\employee2.CSV","r")

with _file:
    _reader = CSV.reader(_file,delimiter="|")
    for row in _reader:
    # The row variable is a list that represents a row in CSV
        print(row)
```

Output:

```
['Vijay Shankar', 'Accounting', 'November']
['Kiran Kumar', 'IT', 'March']
```

11. How to read CSV file using function DictReader()?

F:\Files\names.csv - Notepad++

File Edit Search View Encoding Language Settings Tools Macro Run Plugins Window ?

copyfile.py | csvdb1.py | csvdb2.py | csvexamples.py | names.csv

```
first_name,last_name
Khaniya,Kumar
Zoya,Khan
Julia,Roberts
```

Ans.

```
with open('F:\\files\\names.CSV',mode='r') as _f :
dict_reader = CSV.DictReader(_f)
# iterate over each line as a ordered dictionary
for row in dict_reader:
    # The row variable is a dictionary
    print(dict(row))
```

Output:

```
{'first_name': 'Khaniya', 'last_name': 'Kumar'}
{'first_name': 'Zoya', 'last_name': 'Khan'}
{'first_name': 'Julia', 'last_name': 'Roberts'}
```

12. Explain how to print the file header with an example?

F:\Files\students.csv - Notepad++

File Edit Search View Encoding Language Settings Tools Macro Run Plugins Window ?

copyfile.py | csvdb1.py | csvdb2.py | csvexamples.py | names.csv | students.csv

```
Id,Name,Course,Location,Block
0021,Vijay,C++,CV Raman Hall,A
0101,John,Android,Vivekanand Hall,C
0102,Arun,Python,Albert Eisten Hall,A
0010,Shaun,C,Mahatma Ghandi Hall,B
```

Ans.

```
import CSV
# open file in read mode
with open('F:\\files\\students.CSV', 'r') as read_obj:
    # Pass the file object to DictReader() to get the DictReader object
    CSV_dict_reader = CSV.DictReader(read_obj)
    # Get column names from a CSV file
    column_names = CSV_dict_reader.fieldnames
    print(column_names)
```

Output:

```
['Id', 'Name', 'Course', 'Location', 'Block']
```

13. Explain how to fetch a column using column name from a CSV file?

F:\Files\names.csv - Notepad++

```
first_name,last_name
Khaniya,Kumar
Zoya,Khan
Julia,Roberts
```

Ans. The column name is used to fetch a column from a row. Row is a combination of columns. For example row['Id'] is the first field of the row. Below example demonstrate how to fetch a column from a CSV file:

```
with open('F:\\files\\names.CSV',mode='r') as _f :
    dict_reader = CSV.DictReader(_f)
    # Iterate over each line as a ordered dictionary
    for row in dict_reader:
        print(dict(row))
```

Output:

```
Khaniya
Zoya
Julia
```

14. How to read tab separated file?

F:\Files\employeetab.csv - Notepad++

```
Vijay Shankar	Accounting	November
Kiran Kumar	IT	March
```

Ans. To read the tab separated file the character ("\t") is used as delimiter. For example:

```
_file = open("F:\files\employeetab.CSV","r")

with _file:
    _reader = CSV.reader(_file,delimiter="\t")
    for row in _reader:
        print(row)
```

Output:

```
['Vijay Shankar', 'Accounting', 'November']
['Kiran Kumar', 'IT', 'March']
```

Long Questions and Answers 3/4 Marks

1. Write a program that copy one CSV file to another CSV file?

F:\Files\students.csv - Notepad++

File Edit Search View Encoding Language Settings Tools Macro Run Plugins Window ?

copyfile.py | csvdb1.py | csvdb2.py | csvexamplea.py | names.csv | students.csv

```
Id,Name,Course,Location,Block
0021,Vijay,C++,CV Raman Hall,A
0101,John,Android,Vivekanand Hall,C
0102,Arun,Python,Albert Eisten Hall,A
0010,Shaun,C,Mahatma Ghandi Hall,B
```

Ans.

```
import CSV
# open file in read mode
_copyfile =open('F:\\files\\studentscopy.CSV',mode='w',newline='')

_file= open('F:\\files\\students.CSV', 'r')

# Pass the file object to DictReader() to get the DictReader object
_dict_reader = CSV.DictReader(_file)

# Get column names from a CSV file
column_names = _dict_reader.fieldnames

writer = CSV.DictWriter(_copyfile, fieldnames= column_names)
writer.writeheader()

for row in _dict_reader:
    # Write a row in CSV
    writer.writerow(dict(row))

_file.close()
_copyfile.close()
```

Output:

F:\Files\studentscopy.csv - Notepad++

File Edit Search View Encoding Language Settings Tools Macro Run Plugins Window ?

copyfile.py | csvexamples.py | csvread.py | copycsv.py | studentscopy.csv

```
Id,Name,Course,Location,Block
0021,Vijay,C++,CV Raman Hall,A
0101,John,Android,Vivekanand Hall,C
0102,Arun,Python,Albert Eisten Hall,A
0010,Shaun,C,Mahatma Ghandi Hall,B
```

2. Write a program that deletes a record in the CSV file?

Ans. Steps to delete a record in CSV file:

- Open the source file in the read mode.
- Open another file in write mode and place the row if does not match the criteria.
- Delete the source file.
- Rename the other file to the source file.

```
import CSV
import os

with open('F:\\files\\studentdata.CSV',mode='w',newline='') as _f :

    fnames =['Id','Name','Course','Location','Block']

    writer = CSV.DictWriter(_f, fieldnames=fnames)
    writer.writeheader()

    writer.writerows([
        {'Id': '0021', 'Name': 'Vijay', 'Course': 'C++', 'Location': 'CV Raman Hall',
        'Block':'A'},
        {'Id': '0101', 'Name': 'John', 'Course': 'Android', 'Location': 'Vivekanand Hall',
        'Block': 'C'},
        {'Id': '0102', 'Name': 'Arun', 'Course': 'Python', 'Location': 'Albert Eisten
        Hall', 'Block':'A'},
        {'Id': '0010', 'Name': 'Shaun', 'Course': 'C', 'Location': 'Mahatma Ghandi Hall',
        'Block': 'B'}
    ])

memberName = input("Please enter a member's name to be deleted.")
infile = open('F:\\files\\studentdata.CSV' , 'r')
outfile = open('F:\\files\\temp.CSV' , 'w' , newline='')
writer = CSV.writer(outfile)

for row in CSV.reader(infile):
    if  memberName not in row:
        writer.writerow(row)

infile.close()
outfile.close()

os.remove('F:\\files\\studentdata.CSV')
os.rename('F:\\files\\temp.CSV','F:\\files\\studentdata.CSV')

# os.rename(src, dst)
#src: Source is the name of the file or directory from where values are transferred to
another file.

#dst: Destination is the new name of the file or directory where the values are transferred
from the source file
```

Output:

```
Please enter a member's name to be deleted.
Arun
```

F:\Files\studentdata.csv - Notepad++

```
Id,Name,Course,Location,Block
0021,Vijay,C++,CV Raman Hall,A
0101,John,Android,Vivekanand Hall,C
0010,Shaun,C,Mahatma Ghandi Hall,B
```

3. Write a program that calculates the sum of all debit amount from the transaction file?

Ans.

```
import CSV
with open('F:\\files\\transactions.CSV',mode='w', newline='')as _file:

    fnames = ['TransactionId','date','debit','credit','remark']
    _writer = CSV.DictWriter(_file,fieldnames=fnames)
    _writer.writerows([
{'TransactionId':'131234','date':'12/12/2019','debit':'','credit':'1234','remark':'misc
expense'},
{'TransactionId':'123457','date':'11/12/2019','debit':'20000','credit':'','remark':'bonus'},
{'TransactionId':'133458','date':'01/12/2019','debit':'25000','credit':'','remark':'salary'},
{'TransactionId':'131234','date':'25/11/2019','debit':'','credit':'3000','remark':'Car
maintenance'},
{'TransactionId':'123457','date':'11/12/2019','debit':'','credit':'2500','remark':'clothings'},
{'TransactionId':'133458','date':'01/11/2019','debit':'25000','credit':'2500','remark':'salary'}
    ])

# Read the transactions file
debitamt=[]
with open('F:\\file\\transactions.CSV',mode='r') as _f :
    _reader = CSV.reader(_f)
        # Iterate over each line as a ordered dictionary
    for row in _reader:
        # Row variable is a dictionary that represents a row in CSV

        if(row[2] != ''):
            # Print date and transaction amount
        print(row[1], "\t\t", row[2])
        debitamt.append(float(row[2]))

print("Total debited Amount:  " ,sum(debitamt))
```

Output:

```
11/12/2019              20000
01/12/2019              25000
01/11/2019              25000
Total debited Amount:   70000.0
```

4. Define a function that allows to insert a record in a CSV file using a function.

Ans.
```
import CSV
import os
dberror={"000":"Success",
    "ERCode011":"table not exists",
    "ERCode012":"Column name mismatch",
    "ERCode013":"Column and values mismatch"}

def insertinto(filepath, columns, values):
    if( not isfileexists(filepath) ):
        return "ERCode011"
    _record = {}
    columnnames=[]

    with open(filepath, 'r') as _infile:
        _dictreader = CSV.DictReader(_infile)
        columnnames = _dictreader.fieldnames
        #using all() to  check subset of list
        if(not all(x in columnnames for x in columns)):
            return "ERCode012"
        if(len(columns) != len(values)):
            return "ERCode013"

    # Using zip function to convert lists into dictionary
    _record = dict(zip(columns,values))
    for element in columnnames:
        if(element not in columns):
            _record[element]=''

    with open(filepath, 'a', newline='') as _infile:
        _dictwriter = CSV.DictWriter(_infile,fieldnames=columnnames)
        _dictwriter.writerow(_record)

    return "000"

def isfileexists(filepath):
    if(os.path.exists(filepath)):
        return True
    else:
        return False

#Id,Name,Course,Location,Block
file ='F:\\students.CSV'

cols= ['Id','Name','Course','Location','Block']
vals=['0021','Akash','C++','CV Raman Hall','A']

retcode =insertinto(file,cols,vals)
```

```
print(dberror[retcode])

cols= ['Id','Course','Location']
vals=['C++','CV Raman Hall']

retcode =insertinto(file,cols,vals)
print(dberror[retcode])
```

Output:

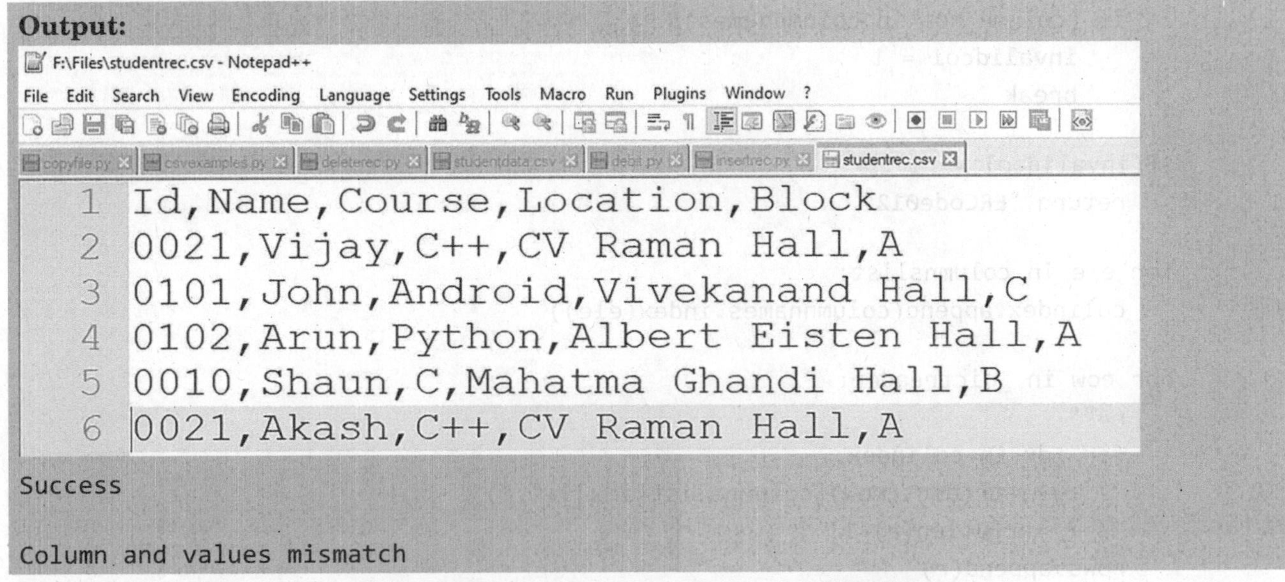


```
Success

Column and values mismatch
```

5. Write a program that allows to select the record(s) from a CSV file

Ans.

```
import csv
import os

dberror={"000":"Success",
    "ERCode011":"table not exists",
    "ERCode012":"Column name mismatch",
    "ERCode013":"Column and values mismatch"}

def select(filepath, columnslist):
    rows=[] #for return the rows selected
    if( not isfileexists(filepath) ):
        return "ERCode011"
    collist=[]
    colindex=[]
    columnnames=[]
    with open(filepath, 'r') as _infile:
        _dictreader = csv.DictReader(_infile)
        columnnames = _dictreader.fieldnames
        #using all() to  check subset of list
        if(columnslist == "all" or columnslist == "*"):
            for row in _dictreader:
                #convert the orderdict to string
                #convert ordered dictionary to dictionary
```

```
                #convert dictionary to list and
                #list to string using join
                rows.append(','.join(list(dict(row).values())))

        return rows
    invalidcol = 0
    for column in  columnslist:
        if (column not in columnnames):
            invalidcol = 1
            break

    if(invalidcol == 1):
        return "ERCode012"

    for ele in columnslist:
        colindex.append(columnnames.index(ele))

    for row in _dictreader:
        r=""
        for idx in colindex:
            r+= str(dict(row)[columnslist[idx]]+",")
            r = r[0:len(r)-1]
        rows.append(r)
    return(rows)

def isfileexists(filepath):
    if(os.path.exists(filepath)):
        return True
    else:
        return False

#Id,Name,Course,Location,Block
file ='F:\\files\\studentrec.csv'

rows= select( file, ['Id','Name','Course','Location'])
print(rows)
print()
rows= select( file, "all")
print(rows)
```

Output:

```
['0021,Vijay,C++,CV Raman Hall', '0101,John,Android,Vivekanand Hall', '0102,Arun,Python,Albert Eisten Hall', '0010,Shaun,C,Mahatma Ghandi Hall', '0021,Akash,C++,CV Raman Hall']

['0021,Vijay,C++,CV Raman Hall,A', '0101,John,Android,Vivekanand Hall,C', '0102,Arun,Python,Albert Eisten Hall,A', '0010,Shaun,C,Mahatma Ghandi Hall,B', '0021,Akash,C++,CV Raman Hall,A']
```

9 MODULES AND PACKAGES

LEARNING OBJECTIVES

- Recall the terms modularity, module, package and pythonpath
- Write a code that creates a module, and imports and uses user-defined modules
- Divide a larger program into packages, sub-packages and modules.
- Generate random numbers by using the functions defined in the random module

DEFINITION

- **Modularity:** Modularity in programming is a mechanism of breaking a large programming task into smaller, manageable subtasks or modules. Modules are clubbed together to create a larger application.
- **Module:** A module is a code that contains Python definitions (function, classes) and statements in a file. This file is saved with the '.py' extension.
- **Package:** A package is a directory that contains Python files and a file with name as _init_.py. Every directory inside a Python path, has a file named _init_.py, which is a package in Python. It is possible to place several modules in a single package.
- **Pythonpath:** Pythonpath is used to locate modules and packages. It is an environment variable that sets path where modules and packages are looked for.
- **Random Module:** This random module has random number generators that implement pseudo-random numbers. The most basic function is random (), which generates a random float value uniformly in a semi-open range [0.0, 1.0), which is from 0 to less than one.

Very Short Questions and Answers — 1 Mark

1. Explain the significance of a module.

Ans. A module allows dividing complex and large programs into smaller parts.

2. Why is docstring used?

Ans. The docstring contains information about the module, class, function and what they are supposed to do or / and how they can be used.

3. How to access a docstring?

Ans. The docstring is accessed through a special attribute called __doc__.

4. Why PYTHONPATH is used?

Ans. PythonPath is used to locate modules and packages.

5. Where are the environment variables stored?

Ans. The default directory is a special directory where system-wide PATH variables are stored. For Windows, the default directory is C:\Program Files\Common Files, and for Linux, it is defined in /etc/environment.

6. Why is a package created?

Ans. For the larger program, it is required to break program into smaller parts (packages, sub-packages and modules). These can be arranged by using the packages. A package is a directory structure that allows storing the modules into sub-packages.

7. Where are user-defined packages stored?

Ans. The site-packages directory is used for storing user-defined Python packages.

8. Mention the standard locations for site-packages.

Ans. For Unix,the OS path is (python home)/lib/pythonX.Y/site-packages and for Windows, the path is (python home)\Lib\site-packages.

9. How to find the Python search path?

Ans. We can retrieve the Python search path by using the below code:

```
import sys
print(sys.path)
```

Output:

```
['', 'E:\\Python3x\\Lib\\idlelib',
   'E:\\Python3x\\python37.zip',
   'E:\\Python3x\\DLLs', 'E:\\Python3x\\lib',
   'E:\\Python3x', 'E:\\Python3x\\lib\\site-packages',
   'E:\\Python3x\\lib\\site-packages\\beautifulsoup4-4.8.0-py3.7.egg',
   'E:\\Python3x\\lib\\site- packages\\soupsieve-1.9.2-py3.7.egg']
```

10. What is the use of __init__.py?

Ans. The __init__.py labeling a directory as a Python package and allows us to define any variable at the package level.

11. Can __init__.py be placed in an empty subpackage?

Ans. Yes, it is allowed to have an empty __init__.py in a subpackage.

12. Mention the module name that contains the following functions.

`pow(), sqrt(), log(), ceil(x), fabs(x), factorial(x), floor(x)`
`fmod(x, y), modf(x), trunc(x), exp(x), log(x[, base]), log10(x), pow(x, y), sqrt(x)`

Ans. The above functions are defined in the math module.

13. Why is the dir()function used?

Ans. The dir()function is used to retrieve built-in properties, it also returns all methods and properties defined in a module.

Short Questions and Answers — 2/3 Marks

1. How to create a module? Explain it with an example.

Ans. A module is a file which is saved as .py extension. It can contain functions, variable, and class. Let's create a module that implements stack and its functions as shown below and save this file as DSstack.py module:

```
stack =[]
def push(val):
    stack.append(val)

def pop():
    if(len(stack) == 0):
        print("Stack Empty")
        return None
    else:
        return stack.pop()
```

```
def peek():
    if(len(stack) == 0):
        print("Stack Empty")
        return None
    else:
        return stack[len(stack)-1]
```

2. Why do we create modules?

Ans. Modules are Python code that can be reused. It is not practical to write a large program in a single file. Modules allow a programmer to split a code into multiple source code files.

A module allows organizing a Python code as a logical unit. For example,the math module. Modules are easy to understand, and they can be reused.

3. How is a module structured?

Ans. A module can contain classes, functions, variables, constant, and docstring. A module can import other modules. The following figure shows the structure of a module:

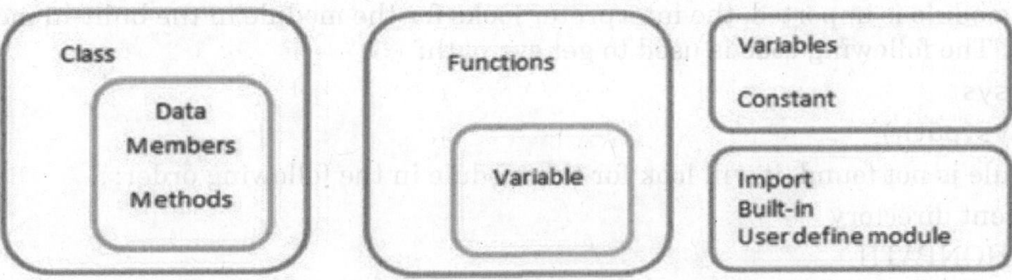

Structure of a module

4. Mention the various ways to import modules and their components.

Ans. Various ways to import modules are:

a. `import <module_name>`

Example:

```
import random
print(random.random())
```

Output:

```
0.537880582094801
```

b. `from <module_name> import <name(s)>`

Example:

```
from random import random, randint
```

c. `import <module_name> as <alt_name>`

Example:

```
import pandas as pd
import numpy as np
pd.Series(np.random.randn(5), index=['1', '2', '3', '4', '5'])
```

d. `from <module_name> import <name> as <alt_name>`

Example:

```
from math import e as exp
print(exp)
```

Output:

```
2.718281828459045
```

e. `from <module_name> import *`

Example:

```
from random import *
randint(5,10)
```

Output:

```
10
```

f. `from <module_name > import <variable>`

Example:

```
from math import pi
print(pi)
```

Output:

```
3.141592653589793
```

5. Explain how Python locates the modules.

Ans. When a module is imported, the interpreter looks for the module in the built-in module directory, that is sys.path. The following code is used to get sys.path:

```
import sys
print(sys.path)
```

If a module is not found, it will look for the module in the following order:

- Current directory
- PYTHONPATH
- Default directory

6. What are the advantages of a module?

Ans.
- The modules allows to reuse of code.
- A programmer can focus on one module at a time not entire the code.
- The entire program can be break into modules make it easy to divide work the among team members.

7. Explain the utility of the dir() function.

Ans. The dir() is a built-in function. It finds out names (class, function, and variable) defined in a module and returns a list of names in the module. For example:

```
import DSstack
print(dir(DSstack))
```

Output:

```
['_builtins_', '_cached_', '_doc_', '_file_', '_loader__',
' name ', ' package ', ' spec ', 'peek', 'pop', 'push', 'stack']
```

8. How is a package different from a module?

Ans. A module is a file (or files) whereas a package is a directory that can contains multiple modules and __init__.py in it.

9. Differentiate between the statement import module and from module import *?

Ans. Let us understands this with an example:

```
import sys
#importing module sys
```

It brings name sys into the program. It does not provide direct access to names (functions, variables, and objects) inside it. It is required to prefix with the module name. For example:

```
sys.exit()
from sys import *
#import names from sys not sys
```

It doesn't bring name sys into the client module (which accesses the module), instead, it brings all names inside sys. To access them, we do not need to add a prefix to the name of the module. For example, function exit() can be used instead of sys.exit().

10. Mention the utility of the help() function.

Ans. The help function is used to display docstring (documentation) of classes, functions, modules, keywords, etc. For example:

```
>>> help(print)
```

Help on built-in function print in module built-ins:

```
print(...)
print(value, ..., sep=' ', end='\n', file=sys.stdout, flush=False)
```

Prints the values to a stream or to sys.stdout by default. Optional keyword arguments are:

- **file:** A file-like object (stream); defaults to the current sys.stdout.
- **sep:** String inserted between values, defaults a space.
- **end:** String appended after the last value, defaults a newline.
- **flush:** Whether to forcibly flush the stream.

11. Mention the module name that contains the following functions.

```
randrange(start, stop[, step])
randint(a, b)
choice(seq)
shuffle(seq)
```

Ans. The random module contains all the above mention functions.

12. Find the possible outcomes of the following code.

Ans.
```
import random
cities =['Delhi', 'Mumbai','Chennai','Kolkata']
pick = 4
for city in cities:
    for j in range(random.randint(1,pick)):
        print(city, end=' ')
    print()
```

a.
```
Delhi Delhi Delhi
Mumbai Mumbai Mumbai Mumbai
Chennai Chennai
Kolkata Kolkata Kolkata Kolkata
```

b.
```
    (blank line)
Mumbai Mumbai Mumbai
Chennai Chennai
Kolkata Kolkata Kolkata Kolkata
```

c.
```
Delhi
Mumbai Mumbai Mumbai Mumbai
Chennai
Kolkata Kolkata
```

d.
```
Delhi
Mumbai Mumbai Mumbai
Chennai Chennai
Kolkata Kolkata Kolkata Kolkata Kolkata
```

Explanation

At least one city will be printed. Hence, option b has blank is ruled out.
Printing 5 time kolkata is not possible, so option d is ruled out.
The possible answers for the above code are a and c

13. Find the possible outcomes of the following code.

```
string ="CBSEONLINE"
num = random.randint(0,3)
n= 9
while string[n] != 'L':
    print(string[n]+string[num]+'#', end='')
    num = num -1
    n= n-1
```

a. ES#NE#IO# **b.** LE#NO#ON# **c.** NS#IE#LO# **d.** EC#NB#IS#

Ans. The answer for the above code is option d.
The answer is combination of last three characters (in reverse order) and first three characters. So, answer is d.

Long Questions and Answers — 3/4 Marks

1. Mention the steps for creating a package.

Ans. The steps of creating packages are:

a. Create the basic structure of the package: Define the layout and identify the module in a package and sub-packages. For example, we want to create a hotel management system. It has three major components, which are as follows:

a. UI for user entry
b. User can book a room
c. Billing of a user

We create the following folders:

```
HotelApp
➢ UI
➢ User entry
➢ Billing
```

b. Create the directory structure and add modules to it: Create the structure defined in step a. Add the files to the sub-packages as shown below:

```
HotelApp/(Directory)
    UI(/Directory)
        Displaymenu.py
        Dataentry.py
    User(/Directory)
        CreateUser.py
        Book room.py
        RoomStatus.py
    Billing(/Directory)
        DisplayBill
```

c. Create the __init__.py for package and subpackage level and add it to the directory:

```
HotelApp(Directory)
➢ UI (Directory) that contains code for data entry and menu display
    • Displaymenu.py
```

- Dataentry.py
- __init__.py

➢ User (Directory) that contains code for booking a room

- CreateUser.py
- Book room.py
- RoomStatus.py
- __init__.py

➢ Billing(Directory)

- DisplayBill
- __init__.py

The overall structure of the package will look like:

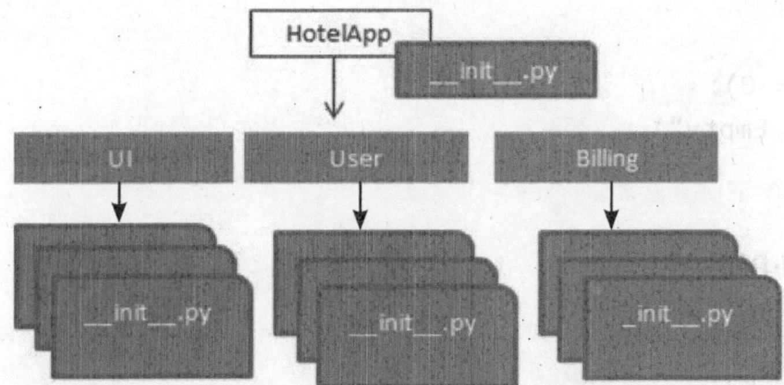

Structure of the package

d. Associate package to the site-packages folder of the Python installation: Copy the package from the site-packages directory of Python installation.

2. Answer the following:

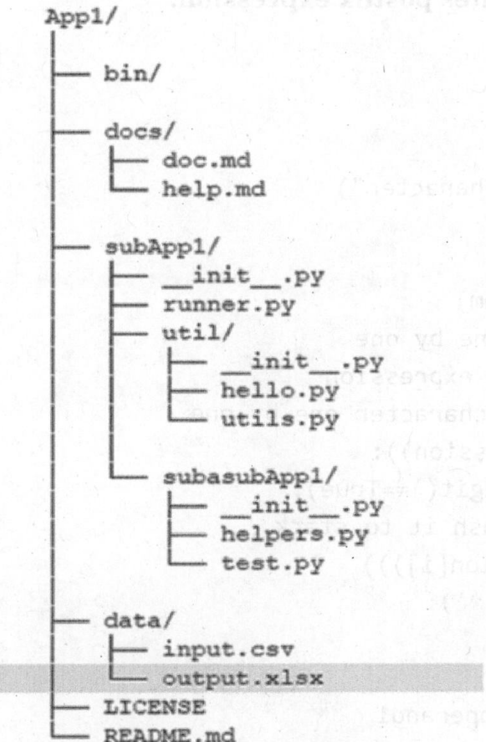

Refer to the above diagram and answer the following:

a. Write an import statement that imports the hello module.

Ans. `from App1.subApp1.utils import hello`

b. Write a statement that calls a method from a runner module.

Ans.
```
import App1.subApp1.runner
runner.method_in_runner()
```

3. Explain how the module is created and used with an example.

Ans. Modules are created by saving a file under the extension .py. For example, this is a module DSstack.py:

```
stack =[]
def push(val):
    stack.append(val)

def pop():
    if(len(stack) == 0):
        print("Stack Empty")
        return None
    else:
        return stack.pop()

def peek():
    if(len(stack) == 0):
        print("Stack Empty")
        return None
    else:
        return stack[len(stack)-1]
```

Create the file that evaluates postfix expression:

```
#import DSstack
from DSstack import *
expression = []
while True:
    item=input("Enter a character")
    if (item==''):
        break
    expression.append(item)
#Adding items to stack one by one
print(expression) #Print expression
#loop for checking each character one by one
for i in range(len(expression)):
    if(expression[i].isdigit()==True):
#if character is digit push it to stack
        push((int(expression[i])))
    elif(expression[i]=='*'):
        operand1=pop()
        operand2=pop()
        res = operand2 * operand1
        push(res)
    elif(expression[i]=='+'):
```

```
        operand1=pop()
        operand2=pop()
        res = operand2 + operand1
        push(res)
    elif(expression[i]=='-'):
        operand1=pop()
        operand2=pop()
        res = operand2 - operand1
        push(res)
    elif(expression[i]=='/'):
        operand1=pop()
        operand2=pop()
        res=operand2/operand1
        stack.push(res)
print('Postfix expression is',stack[0])
```

Output:

```
Enter a character :2
Enter a character :3
Enter a character :+
Enter a character :
['2', '3', '+']
Postfix expression is evaluated to 5
```

Multiple-Choice Questions and Answers

1. **Which of the following is true?**
   a. A module contains python code
   b. Module has .py extension
   c. A module can be used in a file or another module using import
   d. All of these

Ans. Option d, that is, all of these.

2. **Which of the following is not an advantage of using modules?**
   a. It allows reusing the program code
   b. It divides the program into smaller tasks
   c. It reduces the size of a program
   d. It allows to test individual parts

Ans. Option c, that is,It reduces the size of a program.

3. **The code that uses a module is called a _________ of the module.**
   a. Interface
   b. Docstring
   c. Client
   d. Modularity

Ans. Option c, that is, Client.

4. **A _________ is a string literal placed in triple quotes in a module.**
   a. Interface
   b. Modularity

c. Client
d. Docstring

Ans. Option d, that is, Docstring.

5. Find the output of the following piece of code.

```
#module1
def sqr(x):
    b=x**2
    print(b)
#module2
def sqr(x):
    b= x*x
    print(b)
from module1 import sqr
from module2 import sqr
s=5
sqr(s)
```

a. 25
b. 25 25
c. There is a name clash
d. None of the above

Ans. Option c, that is, There is a name clash.

6. Find out which of the following is not a valid namespace?

a. Public namespace
b. Global namespace
c. Local namespace
d. Built-in namespace

Ans. Option a that is, Public namespace.

7. Find the output of the below code.

```
import random
random.choice(1,2,3,4)
```

a. Error
b. any value among 1, 2, 3 or 4
c. integer expect 1, 2, 3 and 4
d. 3

Ans. Option b, that is, any value among 1, 2, 3, or 4.

8. Find the output of the following code.

```
import random
random.choice([4.10, 99.56, 67])
```

a. Error
b. Either of 4.10, 99.56, 67
c. Number expect 4.10, 99.56, 67
d. 99.56

Ans. Option b, that is, Either of 4.10, 99.56, 67.

9. Find the output of the following code.

```
import random
```

```
random.choice('moon')
```

a. moon
b. o
c. m, o or n
d. error

Ans. Option c, that is, m, o or n.

10. Find the output of the following code.

```
import random
random.randint(4.5,9)
```

a. Error
b. An integer between 4.5 and 9, including 9
c. An integer between 4.5 and 9, excluding 9
d. 4.5

Ans. Option a, that is, Error.

Note: The random.randint() only accepts integer value as a parameter.

11. Which of the following is true about a module.

a. Denoted by triple quotes for providing the specification of certain program elements
b. Design and implementation of specific functionality to be incorporated into a program
c. Defines the specification of how it is to be used
d. Any program that reuses code

Ans. Option b, that is, Design and implementation of specific functionality to be incorporated into a program.

12. Which of the following functions randomly re-arranges the items of a list?

a. seed
b. shuffle
c. randomize
d. uniform

Ans. Option b, that is, shuffle.

13. The function random.random() returns only integer value. Is it true or false?

a. True
b. False

Ans. Option b, that is,False.

14. Find the output of the below function.

```
random.randrange(100,10)
```

a. 67
b. 32
c. ValueError
d. 90

Ans. Option c, that is,ValueError(100 > 10) start should be less than stop.

15. Find the return value of random.randrange(4).

a. 0
b. 2.3
c. 3
d. None of the above

Ans. Option a and c, that is,0 or 3.

16. Find the equivalent of random.randrange(3).

a. range(3)
b. random.choice(range(0, 3))
c. random.select(range(3)))
d. random.shuffle(range(3))

Ans. Option b, that is,random.choice(range(0, 3)).

17. Find the output of the following code.

```
random.randint(4)
```

a. only 4
b. 1,2,3 and 4
c. 0,1,2,3
d. error

Ans. Option c, that is, 0, 1, 2, 3.

18. Find the equivalent of the random.randint(3, 6).

a. `random.randrange(3, 6)`
b. `random.choice([3, 6])`
c. `3 + random.randrange(3)`
d. `3 + random.randrange(4)`

Ans. Option d, that is 3 + random.randrange(4).

19. A list passed to the shuffle function is shuffled in-place. Is it true or false?

a. True
b. False

Ans. Option a, that is,True.

20. Which one of the following is an expectable type of argument to the function random.shuffle()?

a. tuple
b. list
c. string
d. integer

Ans. Option b, that is, lists.

21. Which of the following is the range of values that are returned by random.random() function?

a. Greater than 0.0 and lesser than 1.
b. Greater than 0.0 and lesser than equal to 1.0.
c. Greater than or equal to 0.0 and less than equal to 1.0
d. Greater than or equal to 0.0 and less than 1.0

Ans. Option d, that is, Greater than or equal to 0.0 and less than 1.0.

EFFICIENCY AND COMPLEXITIES

LEARNING OBJECTIVES

- Define and explain big O notation, time complexity, space complexity, linear complexity, logarithm complexity, and exponential complexity with examples
- Compute complexity and run-time efficiency
- Identify and distinguish among various time complexities

DEFINITION

- **Algorithm's Complexity or Complexity:** An algorithm's complexity is defined as a function f(n) measuring the time and space consumed by an algorithm in terms of its input size n.
- **Big O notation:** The Big O notation tells how long an algorithm takes to run.
- **Linear complexity:** An algorithm with linear complexity where its runtime is proportional to its input size 'n'. The runtime grows linearly with respect to its input size.
- **Logarithmic complexity:** An algorithm with logarithmic complexity where its runtime is proportional to the logarithm of the input size. The run time grows logarithmically with respect to its input size.
- **Exponential complexity:** An algorithm with exponential complexity where its runtime is proportional to the 2 ^n of its input size n. The time grows exponentially with respect to its input size.

Very Short Questions and Answers — 1 Mark

1. **Why is complexity used?**

Ans. The complexity of an algorithm in computer science is a way of classifying how efficient an algorithm is compared to its alternative ones.

2. **Define Big O notation.**

Ans. The Big O notation tells how long an algorithm takes to run. It is helpful in comparing the efficiency of a different algorithm. The Big O notation is an expression that tell show quickly it grows relative to the input.

3. **Why is the performance of an algorithm measured?**

Ans. There are multiple algorithms that can solve a problem. The performance of an algorithm helps to select the most suitable algorithm among multiple algorithms that can solve a problem.

The performance of an algorithm is a process of making an evaluative judgment about algorithms. The Big O notation is a way to evaluate the performance of an algorithm.

4. **Mention the factors that are used to measure the performance of an algorithm.**

Ans. Performance analysis of an algorithm depends on two factors, that is, the amount of memory used and the amount of time consumed on any CPU for computation. Formally, they are notified as complexities in terms of:

a. Space complexity

b. Time complexity

5. Define space complexity.

Ans. The space complexity of an algorithm is the amount of memory it needs to run till completion, that is, from start of the execution to its termination.

6. Define time complexity.

Ans. Time complexity defines the amount of time taken by an algorithm to run it. It is also related to the time taken by an algorithm against the length of the input.

7. Define computational complexity

Ans. The complexity or computational complexity of an algorithm is the amount of resources (time or space) required to run it.

Short Questions and Answers — 2/3 Marks

1. Why is Big O notation used?

Ans. The Big O notation is used to know how runtime grows with respect to the size of the input 'n':

- O(n) order of the size of the input
- O(n^2) order of the square of the size of the input

2. What does Big O notation indicate?

Ans. Big O notation indicates how long an algorithm takes to run. It mainly focuses on expensive or time-consuming steps and skips the smaller or constant time where n is fairly large.

3. Explain the constant time complexity in the Big O notation with an example.

Ans. The constant time complexity is explained below:

Constant Time O(1): If an algorithm runs in constant time, it means it takes the same amount of time irrespective of the input size, for example:

- Accessing any element in a fixed-sized array
- Enqueue and dequeue operations in a fixed-size array
- Push and pop operations in the fixed-size stack

4. Explain the linear time complexity in Big O notation.

Ans. An algorithm with linear complexity where its runtime is proportional to its input size 'n'.

5. Explain the logarithmic time complexity in Big O notation?

Ans. An algorithm runs in proportional time of the logarithm of the input size, Example: Binary search

6. Explain the Quadratic time complexity in Big O notation.

Ans. An algorithm runs in proportional times to the square of its input. ***Example:***

- Bubble sort
- Selection sort
- Insertion sort

Long Questions and Answers — 3 Marks

1. Explain constant time complexity with an example.

Ans. The constant time complexity O(1) does not depend on the size of the input. It is constant in all cases. To understand this, let's see an example:

```
def sum_2(num1, num2):
    return num1 + num2
```

The function sum_2(4, 5) will return 9. This single step computation sums two numbers. No matter the number is small or large, it returns the sum. It executes only 1 step hence Time Complexity is O(1) or Constant Time Complexity.

2. Explain Linear Time Complexity with an example.

Ans. Linear time complexity O(n) is the time it takes to complete is proportional to the input size.

Consider an example:

```
def list_sum(numlist):
    total = 0                                    #1
    for element in numlist:                      #2
        total += i                               #3
        return total                             #4
```

The function accepts a list of size 10.

Step 1: initializing total: execute 1 statement

Step 2: executes statement total += i 10 times

Total number of statements is executed as 10, that is, len (numlist)

Step 3: return statements: executes 1 statement So, total number of steps are1 + 10 + 1 = 12

```
if
list size is 10 for loop execution 10 times total step 1+ 10 + 1
list size is 100 for loop execution 100 times total step 1+ 100 + 1
list size is 1000 for loop execution 1000 times total step 1+ 1000 + 1
list size is 10000 for loop execution 10000 times total steps 1+10000+1
```

In the computation of total steps do you think first and last (step 1 and step 4) matter if the number of steps is high? Not really.

Time Complexity for 1 + N + 1 = (N + 2) is approximately N. We can neglect additional 2 when N ia large number. Time Complexity is O(N). We can clearly see that for input size n loop executes n time, and that's why it is linear complexity.

3. Explain Logarithmic time complexity with an example.

Ans. Logarithmic time complexity O(log(n)) where the time taken to complete an algorithm is log(n), where n is input size. To understand this, consider an example:

```
                                         Input size
def power2(num):           Step#     16        32        1024
    n = 0                  #1        1         1         1
    while num> 1:          #2        4 x 1     5 x 1     10 x 1
        num = num//2       #3        4 x 1     5 x 1     10 x 1
        n = n+1            #4        4 x 1     5 x 1     10 x 1
    return n               #5        1         1         1
total steps                          14        17        32
```

The number of time loops executed can be derived by using below formula:

$\log_2(16) = \log_2(2^4) = 4$

$\log_2(32) = \log_2(2^5) = 5$

$\log_2(1024) = \log_2(2^{10}) = 10$

When we keep dividing the size of input N by some value, say base, the time complexity turns out to be log(N) to the base.

The time complexity is

$1 + O(\log_2(n)) + 1 \approx O(\log_2(n))$

4. Explain quadratic time complexity n^2 complexity with an example.

Ans. In Quadratic time complexity $O(n^2)$ the time taken to complete an algorithm is the order of n^2 to the input size. To understand it, let's see an example:

```
def bubble_sort(d_list):
    l_len = len(d_list)                              #1
    # Traverse through all array elements            #2
    for i in range(l_len):                           #3
    # traverse the list                              #4
        for j in range(0, l_len-i-1):                #5
        # Swap the element                           #6
            if d_list[j] >d_list[j+1] :              #7
                d_list[j], d_list[j+1]\              #8
                = d_list[j+1], d_list[j]
```

The complexity can be calculated as follows:

Line Number	**Complexity**	**Number of Steps**
line 1	O(1)	1
line 3	O(n)	n
line 5	O(n-1)	n* n - 1
Step 7 and 8		

in worst case it is O(2*n) total step 2n

Total steps 1 + n + (n * n-1) + 2n

$1 + n^2 - n + 2n$

$1 + n^2 - n + 2n$

$1 + n^2 + n$

If n is large, we can ignore 1 and 2n, hence complexity is n^2

The time complexity is the order of $O(n^2)$.

5. Calculate the time taken by an algorithm using the following.

Ans. The complexity of the algorithm $7n^2$

A step takes 10^{-9} second to execute

Input size of data is 1000(n)

Total numbers of steps to be executed n^2 (1000 x 1000)

Time taken = 7 x 1000 x1000 x 10^{-9}

= 7 x 10^{-3} = 7 millisecond

Total time taken is 7 milliseconds

6. Calculate the time taken by an algorithm using the following.

Ans. The complexity of the algorithm n^3

A step takes 10^{-9} second to execute

Input size of data is 1000(n)

Time taken = 1000 x 1000 x1000 x 10^{-9} = 1 second

Total time taken is 1 second

7. Calculate the time taken by an algorithm using the following.

Ans. The complexity of the n log(n) or n log10(n)

A step takes 10^{-9} second to execute

Input size of data is 1000(n)

Time taken

1000 x $\log_{10}$(1000) x 10^{-9} :: $\log_{10}$(1000) = 3.0

= 1000 x 3 x 10^{-9}

```
= 3 x 10-6
Total time taken is 3 microseconds
```

8. Calculate the time taken by an algorithm using the following.

Ans. The complexity of the n $\log_2(n)$

A step takes 10^{-9} second to execute

Input size of data is 1024 (n)

Time taken = 1024 x $\log_2(1024)$ x 10^{-9}

~= 1000 x 10 x 10^{-9} ::$\log_2(1024)$ = 10

= 10^{-5}

= 10 x 10^{-6}

= 10 micro seconds

Total time taken is 10 microseconds

Note: Below code computes $\log_2(1024)$

```
import math
math.log2(1024)
= 10.0
```

9. Calculate the run-time efficiency of the following code.

Ans.

```
i = 1
while i<= n :
    print(i)
    i = i + 1
```

#Ct denotes Constant time

Code	Complexity
i = 1	O(1)
while i<= n :	O(n)
print(i)	n* O(1)
i = i + 1	n* O(1)

Complexity

O(1)+ O(n) + n* O(1)+ n* O(1)

~= 1+ O(n)+ O(n)+ O(n)

= O(n)

10. Find the complexity of the following code.

Code	Complexity
i = n	O(1)
x = 0	O(1)
while i > 0 :	O(n)
print(i)	n*O(1)
i = i -1	n*O(1)
x = x +1	n*O(1)

Ans. Complexity

O(1) + O(1) + O(n) + n*O(1) + n*O(1) + n*O(1)

~= O(n)

11. Calculate the run-time efficiency of the following code.

Ans. The complexity of the func() is 2n

Code	Complexity
`i = 1`	`O(1)`
`while i <= n:`	`O(n)`
`    func() #`	`O(n) * (2*n )`
`    i+=1`	`n*O(1)`

```
Complexity
O(1) + O(n) * O(2*n) + O(1)
= O(1)+ O(n)+(O(n) * O(2n)) +n* O(1)
~= O(n²)
```

12. Calculate the run-time efficiency of the following code.

The complexity of the func is 2n

Code	Complexity
`i = 1`	`O(1)`
`while i <= n:`	`O(n)`
`    j = 1`	`n*O(n)`
`    while j < n - 1`	`n*O(n-1)`
`        func()`	`O(n) * O(n-1) * 2n`
`        j+=1`	`(n -1) * O(1)`
`    i+=1`	`n* O(1)`

Ans.
```
Complexity
O(1) + O(n) + n * O(n) + n * O(n-1) + O(n) * O(n-1) * 2n + (n -1) * O(1) + n * O(1)
1 + n + n *n +(n- 1) + n * (n-1) * 2n + (n -1) * 1 + ( n * 1 )
~= O(n³)
```

13. If the complexity of function in the above example is n^2, compute the complexity.

Ans.
```
1 + n + n * n + (n- 1) + n * (n-1) * n² + (n -1) * 1 + ( n * 1 )
~= O(n⁴)
```

14. Calculate the run-time efficiency of the following code.

The complexity of the func is n^2

Code	Complexity
`i = 1`	`O(1)`
`while i <= n:`	$\log_2(n)$
`    func()`	`# complexity is O(n² )`
`    i = i *2`	

```
# it is called n times? See the explanation below
```

> ***Note:*** In the above statement i= i*2, it cuts the number of iterations by ½ for each iteration, hence the complexity is $\log_2(n)$.

Ans.
```
O(1) + O(1)+ n² * log2(n)
~ = O(n² * log₂(n))
```

15. Calculate the run-time efficiency of the following code.

Code	Complexity
`i = 0`	O(1)
`while i <= n:`	O(n)
`   j= 1`	n* O(1)
`   while j <= n:`	n * O(n)
`      k = 1`	n*n* O(1)
`      while k < = n:`	n* n* O(n)
`         print( i+j+k ,i, j, k)`	n* n*n*O(1)
`         k+=1`	n*n*n*O(1)
`      j+=1`	n*n*n*O(1)
`   i+=1`	n*O(1)

Ans. Complexity

O(1) + O(n) + n * O(1)+ n * O(n)+ n * n * O(1) + n * n * O(n)+n * n* n * O(1) + n * n * n * O(1) + n* n* n* O(1) + n* O(1)

~= $O(n^3)$

16. Calculate the run-time efficiency of the following code.

Code	Complexity
`ListA=[]`	O(1)
`for i in range(n):`	O(n)
`   for j in range(m):`	O(n) * O(m)
`      a = 0`	O(n) * O(m)
`      for k in range(p):`	O(n) * O(m) *O(p)
`         a += ListA[i]`	O(n) * O(m) *O(p)

Ans. Complexity

O(1)+ O(n) + (O(n) * O(m)) + O(n) * O(m) + (O(n) * O(m) *O(p)) + (O(n) * O(m) *O(p))

~= O(n*m*p)

17. Calculate the run-time efficiency of the following code.

Ans. Code **Complexity**

```
A = []                                   O(1)
start = 0                                O(1)
end = n                                  O(1)

while( start < end):

   mid = (start + end) // 2
   if( A[mid] < searchelement):
      start = mid                        O (log(n))
   else:
      end = mid
```

complexity is

3 * O(1) + O(log(n))

= O(log(n))

18. Calculate the run-time efficiency of the following code.

Code	Complexity
`m = A[0]`	O(1)
`for i in range(n):`	O(n)
`    if A[i] >m:`	O(n)
`        m= A[i]`	O(n)

Ans. In worst case there will be n assignment

O(1) + O(n) + O(n) + O(n)

~= O(n)

Note: Statement if (A[i] > m): will execute <= n however complexity will remain O(n).

19. Calculate the run-time efficiency of the following code.

Ans.

```
n1 = int(input("Input for start number: "))
n2 = int(input("Input a   stop number: "))

for num in range(n1,n2):
    isPrime = True
    for i in range(2,num):
        if ( num % i == 0):
            isPrime = False
            break
if (isPrime == True):
    print(num, end=',')
```

Whenever iterating over a sequence or other linear data structure, regardless of how many elements are skipped or how early you break out, the big-O notation is always O(n). Here, the best case is O(1), the average case is O(n/2), and the worst case is O(n).

Whereas in case of iteration in a nested loop, the break has no impact on the magnitude of the complexity. Hence complexity is the magnitude of O(n^2).

Fill in the blanks — 1 Mark

1. In the big O notation of Constant, Time complexity is denoted by ___________.

Ans. O(1)

2. In the big O notation of Logarithmic, Time complexity is denoted by ___________.

Ans. O(log n)

3. In the big O notation of Linear, Time complexity is denoted by ___________.

Ans. O(n)

4. In the big O notation of Quasilinear, Time complexity is denoted by ___________.

Ans. O(n log n)

5. In the big O notation of Quadratic, Time complexity is denoted by ___________.

Ans. O(n^2)

6. In the big O notation of Exponential, Time complexity is denoted by ___________.

Ans. O(2^n)

Multiple-Choice Questions and Answers 1 Mark

1. **Big O notation is used in which of the following?**
   a. upper bound on the growth rate
   b. A function based on the growth of n
   c. Both a and b
   d. None of these

Ans. Option c, that is a and b.

2. **If O(1) is a complexity of an algorithm, it grows __________ with respect to n.**
   a. exponential
   b. polynomial
   c. constant
   d. none of the mentioned

Ans. Option c, that is, constant.

3. **If O(logn) is a complexity of an algorithm then, it grows __________ with respect to n.**
   a. constant
   b. exponential
   c. polynomial
   d. logarithmic

Ans. Option d, that is, logarithmic.
If the growth rate is logarithmic, complexity will be logarithmic.

4. **If O(n) is the complexity of an algorithm, then it grows __________ with respect to n.**
   a. exponential
   b. linear
   c. constant
   d. none of the mentioned

Ans. Option b, that is, linear.

5. **If O(n^2) is the complexity of an algorithm, then it grows __________ with respect to n.**
   a. Linear
   b. Exponential
   c. Quadratic
   d. Constant

Ans. Option c, that is, Quadratic.

6. **What is the time complexity of binary search?**
   a. Logarithmic
   b. Quadratic
   c. constant
   d. exponential

Ans. Option a, that is, Logarithmic.

7. **What is the time complexity of a linear search?**
   a. O(1)
   b. O(n)
   c. exponential
   d. Logarithmic

Ans. Option b, that is, O(n).

8. Time complexity for binary search algorithm is constant. Is this True or False?

a. True

b. False

Ans. Option b, that is, false. (complexity is logarithmic)

9. Which of the following case does not exist in complexity theory?

a. Average case

b. Worst case

c. Best case

d. Null case

Ans. Option d, that is, Null case.

10. The worst case complexity of the linear search algorithm is:

a. O(n)

b. O(n)

c. O(log n)

d. O(n log n)

Ans. Option a that is, O(n).

Explanation: The worst-case complexity of the linear search is O(n).

11. What is the worst case complexity of the Binary search algorithm?

a. O(n)

b. O(n2)

c. O(log n)

d. O(n log n)

Ans. Option c, that is, O(log n).

12. What is the worst-case complexity and best-case complexity of Bubble sort?

a. $O(n^2)$ and O(n)

b. O(n log n) and $O(n^2)$

c. $O(n^2)$ and O(n log n)

d. O(log n) and O(n)

Ans. Option a that is, $O(n^2)$ and O(n).

13. What is the Worst case in linear search?

a. Search element in the middle of the list

b. Search element is not in the list

c. Search element is last in the list

d. b and c

Ans. Option d, that is, b and c.

11 DATA STRUCTURE STACK AND QUEUE

LEARNING OBJECTIVES

- Define and implement data structure, stack, push, pop queue, enqueue and dequeue methods
- Implementing stack and queue using a list in python
- Applying stack for converting infix to postfix and evaluating a postfix expression

DEFINITION

- **Stack:** A stack is a data structure that allows inserting and deleting an element from the same location only at the top. It is called LIFO (Last in First Out).
- **Queue:** A queue is a data structure that allows inserting an element at the rear end of the queue and deleting the element from the front. It is called FIFO (First in First Out).
- **Push:** Push is an operation defined for stack that is used to insert an element at the top of the stack. This operation is implemented by using append() function of the list.
- **Pop:** Pop is an operation defined for stack that is used to remove and return an element from the top of the stack. This operation is implemented using pop() function of the list.
- **Enqueue:** Enqueue is an operation defined for the queue that is used to insert an element at the rear(end) of the queue. This operation is implemented using append() function of the list.
- **Dequeue:** Dequeue is an operation defined for the queue that is used to remove and return an element form the front of the queue. This operation is implemented using 'pop()' function with argument 0, that is pop(0).

Very Short Questions and Answers — 1 Mark

1. How is a data structure different from a predefined data type?

Ans. Python provides various inbuilt data types and users are allowed to perform various operations. For example, an integer data type is used to add, subtract, divide, and multiply. However, there are some problems that cannot be solved using predefined data types.

This is where data structure is handy. A data structure allows us to arrange, retrieve, manipulate, and store data required for the specified problem to be solved.

2. How linear search is performed?

Ans. Linear search is performed where an array or list is traversed one item at a time to find whether an item that exists in an array or list.

3. How to sort a list?

Ans. Python provides inbuilt method sort() that sort elements of the list and places the sorted elements in the list. Sort method returns none as it sorts the list in place.

Short Questions and Answers — 2/3 Marks

1. How is FIFO (First In First Out) implemented in Python?

Ans. The FIFO method works on the first-in-first-out principle where the elements are inserted at the rear and removed from the front. FIFO is implemented using a queue; It can be implemented by creating process enqueue (using inbuilt method insert()) and dequeue (using inbuilt method pop()).

2. How is LIFO (Last In First Out) implemented in python?

Ans. The LIFO method works on the principle of last-in-first-out where the elements are inserted and removed from the top. LIFO is implemented using a stack. It can be implemented by creating process push (using inbuilt method append()) and pop (using inbuilt method pop()).

3. Define the key attribute of a data structure stack.

Ans. Key attribute of a data structure stack are:

- A stack contains items where insertion and deletion are based on LIFO.
- A stack is a linear collection.
- A stack has only two operations: push the item into the stack and pop the item out of the stack.
- A stack has a single entry and exit point named top.

4. Define the key attributes of a data structure queue.

Ans. Key attributes of a data structure queue are:

- A queue contains items where insertion and deletion are based on last-in-first-out (LIFO).
- A queue is a linear collection.
- A queue has only two operations: enqueue that inserts the item into the queue and dequeue to remove the item out of the queue.
- A queue has different entry and exit points.

5. In how many ways you can implement the stack and queue?

Ans. A stack or queue can be created in two ways:

a. Using a static data structure

   Fixed-sized, for example, arrays in C, C++, java

b. Using a dynamic data structure

   List in python, Linklist in C, C++

6. How is the binary search implemented?

Ans. To implement a binary search, a list should be sorted either in ascending or descending order. Binary Search works on the principle of repeatedly dividing the search interval in half so as to minimize the number of iterations. Initially, the interval covers the whole list. If the value to be searched is found in the middle, the index of the value is returned. If the value to be searched is less than the value in the middle, then reduce the search interval to the lower half otherwise reduce it to the upper half. This process is repeated until the value is found or the interval becomes empty.

7. How is the top implemented in a stack using Python's list?

Ans. The list in python is a dynamic data structure; there is no need to maintain the top explicitly. The append method adds an element at the end and pop removes an element from the end, thus the top is automatically maintained. At any point of time, the length of the stack can be obtained using the inbuilt len() method.

8. How is the operation pop different from the peek operation?

Ans. Pop removes an item from the top of the stack and returns it, whereas Peek just returns the item at the top without removing it from the list.

9. Mention the applications of a stack.

Ans. The stack can be used:

- for conversion from infix to postfix, postfix to infix, etc.
- for evaluation of arithmetic expressions.
- for implementing function calls in an operating system.

10. What are the applications of a queue?

Ans. Applications of a queue are:

- CPU scheduling and Disk Scheduling are done using queue and priority queue.

- Queues are used in I/O Buffers, file I/O, and many more. Where data is transferred (asynchronously) between two processes in the operating system.

11. How are stack and queue similar?

Ans. The similarities between stacks and queues are:

- Both are a linear data structure
- Both can be implemented using a list in python

12. How is a stack different from a queue?

Ans. The difference between stacks and queues is as follows:

Stack follows LIFO (last in first out) while queues follow FIFO (first in first out).

Long Questions and Answers 3/4 Marks

1. What are the key characteristics of a data structure?

Ans. The key characteristics of data structure are:

- **Linear or non-linear:** In Linear data structure data is stored, and it data can be arranged in an ordered sequence such as an array where as in non–linear data structure data is stored in an unordered sequence such as a dictionary or a graph.
- **Homogeneous or non-homogeneous:** Homogeneous data structure stores similar data types whereas non-homogeneous data structure stores heterogeneous data types.
- **Static or dynamic:** Static data structures have a fixed size whereas dynamic data structures can shrink or expand depending on the use.

2. Mention the different types of data structures.

Ans. Different types of data structures:

- **Arrays:** An array stores items at adjoining memory locations. It either has a fixed size or it is flexible in length.
- **Stacks:** A stack stores items in the linear order based on last in first out (LIFO).
- **Queues:** A queue stores items in the linear order based on first in first out (FIFO).
- **Linked lists:** A linked list stores items in a linear order. Each element or node keeps the reference of the next item in the list.
- **Trees:** A tree stores items in a hierarchical way. Each node has a link to their children.
- **Graphs:** A graph stores a collection of items in a non-linear fashion. Graphs are made up of a finite set of nodes, also known as vertices and lines that connect them, also known as edges. These are useful for representing real-life systems such as computer networks.
- **Hash tables:** A hash map or a hash table stores items where its values are accessed using its keys; this is treated as a key-value pair.

3. What operations are associated with a data structure?

Ans. Various operations associated with a data structure are:

- **Insert:** Add a new item to the data structure
- **Delete:** Delete an item from the data structure
- **Update:** Update an item in the data structure
- **Traversal:** Iterate over the data structure to process all/some of its items
- **Search:** Iterate over the data structure to search an item
- **Sorting:** Arrange all the items in ascending or descending order or in specific order
- **Merging:** Club two or more similar data structures into one

4. Write a program that searches an item in a list.

Ans.

```
#program linear search
def linearsearch( lst, element):
```

```
    for index in range(len(lst)):
        if( lst[index] == element ):
            return index+1
    #if element not found return -1
    return -1

l = [ 23, 56, 45, 67, 89, 5 , 9, 39, 99]
location = linearsearch(l, 9)
if(location > 0):
    print("The element found at location " + str(location))
else:
    print("Element not found !!!")
```

Output:

```
The element is found at location 7
```

5. Write a program that performs the binary search.

Ans.

```
# Program for recursive binary search and returns the index
# if a search key present otherwise -1

def binSearch(_list, lowrange, upprange, searchkey):
    # Check base case
    if upprange >= lowrange:
        mid = 1+(upprange - lowrange)//2
    # Checks if an element is present in the middle
        if _list[mid] == searchkey:
            return mid

        # If element is smaller than mid, it may present in upper sublist
        elif _list[mid] > searchkey:
            return binSearch(_list, lowrange, mid-1, searchkey)

        # search in upper sublist
        else:
            return binSearch(_list, mid + 1, upprange, searchkey)
    else:
    # Element is not present in the list
        return -1

_list = [2, 3, 5, 7,10, 40 ]
searchkey = 10
# Function call
result = binSearch(_list, 0, len(_list)-1, searchkey)
if (result != -1):
    print ("Element is present at index % d" % result )
else:
    print ("Element is not present in list')
```

Output:

```
The element is present at index 4
```

6. Explain how items are inserted into a fixed size array?

Ans. In fixed-size arrays, insertion can be done by moving elements from the insertion position to the next location and element is placed once all the elements are moved. This is demonstrated below:

For example, if we have a list and we want to insert 5 at location 2, then:

1	4	6	7	8	0	9			

Move the element to the next location.

1	4	6	7	8	0	9			

Step 1:

1	4	6	7	8	0		9		

Step 2:

1	4	6	7	8		0	9		

Step 3:

1	4	6	7		8	0	9		

Step 4:

1	4	6		7	8	0	9		

Step 5:

1	4		6	7	8	0	9		

Step 6:

1		4	6	7	8	0	9		

Step 7:

Insert 5 at location 2

The final list will look like:

1	5	4	6	7	8	0	9		

7. Explain how items are inserted into a list in python?

Ans. A list in Python is a dynamic data structure; it grows and shrinks as items are added or removed.

In case we want to insert an item into the list, we split the list by slicing and adding the item as shown below:

```
_list = [1,4,6,7,8,0,9]
```

Now we want to insert 5 at location 2:

```
_list[:2] + [5]+ _list[2:]
```

Split the list up to the 2nd element and add 5 to it, then add the remaining list index 2 to the end of the list:

Output:

```
[1, 4, 5, 6, 7, 8, 0, 9]
```

Alternatively, we can use the insert method:

```
_list = [1,4,6,7,8,0,9]
_list.insert(2,5)
print(_list)
```

Output:

```
[1, 4, 5, 6, 7, 8, 0, 9]
```

8. Explain how can an item be deleted from fixed-size arrays?

Ans. In fixed-size arrays, deletion can be done by moving an element to its previous location (starting from the location of an element that is to be removed) until the list is exhausted. This is demonstrated below:

For example, in the below list we want to delete 4:

1	4	6	7	8	0	9			

Move the element to the next location.

Step 1:

1	6		7	8	0	9			

Step 2:

1	6	7		8	0	9			

Step 3:

1	6	7	8		0	9			

Step 4:

1	6	7	8	0		9			

Step 5:

1	6	7	8	0	9				

The final list will look like:

1	6	7	8	0	9			

Item 4 has been removed.

9. Explain how are items deleted from the list in python?

Ans. The below code demonstrates to remove an element from the list: Consider an example,

To delete the element 4 from the list:

```
_list = [1,4,6,7,8,0,9]
_list[:1] + _list[2:]
[1, 6, 7, 8, 0, 9]
```

To delete an element from a list:

```
def del_listItem(_list, element):
    found = False
    for index in range(len(_list)):
```

```
        if( _list[index] == element ):
            found = True
            del _list[index]
            break

    return found

l = [1,4,6,7,8,0,9]
element = 4

#checks if an element is deleted
isdeleted = del_listItem(l, element)
if(isdeleted == True):
    print (str(element) + " is deleted ")
else:
    print (str(element) + " not found in list ")
print(l)
```

Output:

```
4 is deleted
[1, 6, 7, 8, 0, 9]
```

10. How to insert an element into a sorted list?

Ans. The Insort() method of the Bisect module allows placing an element in the sorted list as shown in below code:

```
import bisect

def insert_sortlist(_list, num):
    bisect.insort(_list, num)

    return _list

_list = [1, 2, 4]
num = 3

print(insert_sortlist(_list, num))
```

Output:

```
[1, 2, 3, 4]
```

11. Explain how push and pop work in a stack diagrammatically with the help of an illustration.

Ans. The stack can be implemented by using the fixed-size array. Below demonstrates diagrammatically how top moves with push() function in a fixed-sized array:

```
Push(5)
Push(10)
Push(15)
Push(20)
```

			20 ← top
		15 ← top	15
	10 ← top	10	10
5 ← top	5	5	5

The illustration below demonstrate diagrammatically how top moves with function pop() in a fixed-sized array:

```
Pop()
Pop()
Pop()
```

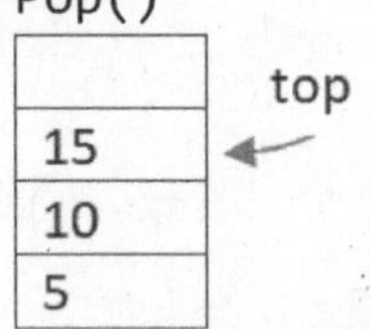

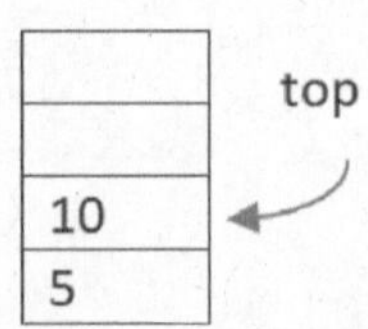

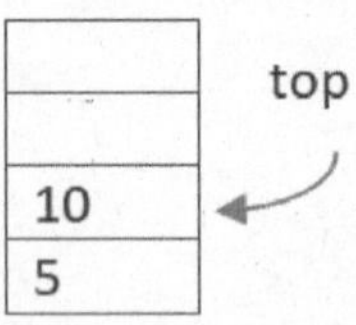

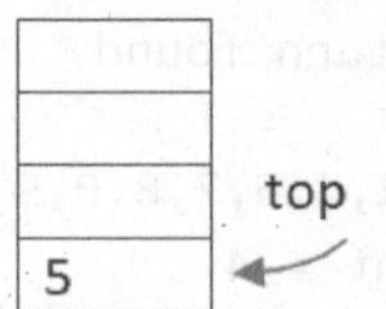

A stack can be implemented using a list. The illustration below demonstrates diagrammatically how top moves with function push() in a list.

```
Push(5)
Push(10)
Push(15)
push(20)
```

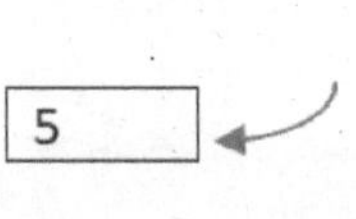

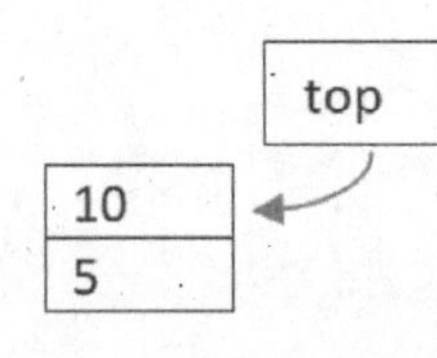

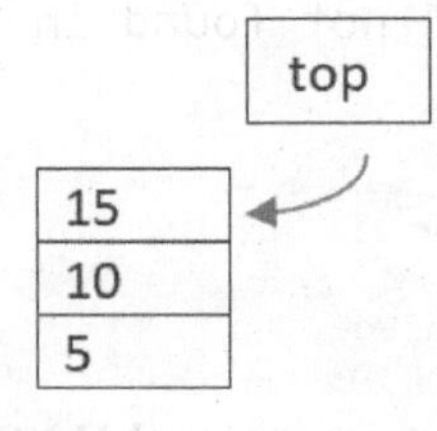

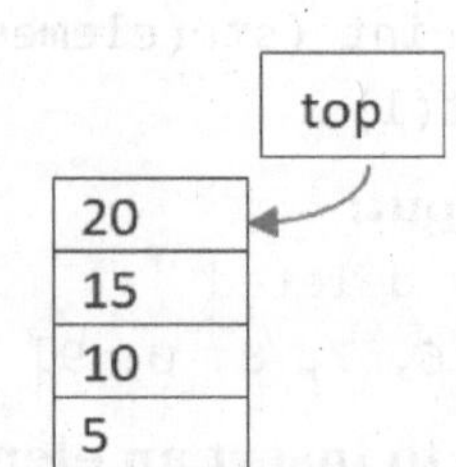

The illustrate below demonstrate diagrammatically how top moves with function pop() in a list:

```
Pop()
Pop()
Pop()
```

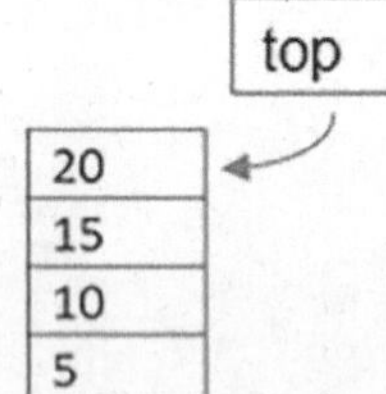

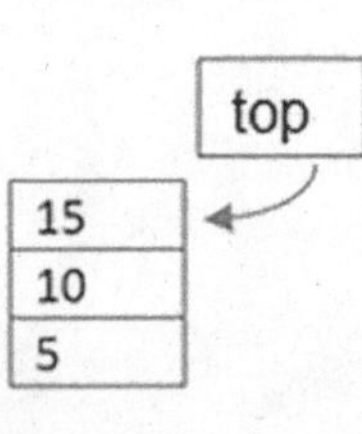

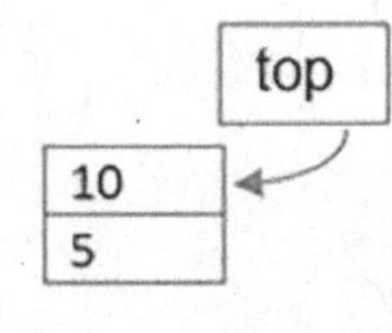

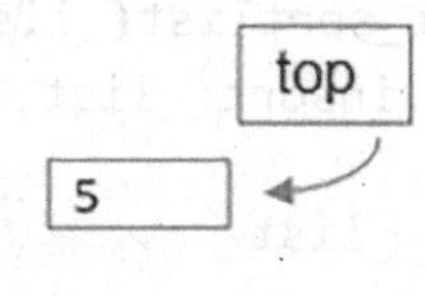

12. How is push() method implemented?

Ans.

```
# create the empty list
stack=[]
def push(val):
    # add element to the end of stack(top)
    stack.append(val)
```

13. Explain the boundary cases in a stack.

Ans. There are two boundary cases in a stack:

a. Stack is empty

b. Stack is full

Stack is empty

When we pop the element from the list, it returns a value. Trying to remove an element from an empty list raises an exception.

```
lis =[]
lis.pop()
```

```
IndexError: pop from empty list
```

Stack is full

We cannot insert an element in a list when a list is exhausted (List is full). A list in Python is dynamic; on a 32-bit machine, it can store 536,870,912 elements. It is large enough. Thus, we ignore to test the stack's full condition.

14. How pop() method is implemented?

Ans.

```
stack =[]

def pop():

    return stack.pop()
```

15. Implement a pop() method that checks if the list is empty?

Ans.

```
stack =[]
def pop():
    #if stack is empty returns none
    if(stack == []):
        return None
    else:
        return stack.pop()
```

16. Write a program that implements the stack.

Ans.

```
#implements stack.py (module)
stack =[]
def push(val):
    # add element to the end of stack (top)
    stack.append(val)

def pop():
    #if stack is empty returns none
    if(stack == []):
        return None
    else:
        return stack.pop()
```

Implementing the stack in stackaap.py

Stackapp.py

```
import stack
stack.push(10)
stack.push(20)

print(stack.pop())
print(stack.pop())
```

Output:

```
20
10
```

17. How is the peek method implemented?

Ans. Peek method returns the element without popping (deleting) it:

```
def peek():
    if ( stack == []):
        return None

    else:
        #return last element
        return stack[len(stack)-1]
```

18. Explain the use of the stack with an example.

Ans. To explain the use of the stack, consider an example where we can use the stack to convert a decimal number into a binary equivalent (a string representation). To convert a decimal number to a binary number, the number is divided until it is greater than 1. It keeps the remainder and arranges the remainder in reverse order. Here, the remainder is stored in the stack because the binary number is in the reverse order of the remainder.

```
stack =[]
def dec_binary(num):
    if num > 1:
        dec_binary(num//2)
        stack.append(str(num % 2))

num = 10
dec_binary(num)
#convert stack to string and print binary string
print("The binary of ", str(num) , " is ",
''.join(stack))
```

2	10	0
2	5	1
2	2	0
2	1	1
	0	

10 = $(1010)_2$

Output:

```
The binary of 10 is 1010
```

19. Write an algorithm for the evaluation of a postfix expression.

Ans. The algorithm for postfix evaluation is as follows:

1. Print operand.
2. Push incoming operator onto the operand stack.
3. If a symbol is a left parenthesis, push it on the operand stack.
4. If the symbol is a right parenthesis, pop it and print the operators until a left parenthesis. Do not print the parenthesis.
5. If the symbol has higher precedence than the top of the operand stack, push it on the operand stack.
6. If no symbol pop, print all operators on the operand stack.

20. Write a program that evaluates a postfix expression.

Ans.

```
exp="2 3 + "

resultstk=[]
res=0

for i in range(len(exp)):
    if(exp[i].isdigit()==True):
        resultstk.append(int(exp[i]))
```

```
        elif(exp[i]=='*'):
            operand1=resultstk.pop()
            operand2 =resultstk.pop()
            res = operand2 * operand1
            resultstk.append(res)

        elif(exp[i]=='+'):
            operand1=resultstk.pop()
            operand2=resultstk.pop()
            res = operand2 + operand1
            resultstk.append(res)

        elif(exp[i]=='-'):
            operand1=resultstk.pop()
            operand2=resultstk.pop()
            res = operand2 - operand1
            resultstk.append(res)

        elif(exp[i]=='/'):
            operand1=resultstk.pop()
            operand2=resultstk.pop()
            res=operand2/operand1
            resultstk.append(res)

print('The   result is',resultstk[0])
```

Output:

```
The result is 5
```

21. Explain how queues work with the help of diagrams.

Ans. A queue can be implemented by using two ways:

1. Fixed sized array
2. Dynamic list

Enqueue and dequeue in Array (Fixed size)

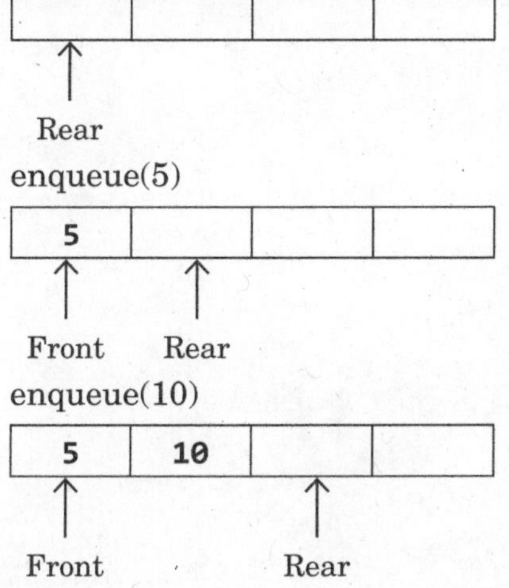

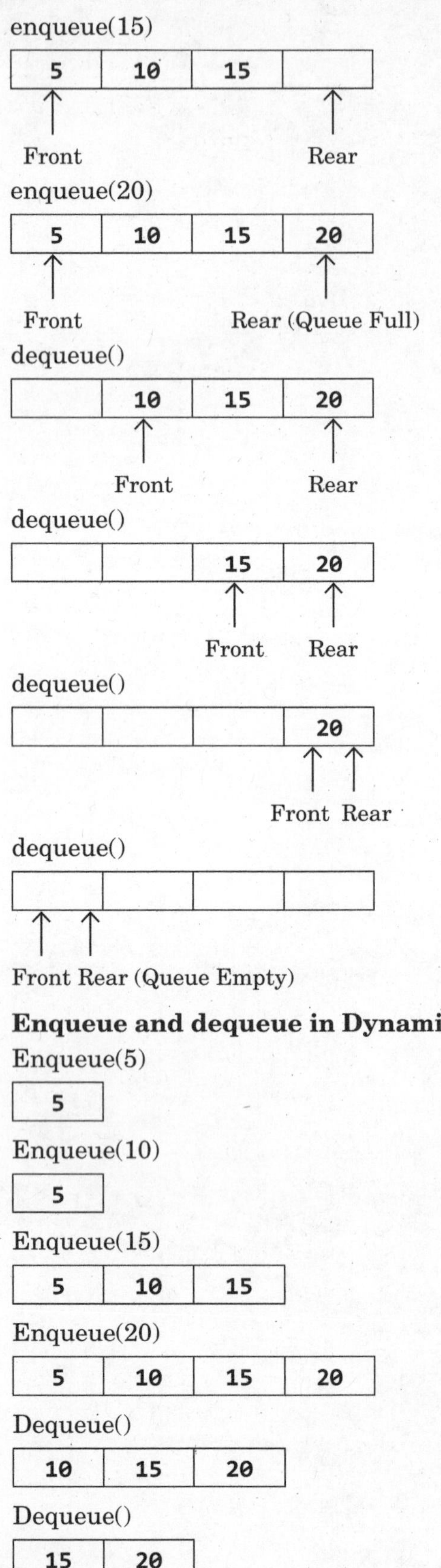
enqueue(15)
5
10
15
Front
Rear
enqueue(20)
5
10
15
20
Front
Rear (Queue Full)
dequeue()
10
15
20
Front
Rear
dequeue()
15
20
Front
Rear
dequeue()
20
Front
Rear
dequeue()
Front
Rear (Queue Empty)
Enqueue and dequeue in Dynamic list
Enqueue(5)
5
Enqueue(10)
5
Enqueue(15)
5
10
15
Enqueue(20)
5
10
15
20
Dequeue()
10
15
20
Dequeue()
15
20

Dequeue()

20

Dequeue()
[] #empty list

22. How to implement enqueue and dequeue functions using list?

Ans.
```
queue =[]
def enqueue(val):
    # add element to the end of stack (rear)
    queue.append(val)

def dequeue():
    #return element from front
    return queue.pop(0)
```

23. What are the boundary cases in a queue?

Ans. There are two boundary cases in the stack:

1. Queue is empty
2. Queue is full

When we dequeue an element from the queue (list), it returns a value but if the list is empty and we try to dequeue an element, it raises an exception.

```
lis =[]
lis.pop(0)
```

IndexError: pop from empty list

Queue is Full

We can't insert an element in a list when a list is exhausted (Queue is Full). List in a Python is dynamic; on a 32-bit machine it can store 536,870,912 elements. It is large enough, so we ignore to test the queue's full condition.

24. Write a program that implements the queue.

Ans.
```
queue =[]
def  enqueue(val):
# add element to the end of stack (rear)
    queue.append(val)

def dequeue():
    #if stack is empty returns none
    if(queue == []):
        return None
    else:
        return queue.pop(0)

def printqueue():
    if ( queue == []):
        print ("Queue Empty...")
    else:
        for element in queue:
            print(element, end=", ")
        print()
```

```
import queue

queue.enqueue(10)
queue.enqueue(20)
queue.enqueue(30)

print("Printing list")
queue.printqueue()

print(queue.dequeue())
print(queue.dequeue())
print(queue.dequeue())
print(queue.dequeue())
```

Output:

```
Printing list 10, 20, 30,

10
20
30
None
```

25. Convert the following infix expression to postfix expression.

Ans. A * B + C

Step	Symbol	Operator Stack	Postfix String	Explanation
1.	A		A	Add A to Postfix String
2.	*	*	A	Push * to operator stack
3.	B	*	A B	Add B to Postfix String
4.	+	* +	A B	Push * to operator stack
5.	C	* +	A B C	Add C to Postfix String
6.			A B C * +	Pop * and + add them to postfix string

26. Convert the following infix expression to postfix expression.

A * (B + C)

Ans.

Step	Symbol	Operator Stack	Postfix String	Explanation
1.	A		A	Add A to Postfix String
2.	*	*	A	Push * to operator stack
3.	(	*(	A	Push (to stack
4.	B	* (	A B	Add B to Postfix String
5.	+	* (+	A B	Push + to stack
6.	C	* (+	A B C	Add C to Postfix String
7.	)	*	A B C +	Pop + and (, do not add (to postfix string
8.			A B C + *	Pop * and add to postfix string

27. Convert the following infix expression to postfix expression.

A - B + C = A B - C +

Ans.

Step	Symbol	Operator Stack	Postfix String	Explanation
1.	A		A	Add A to Postfix String
2.	-	-	A	Push - to operator stack
3.	B	-	A B	Add B to Postfix String
4.	+	+	A B -	Pop - (same precedence) and add - to postfix ; Push +
5.	C	+	A B- C	Add C to Postfix String
6.			A B - C +	Pop + and add to postfix string

28. Convert the following infix expression to postfix expression.

A * B ^ C + D

Ans.

Step	Symbol	Operator Stack	Postfix String	Explanation
1.	A		A	Add A to Postfix String
2.	*	*	A	Push * to operator stack
3.	B	*	A B	Add B to Postfix String
4.	^	* ^	A B	Push ^ to operator stack
5.	C	* ^	A B C ^*	+ has lower precedence pop ^ , * and add to post fix string
6.	+	+	A B C ^ *	Pop + and add to postfix string
7.	D	+	A B C ^ * D	Add D to Postfix String
8.			A B C ^ * D +	Pop + and add to postfix string

29. Convert the following infix expression to postfix expression.

A * (B + C * D) + E => A B C D * + * E +

Ans.

Step	Symbol	Explanation	Postfix String	Operator Stack
1.	A	Add A to Postfix String	A	
2.	*	Push * to operator stack	A	*
3.	(	Push (to operator stack	A	* (
4.	B	Add B to Postfix String	A B	* (
5.	+	Push + to operator stack	A B	* (+
6.	C	Add C to Postfix String	A B C	* (+
7.	*	Push * to operator stack	A B C	* (+ *
8.	D	Push D to the operator stack	A B C D	* (+ *
9.	)	Pop + , * and add +, * to Postfix String	A B C D * +	*
10.	+	Since + has low precedence pop * and add to Postfix String	A B C D * + *	+
11.	E	Add E to Postfix String	A B C D * + * E	+
12.		Pop + add to Postfix String	A B C D * + *E +	

30. Convert the following infix expression to postfix expression.

P/ (Q-R) * S + T

Ans.

Step	Symbol	Operator Stack	Postfix String	Explanation
1.	P		P	Add P to Postfix String
2.	/	/	P	Push / to operator stack
3.	(	/(	P	Add (to Postfix String
4.	Q	/(	P Q	Add Q to Postfix String
5.	-	/(-	P Q	Push - to operator stack
6.	R	/(-	P Q R	Add R to Postfix String
7.	)	/	P Q R-	Pop - and (and add - to postfix string
9.	*	*	P Q R- /	Since / has same precedence Pop / and add / to Postfix String and Push * to operator stack
10.	S	*	P Q R - / S	
11.	+	+	P Q R- / S*	Since * has higher precedence pop * and push + to operator stack Push + to operator stack
12.	T	+	P Q R- / S * T	Add T to Postfix String
			P Q R- / S* T +	Pop + add to postfix string

31. Convert the following infix expression to postfix expression.

A/(B + C) *D – E delhi 2015

Ans.

Step	Symbol	Operator Stack	Postfix String	Explanation
1.	A		A	Add A to Postfix String
2.	/	/	A	Push / to operator stack
3.	(	/(	A	Add (to Postfix String
4.	B	/(	A B	Add B to Postfix String
5.	+	/(+	A B	Push + to operator stack
6.	C	/(+	A B C	Add C to Postfix String
7.	)	/	A B C +	Pop + and Add + to postfix string
8.	*	*	A B C + /	Since / has same precedence Pop / and add / to Postfix String and Push * to operator stack
9.	D	*	A B C + / D	Add D to postfix string
10.	–	–	A B C + / D*	Since * has higher precedence pop * and push – to operator stack Push + to operator stack
11.	E	+	A BC- / D * E	Add T to Postfix String
12.			A B C - / D * E +	Pop + add to postfix string

32. Convert the following infix expression to postfix expression?

P / Q + (R – T) *U

Ans.

Step	Symbol	Operator Stack	Postfix String	Explanation
1.	P		P	Add P to Postfix String
2.	/	/	P	Push / to operator stack
3.	Q	/	P Q	Add Q to Postfix string
4.	+	+	P Q /	Since + has low precedence first Pop / and add / to Postfix String and Push + to operator stack
5.	(	+ (	P Q /	Push (to operator stack
6.	R	+ (	P Q / R	Add R to Postfix String
7.	-	+ (-	P Q / R	Push - to operator stack
8.	T	+ (-	P Q / R T	Add T to Postfix String
9.	)	+	P Q / R T -	Pop - and add to postfix string Pop)
10.	*	+ *	P Q / R T -	Push * to operator stack
11.	U	+ *	P Q / R T - U	Add U to Postfix String
12.			P Q / R T – U*+	Pop * and + and add to postfix String

33. Convert the following infix expression to postfix expression.

U* V + R/ (S-T)

Ans.

Step	Symbol	Operator Stack	Postfix String
1.	U		U
2.	*	*	U V
3.	V	*	U V *
4.	+	+	U V *
5.	(	+ (	U V * R
6.	R	+ (	U V * R
7.	(	+ / (	U V * R
8.	S	+ / (	U V * R S
8.	-	+ / (-	U V * R S
9.	T	+ / (-	U V * R S T
10.	)	+ /	U V * R S T -
11.			U V * R S T - / +

34. Convert the following infix expression to postfix expression.

X/Y +U * (V - W)

Ans.

Step	Symbol	Operator Stack	Postfix String
1.	X		X
2.	/	/	X
3.	Y	/	X Y
4.	+	+	X Y /
5.	U	+	X Y / U
6.	*	+ *	X Y / U
7.	(	+ * (	X Y / U

8.	V	+ * (	XY/UV
8.	-	+ * (-	XY/UV
9.	W	+ * (-	XY/UVW
10.	)	+ *	XY/UVW-
11.			XY/UVW-*+

35. Convert the following infix expression to postfix expression.

`X-Y /(Z + U) * W`

Ans.

Step	Symbol	Operator Stack	Postfix String
1.	X		X
2.	-	-	X
3.	Y	-	XY
4.	/	- /	XY
5.	(	- / (	XY
6.	Z	- / (	XYZ
7.	+	- / (+	XYZ
8.	U	- / (+	XYZU
9.	)	- /	XYZU+
10.	*	- *	XYZU+/
11.	W	- *	XYZU+/W
12.			XYZU+/W*-

36. Convert the following infix expression to postfix expression.

`A + B* (C -D ) /E`

Ans.

Step	Symbol	Operator Stack	Postfix String
1.	A		A
2.	+	+	A
3.	B	+	AB
4.	*	+ *	AB
5.	(	+ * (	AB
6.	C	+ * (	ABC
7.	-	+ * (-	ABC
8.	D	+ * (-	ABCD
9.	)	+ *	ABCD-
10.	/	+ /	ABCD-*
11.	E	+ /	ABCD-*E
12.			ABCD-*E/+

37. Convert the following infix expression to postfix expression.

`(A * B) / C`

Ans.

Step	Symbol	Operator Stack	Postfix String
1.	(	(	
2.	A	(	A
3.	*	(*	A
4.	B	(*	AB

5.	)		AB*
6.	/	/	AB*
7.	C	/	AB*C
			AB*C/

38. Convert the following infix expression to postfix expression.

(X - Y) + (W * Z) / V

Ans.

Step	Symbol	Operator Stack	Postfix String
1.	(	(	
2.	X	(	X
3.	-	(-	X
4.	Y	(-	XY
5.	)		XY-
6.	+	+	XY-
7.	(	+(	XY-
8.	W	+(	XY-W
9.	*	+(*	XY-W
10.	Z	+(*	XY-WZ
11.	)	+	XY-WZ*
12.	/	+/	XY-WZ*
13.	V	+/	XY-WZ*
14.			XY-WZ*/+

39. Convert the following infix expression to postfix expression.

A + B * C ^ D-(E / F -G)

Ans.

Step	Symbol	Operator Stack	Postfix String
1.	A		A
2.	+	+	
3.	B	+	AB
4.	*	+*	AB
5.	C	+*	ABC
6.	^	+*^	ABC
7	D	+*^	ABCD
8.	-	-	ABCD^*+
9.	(	-(	ABCD^*+
10.	E	-(	ABCD^*E
11.	/	-(/	ABCD^*E
12.	F	-(/	ABCD^*EF
13.	-	-(-	ABCD^*EF/
14.	G	-(	ABCD^*EF/-
15.	)	-	ABCD^*EF/-
16.			ABCD^*EF/--

40. Solve the following postfix expression.

`10 3 X 7 1 - X 23 +`

Ans. The answer to the above expression is shown in the below table:

Step	Symbol	Operator	Stack
1.	10	Push 10	10
2.	3	Push 3	10,3
3.	X	Pop 3, Pop 10 Push 10 X 3	30
4.	7	Push 7	7,30
5.	1	Push 1	1,7,30
6.	-	Pop 1 , pop 7 Push 7 - 1	6, 30
7.	X	Pop 6, pop 30 Push 30 X 6	180
8.	23	Push 23	23, 180
9.	+	Pop 23, pop 128 Push 180 + 23	203

41. Solve the following postfix expression.

`5 3 + 2 X 6 9 7 - / -`

Ans. The answer to the above expression is shown in the below table:

Step	Symbol	Operator	Stack
1.	5	Push 5	5
2.	3	Push 3	3,5
3.	+	Pop 3 , Pop 5 Push 5 + 3	8
4.	2	Push 2	2,8
5.	X	Pop 2 , Pop 8 Push 8 X2	16
6.	6	Push 6	6, 16
7.	9	Push 9	9, 6, 16,
8.	7	Push 7	7,9,6,16
9.	-	Pop 9 , Pop 7 Push 9-7	2,6,16
10.	/	Pop 2 ,Pop 6 Push 6 / 2	3,16
11.	-	Pop 3, Pop 16 Push 16- 3	13

42. Solve the following postfix expression.

`3 5 + 6 4 - * 4 1 - 2 ^ +`

Ans. The answer to the above expression is shown in the below table:

Step	Symbol	Operator	Stack
1.	3	Push 5	5
2.	5	Push 3	3,5
3.	+	Pop 3, Pop 5 Push 5+ 3	8
4.	6	Push 6	6,8
5.	4	Push 4	4,6,8
6.	-	Pop 6, Pop 4 Push 6 - 4	2,8
7.	*	Pop 2, Pop 8 Push 8 * 2 = 16	16
8.	4	Push 4	4,16
9.	1	Push 1	1,4,16
10.	-	Pop 1, pop 4 Push 4-1	3,16
11.	2	Push 2	2,3,16
12.	^	Pop 2, Pop 3 Push 3 ^ 2	8,16
13.	+	Pop 8, Pop 16 Push 16 + 8	24

43. Solve the following postfix expression.

`3 1 + 2 ^7 4 - 2 * + 5 -`

Ans. The answer to the above expression is shown in the below table:

Step	Symbol	Operator	Stack
1.	3	Push 3	3
2.	1	Push 1	1,3
3.	+	Pop 1, Pop 3 Push 3+ 1	4
4.	2	Push 2	2, 4
5.	^	Pop 2 Pop 4 Push 4 ^ 2	16
6.	7	Push 7	7,16
7.	4	Push 4	4,7,16
8.	-	Pop 4, Pop 7 Push 7 - 4	3,16
9.	2	Push 2	2,3,16
10.	*	Pop 2, pop 3 Push 3 * 2	6,16
11.	+	Pop 6 ,Pop 16 Push 16 + 6	22
12.	5	Push 5	5,22
13.	-	Pop 5 , Pop 22 Push 22 - 5	17

44. Solve the following postfix expression.

`5 11 - 6 8 + 12 X /`

Ans. The answer to the above expression is shown in the below table:

Step	Symbol	Operator	Stack
1.	5	Push 5	5
2.	11	Push 11	11,5
3.	-	Pop 11, Pop 5 Push 11-5	6
4.	6	Push 6	6,6
5.	8	Push 8	8,6,6
6.	+	Pop 8 , Pop 6 Push 8 + 6	14,6
7.	12	Push 12	12,14,6
8.	X	Pop 12 ,Pop 14 Push 14 x 12	168,6
9.	/	Pop 168 , Pop 6 Push 168 / 6	22

45. Solve the following postfix expression.

Ans. If A = 2, B = 3 , C = 2 , D = 7 , E = 2 , F=2

Step 1. Convert it to postfix expression

Step 2. Evaluate the postfix expression

A + B * C ^ (D / E) / F

```
A                A  B
+        +       A  B
B        +       A  B
*        + *     A  B
C        + *     A  B  C
^        + * ^   A  B  C
(      + * ^ (   A  B  C
D      + * ^ (   A  B  C  D
/    + * ^ ( /   A  B  C  D
E    + * ^ ( /   A  B  C  D  E
)        + * ^   A  B  C  D  E  /
/        + /     A  B  C  D  E  /  ^  *
F        + /     A  B  C  D  E  /  ^  *  F
                 A  B  C  D  E  /  ^  *  F  /  +
```

The equivalent expression is:

2 3 2 7 2 / ^ * 2 / +

The answer to the above expression is shown in the below table:

Step	Symbol	Operator	Stack
1.	2	Push 2	2
2.	3	Push 3	Push 2

3.	2	Push 2	2,3,2
4.	7	Push 7	7,2,3,2
5.	2	Push 2	2,7,2,3,2
6.	/	Pop 2, Pop 7 Push 7/2	3,2,3,2
7.	^	Pop 3, Pop 2 Push 2 ^ 3	8,3,2
8.	*	Pop 8, Pop 3 Push 3 * 8	24,2
9.	2	Push 2	2,24,2
10.	/	Pop 2, Pop 24 Push 24/ 2	12,2
11.	+	Pop 12, Pop 2 Push 12 + 2	14

46. Convert the following infix expression to postfix expression.

P + Q - R / S

Ans.

Step	Symbol	Operator Stack	Postfix String
1.	P		P
2.	+	+	
3.	Q	+	P Q
4.	-	-	P Q +
5.	R	-	P Q + R
6.	/	- /	P Q + R
7.	S	- /	P Q + R S
8.			P Q + R S / -

47. Convert the following infix expression to postfix expression.

(X + Y) / (C * D) - E

Ans.

Step	Symbol	Operator Stack	Postfix String
1.	(	(	
2.	X	(	X
3.	+	(+	X
4.	Y	(+	X Y
5.	)		X Y +
6.	/	/	X Y +
7.	(	/ (	X Y +
8.	C	/ (	X Y + C
9.	*	/ (*	X Y + C
10.	D	/ (*	X Y + C D
11.	)	/	X Y + C D *
12.	-	-	X Y + C D * /
13.	E	-	X Y + C D * /E
14.			X Y + C D * E -

48. Solve the following postfix expression.

```
10 20 + 25 15 - * 30 /
```

Ans. The answer to the above expression is shown in the below table:

Step	Symbol	Operator	Stack
1.	10	Push 10	10
2.	20	Push 20	20,10
3.	+	Pop 20, Pop 10 Push 20 +10	30
4.	25	Push 25	25,30
5.	15	Push 15	15,25,30
6.	-	Pop 15, pop 25 Push 25- 15	10,30
7.	*	Pop 10, Pop 30 Push 30 *10	300
8.	30	Push 30	30,300
9.	/	Pop 30 , Pop 300 Push 300 /30	10
10.	/	Pop 2, Pop 24 Push 24/ 2	12,2
11.	+	Pop 12, Pop 2 Push 12 + 2	14

49. Solve the following postfix expression.

```
20 10 + 5 2 * - 10 /
```

Ans. The answer to the above expression is shown in the below table:

Step	Symbol	Operator	Stack
1.	20	Push 20	20
2.	10	Push 10	10,20
3.	+	Pop 10 ,Pop 20 Push 20 + 10	30
4.	5	Push 5	5,30
5.	2	Push 2	2,5,30
6.	*	Pop 2, pop 5 Push 2 * 5	10,30
7.	-	Pop 10, Pop 30 Push 30-10	20
8.	10	Push 10	10,20
9.	/	Pop 10 ,Pop 20 Push 20 /10	2

50. Solve the following postfix expression.

```
120 45 20 + 25 15 - + *
```

Ans.

Step	Symbol	Operator	Stack
1.	120	Push 120	120

2.	45	Push 45	45,120
3.	20	Push 20	20,45,120
4.	+	Pop 20, Pop 45 Push 45 + 20	65, 120
5.	25	Push 25	25,65,120
6.	15	Push 15	15,25,65,120
7.	-	Pop 15, pop 25 Push 25 -15	10,65,120
8.	+	Pop 10, Pop 65 Push 65 +10	75,120
9.	*	Pop 75, Pop 120 Push 120 * 75	9000

51. Solve the following postfix expression.

```
If P= 5 Q =3 R = 5 S = 4 T = 2 PQ - RS + T * +
The equivalent expression is:
5 3 - 5 4 + 2 * +
```

Ans. The answer of the above expression is shown in the below table:

Step	Symbol	Operator	Stack
1.	5	Push 5	5
2.	3	Push 3	3,5
3.	-	Pop 3 ,Pop 5 Push 5 -3	2
4.	5	Push 5	5,2
5.	4	Push 4	4,5,2
6.	+	Pop 4 ,Pop 5 Push 5 + 4	9,2
7.	2	Push 2	2,9,2
8.	*	Pop 2, Pop 9 Push 9 * 2	18,2
9.	+	Pop 18, Pop 2 Push 2 + 18	20

52. Solve the following postfix expression.

```
30 5 2 ^ 12 6 / + -
```

Ans. The answer of the above expression is shown in the below table:

Step	Symbol	Operator	Stack
1.	30	Push 30	30
2.	5	Push 5	5,30
3.	2	Push 2	2,5,30
4.	^	Pop 2, Pop 5 Push 5 ^2	25,30
5.	12	Push 12	12,25,30
6.	6	Push 6	6,12,25,30

7.	/	Pop 6 ,Pop 12 Push 12 / 6	2,25,30
8.	+	Pop 2 ,Pop 25 Push 25 + 2	27,30
9.	-	Pop 27 ,Pop 30 Push 30 - 27	3

53. Solve the following postfix expression.

`4 10 5 + X 15 3 / -`

Ans. The answer to the above expression is shown in the below table:

Step	Symbol	Operator	Stack
1.	4	Push 4	4
2.	10	Push 10	4,10
3.	5	Push 5	5,10,4
4.	+	Pop 5 ,Pop 10 Push 10 + 5	15,4
5.	x	Pop 15 ,Pop 4 Push 15 x 4	60
6.	15	Push 15	15,60
7.	3	Push 3	3,15,60
8.	/	Pop 3, Pop 15 Push 15 / 3	5, 60
9.	-	Pop 60 ,Pop 5 Push 60 -5	55

54. Solve the following postfix expression.

`100 40 8 /20 10 - + *`

Ans. The answer to the above expression is shown in the below table:

Step	Symbol	Operator	Stack
1.	100	Push 100	100
2.	40	Push 40	40,100
3.	8	Push 8	8,40,100
4.	/	Pop 8 ,Pop 40 Push 40 / 8	5,100
5.	20	Push 20	20,5,100
6.	10	Push 10	10,20,5,100
7.	-	Pop 10, Pop 20 Push 20- 10	10,5,100
8.	+	Pop 10 ,Pop 5 Push 5 + 10	15,100
9.	*	Pop 15 ,Pop 100 Push 100 * 1500	1500

55. Solve the following postfix expression.

`5 2 * 50 5 / 5 - +`

Ans. The answer to the above expression is shown in the below table:

Step	Symbol	Operator	Stack
1.	5	Push 5	5
2.	2	Push 2	2,5
3.	*	Pop 2, Pop 5 Push 5 * 2	10
4.	50	Push 50	50,10
5.	5	Push 5	5,50,10
6.	/	Pop 5 , Pop50 Push 50 / 5	10,10
7.	5	Push 5	5,10,10
8.	-	Pop 5 ,Pop 10 Push 10 - 5	5,10
9.	+	Pop 5 , Pop 10 Push 10 + 5	15

56. Solve the following postfix expression.

`60 6 / 5 2 * 5 - +`

Ans. The answer to the above expression is shown in the below table:

Step	Symbol	Operator	Stack
1.	60	Push 60	60
2.	6	Push 6	6,60
3.	/	Pop 6, Pop 60 Push 60 /6	10
4.	5	Push 5	5,10
5.	2	Push 2	2,5,10
6.	*	Pop 2 , Pop 5 Push 5 * 2	10,10
7.	5	Push 5	5,10,10
8.	-	Pop 5 ,Pop 10 Push 10 - 5	5,10
9.	+	Pop 5 , Pop 10 Push 10 + 5	15

57. Solve the following postfix expression.

`5 3 2 * 4 2 / - *`

Ans. The answer to the above expression is shown in the below table:

Step	Symbol	Operator	Stack
1.	5	Push 5	5
2.	3	Push 3	3,5
3.	2	Push 2	2,3,5
4.	*	Pop 2, Pop 3 Push 3 *2	6,5
5.	4	Push 4	4,6,5
6.	2	Push 2	2,4,6,5
7.	/	Pop 2, Pop 4 Push 4/ 2	2,6,5

8.	-	Pop 2, Pop 6 Push 6 - 2	4,5
9.	*	Pop 4 ,Pop 5 Push 5 * 4	20

58. Solve the following postfix expression.

`50 60 + 20 10 - *`

Ans. The answer to the above expression is shown in the below table:

Step	Symbol	Operator	Stack
1.	50	Push 50	50
2.	60	Push 60	60,50
3.	+	Pop 60, Pop 50 Push 60 + 50	110
4.	20	Push 20	20,110
5.	10	Push 10	10,20,110
6.	-	Pop 10, Pop 20 Push 20 - 10	10,110
7.	*	Pop 10, Pop 110 Push 110 * 10	1100

59. Solve the following postfix expression.

`False NOT True And True False OR AND`

Ans. The answer to the above expression is shown in the below table:

Step	Symbol	Operator	Stack
1.	False	Push False	False
2.	NOT	Pop False Push NOT False	True
3.	True	Push True	True, True
4.	AND	Pop True, Pop True Push True AND True	True
5.	True	Push True	True, True
6.	False	Push False	False,True, True
7.	OR	Pop False,Pop True Push Ture OR False	True, True
8.	AND	Pop True,Pop True Push Ture AND True	

60. Solve the following postfix expression.

`True False NOT AND False True OR AND`

Ans. The answer to the above expression is shown in the below table:

Step	Symbol	Operator	Stack
1.	True	Push True	True
2.	False	Push False	False, True
3.	NOT	Pop False Push NOT False	True, True
4.	AND	Pop True, Pop True Push True AND True	True
5.	False	Push False	False, True
6.	True	Push True	True, False, True
7.	OR	Pop True, Pop False Push True OR False	True,True
8.	AND	Pop True, Pop True Push True AND True	True

12 COMPUTER NETWORKS

LEARNING OBJECTIVES

- Define key terms in networking such as WWW, Internet, client-server model, switching
- Define networking devices, their usages and differentiate between various networking devices
- Describe the application-level protocols and explain how they works
- Describe the various mobile communication technologies with their advantages and disadvantages

DEFINITION

- **WWW (World Wide Web):** The World Wide Web (WWW) or web is a way to access data (files, audio, video, website) through the Internet. The web is built on the Internet for sharing information. The HTTP protocol is one of the most commonly used protocol by the web to communicate information over the Internet.
- **Internet:** The Internet is a network of networks that is spread worldwide. This allows users to interact directly with other users or devices (phone, computers, and laptops).
- **Server:** A server provides a service (it serve the resources) to its clients. A server is a program that resides on a computer or cloud.
- **Client:** A client is a program or a computer hardware device that requests a resource from the server.
- **Client-Server model:** A client-server model splits the program into two layers: front-end (a client) and backend (a server). It allows accessing resources such as files, videos, images, or some other services from a central computer called a server. The client requests the resources and the server responds to its clients by providing resources.
- **Protocol:** A protocol is a set of rules for communication between two devices over the network.
- **LAN:** Local area network is a group of computers or devices connected, usually within the same office building. The LAN requires a high-speed connection. Usually, LAN uses Fast Ethernet (100 Mbps) or Ethernet (10 Mbps) and at few locations use Gigabit Ethernet (1000 Mbps) connections.
- **MAN:** Metropolitan area network spans across several buildings in the same city or a town.
- **WAN:** Wide area network connects multiple LANs. A LAN may be limited to a corporation or an organization or it may be accessible to the public. The internet is an example of a worldwide WAN, which is public.
- **Switching:** An Internet is networks of network and it is required to send the data from one network to another network. Switching is the mechanism of sending data between different computer networks or their segments.
- **Circuit switching:** The physical path between the sender and receiver is established, between the caller and receiver. It is connected throughout the conversation. Once a message is delivered switches are released.
- **Packet switching:** Packet switching is connectionless and it does not establish any physical connection before the transmission begins. In packet switching a message is divided into small packets, which are routed from source to destination. Each packet may follow a different route to reach the destination. The packets received at the destination may not reach in order; however, they are rearranged by the upper layer.
- **Hub:** Hub connects multiple devices in a network. The hub sends data packets to all the connected devices. A hub is a simple network connecting device that connects other LAN components with identical protocols.
- **NIC:** Network Interface Card (NIC) is a circuit board or chip installed on a computer and is used to connect to a network.
- **MAC address:** Each NIC has a hardware address which is known as Media Access Control (MAC). A MAC address is hard-coded or hardwired into the Network Interface Card (NIC), and it is unique. The MAC address is given to an adapter by the manufacturer.

- **Switch:** A switch reads the hardware addresses of an incoming packet(s) to transmit them to the appropriate destination. It is more intelligent than a HUB, which just replicates messages for each connected device.
- **Router:** A router is a general-purpose device that interconnects two or more heterogeneous networks. Every router has its Internet Protocol (IP) address. The router keeps a routing table and knows where to route a packet.
- **Bridge:** Bridges can connect two or more network segments. It stores and forward frames between the different segments. It uses hardware MAC (Media Access Control) addresses for transmitting frames. Bridges can be used to connect two or more physical LANs into one larger logical LAN.
- **Repeater:** Repeater is an electronic device that amplifies the signals it receive. It works on the physical layer.
- **SMTP:** SMTP stands for Simple Mail Transfer Protocol; it is used to send e-mails to a mail server.
- **POP:** POP stands for Post Office Protocol, a protocol that is used to retrieve e-mail(s) from a mail server.
- **IMAP:** IMAP stands for Internet Message Access Protocol, a protocol that is used to retrieve e-mails from an e-mail server.
- **URI:** URI stands for Uniform Resource Identifier. It is a set of characters (string) that identifies a particular resource. A URI identifies resources either by location, or a name, or both. An URL is an example of an URI.
- **URL:** A URL stands for Uniform Resource Locator. It is a web resource that specifies its location on a computer network.
- **Web address:** Web address is a specific location of a web domain on the Internet, for example, http://computerscienceforcbse.com
- **Web page:** Web Page (web document) refers to a single page (A web page contains HTML, JavaScript, CSS, images, and more) on the Internet.
- **Website:** A Website refers to an entire web domain and all its sub-levels. It contains single or multiple web pages.
- **Data Channel:** Data channel is a medium that carries data (signals) from one end-point to another end-point.
- **Baud Rate:** The baud rate, is data transfer rate through a communication channel. In a serial port "9600 baud" means that is capable of transferring a maximum of 9600 bits per second
- **Data Rate:** Data rate is the speed at which data is transferred in a channel. It is measured in terms of bits per Second or bps.
- **bps:** Bits per second
- **Bps:** Bytes per second (Note capital B)
- **Bandwidth:** The amount of data transferred per unit time. It simply indicates the data transfer rate.
- **Data Transfer Rates:** It is the amount of data transferred per second through a communication channel. It is measured in bits per second (bps)

Very Short Questions and Answers — 1 Mark

1. Expand the following

a) Hz, kHz, MHz

Ans.
- Hz: Hertz
- kHz: Kilo Hertz
- MHz: MegaHertz

b) TCP/IP, ICMP, HTTP

Ans.
- TCP/IP: Transmission Control Protocol
- IP: Internet Protocol
- ICMP: Internet Control Message Protocol
- HTTP: HyperText Transfer Protocol

c) GSM, GPRS, WLL

Ans.
- **GSM:** Global System for Mobile Communication
- **GPRS:** General Packet Radio Service
- **WLL:** Wireless Local Loop

d) NIC, MAC, ARP

Ans.
- **NIC:** Network Interface Card
- **MAC:** Media Access Control address
- **ARP:** Address Resolution Protocol

e) **LAN,MAN,WAN**

Ans.
- **LAN:** Local Area Network
- **MAN:** Metropolitan Area Network
- **WAN:** Wide Area Network

f) **Kbps, Mbps**

Ans.
- **Kbps**: Kilobits per second
- **Mbps:** Megabits per second

g) **FTP,PPP,VoIP**

Ans.
- **FTP:** File Transfer Protocol
- **PPP:** Point to Point Protocol
- **VoIP:** Voice over Internet Protocol

h) **SMTP,POP3,IMAP**

Ans.
- **SMTP**: Simple Mail Transfer Protocol
- **POP3**: Post Office Protocol Version 3
- **IMAP**: Internet Mail Access Protocol

2. Write a brief on ARPAnet?

Ans. ARPANET or ARPAnet stands for Advanced Research Projects Agency Network. It was developed in 1966 by the United States of America for people to have easier access to their computers and other computing devices and to build effective communication methods for the military. Technically, it was the a first wide-area network that uses the packet-switching for data transmission and it is the first computer network that implemented the TCP/IP protocol suite.

3. Who has started the project APRANET?

Ans. The J. C. R. Licklider, Bob Taylor started a project called ARPANET project in 1966 to enable access to remote computers.

4. Mention the basic purpose of developing Arpanet?

Ans. The basic purpose of developing the Arpanet was to communicate with the computers at different locations mainly among scientific users.

The main idea was to send the message by splitting into small units called **packets**. These packets could be routed through the different paths and reconstruct the message back at their destination.

5. Differentiate between Arpanet and Internet?

Ans. The Internet is a network of massive networks, a networking infrastructure. The ARPANet was created for a smaller group for linking scientific and academic researchers in the United States. The internet is used for all the purposes, whereas APRAnet was developed for limited purposes.

6. How was Internet evolved with APRANET?

Ans. The ARPANET uses a packet-switching network and TCP/IP protocol suite for data transmission both of these technologies leads to the technical foundation for the Internet.

7. Mention the components of a network?

Ans. A network is a collection of several devices. The key components of a network are:
- Devices (Laptop, iPad, Smartphone)
- Cables
- Switches
- Routers
- Gateways

8. What is WWW?

Ans. World Wide Web is used for communication between web clients (Browsers) and servers.

9. How the client and server communicate with each other using HTTP?

Ans. The client sends HTTP requests to the server. HTTP uses TCP to serve resources independently. For each request, a new TCP connection is created. The server received the request to create the response and send it back to the client.

10. Are WWW and Internet the same?

Ans. The Internet and World Wide Web are not the same. The Internet is a massive network of networks, a networking infrastructure. The World Wide Web, WWW, or Web is a mechanism of accessing information over the Internet.

11. What are the major components of the Internet?

Ans. The Internet has three major components these are:

a. Hardware b. Network protocols c. Transmission media

12. Mention some hardware devices which are used to access the Internet?

Ans. Hardware includes devices such as laptops, smartphones, clients, and servers that are endpoints. Hubs, Switches, Routers, Gateways are mostly used with the internet for data transmission.

13. What is a networking protocol? Give an example.

Ans. Protocols are responsible for translating a text into electronic signals that can be transmitted over the wired Internet and translate it back to text. The protocol suite, TCP/IP, is a set of rules that allow communication between two devices in a network.

14. Mention the components used for transmission?

Ans. The transmission lines or physical media such as cables and fiber optics or wireless media such as satellite, Wi-Fi and, cell phone towers.

15. Explain how data is transmitted over the Internet?

Ans. The data are transmitted from one device to another by using packet switching. A unique IP address is assigned to each device that is connected to the Internet. The IP address allows to identify a device uniquely in a network. The IP protocol delivers the packets and TCP protocol ensures that packets are delivered reliably.

A packet contains the IP address and the port number (A unique number of a protocol) of the destination. The router finds the IP address of the destination assigned to each packet and determines where to send it. Finally, the packet reaches the destination, translates signals to text, and displays at the application level.

16. Which communication technology is used to communicate with each other in the network?

Ans. Packet switching and **circuit switching** are the techniques used to connect the multiple communicating devices.

17. Mention the technique used for transmitting the voice and data in a network?

Ans. Circuit Switching is designed for voice communication and it is not suitable for data transmission. Packet switching is suitable for data transmission. Circuit switching is connection-oriented; however, Packet Switching is connectionless.

18. Define bandwidth?

Ans. Bandwidth in electronics, communications is a range of frequencies (signal) that can pass through a medium, which is measured in Hz (Hertz) for analog communication. The transmitted signal can be a voice, message, video, and other data.

In the field of the computer-networking bandwidth is called also known as Data Transfer Rate which is measured in the bps (bits per second).

19. Define Data Transfer Rate?

Ans. DTR is an amount of digital data, which is moved from source to destination. It is measured as bps (bits per second) or baud rate.

20. Define the term channel?

Ans. A channel is a medium that is used to carry signals or data from source to destination.

21. Define transmission media?

Ans. Transmission media is a medium that transmits the data from a transmitting device to a receiving device.

22. Mention the two types of transmission media?

Ans. The two types of transmission media are:

a. Guided b. Unguided

23. Mention the component of a network.

Ans. A network is a collection of several devices. The key components of a network are devices, cables, switches, routers, gateway, and many more.

24. Give an example of the URL and domain name.

Ans. An example of an URL is http://cbse.nic.in/newsite/index.html. An example of a domain name is cbse.nic.in.

25. How are IP and MAC linked?

Ans. The IP addresses are the addresses of networking software, whereas a MAC address is a address of the hardware of network adapters.

26. Which protocol is used to convert IP to MAC address?

Ans. Address Resolution Protocol (ARP) translates an IP address into a MAC address.

27. How do bridges help to overcome the problem with hubs?

Ans. Hub does not filter the traffic whereas bridges filter the traffic based on MAC address.

28. How is a router helpful over a switch?

Ans. A switch does not stop data packets to other LAN segments, whereas a router can filter traffic on the basis of an IP address and route the data packet for the intended destination.

29. Why is the repeater required?

Ans. When a signal travels in a network over a while it may lose its strength. Repeater boosts signal strength and retransmits it. A repeater receives signals and retransmits it with a higher power to cover longer distances which can be more than 100 meters for a standard LAN cables.

30. Why is Access Point used?

Ans. An access point is a network device with a built-in antenna, transmitter, and adapter. It is used to create a wireless LAN (WLAN). An access point is used to connect between Wireless LANs and a wired Ethernet LAN.

31. Explain how a device is connected to a wireless network.

Ans. To connect to a wireless network AP(Access Port), and SSID (service set identifier). The AP broadcasts the SSID, which allows wireless clients to connect in an area. The SSID is used to identify all devices that belong to the same network. All the client devices must be configured with the SSID to be authenticated with an access point.

Short Questions and Answers — 2 Marks

1. Differentiate between the network and the Internet.

Ans.

Network	Internet
A network is where two or more devices are connected and able to exchange information.	The Internet is a network of networks.
A network covers a limited area.	The Internet is spread all over the world.
A network is used for connecting a few devices and it is inexpensive.	The Internet needs inter-networking devices and they are expensive.

2. Define Circuit Switching?

Ans. Circuit switching establishes a physical connection between a sender and receiver. The example of circuit switching is a telephonic conversation. In a telephone conversation, a connection is established and it remains connected throughout the whole conversation. Once a message is delivered switches are released.

3. Define Packet Switching?

Ans. Packet Switching is connectionless. It does not establish a physical connection between a sender and receiver before the transmission begins. In the packet switching a message is divided into small packets. These packets are routed from source to destination. The packets may take a different route to reach the destination. The packets received at the destination may not reach in order however they will be re-arranged by the upper layer.

4. Differentiate between Circuit Switching and Packet Switching?

Ans.

Circuit Switching	Packet Switching
It is connection-oriented. The path is established between the source and destination before the transmission of the messages.	It is Connectionless, for each packet dynamic route is decided for transmission.
It was designed for voice communication	It was designed for data communication.
A path is established before transmission and not during the duration of the session.	Each packet may travel through a different route to reach its destination.

5. What are the four components of data communication?

Ans. The four components are:

a. Message: It is the information to be communicated.

b. Sender: It is a device that sends the data messages.

c. Receiver: It is a device that receives the data messages.

d. Transmission Medium: It is a physical path by which a message travels from sender to receiver.

6. Mention the different units of Data Transfer Rate.

Ans. Units for DTR are:

Denoted by	Full Form	Rate
kbps	Kilo **bits** per second	Thousand bits per second
Kbps	Kilo **bytes** per second	Thousand bytes per second
Mbps	Mega**bits** per second	Million bits per second
Mbps	Mega**bytes** per second	Million bytes per second
Gbps	Giga**bits** per second	1 Gbps is equal to 1,000 Megabits per second (Mbps), or 1,000,000,000 bits per second.

7. Mention the different units to measure bandwidth.

Ans. Table of units for bandwidth:

Short	Full Form	Represents
KHz	kilohertz	a thousand cycles per second
MHz	megahertz	a thousand kHz
GHz	gigahertz	a thousand MHz
THz	terahertz	a thousand GHz

8. Write a brief note on Twisted Pair Cable

Ans. Twisted pair cable is widely used for voice transmissions. Twisted pair is widely used in networking. There are two types of twisted-pair cables

a. UTP (Unshielded twisted pair)

b. STP (Shielded twisted pair)

9. Differentiate between UTP and STP?

Ans. UTP has four pairs of copper wires which are twisted to protect them from interference, inside a plastic sheath. The UTP has a plastic sheath (casing) that is thin in size for protection. STP contains an extra copper braid jacket or foil wrapped around the shield to save from interference.

Note: STP cables is expensive compared to UTP however, it is used for higher transmission rates over long distances.

10. Mention the advantage of Twisted Pair Cable

Ans. Advantages offered by twisted pair cables are:

- Light Weight
- Economical
- Easy to install
- Greater speeds than coaxial cables.

11. Mention the applications of Twisted-Pair Cables?

Ans. The Twisted-Pair Cables are mostly used in:

- LAN
- Telephone lines
- DSL(Digital Subscriber Lines)

12. Write a brief note on Coaxial Cable

Ans. Coaxial cables are copper cables with metal shielding designed to provide immunity against noise and greater bandwidth. They can transmit signals at higher speed and over large distances compared to twisted pair cables.

Coaxial cables have a core of solid copper conductor for transmitting signals. This is covered by an insulating material. The insulator is covered by a braided metal that shields it against noise. The outer conductor is enclosed by an insulating plastic cover. Here is the pictorial representation of the co-axial cable.

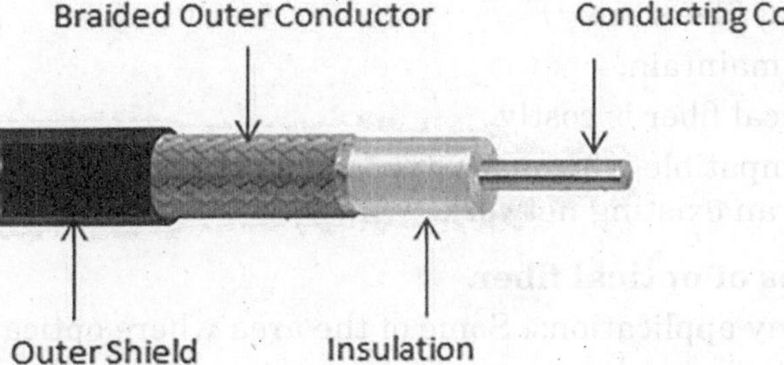

13. Mention the advantage of coaxial Cables

Ans. Advantages of coaxial cable:

- Coaxial cable has a sufficient frequency range to support multiple channels, which allows for much greater throughput.
- Support multiple frequency range with greater throughput.
- High bandwidth compared to twisted-pair.
- It supports voice, data, and even video services.
- Lower error rates due to shield and better noise immunity

14. Mention the applications of coaxial cables.

Ans. The **coaxial cables** are mostly used in:

- Cable TV networks
- Analog and Digital telephone networks:
- Ethernet LANs
- MANs

15. Mention the disadvantage of coaxial cable?

Ans. The coaxial cable has the following disadvantages:

- They're prone to lightning strikes.
- They cover less distance than fiber optic cables.

16. Write a brief note on optical fibers

Ans. Optical fiber uses light waves for the transmission. It is suitable for voice, data, audio, video transmissions. It offers many benefits over other cables like greater high bandwidth, greater transmission speed. Signals in optical fibers can travel over long distances. The optical fiber cable is cheaper as compared to twisted pair cables and co-axial however its installation makes it costliest from the other cables.

Optical fiber consists of a core and a cladding layer, usually coated with a layer of acrylate polymer or polyimide. The Layered structure of an optical fiber cable is shown below

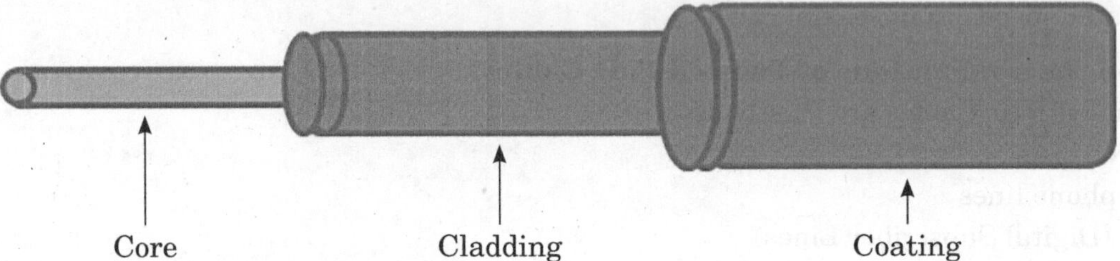

A solid dielectric material surrounds the core, which is called cladding that is encased in the coating.

17. Mention the advantages of optical fibers.

Ans. Optical fiber offers the following advantages:

- They have high speed and high bandwidth.
- They are highly secure.
- They can cover long-distance (including cities and counties) with zero interference.

18. Mention the disadvantages of optical fiber?

Ans. Disadvantages of the optical fibers are:

- Difficult to Install and maintain.
- The Installation of optical fiber is costly.
- Optical fibers are incompatible with many types of electronic networking equipment, at times it is difficult to retrofit it to an existing network.

19. Mention the applications of optical fiber.

Ans. The optical fibers have many applications. Some of the area where optical fiber is used are:

- Telephone systems
- Submarine cable networks (Undersea cables)
- For data linking in computer networks, CATV Systems
- CCTV surveillance cameras

20. Define Radio link?

Ans. A radio link (wireless Point-to-Point connection) is a wireless connection between two communicating nodes in a data network. Each node can send and receive communication with the help of a highly directive antenna.

Each node or radio unit consists of a transceiver and a sender with a directive antenna, the radio link operates with a microwave. The microwaves ranges from 6 to 23 GHz. Depending on the frequency of the signal, the communication range of a radio link varies within a few meters to hundreds of kilometers.

21. Mention the advantages of radio links.

Ans. Advantages of radio link are:

- Radio links are quick to deploy since no physical cable to be laid out.

- It is a cost-efficient solution compare to fiber.
- Radio links allows to communication from few meters to hundreds of kilometer.

22. Mention the disadvantages of radio link?

Ans. Disadvantages offered by radio link are:

- The radio links require direct link so-called line-of-sight for optimum performance.
- It is less stable in bad weather, which can interrupt the connection, particularly at higher frequencies.
- Obstacles such as buildings, in between, can disturb the transmission
- It may contain a very high signal to noise ratio.

23. Write a brief note on satellite links.

Ans. Satellite links are used for very large distances and global coverage. The satellite is used as a repeater. A ground station relays uplink signals. The satellite receives these signals and re-transmits it on a downlink frequency to receiving ground station(s). The diagram shown below illustrates the satellite communication.

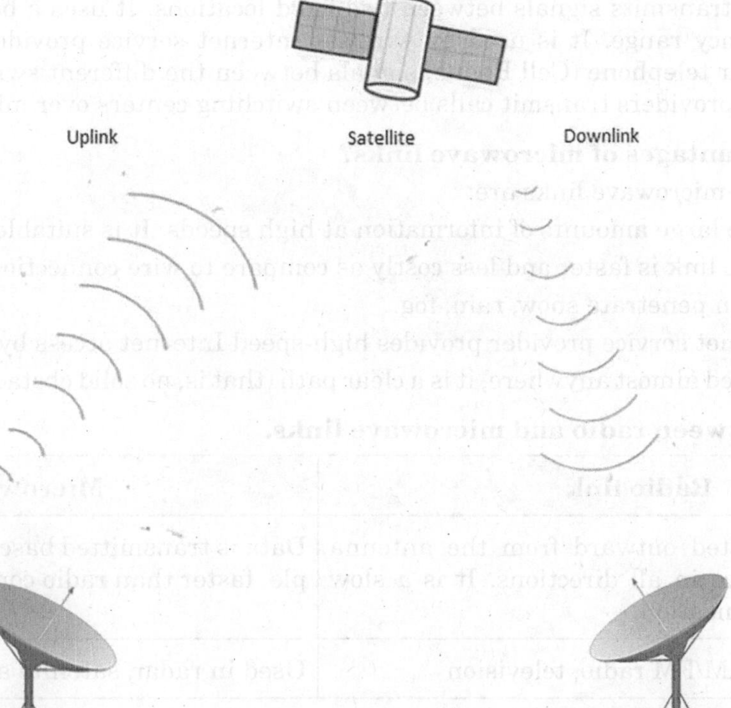

If digital communications signaling is used, the signal may be regenerated before it is re-transmitted to Earth.

24. Mention the places where satellite link communication are used?

Ans. Places where satellite link communication is used are:

- Radio
- Television
- Telephone
- Military applications /Operations
- Internet

25. Differentiate between Satellite Link and Optical fiber.

Ans.

Optical Fiber	Satellite Link
Optical Fiber is faster.	The Satellite link is slow.
Optical Fiber has higher bandwidth.	The Satellite link has Lower Bandwidth.
Fiber Optics are easy to maintain and repair.	The Satellite cannot be repaired.
Fiber Optics initial cost is low.	The cost of the satellite is very high.
For an optical fiber, there is no mobile terminal needed since the cable is to be laid physically.	Satellite provides global mobile communication. For example, GPS
The Satellite suffers from propagation delay. Optical fiber has no such delays	Satellite is suitable for rough terrain and remote areas where it is difficult to use fiber optics and microwaves.

26. Write a brief note on a microwave link.

Ans. A microwave link transmits signals between two fixed locations. It uses a beam of radio waves in the microwave frequency range. It is used by wireless internet service providers since Microwave links can carry a cellular telephone (Cell Phone) signals between the different switching center or cell sites. Telephone service providers transmit calls between switching centers over microwave links.

27. Mention the advantages of microwave links?

Ans. Key advantages of microwave links are:

- They can move large amounts of information at high speeds. It is suitable for the broadband.
- The microwave link is faster and less costly as compare to wire connection (a cable connection).
- Microwaves can penetrate snow, rain, fog.
- Wireless Internet service provider provides high-speed Internet access by using microwave links.
- They can be used almost anywhere, it is a clear path (that is, no solid obstacles) between the locations.

28. Differentiate between radio and microwave links.

Radio link	Microwave link
Data is transmitted outward from the antenna through free space in all directions. It is a slow means of communication.	Data is transmitted based on a line of sight principle, faster than radio communication.
Used in Mobile, AM/FM radio, television	Used in radar, satellite and space communication

29. Mention where a satellite and microwave links are used?

Ans. Microwave links are used in point to point communication, whereas satellite link is used in television, radar, satellite and space communication.

30. Explain the functioning of modem?

Ans. Modem stands for **MO**dulator/**DEM**odulator, it is a hardware device used by a computer to send and receive information through telephone lines. While receiving a signal modem converts digital data into an analog audio signal this is called modulation. When an analog signal is received modem converts it back to a digital signal this is called demodulation.

31. Why modem is used?

Ans. The computer is a digital device and telephone lines are used to carry the analog signals. Here modem act as a translator between telephone lines and computer by using modulation and demodulation process.

32. Define RJ45 and where it is used?

Ans. The RJ45 connector connects each end of the Ethernet cable.

33. Define Ethernet card and why it is used?

Ans. An Ethernet card or a NIC (circuitry/board) is used to connect to a network. It is implemented in the physical layer circuitry for communicating with data link layers/physical standards such as Ethernet or Wi-Fi.

Each NIC card can transmit and control the flow of data on the network. The card receives the signals and translates them into the data that is displayed by the computer or device.

34. Explain how NIC works?

Ans. NIC or network card converts data to electrical pulses and send them to ethernet or wireless. This process is also known as Encoding. It decodes the data received from media send it to the computer.

35. List the various network devices.

Ans. Various network devices are:

- Hub
- Switch
- Router
- Bridge
- Repeater
- Access Point

36. How does a Wi-Fi card work?

Ans. The Wi-Fi card acts as a receiver and transmitter. It allows laptop to connect to the Internet without a cable connection via a signal transmitted by a wireless router or cell tower. It receives the wireless signal and transmits a signal to the wireless network, thus enables users to access the web with laptop using wireless card. The wi-fi cards are inbuilt or can used as external device.

37. Write a brief note on Hub.

Ans. A Hub is used to connect the multiple networking devices. It connects various LAN components that work on identical protocols. It acts as a repeater as well as amplifies the strength of a signal which has travelled a long distance through connecting cables.

38. Explain the different types of hubs.

Ans. Different types of hub are:

- **Passive Hub:** It is used to forward signal to the network without boosting and cleaning the signals.
- **Active Hub:** It cleans and boosts the signal and forward it to the network. It serves as a repeater and wiring center. These hubs allow extending the distance between nodes up to its maximum capacity.

39. Write a brief note on switch.

Ans. A switch is a multiport device and it improves network efficiency. Switches are more intelligent than hubs. It can read a hardware address of the incoming packets and transmit them to the destination. It is a data link layer device. It checks the error before forwarding data, packets selectively to correct port only.

40. Write a brief note on router.

Ans. A router is a device that routes data packets based on their IP addresses. It is a Network Layer device that connects LANs and WANs. Routers perform routing based on the routing table to make decisions on routing the data packets to the destination.

41. Write a brief note on the gateway.

Ans. A gateway connects different types of networks. It accepts data from a system, interprets it, and transmit it to another system. Gateways are also known as protocol converters, which works at a network layer. Gateways perform more complex operations than a switch or router.

42. What do you mean by bridge?

Ans. A bridge is a repeater, which filters the content by reading the MAC addresses of the source and the destination. It is also used to interconnect two LANs working on the same protocol.

43. Write a brief note on the repeater?

Ans. Repeater works at the physical layer. It does not amplify the signal but regenerates the signal bit by bit before it becomes too weak or corrupted, it regenerates the original message. The signal re-generation allows transmitting signals for longer distances.

44. Differentiate between the following.

1) Hub and Switch

Switch	Hub
A switch is more efficient and intelligent. A Switch can join multiple devices with one LAN.	A Hub connects multiple Ethernet devices as a single segment.
Switches are smarter than the hub and can determine the target and forward data.	A Hub is a dumb device as it just forwards packets.

2) Hub and Router

Hub	Router
Hub transfers data as bits or electrical signals.	The router sends data packets.
A hub is a passive device.	A router is a networking device.

3) Switch and Router

Switch	Router
A switch can only be used with wired networks	A router can link wired network or wireless network. A router has additional features but costs higher than a switch.
Switches are designed to connect devices within a network.	Routers are designed to connect multiple networks

45. Why bridges are better than hub?

Ans. Hub does not filter traffic whereas, bridges filter the traffic based on MAC address.

46. How is a router helpful over a switch.

Ans. A switch does not stop travelling data packets to other LAN segments, whereas a router can filter traffic based on the IP address and route the data packet for the intended destination.

47. Why do we need a repeater?

Ans. When a signal travels a long distance, it may lose its strength. Repeater boosts the signal strength and retransmits it. It receives signals and retransmits it with a higher power to cover longer distances which can be more than 100 meters for standard LAN cables.

48. Mention the different types of network.

Ans. A network and its type are based on their number of nodes in a network, data transfer speed, their reach (distance) and, other characteristics. Private networks are networks that belong to a single organization.

Networks can be divided into four categories

a. PAN (Personal area Network)
b. LAN (Local area network)
c. MAN (Metropolitan area network)
d. WAN (Wide area network)

49. Write a short note on PAN.

Ans. PAN (personal area network) is a network for interconnecting electronic devices based on a person's workspace. It transmits data between laptops, smartphones, tablets, and PDA (personal digital assistants). PAN can be used for communication to the internet and among the personal devices as one network

The variant of PAN are:

- Wireless (WPAN)
- Wired interfaces such as USB.

A WPAN (wireless personal area network) is carried over a short-distance wireless network technology such as Bluetooth, Wireless USB, IrDA, or ZigBee. The WPAN can reach out from a few centimeters to a few meters.

50. Write a short note on the Local Area Network (LAN).

Ans. LAN stands for Local Area Network. It is designed for a small geographic area (this belongs to an organization) where nodes are connected through Ethernet or Wi-Fi in general. Data transfer in LAN can speed up to 10 Mbps (such as for an Ethernet network) and 1 Gbps (as with FDDI or Gigabit Ethernet). A LAN can connect 100, or even 1000, users.

51. Write a short note on MAN.

Ans. MAN stands for Metropolitan Area Network. It is designed to connect multiple LANs within the area of up to a few kilometers at high speeds.

It connects two remote nodes as a local area network. MAN consist of switches or routers with high-speed links (usually fiber optic cables).

52. Write a short note on WAN.

Ans. A WAN stands for Wide Area Network, it connects multiple LANs over great geographic distances. The speed for a WAN varies based on the nodes or distance. WANs operate by using gateways, routers, which can "choose" the most appropriate path for data packets to take to the destination network node. The well-known example of WAN is the Internet.

WAN works in two modes:

a. The peer-to-peer network where communication between two computers is carried, without a central computer, and each computer has the same role.

b. In a client-server model, a central computer provides resources to its users.

53. Differentiate between LAN and MAN.

Ans.

LAN	MAN
LAN is a private network.	MAN can be a private or public network.
LAN has higher speed than MAN.	MAN has lesser speed than LAN.
LAN has a shorter propagation delay.	MAN has a greater propagation delay than LAN.
LAN has less congestion and it has more fault-tolerance.	Man has more congestion and less fault tolerance.

54. Compare the LAN, MAN, and WAN.

Ans.

COMPARISON	LAN	MAN	WAN
Area covered	A small geographical area.	It covers large region cities or towns.	It spans across the globe and connects countries and subcontinent. For example, Internet.
Ownership	Private	Private or Public	Public or Private
Network speed	High	Moderate	Low
Propagation delay in network	Short	Moderate	Longest
Fault tolerance in networks	More Tolerant	Less Tolerant the LAN	Less Tolerant
Devices for transmission	Ethernet Cables or Wi-Fi	Wire/Cable	Wire/Cable and modem
Congestion in network	Less	More	Most

55. What is BUS Topology? Mention its features, advantages, and disadvantages.

Ans. In Bus topology, every computer in a network is connected through a single cable. This topology has exactly two endpoints and is called BUS or Linear Bus topology, as shown below:

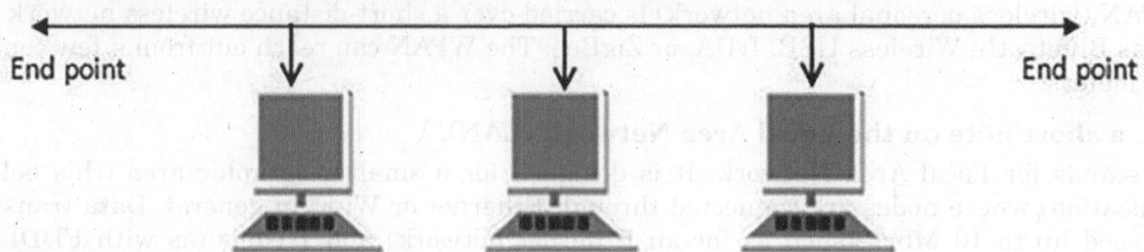

Key features:

- It transmits data in one direction only.
- Each device is connected through a single cable.

Advantages:

- It is economical.
- It is suitable for small networks.
- It is easy to expand the two cables together.

Disadvantages:

- If cables fail, it causes the whole network to fail.
- For heavy network traffic, the performance of the network decreases.
- The length of the cable is limited.

56. Mention the features, advantages, and disadvantages of Ring Topology.

Ans. Ring topology is where all devices are connected to each other in a ring and the last node is connected to the first one as shown below:

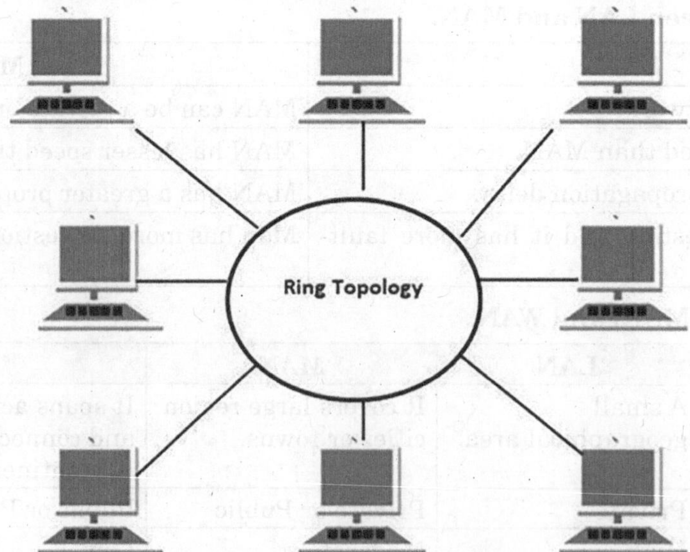

Key features:

- In a ring topology, data is transferred through each node of the network, till the destination node.
- The transmission in the ring topology is unidirectional. Using Dual Ring Topology, it can be made bidirectional by having two connections between each Network Node, thus if one ring fails, the second one can act as a backup.

Advantages:

- Economical for installation and expansion.

- ➢ It performs well even if traffic is high.
- ➢ It is easy to add new nodes.

Disadvantages:

- ➢ If one node fails, it disturbs the whole network.
- ➢ It is not easy to troubleshoot problems in a ring topology.
- ➢ Deleting and adding a node disturbs the network activity.

57. Mention the features of STAR Topology?

Ans. In the star topology, all computers are connected to a single central node through cables. This central node is connected to all other nodes. Star topology is shown in the below diagram:

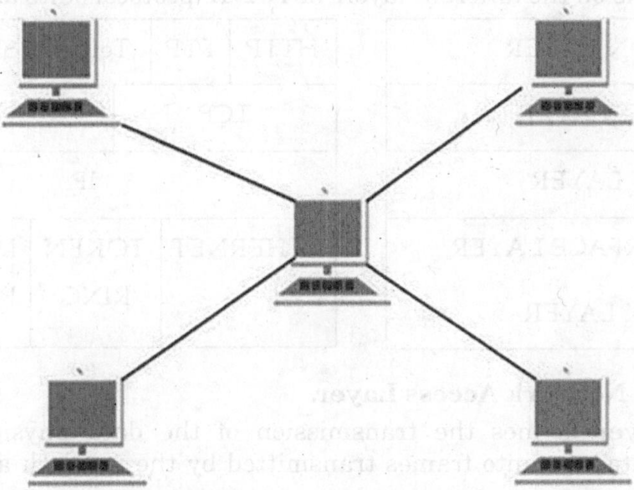

Key features:

- ➢ Every node has a dedicated connection to the central node.
- ➢ Twisted pair, Coaxial cable, or Optical Fiber is used for wired connections.

58. Mention the advantages and disadvantages of star topology.

Ans. Advantages:

- ➢ It is easy to set up and modify.
- ➢ It has fast performance due to low network traffic between the central node and the other nodes.
- ➢ It is easy to troubleshoot.
- ➢ If a node fails, the rest nodes can work smoothly.

Disadvantages:

- ➢ The installation cost and maintenance of star topology are high.
- ➢ If the central node fails, then the whole network goes down.
- ➢ The performance is based on a central node's capacity.

59. Explain the TCP/IP Protocol Suite.

Ans. TCP/IP, protocol transmits the data between source and destination over the internet. It is a suite of related protocols, not a single protocol. Currently, the Internet Engineering Task Force, or IETF, manages the TCP/IP protocol suite. The TCP/IP suite is a four-layer model of networking as shown in the below diagram

Application
Transport
Internet
Data link Layer/ Network interface layer

In the diagram shown above, the lowest layer is the Network Interface layer. It works with a wide variety of Network Interface layer level protocols such as Ethernet, Token Ring, and FDDI (it is an older standard for fiber-optic networks).

The TCP /IP suite, support lot of protocol that is used at various layers as shown in the below diagram:

HTTP	FTP	Telnet	SMTP	DNS
TCP		UDP		
IP				
Ethernet	Token Ring	Link-layer protocols		

All these protocols works on the different layers of TCP/IP protocol suite as shown in the below diagram

APPLICATION LAYER	HTTP	FTP	Telnet	SMTP	DNS
TRANSPORT LAYER	TCP		UDP		
INTERNET LAYER	IP				
NETWORK INTERFACE LAYER/ DATA LINK LAYER	ETHERNET	TOKEN RING	LINK LAYER PROTOCOLS		

60. Write a brief note on Network Access Layer.

Ans. **Network Access Layer** defines the transmission of the data physically through a network. It encapsulates the IP datagram into frames transmitted by the network and maps of the IP addresses into physical addresses.

The Ethernet, FDDI, token ring, X.25, frame relay protocols work with this layer.

61. Write a brief note on the Internet Access layer.

Ans. Internet Access layer is also known as the network layer. It sends the data packets from source to destination. The packets may take different routes to arrive at the destination.

62. Write a brief note on Transport Layer.

Ans. Transport layer is responsible for the flow control, reliability, and correctness of data sent over the network. The TCP and UDP works at transport let go through them one by one:

a. Transmission Control Protocol (TCP)

TCP creates a virtual circuit between the sender and receiver, for which connection remains active for the entire duration of the data transmission. The TCP divides the whole data into smaller units called segments, each segment has a sequence number. At the receiving end, all segments are recollected and re-arranged in the order to get the original message.

TCP is a reliable protocol, it ensures that packets are delivered. In case of error, it re-transmits the damaged packets until it is a success or it is un-recoverable Once the transmission is completed the virtual circuit is discarded.

b. User Datagram Protocol (UDP)

UDP provides end-to-end delivery of data. It discovers the error, and the ICMP protocol is responsible for sending reports the error to the sender, that datagram has been damaged.

63. Write a brief note on Application Layer.

Ans. An application layer is a topmost layer in the TCP/IP model. This layer allows the user to interact with the application.

The application layer interacts with the communication system. For example: at an application layer, an application web browser uses the **HTTP** protocol to interact with the server (a computer on a network).

64. Write a brief note on IP protocol.

Ans. Internet Protocol (IP), is a Network layer protocol. It delivers packets to network devices. The IP protocol uses an IP address to identify the individual device, not the MAC (physical) addresses. The Address Resolution Protocol (ARP) converts an IP address to MAC addresses.

The IP address has a network part and a host part that help to route a packet to the destination. IP is a routable protocol hence it can forward a packet to another network even if a host is not on the current network.

65. Write a brief note on TCP protocol.

Ans. TCP stands for Transmission Control Protocol. It is a connection-oriented protocol that works at the transport layer. TCP ensures the packets delivered reliably on the same network or a different network. In case if a packet does not arrive, it resends the packet until it has been delivered successfully or an unrecoverable error has occurred.

It establishes a connection with the receiving device and then sent the packets. It ensures that each packet is delivered to the destination. It does one-to-one communication that means it allows a single network device to exchange data with another single network device on another network. TCP is not used for broadcasting messages to multiple network devices.

66. How are IP and MAC linked?

Ans. The IP addresses are the addresses of networking software, whereas a MAC address is a address of hardware of network adapters such as NIC cards.

67. Explain how Simple Mail Transfer Protocol (SMTP) works?

Ans. Simple Mail Transfer Protocol (SMTP), works at an application layer of the TCP/IP protocol. It follows a process known as **store and forward**; SMTP client sends an email to its server called the mail server. It works with a Mail Transfer Agent (MTA) to send an email to the recipient's email inbox.

Note: **Store and forward** is a technique, where information is sent to an intermediate node and kept there later it is forwarded to the final destination node.

68. Explain the steps in the sending an e-mail from a client to a server (mailbox).

Ans. Here are the steps to send an email to the mailbox (mail server)

- A message is sent to the host; if it is only one host, only one copy is sent. If there are multiple clients the message is sent to multiple clients.
- A message is sent to the receiver (host) over a TCP Connection.
- The receiver (host) accepts incoming email and it is distributed to destined mailboxes.
- If the message is not sent, it resend it until the email's lifetime is expired, the sender is informed about a malformed email address.

69. How does IMAP work.

Ans. Internet Message Access Protocol **(IMAP)**, fetches the email from an email server. The flow of emails from the server to its clients is:

- Email client sends a connection request to the server. Once the connection is established, it fetches content from the user and caches it locally, for example, it marks the new emails, message summaries.
- Read or deletes an email.
- Disconnects from the server.

70. Write a brief note on POP or POP3 protocol.

Ans. Post Office Protocol) is also known as the POP3 protocol. It is used by a mail server in conjunction with SMTP to receive and hold mail for hosts. POP3 mail server receives e-mails and filters them into appropriate user folders. POP3 has two modes: keep and delete. In the delete mode, once a file is accessed by the client, it is deleted from the host whereas, keep mode allows to keep emails even fetched by its client.

71. How do POP or POP3 protocol work?

Ans. POP or POP3 protocols are used to fetch the emails from the server to the client. The steps to fetch emails to a client are:

- Sends a connection request to the server.
- Retrieves all e-mail(s).
- Stores email locally as a new mail.
- Delete/keep a mail from a server.
- Disconnects from the server.

Note: The POP protocol email may be deleted from the server once an email is fetched by its client.

72. How do the client and server communicate with each other by using HTTP?

Ans. The client sends an HTTP request to the server. The Server creates a response and sent the HTTP response. HTTP uses TCP to serve resources independently. For each request, a new TCP connection is created.

73. Why we use remote desktop?

Ans. Remote desktop is an application program or an operating system feature, which enables a user to connect to a computer from a different location and works as it is local.

The remote desktop access capabilities, and is used for the following:

- Fix a computer problem from a different location.
- Access a workplace/home machine when traveling.
- Access computer at home from other locations or vice versa.
- Perform administrative tasks remotely.
- Demonstrate how to use some software applications.

74. How VoIP works?

Ans. Voice over IP (VoIP) uses codecs that allow encapsulating audio data into data packets and transmitting them to an IP network. They are un-encapsulated at another endpoint of the connection.

75. Give an example where VoIP is used.

Ans. Voice over IP (VoIP) transmits voice and multimedia content over Internet Protocol (IP) networks. The VoIP is used to connect private branch exchanges (PBXs).VoIP is interchangeably called IP telephony.

76. Mention the advantages of VoIP?

Ans. VoIP eliminates circuit-switching networks for voice. It uses data packets thus reduces the cost to deliver voice services over networks and allows enterprises to operate a single voice and data network.

77. Explain how FTP works?

Ans. File Transfer Protocol (FTP) is used for transmitting files between devices (computers, laptops, servers) on the Internet by using TCP/IP connections. Clients send a request to servers to download a file. Using FTP, client can download, upload, delete, copy, rename, and move files on a server. A user can either log on to the FTP server or use it without logging in; this is known as anonymous FTP.

FTP works in two modes:

a. Active Mode

In Active mode a client initiates a session by command channel request, the server initiates a connection to the client and start transferring the data as shown in below diagram

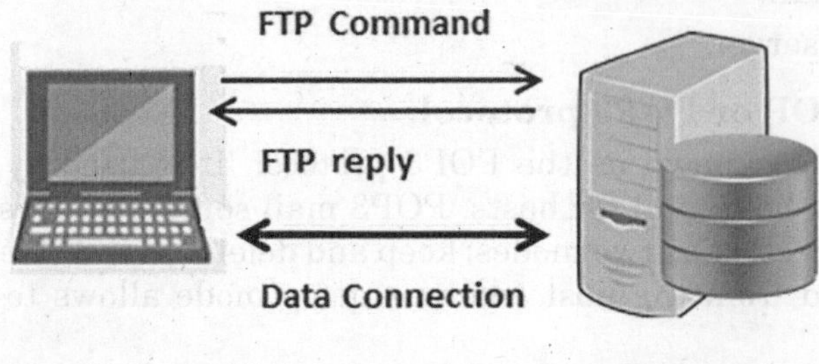

Active mode

b. Passive Mode

In this mode, the server initiates the command channel to open a data channel with the client.

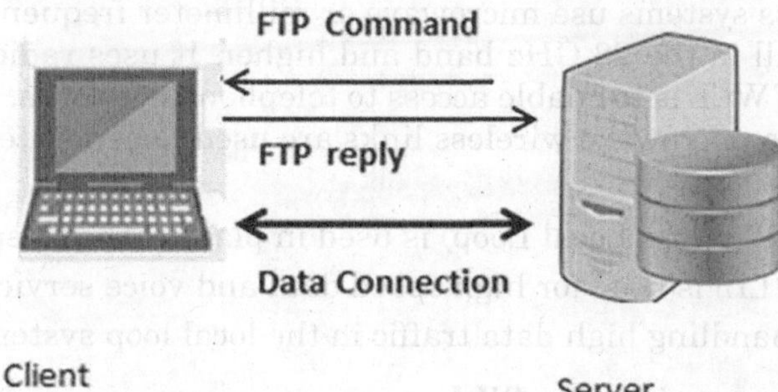

78. Differentiate between Active FTP and Passive FTP:

Active FTP	Passive FTP
In the active FTP, a client establishes the command channel and the server establishes the data channel.	In passive FTP, both the command channel and the data channel are established by the client.
Active FTP provides security to the FTP server.	Passive FTP does not provide security to the FTP server.
Active FTP may cause problems because of firewalls.	Passive FTP does not have any connection issues from firewalls.

79. Define SCP.

Ans. Secure Copy Protocol (SCP), transfers the files securely from a local device to a remote host. It runs on Port 22. The data remains confidential. SCP is secure; it can block packet sniffers that can extract/steal information through data packets. The SCP uses SSH that allows the inclusion of the time stamp for the file to be uploaded.

80. Mention the key difference between SCP and FTP?

Ans. SCP allows transferring files to a remote machine. It looks similar to the File Transfer Protocol (FTP) but it adds features like security and authentication.

81. What is PPP in networking?

Ans. Point-to-Point Protocol (PPP), is a data link layer communication protocol that transmits data using frames. It allows multi-protocol data transfer between directly connected devices without any host.

82. Define remote login?

Ans. Remote login is an internet application. It allows login a host from a remote device using login credentials.

Various software uses remote login are:

- **Remote desktop**

  The Remote Desktop enables one to connect another device on the network through remote, shares the control of its keyboard, mouse, and display the view.

- **Telnet**

  Telnet is a protocol which enables connecting the remote hosts over a TCP/IP protocol. It works as client-server, where a telnet clients connect to the telnet server and the client becomes a virtual terminal, the client needs to provide the credentials or log in as a guest in some cases.

83. Explain Wireless Local Loop(WLL).

Ans. A broadband connection provides all telecommunication services like the internet, telephone, fax, and radio. The broadband services are used for connection are called **fixed wireless access systems**. In a

Fixed Wireless Access System (FWA), the Wireless Local Loops (WLL) are most popular. It is also called a fixed wireless loop

The modern fixed wireless systems use microwave or millimeter frequencies. The wavelengths of these frequencies are very small in the 28 GHz band and higher. It uses radio connectivity instead of wired cable. The key function of WLL is to enable access to telephone networks. It supports subscribers of fixed and defined locations. The microwave wireless links are used to generate a Wireless Local Loop (WLL). It uses:

- NWLL (Narrowband Wireless Local Loop) is used in place of the telephone systems.
- BWLL (Broadband WLL) is used for high speed data and voice services.

Thus, WLL is useful for handling high data traffic in the local loop system.

84. Mentioned the services provided by WLL.

Ans. Services provided by a WLL are:

- Internet connection via modem
- Voice service
- Data service
- Fax service

85. Describe the components of WLL.

Ans. Components of WLL are:

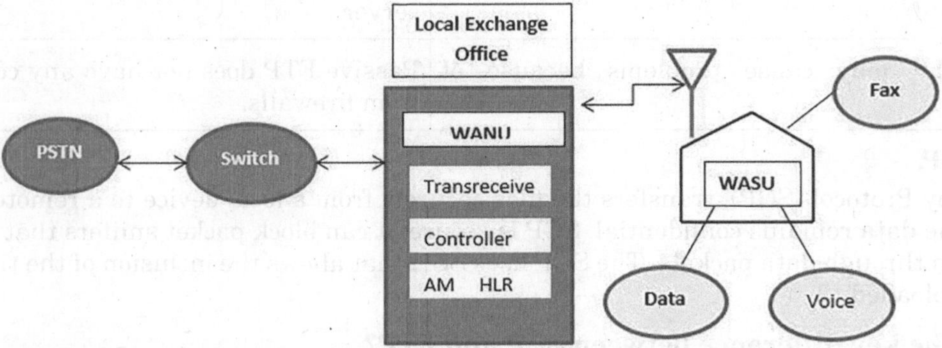

- **PSTN:** Public Switched Telephone Network (PSTN) is a circuit-switched network. It is a network of interconnected circuit-switched telephone networks.
- **Switch Function:** Switches the PSTN among various WANUs.
- **WANU:** Wireless Access Network (WANU). It is installed with LCO (Local Cable Operators), it performs Operations like, authenticate, maintenance, routing, Trans receiving data and voice

  Key functions of WANUs are

  - **Transreceiver**: It receives and transmits data.
  - **WLL Controller:** It controls the WLL components with WASU.
  - **AM:** Access Manager is responsible for the authentication of the users.
  - **HLR:** (Home Location Register) is responsible for storing the details of all local WASUs.
- **WASU:** Wireless Access Subscriber Units is installed at the subscriber location. It provides power supply locally and connects the subscriber to WANU.

86. Mention the advantages of WLL.

Ans. Advantages offered by WLL

- It eliminates the need to lay out the cables for network connection.
- It is a low-cost solution since there is no use of conventional copper wires.
- It uses the encryption techniques for wireless communication hence it is secure
- It is scalable as it does not require wires for scaling it.
- WLL can be installed in quick time, maybe in a couple of hours.

87. Define GSM?

Ans. GSM stands for Global System for Mobile Communication. This is a digital cellular technology that is used for transmitting mainly voice and data. It uses narrowband Time Division Multiple Access (TDMA) for transmitting signals

88. What are the features of GSM?

Ans. Features of GSM are:

- It allows international roaming
- It allows using low-cost mobile sets and Mobile base stations (BSs)
- It provides high-quality voice
- It improves the efficiency of spectrum
- It is compatible with Integrated Services Digital Network (ISDN) and other services offered by telephone companies

89. What is GPRS?

Ans. GPRS stands for General Packet Radio Service. It enhances the existing GSM network infrastructure. It is a connection-less packet data service. GPRS is based on Internet Protocols(IP) and enables its users to use a large range of applications.

GPRS does not use the dedicated radio channel for its mobile data for a fixed amount of time; it uses the radio resources concurrently which are shared among several users. This efficient use of radio resources enable the enormous number of GPRS users to share the same bandwidth from a single cell.

90. Differentiate between GSM and GPRS?

Ans.

GSM	GPRS
GSM is a circuit switching system.	GPRS is a packet switching system.
GSM uses SMS to transmit data.	GPRS supports data services.
It is less effective in using the network resources.	It efficiently uses the wireless network channel resources.

91. Write a brief note on 1G (First Generation) cell phone technology.

Ans. 1G is the first generation of cellular phone technology. It was introduced in the year 1987 by Telstra (formerly known as Telecom). 1G is based on analog technology. It has many drawbacks like poor battery life, call drops, and poor voice quality are the shortcomings of 1G. The maximum speed of 1G is 2.4 Kbps.

92. Write a brief note on 2G (Second Generation) cell phone technology.

Ans. 2G networks are digital. It is implemented using CDMA or GSM. The main aim was to provide reliable and secure communication. It provides SMS and MMS. The max speed of 2G with General Packet Radio Service (GPRS) is 50 Kbps or 1 Mbps.

93. Write a brief note on 3G (Third Generation) cell phone technology.

Ans. 3G allows video downloading, web browsing, email, and picture sharing. It increases the data transmission rate at a lower cost. 3G uses a new technology called Universal Mobile Telecommunications System (UMTS). The most popular feature of 3G is multimedia support along with streaming.

94. Mention the key features of 4G (Fourth Generation) cell phone technology.

Ans. 4G provides high speed, IP telephony, video conferencing, high-definition mobile TV, gaming services, cloud computing, and 3D television.

95. Mention the expected key features of 5G (Fifth Generation) cell phone technology?

Ans. 5G is designed for faster data speeds, lower latency, and higher density of connections. Other improvements include device-to-device communication, improved overall wireless coverage, and better battery consumption. The maximum speed for 5G could be up to 35.46 GBps.

96. Write a short note on Wi-Fi.

Ans. Wi-Fi stands for wireless fidelity. Wi-Fi is wireless networking technology. The Wi-Fi technology allows exchanging information between devices. It was developed for laptops (i.e. mobile computing devices). A Wi-Fi connection is accessed through an access point. It is also known as a wireless LAN. Wi-Fi allows local area networks to operate without cable and wiring.

The wireless network adaptor transfers the data into a radio signal and transfers the data through the antenna for its users.

Any Wi-Fi system has three major components:

a. The Radio signals

b. An Antenna

c. Router

The radio signals are transmitted through antennas and routers. These signals are received by Wi-Fi receivers (for example Wi-Fi cards) these are pre-installed on the laptop and cell phones nowadays. Whenever a Wi-Fi card receives signals from the router, it connects the device. The Wi-Fi cards read the signal and it creates an internet connection between user and network.

97. Mention the advantages offered by Wi-Fi

Ans. Advantages offered by Wi-Fi are:

- Devices are moved from one place to another place without losing connection.
- Wi-Fi allows communicating devices without wire can reduce the cost of wires.
- Setting and configurating Wi-Fi is easier than the cabling process.
- It is safe and it does not interfere with any other network.
- It allows to connect internet wirelessly and via hot spots.

98. Mention the disadvantages of the WI-FI.

Ans. Disadvantages of using Wi-Fi are:

- The radiations generated by Wi-Fi can be harmful to human health.
- The data can't be transferred for longer distances.
- It is expensive as compared to the wired connection.

99. Write a brief note on the WiMax.

Ans. WiMAX stands for Worldwide Interoperability for Microwave Access (AXess), it is based on IEEE 802.16 for point-to-multipoint broadband wireless communications. It provides high-speed data over a wide area. For users on the move such as mobile users. It is a standard for Wireless Metropolitan Area Networks (WMANs).

Long Questions and Answers 3/4 Marks

1. Explain why optical fiber is better than other types of cables.

Ans. Optical fibers is better than other types cables because of following reasons:

- The transmission bandwidth is higher than the metal cables.
- The data transmission rate is higher than other guided and unguided media.
- It is useful for long-distance transmissions due to less power loss.
- They cannot be tapped hence they are secure.
- They are not affected by electrical noise as they are immune to electromagnetic interference.
- They are lighter in weight, occupy lesser space, and flexible with higher capacity compared to copper wire cables.
- They are safe, since no di-electric, no spark hazards are present.
- Fiber optic cables are durable and long-lasting compare to copper cables.

2. Compare 1G, 2G, 3G, and 4G.

Ans.

Generation	Standards	Technology	SMS	Voice Switching	Data Switching	Data Rate
1G	TACS, AMPS	Analog	No	Circuit	Circuit	-
2G	GSM, GPRS, CDMA, EDGE	Digital	Yes	Circuit	Circuit	236 kbps
3G	UTMS, HSPDA, CDMA	Digital	Yes	Circuit	Packet	384 kbps
4G	IEEE 802.16, LTE	Digital	Yes	Packet	Packet	Up to 1 GBps

3. A company named as: Inc.com, it has four buildings on the campus as shown in the below diagram

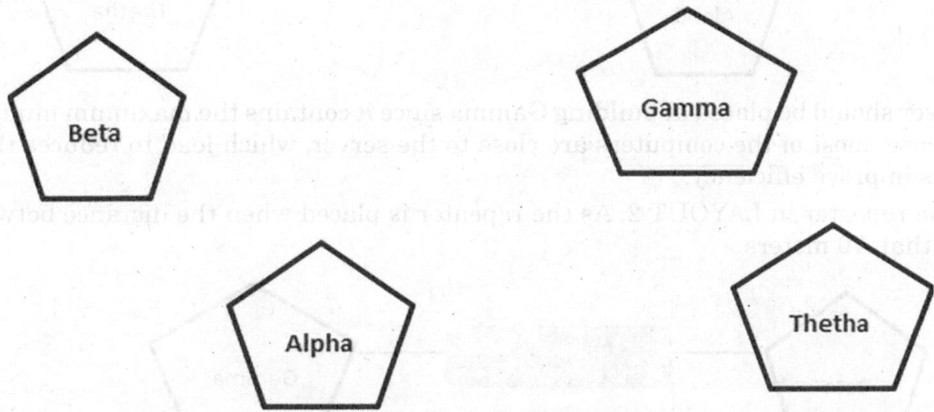

	Distance in meters
Alpha to Beta	50
Alpha to Gamma	150
Gamma to theta	25
Beta to theta	170
Alpha to theta	125
Beta to gamma	90

Building name	Number of computers
Alpha	50
Beta	25
Gamma	125
Theta	50

See the table given and answer the following:

a. Suggest the cable layout between the buildings.

b. Suggest the building to host the server.

c. Suggest where the following devices you will place and why? Repeater and Hub

Ans. a. Cable Layout 1

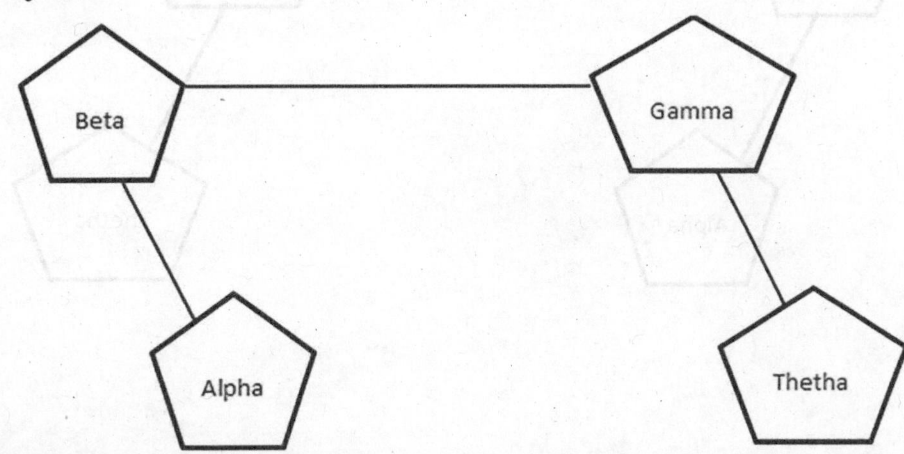

Cable Layout 2

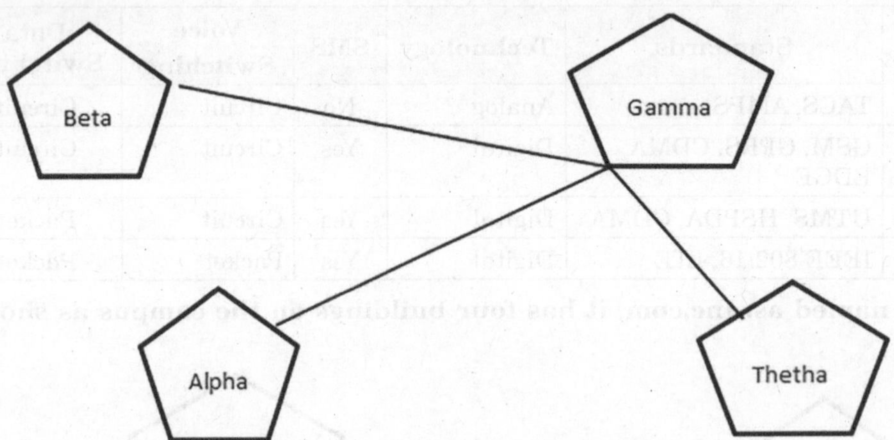

b. The server should be placed at building Gamma since it contains the maximum number of computers. In this case, most of the computers are close to the server, which lead to reduces the cost of cabling and thus improve efficiency.

c. Place the repeater in LAYOUT 2, As the repeater is placed when the distance between two nodes is greater than 70 meters

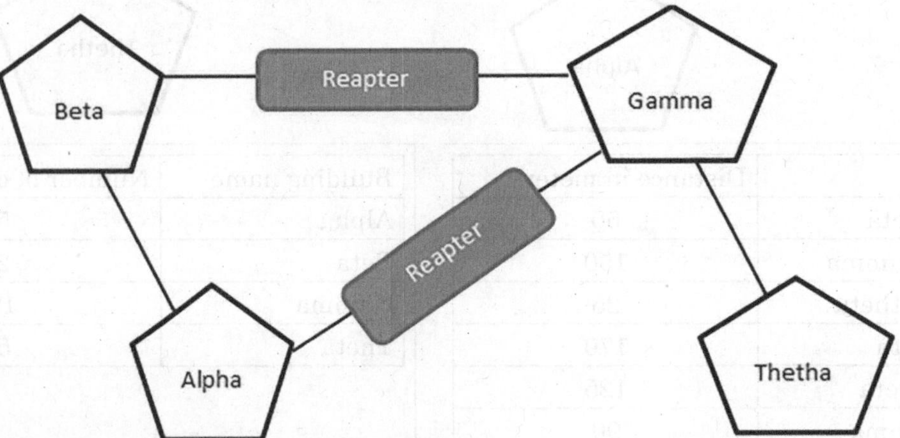

Placing repeater in layout 1

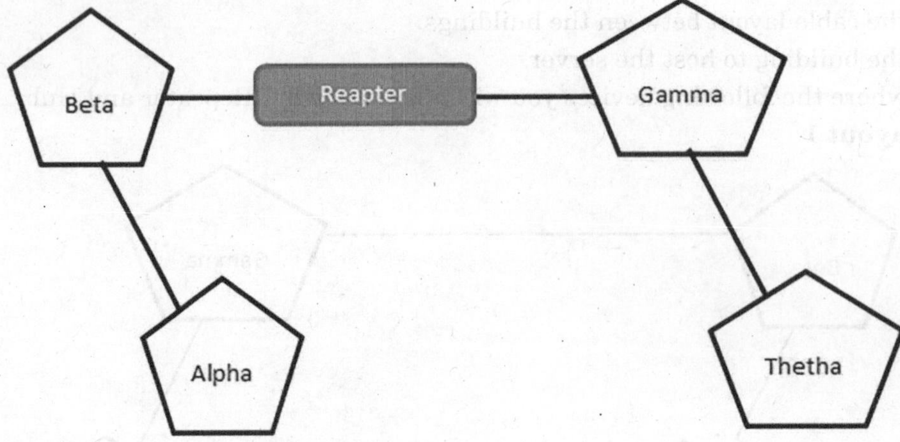

Placing hubs in layout 2

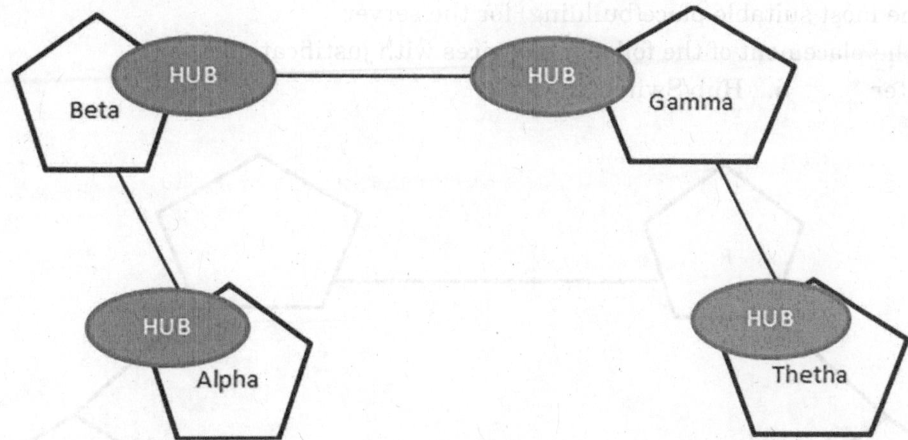

Placing hubs in layout 2

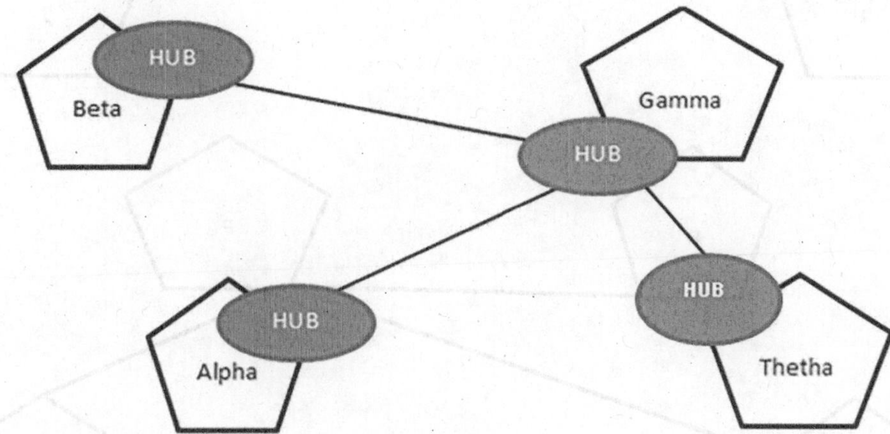

4. **The 'ABC Inc.' has four buildings on its campus.**

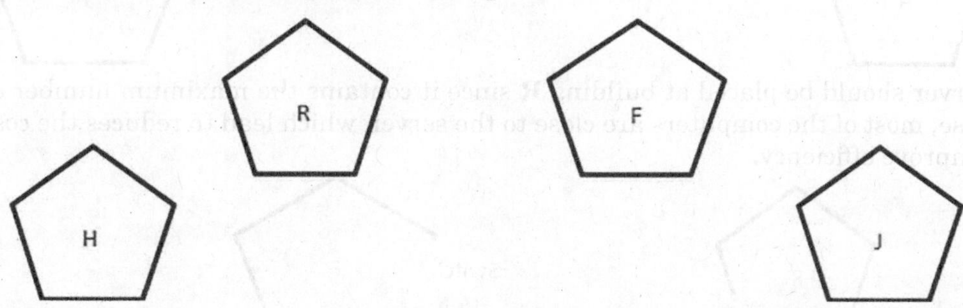

	Distance in meters
H to R	50
R to F	60
F to J	25
J to H	170
H to F	125
R to J	90

	Number of computers
H	15
R	105
F	25
J	28

a. Suggest the cable layouts between buildings
b. Suggest the most suitable place(building) for the server
c. Suggests the placement of the following devices with justification
i. Repeater ii. Hub/Switch

Ans. a) Layout 1

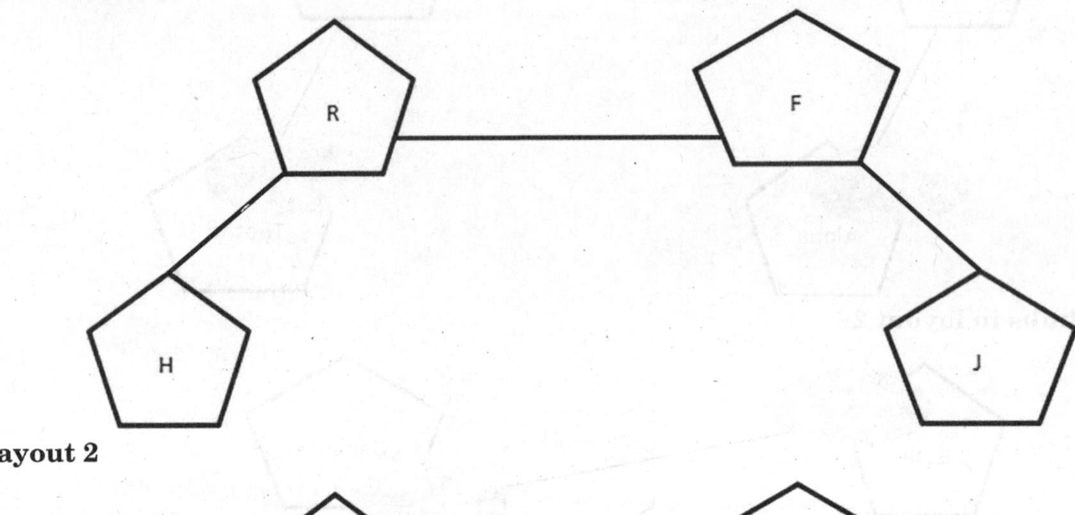

Layout 2

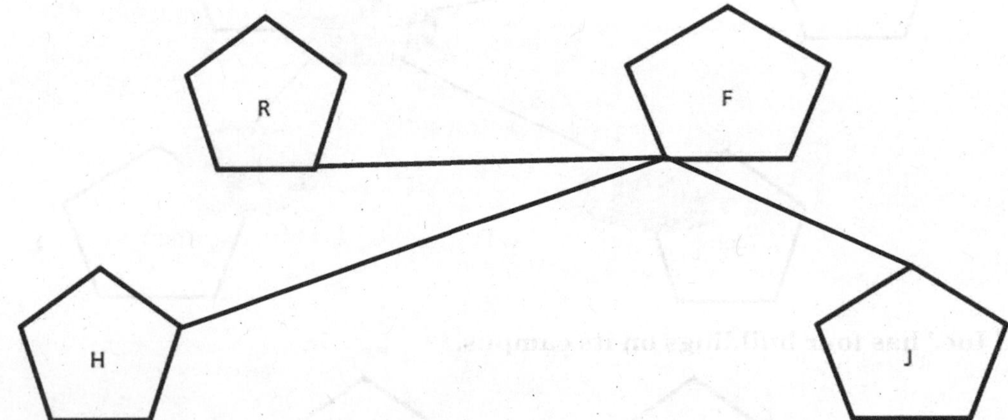

b) The server should be placed at building **R** since it contains the maximum number of computers. In this case, most of the computers are close to the server, which lead to reduces the cost of cabling and thus improve efficiency.

c)

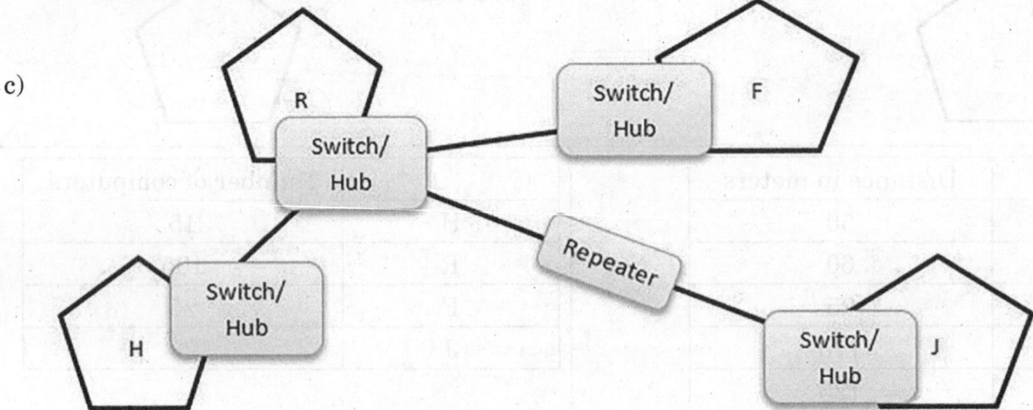

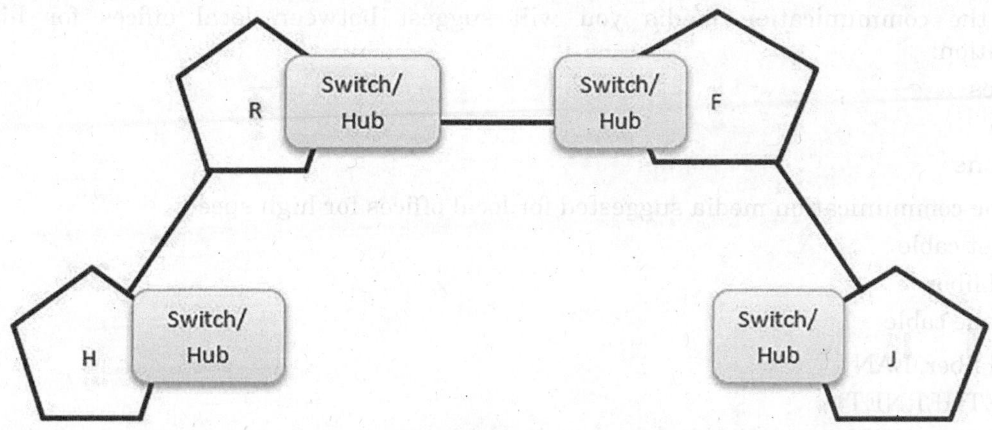

5. What do you suggest for the following conditions?

a) If the company wants to expand its office to another location in the same city what you will suggest.

b) An office in hilly terrain in the city what you would suggest and why?

Ans. a. If a company wants to expand its offices in other location in the same city, the company can use:

i. MAN

ii. An Optical fiber (for higher speed)

b. For hilly terrain WLL or satellite link can be used.

6. ABC company is located at Delhi and Mumbai, in Mumbai, there are 3 buildings PROD (PRODUCTION), HR n FIN (HR and FINANCE) and PR (PUBLIC RELATIONS) as shown in below diagram

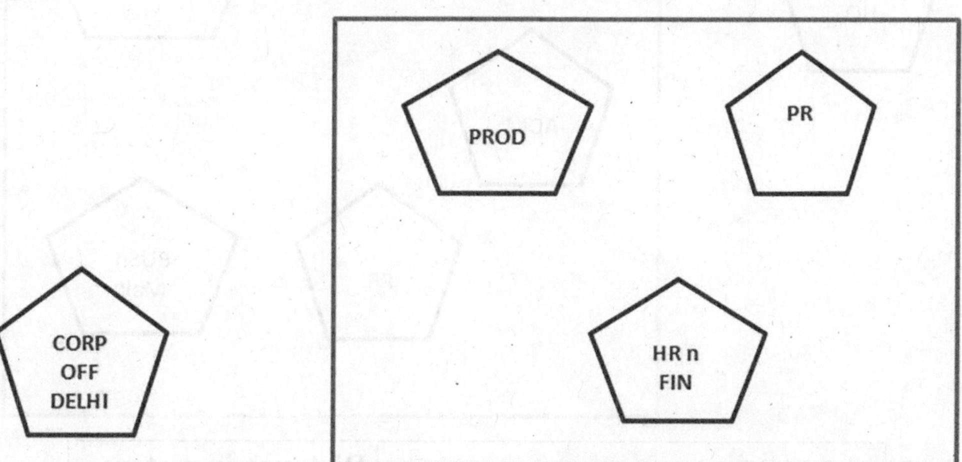

	Distance
PROD To FIN	50 Mtrs
PROD To PR	5 kms
PROD To CORP OFF	1485 kms
FIN To PR	5 kms

	Number of computers
PROD	135
CORP	25
FIN	10
PR	40

a. Suggest the type of network to use (LAN WAN AND MAN) between these offices.

I. Prod and PR unit

II. Prod to FIN N HR

III. PROD AND CROP OFF DELHI

b. Which of the communication media you will suggest between local offices for high-speed communication:
   i. Switches
   ii. Modem
   iii. Telephone

c. Which of the communication media suggested for local offices for high speed:
   i. Ethernet cable
   ii. Optical fiber
   iii. Telephone cable

Ans. a) i. Optical fiber, LAN
   ii. LAN (ETHERNET)
   iii. Optical fiber, WAN or satellite link

b) Switches

c) Optical fiber

7. An education company located at Delhi and Chennai. Chennai has four buildings ADM(ADMINISTRATION), ENG(ENGINEERING), BUS n MAT (BUSINESS and MARKETING), PR(PUBLIC RELATIONS) as shown in below diagram

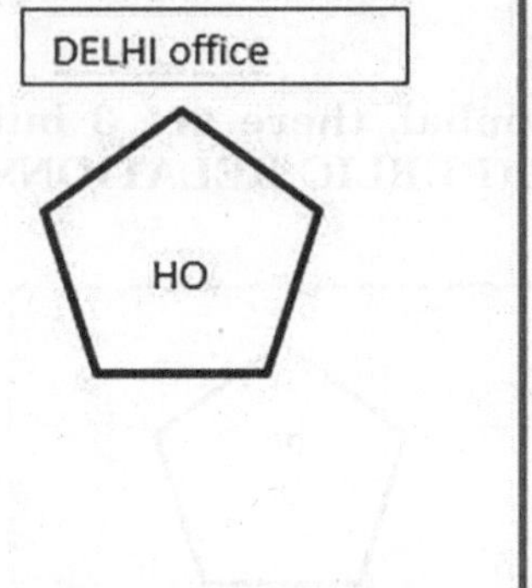

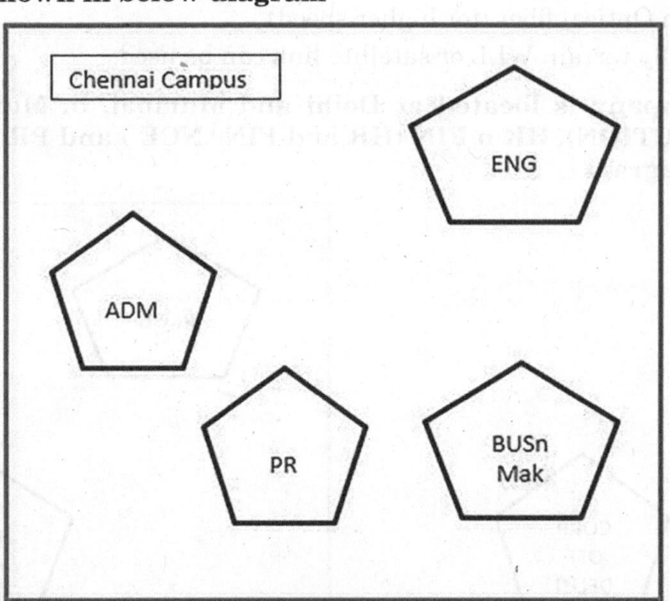

	Distance in meters
ADM to ENG	53 M
ADM to BUSnMak	98 M
ADM to PR	55 M
ENG to BUSnMAK	53 M
ENG to PR	50 M
BUSnMAK to PR	42 M
DELHI HO to CHENNAI CAMPUS	2000KM

Building	Number of computers
ADM	115
ENG	70
BUSnMAK	35
PR	18
DELHI HO	25

a. Suggest the most appropriate location to place the server in Chennai campus?

b. Suggest the cable layout to connect the buildings in Chennai campus?

c. What devices you will suggest for internet security?

d. Which of the following you would suggest for the video communication between the administrative office of Delhi and Chennai campus

   i. Cable

   ii. E-mail

   iii. Video conferencing

   iv. Text chat

Ans. a) The server should be placed at ADM building as it has a maximum number of computers. Alternatively, the server can be placed at PR building as it has shorter distances from the another buildings.

b) **LAYOUT 1**

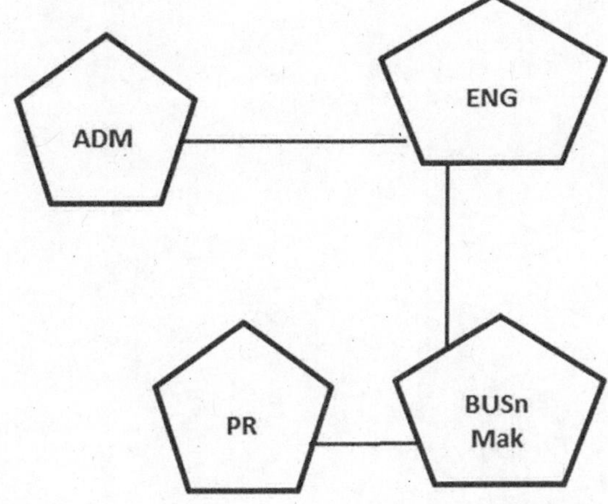

LAYOUT 2

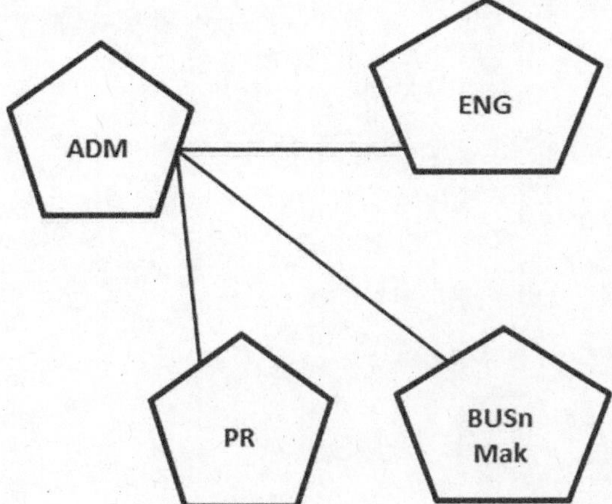

LAYOUT 3

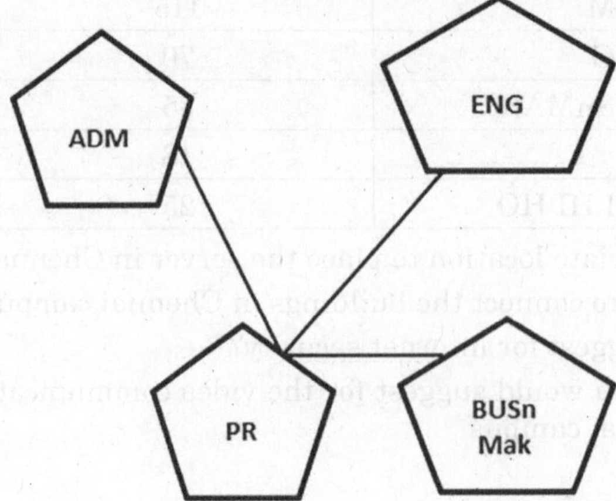

Note: Layout 3 is used since PR building has lesser distances from other buildings.

c. Firewall and router

d. Video conferencing

NETWORK SECURITIES CONCEPTS

LEARNING OBJECTIVES

- Identify threats (Viruses, Worms, Trojan horse, and Spams), risks and preventive actions from these threats.
- Describe the various cyber crimes and their remedial action.
- Define IP, its sub-types and IPR issues
- Recall and define terms HTTP. XML, Client server, Web Server,web browser, web scripting.
- Define and classify the hosting, domain and its subtypes
- Define the payment options like net banking, RGTS, NEFT, IMPS, e-wallets, UPI, Payment Applications.

DEFINITION

- **Threat:** A potential security risk to a device or a network.
- **Malware:** A general term for malicious software.
- **Computer Fraud:** Intentional deception for personal gain via the user's computing device.
- **Privacy violation**: Exposing personal or financial details (phone number, bank account details, email addresses) on websites, social media, etc.
- **Identify theft:** Stealing personal information from somebody and impersonating that person.
- **Spam** An unauthorized email which contains malicious links or advertisements.
- **Web services**: Web service is a standardized way to exchange information between the client and server applications over the internet.
- **Domain Names** It is an easy name of an IP address of a website.
- **URL**: The URL is used to specify addresses of a location on the World Wide Web.
- **Website** It is a set of web pages and other web resources located in a single domain.
- **Web browser**, A web browser is a software application, that is used for surfing on the internet
- **Web Servers**; A computer application program that runs websites and serves the HTTP request over TCP /IP protocol.
- **Web Hosting**, Allocating web resources on the web server that enable accessing the website over the internet.
- **Web Scripting** it is computer language that adds the dynamic capabilities to a web page.

Very Short Questions and Answers — 1 Mark

1. Define cybercrime.

Ans. Cybercrime is a set of criminal or malicious activities which are carried out using computing device(s) using the Internet. Phishing, spamming, and hacking are used to commit online fraud, hate crimes, identity theft, and more.

2. Define online fraud.

Ans. Online fraud is an act of stealing money from the victim's bank account using the internet.

3. Define phishing.

Ans. Phishing is a malicious act where a cyber criminal sends emails to get personal information, like passwords and credit card numbers. These emails look legitimate and appear to be sent from a genuine organization.

4. Define cyber-bullying.

Ans. Cyber-bullying is a set of activities that includes adolescent harassment, threats, defamation by using technology like phone, internet, instant messaging, and social networking sites.

5. Define identity theft.

Ans. Identity theft is a set of activities to steal someone's ID, password and other personal information to commit fraud.

6. What is Intellectual property?

Ans. Intellectual property (IP) refers to designs, inventions, innovation, artistic works, logos, symbols, images, and names used for trade and commerce to represent an individual, a company or product.

7. Define cyber terrorism.

Ans. Cyber terrorism is a set of activities that are carried out to threaten or extort by attacking device(s) of an organization or an individual.

8. Define hacking.

Ans. Hacking refers to performing the strategic activities in order to get unauthorized access to data, with the intent to corrupt or damage the data. It may change the data or send inappropriate messages with wrong or unlawful intent.

9. Define cyber-security.

Ans. Cyber-security is a set of practices which are followed to protect the devices, including software, hardware and data stored in devices that are connected to the internet from cyber-attacks, and unauthorized access.

10. Define Security Threat.

Ans. A Security threat is a potential risk of attack designed by hackers to gain unauthorized access to a device or network. These attacks are in two forms

a. Physical attacks

   For example – damaging devices physically

b. Non-physical attacks

   For example – virus attack.

11. Explain the physical threats and their types.

Ans. Physical threat may result in loss or physical damage to the devices

Physical threats are of three types:

a. Internal Threats: Spikes (power), fire, high temperature, and humidity in the rooms etc.
b. External Threats: Floods, earthquakes, lightning, and so on.
c. Human Threats: Harming devices (accidental or intentional) or theft.

12. Name some non-physical threats.

Ans. Non-physical threats are also called as **logical threats.** Some non-physical threats are:

- Virus
- Spyware
- Trojans
- Worms
- Adware
- Denial of Service Attacks (DoS)
- Distributed DoS Attacks (DDoS)
- Phishing

13. Mention some implication of non-physical threats

Ans. Implication of non-physical attacks are:

- Data corruption
- Data Loss
- Disrupt operations and impact the working of computer systems
- Stealing of sensitive information
- Illegal monitoring and spying of devices
- Cyber Security Breaches

14. Mention the key threats for computing devices.

Ans. Key threats for computing devices are:

- Malware
- Spyware
- Spam
- Phishing

15. Explain malware and how they attack.

Ans. Malware is a type of malicious code which includes viruses, worms, and Trojan horses. They are spread through an infected device, email, and instant messaging. Worms are sent through email, instant messages, and malicious websites. Virus-infected files are downloaded from peer-to-peer connections, thus allowing a Trojan horse to infect devices. Malware will also seek to exploit existing vulnerabilities on systems making their entry quiet and easy.

16. What is a computer virus?

Ans. A **computer virus** or **virus program** is malicious software which is installed or loaded onto a victim's computer without his/her knowledge and performs some malicious actions. It can self-replicate, and attach it with other programs or executable files, infecting them in the process.

A **computer virus** program transmits itself among **computers** via the internet or network. It can also spread through removable storage. For example, Pen Drive, DVD, etc. often causing damage to system files and data.

17. What are the effects of the virus on the computer?

Ans. The most common effect on an infected device are slow performance, data loss, frequent system crash, high memory and disk usage most of the time.

18. Define Trojan Horses.

Ans. Trojan horse is a malicious program downloaded and installed on a computer and appears to be harmless, but in fact it is malicious. It performs some unexpected changes to computer settings and other unusual activity, even when a device is idle.

The Trojan horse is installed when a user clicks on the email attachment or download link; the hidden Trojan horse is transferred to the user's device. The code inside, the malicious code is executed and attackers tasks are carried out.

19. Explain how a Trojan horse works.

Ans. The user unknowingly downloads it from server-side with free software or download trap by using website links, banner ads, or through a pop-up advertisement. The Trojan horse cannot attach itself; to an executable file (.exe); the program must be installed to attack the system.

Most attackers (Trojan horse developers) use email-spamming techniques. Here they send thousands of emails. As soon as the email is opened or attachment has been downloaded, the Trojan server is installed and will run automatically when the computer is turned on.

20. Define worm and explain how do they work.

Ans. A worm is a malware that is transmitted by exploiting software vulnerabilities. It could arrive through attachments in spam emails or other sources. Once opened, it provides a link to another malicious website or automatically downloads a computer worm. Once it's installed, it infects the machine without the user's knowledge.

Worms harm the system by modifying and deleting files or by injecting other malicious software onto a device. Sometimes it makes copies of itself and starts depleting system resources, like bandwidth (by overloading a shared network) or hard drive. It can also steal data, or install a backdoor that allows a hacker to gain control over device and system settings.

21. Define spyware.

Ans. A spyware is malicious software that is designed to gather confidential information, user behavior etc, from the devices without the consent or knowledge of the user and forward (sell) the data to the third party.

22. Why is spyware used?

Ans. Spyware is used for stealing victim's information and storing its movements on the Web and promoting pop-up advertisements to users. The presence of spyware is hidden from the user and it is difficult to detect spyware.

23. Mention the preventive steps that can be used to safeguard from spyware.

Ans. Here is the list of actions that can safeguard from the spyware, these are:

- Configure the firewall to block unsolicited requests.
- Use anti-spyware to protect from spyware.
- Do not click on pop-ups or accept a suspicious error dialog while surfing.
- Do not fall for a free deal offer, it may be a trap for malware.
- Ensure that security and software patches are up to date.

24. What is adware?

Ans. The adware is malicious software which shows unwanted advertisements to the user. These advertisements are produced by adware in the form of a pop-up or a window that a user cannot close.

25. What is a Denial-of-Service (DoS) attack?

Ans. A **Denial-of-Service (DoS)** attack aims to make computers or other devices unavailable to its intended users by disrupting its normal functioning. The attack is created by sending lots of ping requests to the intended device (mostly servers). A DoS attack is launched by using a single device.

26. Explain what is buffer flow attack?

Ans. Buffer flow attack is designed to create a memory buffer overflow causing a device(s) to consume all the available resources, memory, CPU time, hard disk space. This leads to system crashes, sluggish behavior, or other damaging behaviors, resulting in **Denial-of-Service (DoS)**.

27. Explain what is Flood attack.

Ans. Flooding is a **Denial of Service** (DoS) attack. This is designed by flooding a server with large amounts of traffic to bring a network or service down. In the flooding attack, the network is burdened with packets triggering incomplete connection requests so that it can no longer serve the genuine connection requests.

The flooding causes the memory buffer to be full. As, at the server or host end; no further connections can be created, this results into **Denial of Service** (DoS).

28. Define Distributed Denial-of-Service (DDoS).

Ans. A Distributed Denial-of-Service (DDoS) attack is a malicious attempt to generate huge traffic by utilizing multiple compromised computer systems or devices. A DDoS attack is like creating a traffic jam by blocking up the highway, this prevents regular traffic to reach its desired destination.

29. Explain what is a phishing attack.

Ans. Phishing attack is an attack mostly carried out to steal user data, including credentials and credit card numbers, etc. An attacker acting as a legitimate organization, individual, and trusted entity, dupes a victim into opening the instant message, chat message, an email, or text message. The recipient clicks on a malicious link and this leads to the download or installation of malware once the victim reveals the sensitive information.

This 'identify theft' could lead to the stealing of funds and unauthorized purchases.

30. Define spam

Ans. As the name suggests **spams** are unsolicited bulk email messages. These messages are sent through chat apps, email, instant messaging, or any other digital communication tool. It is mostly used by advertisers.

31. Explain how spam email leads to threats?

Ans. Spam email can be a serious security threat. It contains viruses, Trojan horses, worms, spyware, and other specific attacks for obtaining personal identification or confidential information.

32. How to know if an email is a spam?

Ans. The following helps to identify if an email is a spam:

- Messages that do not include your email address in the TO or CC fields are common forms of spam.
- Some spam can contain offensive language or links to Web sites with inappropriate content.
- Also, some spam may include hidden text that only becomes visible if you highlight the content. This is a common trick spammers use to get their email to pass through spam filters without detection.

33. Mention the proactive steps to safeguards from the spam.

Ans. Steps to safeguards from spams are:

- Install Spam filtering and blocking software.
- If you suspect an email is spam do not click on the link or attachment and do not respond to it, just delete it.
- Read emails in plain text or disable the preview panel.
- Reject all the Instant Messages from an unknown source.
- Do not click on URL links within IM (Instant Messaging Application) unless they are from a known source and expected.
- Keep software and security patches up to date.

34. Define firewall

Ans. Firewall is a system which is designed to prevent unauthorized access. It can be implemented in either software or hardware form, or it is a combination of both. A firewall prevents unauthorized users to access private networks connected to the internet, especially an intranet.

Firewall tracks incoming and outgoing data packets, in this way a firewall functions as a network security tool, which allows or blocks packets on the basis of security rules.

35. Why a firewall is required?

Ans. A firewall acts as a shield against unauthorized access to and from a private network as all messages that enter or leave the intranet go through the firewall. Based on the defined rules it examines each message and blocks messages that do not meet the specified security criteria.

36. Mention the benefits of Firewall Security

Ans. Various benefits which firewall offers are:

- **Monitors Traffic:** It monitors incoming and outgoing traffic in a network or device.
- **Blocks Trojans:** It helps to block the Trojan horses, malware.
- **Stops Hackers:** It helps to keep hackers away from the networks.
- **Stops Key loggers:** It reduces the risk of key logger monitoring.

37. Define software firewall

Ans. Software firewall is installed on a local device; it is not hardware (or a cloud server). The key advantage of these firewalls is they isolate each network endpoint (device) from each other.

38. Define hardware firewall

Ans. Hardware firewall is a physical appliance which acts as a traffic router to monitor the data packets before they are connected to the network's servers. They provide security by intercepting malicious traffic outside the network and discard the traffic. Hardware firewalls have limited capacity to handle simultaneous connections.

39. Define HTTPS

Ans. HTTPS stands for **Hypertext Transfer Protocol Secure**. HTTPS uses a **Secure Socket Layer (SSL)** for security purposes. The secure site uses **HTTPS,** for example websites of banks, investment websites, e-commerce websites, and other websites where a user is required to log in. The secure websites use the HTTPS to encrypt data. In simpler terms encryption is converting data into non-understandable for humans.

If someone captures the data while transferring via HTTPS, it would be non-understandable or unrecognizable by a hacker.

40. Why is HTTPS safe?

Ans. HTTPS (hypertext transfer protocol secure) is a secure version of HTTP. HTTPS is encrypted and enhances the security of data transfer. Data such as bank account numbers, unique ids, OTPs are sensitive and should be transported securely, thus HTTPs is used over the Internet. With HTTPS, data is encrypted in a way that if a packet is sniffed or intercepted, the hacker will come across a different set of characters (these characters are non-understandable for the intruder), thus the hacker will not able to understand what is the text.

Consider an example:

String before encryption:

HTTPs is secure

String after encryption:

IRyiEhVpa6VnKyExMiEgNveroy/Kn3bo3OfghBPDc1gU5X73xMsJormzz

(It is just for example not an actual encryption)

This above string is encrypted and cannot be understood by a hacker.

41. Mention some general clues to find out if an email is a phishing email.

Ans. Few tips to identify if the email is phishing or not:

- **Similar name of the brand is used and not using HTTPS**

  Many phishing emails use a name of a legitimate company name but with a small tweak with it. For example: http://icicbank/renewal; you can see that the bank name is ICIC in URL (it is not a valid bank name, it should be ICICI). All the sites that are involved in password changes or financial transactions uses HTTPS. If the ***HTTPS*** is not used in the URL indicating it is not a secure site.

- **Low-resolution logo**

  Phishers cannot cut and paste the logos of agencies, banks in their phishing emails. If the logo is of low quality, unclear, fuzzy, or different this is a sign that the person contacting does not work for that company.

- **Email from a different domain**

  The email doesn't contain the domain name to whatever company is supposedly sending the message. Again, this is a sign that a scammer is trying to trick with the user. One needs to be careful when hovering. Do not accidentally click on the link.

42. Explain how Identity theft and financial fraud are related.

Ans. Identity theft and financial fraud can be separate or related crimes. When a person's identity is used for any unlawful activity, for example, an offender sends an email to a user, pretending as an employee from a bank and ask for his/her bank account details. If a user discloses its details the offender takes all the money of the victim and fraud can take place.

Now an offender uses the victim's details to open an additional bank account which is used for money laundering. This is another way of identity theft. This shows how identity theft is interrelated to fraud.

43. Explain what debit or credit card frauds are.

Ans. Debit card or Credit fraud happens when the criminal gets a debit card or credit number along with the personal identification number (PIN) to make unauthorized purchases from the victim's account.

The **Credit card cloning**, or **Skimming** where someone obtains card holder's credit card details and copies these details to a bogus card and uses them for purchasing.

44. Define hacking.

Ans. Hacking is an act or series of activities that exploit vulnerabilities in a device or a device in a private network. In a simpler term, it is unauthorized access or control over devices or network security systems for the illicit (illegal and unlawful) purposes

45. Mention the various sources of Malware

Ans. The sources of malware are:

- **Malicious download:** Malicious or unintended download of software from the internet
- **Unsolicited emails:** The embedded links and attachments in emails.
- **Media:** Removable (USB drives) or integrated media such as HDD.
- **Self-propagatio**n: Malware can move from network to network or devices to devices on its own, thus spreading in a self-propagating way.

46. Mention the steps to curb phishing attacks.

Ans. Steps to curb phishing attacks are:

- Do not open, or click on suspicious email attachments or links.
- Install a firewall, antivirus, anti-malware, and security tools.
- Do not reveal the personal information identity, such as PIN, OTP, credit card number, PAN number, and more.
- Ensure that sites are legitimate and contain 'HTTPS' in URL.

47. How to secure a system from cyber criminals?

Ans. The following steps can safeguard our system from cyber criminals:

- Use a firewall
- Use a strong password
- Keep the OS and software updated
- Manage social media settings

48. How do people unknowingly commit a cybercrime?

Ans. The following can lead to committing cybercrime unknowingly:

- Adult chats with minors or without consent in public/private platforms with majors.
- Cyber-bullying and cyber-stalking causing mental harassment are classified as a crime.
- Intrusion or hack into a computer or private network without permission.

49. Suggest few steps that can help to prevent identity thefts.

Ans. Steps to prevent identity thefts are:

- Use a strong and unique password.
- Do not post confidential information online.
- Ensure appropriate privacy setting for social media.
- Use trusted web sites.
- Install anti-virus, malware, and spyware tools.
- Install patches on OS and keep browsers updated.
- Download mobile applications only from trusted sites.

50. What measures should one take to curb online frauds?

Ans. The following measures should be taken to curb online frauds:

- URLs should contain HTTPS, shown in the address bar of the browser to make sure your data is encrypted.
- ICT training should be imparted to the users.
- Install a firewall and set up privacy settings.
- Use the latest version of the browser settings for browsers.

- Do not click on suspicious links.
- Do not respond to suspicious emails.

51. Mention the steps that can prevent cybercrime.

Ans. The following steps can prevent cybercrime:

- Beware of unsolicited text messages or voice messages. Avoid these messages or reply cautiously.
- Download from trustworthy sources only.
- Always use trusted payment services and legitimate sites for online payments and online shopping.
- Ignore or report if someone asks for personal information or requests OTP, CVV, password, or pin through a call or an email.
- Do not click on suspicious links and attachments.
- Check feedback and ratings to assess web sites.

52. Who is a hacker?

Ans. A hacker is an expert with the abilities to gain unauthorized access to systems or networks to find vulnerabilities or may exploit them for gains.

53. Who is an Ethical Hacker?

Ans. Ethical Hacker finds vulnerabilities or weaknesses in devices and/or computer networks and may suggest the counter measures to protect the weaknesses. An ethical hacker performs its tasks with consent of an individual or organization.

An Ethical hacker must abide by the following rules:

- The hacker should obtain written permission from the owner before hacking.
- The hacker should protect the privacy of the organization being hacked.
- The hacker should report issues transparently for all the identified issues to the organization.

54. Name the different types of intellectual property.

Ans. Intellectual property are:

- Trade Secrets
- Trademarks
- Patents
- Copyrights

55. Define Intellectual property

Ans. Intellectual property (IP) is a product of a human intellect that includes creative concepts, inventions, trademarks, industrial models, literature, songs, music, symbols (logo), brand, names, and art works used in trade and commerce

56. Define Trade secrets?

Ans. A trade secret is a type of IP; it can be in the form of design, pattern, instrument, the formula, commercial way/method that can be used to obtain business or economic advantage over competitors and confidential information.

57. Define Trademark.

Ans. A trademark is a legally registered name or symbol of an enterprise, which is created to identify the products or services of a particular enterprise from others.

58. Define the term Patent.

Ans. A patent provides ownership of an invention to its inventor and prohibits others from imitating (copying) or selling the invention. A patent is granted for a specific time.

59. Define Copyright.

Ans. A copyright is an exclusive and assignable legal right for publishing and printing artistic material and recording literary, artistic, or musical stuff. A copyright is granted to the creator for a fixed number of years.

60. Differentiate between patent and copyright.

Ans.

Patent	Copyright
A patent is referred to an innovation or an invention.	Copyright refers to the expression of an idea, literary or an art work.
A patent is a right granted by a government or its body.	Copyright occurs automatically or it may be registered.

61. Explain how digital piracy leads to illegal downloads?

Ans. Digital Piracy is using someone else's piece of work, such as songs, movies, music, games, documents, proprietary software, for free or distribute it for free or on a subsided fees without permission. It is how piracy leads to illegal downloads.

62. What do you mean by Intellectual property rights (IPR)?

Ans. **Intellectual property rights (IPR)** are the exclusive right of the creator (owner) over the use of any art form for certain duration by granting those patents, copyrights, and trademarks. Intellectual property rights include patents, copyright, industrial design rights, trademarks, plant variety rights, geographical indications, and in some jurisdictions trade secrets.

63. Why are Intellectual property rights (IPR) important?

Ans. **Intellectual property rights (IPR)** allow its owners to use their rights to retrieve the full benefits of their inventions and spending on R&D.

The protection provided by the IP encourages innovation without defending these innovations individuals and businesses would not be enjoying it to the fullest and it will discourage them to invest time and money on the innovations.

64. Why are Intellectual property rights (IPR) significant?

Ans. The strong **Intellectual property rights (IPR)** help to educate consumers about the reliability, effectiveness, and safety of their purchases. Enforcing **Intellectual property rights (IPR)** ensures that products are of high-quality and authentic. This is helpful for consumers to recognize the brand.

65. How does one protect its Intellectual property rights (IPR)?

Ans. Different ways to protect intellectual property rights are:

- ➢ Register the patents, copyrights, and trademarks
- ➢ Register domain names, business, and product
- ➢ For a business ask employees to sign a confidentiality, non-disclosure, or licensing contract(s) with employers and partners
- ➢ Implement a firewall, set the browser security, implement access point security and other security features

66. What are Intellectual property rights (IPR) for an enterprise?

Ans. IPR for a company are exclusive rights to use its ideas, design, or other intangible assets without worrying about competition, for a specific time. These rights include patents, trademarks, copyrights, and trade secrets.

67. What is IPR in law?

Ans. The role of the IPR in law is to protect the exclusive rights for owners of inventions, designs, and artistic works. An IP law enforces legal rights and protects the exclusive control of intangible assets.

68. Differentiate between intellectual property and copyright.

Ans. Intellectual property is protected by laws specific to the expression of an idea.

Copyright is the law specific to the expression of ideas in visual or audio form. Unlike a trademark that indicates a specific item or design is protected, copyright covers a different expression of thought.

69. What cannot be protected by copyright?

Ans. List of items that cannot be copyrighted are:

- Titles, names, slogans and short phrases
- Font design, familiar symbols or designs
- Ingredients or contents,
- Blank forms, facts, etc.

70. Why do we need to protect IPR?

Ans. The protection of Intellectual Property Rights (IPR) is important for the economy and its further growth in areas such as research, innovation, and employment. Effective IPR enforcement is also essential to health and safety. For these reasons, IP rights are worth protecting, both domestically and internationally.

71. What counts as copyright infringement?

Ans. Under the law, infringement of copyright is:

- Copy the copyrighted work
- Lending, renting or issuing copies of the work for money / without money to the public
- Performing some other's art work in public
- Adapting the other's copyrighted work by a third party who is not the owner of the copyright or does not have permission to use it

72. Is it necessary to register a work to claim copyright?

Ans. Copyright comes into existence as soon as a work is created, published and performed and no formality (paperwork) is required to be completed for acquiring copyright. If a certificate of registration of copyright is obtained it can be produced in case of a dispute, which is served as prima facie (clear cut) evidence of the ownership of a copyright in a court of law regarding the dispute.

73. Which steps are taken to secure IPR and rights?

Ans. Steps to protect the **Intellectual Property Rights (IPR)**:

- Apply for a Trademark
- Register the Patent, Trade Secrets, and Creative works
- Protect Business Ideas and Trade Secrets as a secret
- Ask employees and partners to sign a non-disclosure agreement
- Ensure the cyber security measures are implemented in a device or network

74. Mention the indicators that might indicate if a computer has been infected.

Ans. The list of indicators that a computer has been infected are:

- The computer runs slower than normal
- The computer does not respond often
- The device frequently restarts
- Your computer restarts on its own and then fails to run normally
- The unusual error messages

75. Mention the steps that protects a computer lab in a school from threats?

Ans. Steps to protect the school's lab from threats are:

- Keep software and Operating System (OS) security patches up to date
- Configure security settings for:
  - Operating system
  - Internet browser
  - Security software
- Schools should develop security policies and policy for online behavior
- Students should adopt them and promote online safety

76. Explain what is HTML?

Ans. **HTML** (HyperText Markup **Language**) is a markup **language**, it is used to construct the web page. Web pages can be viewed in a web browser. A web page includes text, links, images, and audio and video. **HTML** is used to mark and describe the content browser can display them correctly.

77. What is the use of HTML?

Ans. HTML stands for HyperText Markup Language. It was developed by 'Tim Berners-Lee' in 1990. It is used to create web pages for the World Wide Web. A web page contains the connections (links) to other pages called hyperlinks. Html is used to create portals, blogs, e-commerce websites, and many more.

78. How webpage is structured?

Ans. HTML is a markup language It uses simple tags to markup and format it's content. These tags are enclosed in angular brackets, for example <html>. Below is the simple structure of the HTML. There are several other tags in the HTML. Here we are discussing bare minimum required tags to define a web page

```
<!DOCTYPE html>

<html>
    <head>
        <title> </title>
    </head>

    <body>

    </body>
</html>
```

<!DOCTYPE html>: This tag is used to tell the HTML version. This currently telling that the version is HTML 5.

<html>: This is the root element, it enclosed the entire web page.

<head>: This tag contains metadata, meta tag title, script, etc. Below is the list of the tags used in a head section

- <style>
- <title>
- <noscript>
- <script>
- <meta>

<body>: This tag is used to enclose the elements and content (text, images, video and many more) of the webpage enclosed in the tags. These tags can be nested.

79. Explain how to create a web page and view it?

Ans. Here is the sample HTML file

```
<html>
    <head>
        <title >Html page</title>
    </head>

    <body>
```

```
        <h1>Html</h1>
        <a href="http://google.com">Link to google</a>

    </body>
</html>
```

Save this code into file with . html or .htm extension this can be viewed in a browser.

The web page looks like this.

Html page × +

← → C file:///F:/webpagesl/sample.html

Html

Link to google

80. Mention the advantages of HTML?

Ans. Here is a list of the Advantages of HTML

- HTML is free
- It is easy to learn and use.
- HTML is easy to understand and change the code
- HTML is supported by all browsers
- HTML is Lightweight
- Changes are displayed immediately

81. What is HTTP?

Ans. HTTP is a client-server protocol. It is used to transfer the HTML (web pages) over the WWW(World Wide Web). An HTTP client browser sends a request to an HTTP /web server. The server creates a document that includes text, images, videos, scripts, and more, returns a document as a response. The entire cycle is shown in the below figure

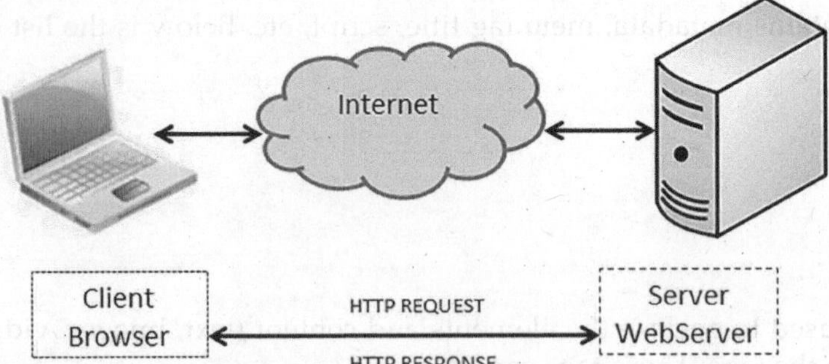

82. Explain how HTTP Protocol works?

Ans. When a user enters a URL in the address bar of a browser, the browser translates the URL into a request and sends the request to the server.HTTP is a pull protocol, that means the client pulls information from the server (instead of server pushes resources to the clients.)

Once the request message reaches the server, it can take one of the following actions:

- The server receives a request maps the request to the path returns the file requested by the client.
- The server receives a request the server-side scripts run and perform the business logic, database access and, build the response and return it to the client.
- If the server cannot satisfy the request, it returns an error message.

83. Explain what is Client-Server Model?

Ans. A client-server model splits the program into two layers: front-end (a client) and back-end (a server). This model allows accessing resources such as files, videos, images, or some other services from a central computer called a server. The client requests the resources and the server responds to its clients by providing resources.

84. Explain what is a Server?

Ans. Server is a computer or device that can be accessed remotely and it stores resources. It serves resources to its clients. **Servers** are dedicated most of the time, which means it does not perform other tasks than serving the clients.

85. Explain Web server in simple words?

Ans. A **Web server** is a software that serves its clients using HTTP (Hypertext Transfer Protocol) on the World Wide Web (WWW). **Web server** software manages the accesses of the hosted files. The computer(s) that host Web sites must have **Web server** software.

86. Explain what is a client in the client-server model?

Ans. A client is a program or a hardware device that requests a resource from the server and the server sends the resources as a response.

87. Explain the key components of the web server?

Ans. Below is the list of key components of a web server

- File storage(s) files (images, HTML pages, scripts, CSS)
- An HTTP server,
- Hardware resources like CPU, RAM, etc.
- Other software, all of them working together to serve their clients.

88. What is the role of a web server?

Ans. A web server is a computer program that can process the HTTP request and return the HTTP response. It is connected through the Internet and supports data interchange with other devices connected to the world wide web.

89. Explain what is HTTP Server?

Ans. A HTTP server processes the client requests via HTTP, The key functions of an HTTP server is to store the web resources, process the request, and send the web pages to clients. Pages delivered are HTML documents, including images, style sheets, scripts, and text content.

90. What is a web browser?

Ans. A **web browser** (Chrome, IE, Mozilla Firefox, Safari are examples of a browser) is application software used to access and view websites. The Browser sends a request to the server. It also interprets the response from the server and renders (display) the content.

91. Differniate between web browser and web server?

Ans. The ***browser*** is used to view and explore web pages on the internet, whereas ***webserver*** is a (computing devices) stores the web content. The web server serves the request sent by the browser.

92. List, the most popular Web browsers?

Ans. Here is a list of the most commonly used browsers are

- Internet Explorer.
- Google Chrome.
- Mozilla Firefox.
- Safari.
- Opera.

93. Why do we need Web browsers?

Ans. A web browser is used for surfing the internet online buying, learning, entertainment and much more.

A non-technical person cannot access websites and the internet without a browser. The browser renders the HTML and display the content of a web page.

94. How to access a website or a web page?

Ans. The web resources are hosted to the webserver. It is a computer with fixed (static) IP address, the browser sends a request(s) via HTTP. Once the request is reached to the web server (or *HTTP server)* it accepts the request. Finds the requested resources (documents) and sends back the response to the browser, also through HTTP. Once a browser receives the request, it interprets and displays the content.

95. What do we mean by hosting?

Ans. Web hosting is transferring a website or web pages on the server using internet by organizations and individuals using FTP or by uploading files. Once a website is hosted it can be accessed through the internet.

96. Differentiate between domain and hosting?

Ans. Web Hosting is buying a space usually called a server or cloud to store files and serve the request through the Internet. Domain Registration is where an individual or organization buys or leases a name in a human-readable form It is known as a **domain** name. Each domain has a corresponding unique IP address on the Internet to access it.

97. What are the types of web hosting?

Ans. Here are the list of commonly used types of web hosting

- Shared hosting.
- Virtual private server (VPS) hosting
- Dedicated server hosting.
- Cloud hosting.

98. Explain what is a shared hosting?

Ans. Sharing hosting is where websites are stored on the same server with other websites. In the shared hosting, all domains share the same resources of the server, such as CPU (Central Processing Unit) and RAM (Random Access Memory). The cost of shared hosting is low because all the resources are shared. Shared hosting is suitable for website owners who do not attract large traffic.

99. Explain what is a virtual private server (VPS) hosting?

Ans. A VPS(Virtual Private Server) is a virtualization technology that provides dedicated (private) resources to multiple users. It offers the customization of the storage space. It provides its own space on the server to each website is hosted however, it shares the same physical server. It is a service that allows us to provide dedicated space without technical skills.

100. What is dedicated server hosting?

Ans. Dedicated hosting where the owner completely owns the server space. The server is exclusively rented by the owner. It means the owner has the full root and admin access. It can be controlled by its owner completely, however the price is higher compare to shared hosting.

101. Explain what is Cloud hosting?

Ans. The Cloud hosting enable access of resources through the network and enables the user to consume the resource like a service. The advantage of cloud-based hosting is scalable this means it can extend the resources as and when required and website owner only pays for what they have used.

102. Explain what is a domain name?

Ans. A domain name is the name of the website name. Technically a domain name is an IP address, this allows users to access the website over the internet. It is difficult for us to remember the IP address, that is defined as *xxx.xxx.xxx.xxx* to overcome the problem domain names were developed. They are used to identify IP addresses over the internet. It is a combination of the letters and numbers or combination of both with their extension .com, .net, and more. The domain has a unique name that must be registered before using it. Every domain name is unique

103. Why domain name is required?

Ans. The domain name is a unique identity of an individual or organization. Another reason to have a domain name is to help businesses to register as a name. It protects and trademarks, copyrights, builds credibility, search engine positioning, increase brand awareness and online presence.

104. Classifies the different types of domains?

Ans. The domains can be classified into the four sub-categories these are mentioned below:s

- **Generic**: These are for general purposes ends with .net, .org, .com, .info
- **Generic restricted:** These domains are for specific purposes end with (.biz, .name, .pro)
- **Sponsored:** These domains are used by businesses involved with the specific industry ends with .gov, .int, .edu,.mil, .asia, .mobi, travel, .tel, .jobs
- **Infrastructure:** These domains are used for DNS infrastructure ends with (.arpa).

105. Why WHOIS service is used?

Ans. Whois is an Internet database of domains and their associated server. The WHOIS search is to find out the following

- When the domain was registered?
- Who has registered the domain?.
- Contact information, when the domain will expire, and more.

106. Explain what is an URL?

Ans. **URL** stands for *Uniform Resource Locator*. It is the address of web resources to uniquely identify it on WWW (world wide web). It is also known as the web address of a resource. URLs consist of multiple parts – including a domain name, protocol, resource's name, including path. It tells a web browser where the resources are located.

107. Mention the few examples of URL

Ans. Here are the few examples of URL

- http://www.test123.com/docs/index.html,
- ftp://www.ftptest123.org/docs/test.txt
- mailto:user@test123.com
- telnet://www.test123.com/

108. Explain how is an URL structured?

Ans. A URL has multiple parts these are

- **Protocol:** The first part of a URL identifies what protocol is used
- **Domain name:** The second part identifies the IP address or domain name
- **Port:** This is number uniquely identifies the application
- **File-path:** this part is a path (absolute or relative) where the resource is located.

Below are the example of the URLs

http://www.test123.com:8080/docs/index.html

Protocol domain port file

File-path

ftp://www.ftptest123.org/docs/test.txt

Protocol domain file

109. List the protocol used in an URL?

Ans. URL includes the following protocols

- HTTP (Hypertext Transfer Protocol)
- HTTPS (HTTP Secure)

- FTP for transferring the files on a File Transfer Protocol (FTP) server,
- Telnet (To access remote computers).
- Mailto

110. What is XML?

XML stands for e**X**tensible **M**arkup **L**anguage. It is designed to store data in self-descriptive way and transport data. It is a markup language and it is used to create the own data type. XML data are self-defining or self-describing. The structure is embedded within the data itself. In data transmission for example B2B (Business to Business XML is sent, at the receiving end no pre-build structure is required for storing the data; it is dynamically understood within the XML. Below is a sample xml.

```
<?xml version="1.0"?>
<catalog>
    <book id="000001">
        <author>Ashish, Bhargava</author>
        <title>Python Companion class XI</title>
        <genre>Computer</genre>
        <price>350</price>
        <publish_date>2014-08-16</publish_date>
        <description>Python Book for class XI</description>
    </book>
    <book id="000002">
        <author>Ashish, Bhargava</author>
        <title>Python Companion class XII</title>
        <genre>Computer</genre>
        <price>450</price>
        <publish_date>2014-08-16</publish_date>
        <description>Python Book for class XI</description>
    </book>
</catalog>
```

The above xml define a catalog of books. It contains the two books. Each book has multiple fields these are, author, title, genre, publish date and description

Each element is defined within start tag and end tag for example <author></author>

111. Mention the advantages of XML

Ans. XML offers many advantages as listed below

- XML is written in plain text, hence it is *platform* independent (it can be created and consumed by a different platform such as windows, Linux, Mac etc.)
- XML is language-independent, it can be created, parsed read by any other language, for example, Java, C#, Python, and many more.
- XML supports Unicode. This allows XML to transmit data written in any human language.
- It is easy to edit the data using XML.
- The data in XML files can be changed at any point of time without affecting the data presentation.
- There are DTD (Document type definition) and Schema is used for validating the XML. This ensures the XML document is free from the syntax error.

112. Disadvantages of XML

Ans. Here is a list of disadvantages of XML

- XML syntax is verbose and redundant compared to JSON (JSON keep data as key-value pair). This causes high storage and transportation costs when the volume of data is large.
- It does not support arrays.
- The XML document is less readable, such as JSON.

113. Mention where XML is used?

Ans.
- It is widely used in B2B (Business to Business) for exchanging the data.
- It is used by the various programs and devices to, transmit, store, and display data.
- **XML** is a standard for Office file formats that include Google Docs and Microsoft Office and files.

114. Mention the similarities between HTML and XML?

Ans.
- HTML and XML both are markup languages.
- HTML and XML are derived from SGML (Standard Generalized Markup Language).
- HTML and XML use tags to define the content which is consumed by other applications.

115. Define what is a website?

Ans. It is a page or collection of pages (all the resources are like HTML, CSS cascading style sheet, script files, images) on the server and accessed through the World Wide Web. It is used for displaying information, display articles, news, buying online products, perform online banking, watching sports, and many more. A website can be accessed using a Uniform Resource Locator (URL). The browser access a website through an URL.

116. Explain what is Static and Dynamic Website?

Ans. There are two types of websites based on their behavior
- Static
- Dynamic

A static site is a plain HTML and the code of the page is displayed to the user. This type of website is usually not updated or frequency is very less.

A dynamic site uses server-side scripting language such as PHP, ASP, JSP, etc. to create its content In dynamic sites the content is created by the server-side scripting language, it can call a database or take other actions taken to build the response.

117. Mention the advantages of the Static sites

Ans. Here is a list of the advantages of the static site
- It is suitable for small businesses.
- A lot of themes and template available to design these types of sites
- These sites can be designed with different layouts for the different types of businesses. These sites allow various themes
- These websites are created in day to one week. Static sites are can build faster compare to dynamic websites

118. Mention the disadvantages of Static sites

Ans. Here is a list of the advantages of the static site
- The main problem is scalability. The static sites are not suitable to add the content frequently
- Changes in the layout may not be easy also adding or deleting some part may not be easy
- To create the additional pages can take considerable time, effort, and cost.

119. Mention the advantages of dynamic sites

Ans. Here is a list of the advantages of the static site
- **Easy to add new content**

  The main advantages of dynamic sites that they are scalable and it is easy to add or remove products without changing the layout.

  The server-side script is used to connect to the database this will help to build a content management system – The admin interface allows the client to manage data via web-based administered pages. With the help of CMS (database of content,) dynamic website can be easily updated
- **Make the site design with less effort**

  Most dynamic sites use pre-defined platforms like Wordpress and themes. Selecting a new theme for an instant makeover without much effort

- **Sites can be more interactive**

  Providing an innovative and interactive experience to visitors helps to retain the customer. A dynamic site can enhance the personalized user experience. Shows them recently viewed items and pages or suggests the personalized product.

120. Mention the disadvantages of dynamic sites

Ans. Here is a list of the advantages of the static site

- The costs are higher than a static site.
- It requires to have more design and technical skill to build it
- Initially, it consumes more time to develop
- The dynamic site may be little, slow, however a good design can improve the performance

121. Explain what is web services?

Ans. A web service is a set of standards and protocols that are used for exchanging the data between applications. It includes software, application, or cloud technology that can be accessed through the HTTP or HTTPS (web protocols) to, communicate, inter-operate and data exchange messages over the internet.

122. Mention the different types of Web Services?

Ans. There are two types of web services: SOAP, and RESTful web services that are used:

SOAP It stands for Simple Object Access Protocol, It is an XML-based Web service protocol that is used to exchange messages, documents, and data over HTTP (HyperText Transport Protocol) or SMTP (Simple Mail Transfer Protocol). It allows exchange messages on dissimilar systems using the XML.

The restful web service is based on **RE**presentational **S**tate **T**ransfer (REST), and it provides connectivity and communication between devices over the internet for API-based tasks. The RESTful services use HTTP protocol for exchanging messages

123. Explain the SOAP Web Services

Ans. This web service uses Web Services Description Language (WSDL) This describes how SOAP requests generated by client–side and responses (generated at server-side) are created. It uses XML over HTTP and SMTP for transmission

124. Mention the pros and cons of the SOAP

Ans. Pros: It is easy to consume, uses standards like (WSDL, etc.), distributed computing.

Cons: It is difficult to set-up, more complex coding is required to develop

125. Mention the RESTful Web Services

Ans. It is a client-server model which is a transfer of representations of resources through requests and responses. Here each object has each unique URL represents It uses HTTP and its HTTP methods like GET, POST, PUT or DELETE.

126. Mention the Pros and cons of the restful web services?

Ans. Pros: It is a lightweight, human-readable and easy to build.

Cons: It is a point-to-point communication protocol and it's lack of standards.

127. Why are Web services used?

Ans. Web services are created that enable accessing the functionality of the service over the network (internet). Once these services are available over the network. The other applications can consume the functionality of the program. **Web services** allow different technologies to communicate with each other and share services and data among themselves.

128. Differentiate between an API and a Web service?

Ans. The Web service is a framework or facilitates interaction between two applications over a network. An API is an interface (set of rules) between these applications that enable them to communicate with each other. The Web service REST, SOAP as a means of communication.

129. Explain what is web scripting?

Ans. HTML is used for creating the web pages. HTML is static, consists of text and images. The websites that are designed for creating interactive content for better user experiences. Web Scripting adds the dynamic content to web pages using scripting. A script is used for event handling, form validations, changes the behavior of the web pages, add and delete elements from the webpage, etc. **Web scripting** uses small functions or programs allows users to interact with a web page.

Web scripts are placed at the client-side and the server-side. Javascript and VBscript are used on the client-side and ASP, JSP, PHP is used at the server-side.

130. Mention the scripting language for websites?

Ans. The web script can classify into

1) Server-side scripting

2) Client-side script

Examples of the Server-side scripting s are: *JSP, ASP, PHP*

Examples of the client-side scripting are *JavaScript, AJAX, jQuery,* etc.

131. Explain what is client-side scripting?

Ans. **Client-side scripting**, like VBScript, JavaScript, are embedded into the web page it is executed in the client's browser instead of the web-server, this enables the user to interact with web applications.

132. How to embed the client-side script in HTML?

Ans. The script tag is used to define the script. The script tag mostly defined inside the head tag. A JavaScript program may be embedded in a Web page with the HTML tag as shown below

```
<script language="JavaScript"> Or <script language="VBScript">
```

To display the dynamic (interactive) pages, JavaScript is combined with XML for exchanging information between server and client. The XMLHttpRequest enables asynchronous data requests This approach, is called Ajax (asynchronous JavaScript and XML).

133. What is server-side scripting?

Ans. **Server-side scripting** in web development are script that are executed on a webserver to build a customized response. The server-side scripts enable web pages to connect with a database(s), other servers run some business logic. Scripts can be developed by **server-side scripting** languages like PHP, JSP, ASP, etc. The server-side script is used to dynamically create pages on the fly. New pages can be created instantly, based on user interaction. If a browser does not support the client-side scripts than server-side is a must.

134. Explain what is ASP?

Ans. ASP stands for Active Server Page. It allows C# code in the HTML. It enables a web page to add dynamic and interactive web pages. ASP uses server-side scripting to dynamically produce web pages that are not affected by the type of browser the visitor is using. The ASP pages are saved with .asp extension

135. Explain what is PHP?

Ans. PHP stands for Hypertext Pre-processor. PHP is an open-source server-side scripting language and HTML can embed PHP scripting to create dynamic web pages. A PHP is saved as .php extension.

136. What is JSP?

Ans. It stands for Java Server Pages. It is a server-side script and use to create dynamic web content by inserting JAVA code into HTML pages. It is a collection of various technologies that create dynamic web pages based on HTML, XML, SOAP, or other document types.

137. What is JavaScript and why it is used?

Ans. **JavaScript** is a programming language. It can be used on the client-side and server-side. It can handle events that allows to make web pages interactive, this helps to improve the user experience. To recap, **JavaScript** adds behavior to web pages

138. Explain VBScript

Ans. VBScript is **used to** make webpage interactive it is used at client-side., if the VBS file is used for client-side scripting, IE (Internet Explorer) can interpret it. **VBScript** is a Microsoft technology that requires Microsoft's IE/ Edge

139. Explain what is web2.0?

Ans. The web2.0 is where websites and applications are created that allows people to create, collaborate, share, & communicate. Web2.0 differs from other previously created websites as it does not require knowledge of web designing, and publishing skills. The aim is to make publishing easy and simple for the people to reach them quickly to their audiences.

The example of web2.0 applications include wikis, blogs, social networking, micro-blogging sites, podcasting & content hosting services.

140. How is Web 2.0 and social media are related?

Ans. A Web 2.0 website allows users to collaborate and interact with each other. This can be achieved through social media, blogging, and micro-blogging sites. These types of websites enabling to create the virtual communities that may help people to use these websites interactively. Most of the websites in Web 1.0-era were limited to view the content passively.

141. Mention the most popular websites for web2.0?

Ans. YouTube, Facebook, Wikipedia, MySpace, Twitter, Flickr, are the most popular websites

142. Mention the advantage offered by web2.0 technologies to the users?

Ans. The web2.0 technologies make it easy to communicate it helps to spread the information larger audience or selected group of users.

143. Explain the social impact the web2.0

Ans. The Web2.0 applications such as blogging, and social networking, micro-blogging sites can help disseminate information over the internet quickly compare to traditional methods (e.g., pamphlets, static websites, postal letters, etc.) of information delivery. This helps a lot of people do networking, they can raise their voices, participating in discussions, and build communities.

144. Explain what is e-commerce application?

Ans. It is also known as internet **commerce or usually e**lectronic **commerce**. It is selling and buying of goods using the internet, and transfer the cost of the good(s) to execute these transactions.

145. What are the various ways to make payment using e-commerce?

Ans.
- ➢ Credit / Debit cards
- ➢ Smart card
- ➢ E-Wallet
- ➢ Net Banking
- ➢ Mobile Apps

146. How to use a debit or credit card making a payment when buying a product from an e-commerce site?

Ans. Credit Cards or Debit Cards are the most popular methods used to make the payment on e-commerce sites. Once the user selects the goods for buying at the billing user opt for credit card or debit cards the customer has to provide the credit card number or debit card number and date of expiry. The User also needs to provide the CVV for security.

147. Explain what smart card is and how they work?

Ans. These cards are preloaded money with stores the user's details. When the transaction is made, the transaction amount is detected from the user's bank account.

148. What is an e-wallet and how making payment through an E-wallet?

Ans. It is a prepaid account that stores multiple bank account numbers, credit cards, and debit card details in a secure environment. This eliminates the need of entering details every time user makes payments.

The advantage of e-wallet is once the customer has registered and created an E-Wallet profile allows the users to make payments faster.

149. What is net banking how payments are made using it?

Ans. It is a method for paying directly from the customer's bank account. Once the user is registered with the bank for the net banking facility he can use it. Once goods are purchased and the net-banking option is selected the customer is redirected to the banking site and the user provides its credentials. Once the transaction is completed the user will be redirected back to the e-commerce site. The net-banking does not require any card for the transaction.

150. Explain What is RTGS in simple words?

Ans. It is an electronic way of transferring the funds. It transaction takes place on a real-time basis. The **RTGS** is used for high-value transactions, the minimum for transfer the amount is Rs 2 lakh. The beneficiary account receives funds, on a real-time basis.

151. Explain what is RTGS and how it works?

Ans. RTGS stands for Real-time gross settlement. It is settling payments on an individual basis. Once payments are made through RTGS it is final and irrevocable.

152. Explain what is RTGS and its advantages?

Ans. Here are the few advantages of using **RTGS**:

- The funds are transferred in real-time.
- The transfer is online. RTGS is primarily used for high-value transactions.
- It is a highly reliable way to transmit since they are managed by the RBI

153. What is NEFT and how it works?

Ans. NEFT stands for National Electronic Funds Transfer. It is an electronic fund transfer system. It is maintained by the RBI (Reserve Bank of India). **NEFT** allows transferring of the funds to the bank's customers in India between to another **NEFT**-enabled bank account on a one-to-one basis. It is accomplished by an electronic message.

154. Who is eligible to transfer the funds using NEFT?

Ans. Here is the list of who can transfer the funds using NEFT

- Individuals
- Firms or corporate offices
- Walk-in customer (The individual without an account)

155. Compare RTGS and NEFT?

Ans. RTGS sends the money in a one-to-one fashion, whereas the NEFT uses DNS Deferred Net Settlement) where all the orders are executed in batches after a time interval.RTGS is faster than NEFT and happens in real-time.

156. Define IMPS?

Ans. IMPS stands for Immediate Payment Service. It is an instant payment inter-bank electronic funds transfer system. **IMPS** services can be used using a mobile phone, bank's website sites, an inter-bank electronic fund transfer service through mobile phones.

157. Mention the reasons to use IMPS?

Ans. IMPS can be used for the following reasons

- IMPS is safe and secure
- It is cost-effective.
- It allows transferring small amounts as there is no minimum amount limit for transactions
- It is available for 24 hours, including bank holidays.
- It allows intrabank and interbank payments

158. What Is Mobile Banking?

Ans. Mobile banking is where the financial transactions are carried through a mobile device (cell phone, tablet, etc.). Mobile banking is used for paying bills or transfer the money. It enables users to bank anywhere and at any time.

159. Differentiate between mobile banking and internet banking

Ans. The mobile banking is accessed through an application on the smartphone, It requires to download the mobile banking app (an application) from a bank. Whereas internet banking is accessed through a browser, typically on a computer.

160. What are mobile payment services?

Ans. Mobile payment is also known as **mobile** money, **mobile** money transfer, and **mobile** wallet are different payment service operated under financial regulation and perform through a **mobile** device. Mobile payment services are replacing cash, bank cheque, or physical credit card payments.

161. Explain what is digital wallet?

Ans. Digital wallet that electronically stores debit, credit card, loyalty card numbers, etc. on the server or cloud. The customer's money stays in its bank or credit card account. Digital wallets keep the user's details that make the transactions easier. Examples of digital-wallets are Masterpass Google Pay, Visa Checkout. Digital wallets allow user to go cashless or card less.

162. Explain what is mobile wallet?

Ans. A mobile wallet is installed on a smartphone as an application that allows you to TAP TO PAY at physical stores, often using NFC (Near Field Communication) technology. The payment is made through a QR code with a smartphone or a device such as a smart watch or a fitness tracker.

163. Explain the Unified Payments Interface

Ans. UPI stands for Unified Payments Interface. It is a real-time payment system that transfers the funds instantly. It enables the transfer of funds through the mobile. The UPI allows multiple bank accounts into a single mobile application.

164. Explain what is a Payment App?

Ans. A payment application or an e-Wallet (mobile wallet) is a payment service. It is operated as per financial regulation using a mobile device. The Payments Apps where the mobile wallet is used for the payment of a transaction using a device.

165. Explain how Payment Applications (Apps) work?

Ans. A Payment App can conduct any transaction from a linked bank account or money can be deposited before conducting the financial transaction

These apps have two components, these are software and information (Individual's details). These apps are secure as they provide encrypt the personal information and financial transaction that has been made.

166. Mention the different types of Payment Applications?

Ans. Here is a list of different types of payment application

- Digital wallets
- e-wallets
- Mobile Wallets
- UPI

167. Explain what is E-Wallets

Ans. These are prepaid wallets. The money is loaded before any financial transaction. It can either be accessed through e-wallet's application or applications using smartphones, tablets, or laptops The key functions of e-wallet are:

- E-money(Storing funds)
- Storing debit or credit card details

- Loyalty credits or coupons
- Payment at physical or online store
- Peer-to-peer transfer,

168. Mention the few Mobile Apps used for making payments?

Ans. Here is the list of the payment application

- Paytm
- Google Pay
- Amazon Pay
- JIO Money
- Freecharge
- Yono SBI
- Airtel Money
- PhonePe
- Axis Bank Lime Pay
- ICICI Pockets Citrus and so on

Long Questions and Answers 3/4 Marks

1. Identify the clue that helps to find if an email is a spam?

Mrs. Hope Natalie <ccmv12@buybaysave.com> (1) Tue, Jul 13, 2010 at 10:45 AM

Lotto Results (2)

New Zealand Lotto Promos
Saturday lotto
Draw 1205 -Saturday, july 10, 2010

CONGRATULATION!

We are pleased to announce to you the draw of the NEW ZEALAND ONLINE LOTTERY Program held on Saturday, july 10, 2010.

Your e-mail address attached to ticket number: 564756063211- 884 with Serial number: 6312/08 which emerged the New Zealand Jackpot winning number: 2,10,11,18,22,25,16,5. Supplementary Strike Numbers: 25,2,18,22. please check the website below to confirm your Winning Numbers

http://lotto.nzpages.co.nz/index.html

You won $786,000.00 in Division 1 NZ LOTTO Promotions (3)

For the immediate release of your payment, you are to forward this message details to our payment agent. Including your Full Names, Contact Address, Telephone Numbers, and Country of Resident to

Mr. Charlie Leonard
Payment Agent
Email: hz1lotto@gmail.com

Good luck from me and members of staff of the NEW ZEALAND LOTTO DEPARTMENT (NZ LOTTO PROMOS).

Yours Faithfully,
Mrs. Hope Natalie

- The email is sent from http://lotto.nzpages.co.nz/ however email is sent from another domain buybaysave
- The email is not addressed to the recipient. If the user has bought the ticket from the site, they would know the recipient's name. Again, they don't know the recipient's name
- Asking for full name, contact address, telephone numbers if they know the recipient is a winner they should know all the details.

2. Explain the different types of hackers?

Ans. There are three types of hackers:

a. **White hat hacker:** White hat hackers are known as ethical hackers. They're often employed to work on a contract as security specialists to find the vulnerabilities. White hat hackers plan and implement strategies for vulnerability assessments.

b. **Grey hat hacker:** Grey hat hackers do not hack the system for malicious purposes. They seek out vulnerabilities in a system without the owner's permission or knowledge. However, they report any issues to the owner, at times they might ask for compensation or incentive. Since grey hat hackers do not have permission their actions are considered as illegal, despite some alarming findings they might reveal.

c. **Black hat hacker:** Black hat hackers create malware, which is used to infiltrate devices or networks. Their intent is personal or financial gain. They can also do for a thrill, protest, personal enmity. Once accessing the targets and based on their motives, black hat hackers can either, manipulate, steal, or destroy data.

3. Mention what is covered under IPR?

Ans. IPR includes the following:

- Copyright
- Patents
- Industrial design rights
- Plant variety rights
- Trademarks
- Trade secrets
- Geographical indications

4. Mention the preventive actions from a Malware attack.

Ans. Preventive actions from the malware attack are:

- Open the email or IM attachments from trusted sources
- Scan the email attachments by the internet security program before opening it
- Delete unwanted messages send by unknown sources
- Do not click on links from the unknown source
- Download or transfer files from well-known sources
- Use a firewall
- Keep OS security patches up to date

5. Explain what is HTTP and Request and Response cycle of HTTP.

Ans. Http is an application layer protocol.

It is used to communicate and exchange data for web applications

Its work over TCP /IP protocol

Steps in the HTTP Request and Response cycle

- The TCP creates a connection to the server,
- Converts messages into small packets
- IP protocol sends these packets to the destination
- TCP protocol re-assemble all the packets and forward it to the application layer
- At application layer a server builds a response
- TCP creates a connection to the client and converts messages into packets
- IP protocol sends these packets to the client
- At application layer client display the response.

The same steps can visualize using below diagram

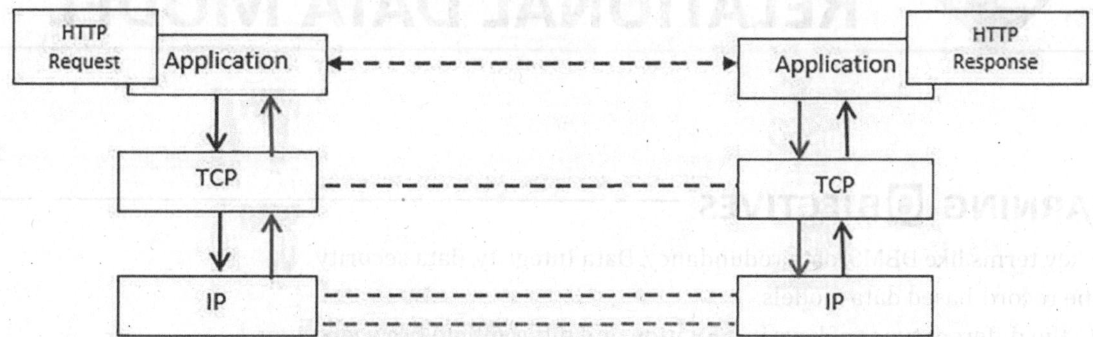

6. Identify the protocol, port, file, from the below URLs

1 ftp://www.ftptest123.org/docs/test.txt

2. mailto:user@test123.com

3. telnet://www.test123.com/

Ans. ftp://www.ftptest123.org/docs/test.txt

Protocol domain file

mailto:user@test123.com

Protocol domain

telnet://www.test123.com/

Protocol domain

7. Differentiate between client-side and server-side scripting

Ans. Here is the list of key differences between client-side and server-side scripting

BASIS FOR COMPARISON	SERVER-SIDE SCRIPTING	CLIENT-SIDE SCRIPTING
Basic	Works are server-side was not visible to the users.	Works at the client site and visible among the users.
Processing	It requires interaction with the database server and other servers.	Works locally executed by a browser
Languages used	PHP, ASP.net, Ruby on Rails, ColdFusion, Python, etc.	JavaScript, Jquery.HTML, CSS etc.
Impact	Provide dynamic websites.	Process the few steps at client- side and reduce the load on the server
Security	Relatively secure	It is not secure

8. Differentiate between HTML and XML

Ans. Here is the list of differences between HTML and XML

HTML	XML
HTML is used to display the content and focuses on how data looks.	XML language and platform-independent that is used for transport and store the data
HTML has pre-defined tags is the standard markup for the web	XML is used for creating own data type
HTML ignores small /minor syntax errors.	XML is strict It does not allow errors.
It is not case sensitive.	It is case sensitive.
Tags in HTML are predefined.	XML tags are user-defined.
It does not preserve white spaces.	White space can be preserved in XML.
HTML, closing tag is not necessary.	In XML, the closing tag is must.

14 RELATIONAL DATA MODEL

LEARNING OBJECTIVES

- Define key terms like DBMS, data redundancy, Data Integrity, data security
- Describe record-based data models
- Identify thę different types of keys in a relation and differentiate between them.
- Identify the Degree, Cardinality in a relation
- Define the advantages offered by DBMS

DEFINITION

- **Data Redudunacy:** The duplication of the data is called data redundancy
- **Relation:** In a relational data model the data are stored in a table and relationships among them are represented by the collection of interrelated tables. Each table is a collection of rows and a row has a column that represents the attributes of an entity. A row represents a record.
- **Tuple:** A tuple in a relation that stores a single record or an entity is called a tuple.
- **Attribute:** In Relation Data Model data is stored data in rows and columns in a table. The columns are known as attributes.
- **Degree:** A degree is the number of attributes in the relation or the table.
- **Cardinality:** It is the number of tuples in a relation or a table.
- **Domain:** An attribute which has a pre-defined set of values is called attribute domain

Very Short Questions and Answers — 1 Mark

1. Define what is a DBMS?

Ans. A database management system stores the interrelated data. It enables users to read, update, create, and delete data in a database. It also provides a set of programs to access the data, define, create, maintain, and control access to the database. Overall DBMS provides a platform that is convenient and efficient to use.

2. Why do we need DBMS?

Ans. A DBMS enhances the accessibility of data, share the data quickly and effectively with the concurrent users. It provides integrity, security, consistency, data accuracy. DBMSs can be accessed through various programming languages and helps work on logic and data is managed by the DBMS.

3. How the DBMS is helpful to reduce data redundancy?

Ans. In the absence of a database management system, data or records are kept in different places. The DBMS does not make separate copies of the same data, hence it reduces the data redundancy.

4. How DBMS ensures data security?

Ans. DBMS provides DCL (Data Control Language) that enables access control. It provides appropriate access rights to the user and ensures that data is secure.

5. Explain what is Data Integrity

Ans. DBMS allows to access the data to multiple users, they can access and update the data using a DBMS.

Here DBMS ensures that data is accurate and consistent with the database. The data consistency means the data remains valid as per defined rules, that includes constraints, triggers, cascade, or their combination.

Short Questions and Answers 2 Marks

1. Explain hierarchical data model

Ans. In this model, data is stored in a tree structure. Each record has a parent, whereas a parent has children (multiple child records).

Let's say data models in DBMS can be classified into Record based and object-based, and these types are further classified into its subtypes hence the relationship becomes one-to-many.

Sample Hierarchical Model Diagram:

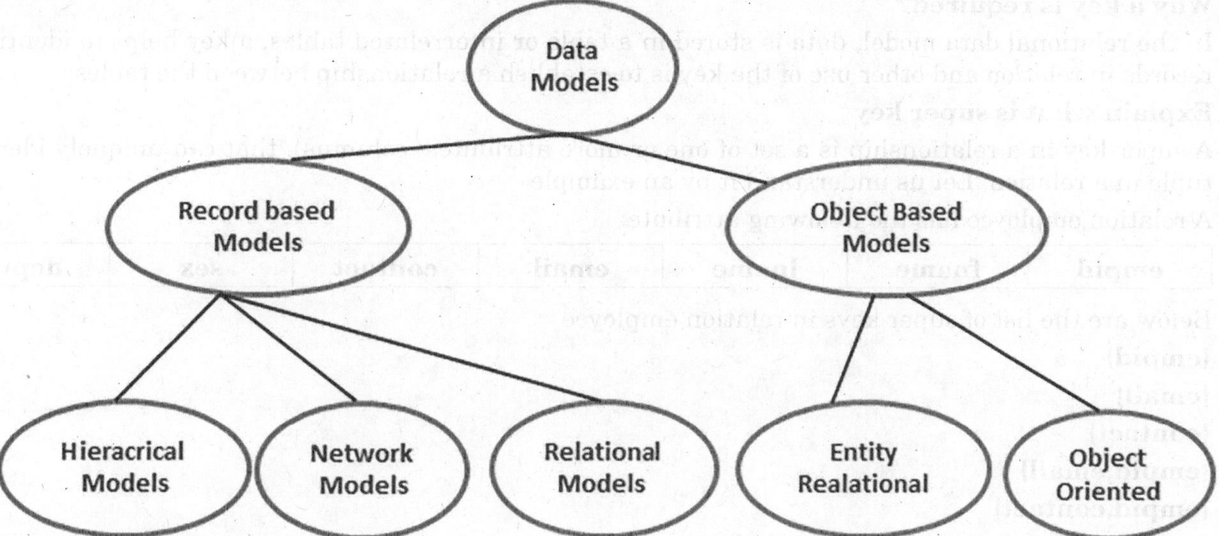

The main drawback of this model is that it can have only one to one relationships between nodes.

2. Explain the network data model

Ans. In this model, data is stored in a graph, and a record has more than one parent node.

This database model is used to map many-to-many data relationships. Multiple parents are possible in many-to-many relationships

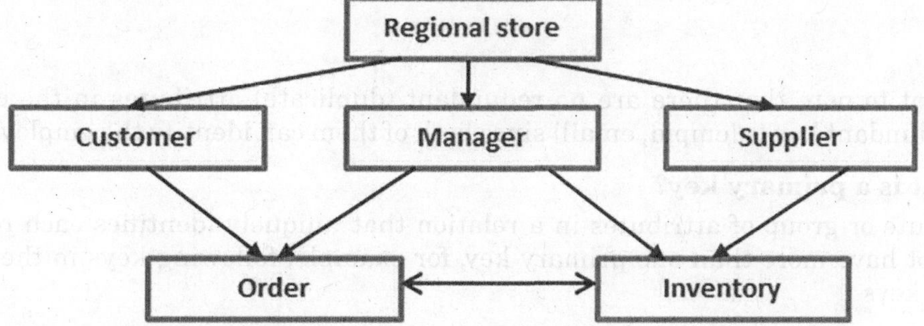

3. Explain Relational data model

Ans. A Relational database model was developed by E. F. Codd. In a Relational database stores data into tables. A table is a collection of records and each record in a table contains the attributes or fields. A relational database enables defining the structure of the data, storage and retrieval operations, and integrity constraints.

4. Define the properties of the Relational data model

Ans.
- Data is presented as a collection of relations.
- Each relation is a table.
- Columns are attributes in a table (for example, attributes of a relation student are name, address, etc.).
- Each row ("tuple") represents a single entity, hence two tuple rows should not be identical.
- The rows are unordered in a relation
- Each column value must be atomic
- All the attribute name should be distinct in a relation
- Each table has a set of attributes that allow identifying the rows uniquely.
- Different tables in the relation database are related through keys

5. Why a key is required?

Ans. In the relational data model, data is stored in a table or interrelated tables, a key helps to identify the records in relation and other use of the key is to establish a relationship between the tables

6. Explain what is super key

Ans. A super key in a relationship is a set of one or more attributes (columns), that can uniquely identify a tuple in a relation. Let us understand it by an example

A relation employee has the following attribute

empid	fname	lname	email	contact	sex	deptid

Below are the list of super keys in relation employee

{empid}
{email}
{contact}
{empid,email}
{empid,contact}
{email,contact}
{empid,email,contact}

7. Explain what is candidate key?

Ans. It is a minimal set of attribute that can uniquely identify a tuple in a relation is called candidate key, for example, following keys in the relation employee are candidate keys

{empid}
{email}
{contact}

Here important to note that there are no redundant (duplicate) attributes in the candidate key. The example of redundant key is {empid, email} since both of them can identify the employee record uniquely.

8. Explain what is a primary key?

Ans. It is an attribute or group of attributes in a relation that uniquely identifies each row in a relation. A relation cannot have more than one primary key, for example, following keys in the relation employee are candidate keys

{empid}
{email}
{contact}

We can pick one of the keys as the primary key, usually an id is picked as the primary key.

9. Mention what are the rules applied for a primary key in a relation?

Ans. Here is the list of rules applied for primary key

- Any two rows in a table cannot same value for a primary key

- The primary key does not contain the null value
- Each row can have only one primary key

10. Explain what is an alternate key?

Ans. There may be multiple attributes that can identify a row uniquely these are called candidate key(s), once a primary key is identified, rest of the candidates key are alternate keys. For example, in the employee relation

Candidate key

{empid}

{email}

{contact}

Out of these keys, the primary key is selected as Primary key that is

{empid}

Alternate keys are

{email}

{contact}

11. What is the Foreign key?

Ans. A foreign key is an attribute that is a primary key of another relation. It creates a relationship between two relations or tables. It is a cross-reference between two tables as it references the primary key of another table. For example, let us consider two relations Teacher and department

Teacher

Table: Teacher — Foreign Key (DeptCode)

TeacherID	F_name	L_name	Deptcode
T002	Mukesh	Sharma	D001
T004	Vivek	Rai	D005
T001	Vikas	Verma	D002

Table: Department — Primary Key **DeptCode**

DeptCode	Dept_Name
001	Physics
002	Computer science
005	Economics

The attribute deptcode is the primary of the department table and foreign key for the table teacher. We can join these two relations to find if a teacher belongs to which department.

12. Compare and contrast primary key and candidate key

Ans. Both Primary and Candidate keys are used identify that records uniquely from the tables. These keys are also used to create a relationship between tables.

Here is the list of differences between the Primary Key and the Candidate key.

Primary Key	Candidate key
A table can have only one primary key.	A table can have multiple candidate keys.
A Primary key cannot be null.	A Candidate key can have a null value.
A Primary Key is a candidate key.	A Candidate key may or may not be a primary key.

13. Differentiate between primary key and foreign key

Ans. Here is the list of differences between the Primary Key and Candidate key.

Primary Key	Foreign Key
It identifies a record uniquely in the table.	It is the primary key of another table.
A relation can have the single **primary key** in a table.	A relation can have **multiple foreign** keys in a table.

Long Questions and Answers 3/4 Marks

1. Find the following from a relation employee?

empid	fname	lname	email	contact	sex	deptid
1	Akash	Jain	ajain@abcinc.com	999087645	M	1
2	Mukesh	Verma	mverma@abcinc.com	789035671	M	2
3	Aparna	Jain	ajain@abcinc.com	991090387	F	1
4	Jay	Arora	jarora@abcinc.com	987549875	M	2
5	Jyoti	Sharma	jsharma@abcinc.com	983456778	F	1

1. **Cardinality**
2. **Degree**
3. **Domain values for attribute sex**
4. **Identify primary key**
5. **All the candidate keys**

Ans. 1. 5

2. 7
3. M, F
4. Empid
5. Empid, Email, Contact

2. Find the following from a relation supplier?
Relation supplier

Supid	fname	area	email	contact	itemid
1	James	east	ajain@abcinc.com	999087645	3
2	Sameer	east	mverma@abcinc.com	789035671	5
3	Jayesh	northeast	ajain@gmail.com	991090387	6
4	Mahesh	north	jarora@abcinc.com	987549875	5
5	Piyush	south	jsharma@abcinc.com	983456778	7

1. **Degree**
2. **Cardinality**
3. **Domain values for attribute area**
4. **Identify primary key**
5. **All the candidate keys**

Ans. 1. 6

2. 5
3. East, Northeast, South, North
4. SupId
5. Supid, email, contact

3. Mention what are the advantages of database base management system?

Ans. Using DBMS has the following advantages

➢ **Reducing Data Redundancy**

The multiple copies of the same data or file is called data redundancy. The DBMS keeps a single copy of data any changes made to data are reflected immediately and there is no chance of duplicate data.

- **Sharing of Data**

  Many users are allowed to access the database simultaneously this allowing sharing the data after a user has been authorized.
- **Data Integrity**

  DBMS ensures data integrity by ensuring data is accurate and consistent with the database.
- **Data Security**

  Unauthorized users are not allowed to access the database. Only authorized users are allowed to access the database after they are authenticated.
- **Backup and Recovery**

  DBMS manages the backup and recovery of data of its own. The user needs not to take backup periodically. In the case of database crash or system, failure DBMS restores it to its previous state.
- **Data Consistency**

  The DBMS ensures the there is no data redundancy and data is updated immediately hence data remain consistent, even after using it is used simultaneously.

15 SQL

LEARNING OBJECTIVES

- Classify the SQL commands and describe their syntax
- Write the queries using SQL command
- Recall DML and DDL commands and their syntax
- Define the various keys and constraints in the relational database management system
- Build queries based on the logical structure of the database table(s)
- Write queries using aggregate functions having clause and order by clause
- Classify the data types and their subtypes in MYSQL

DEFINITION

- **DDL:** DDL is **Data Definition Language** and it is used to create the database tables, view, index, triggers, and stored procedure and alter or drop (delete) tables and databases.
- **Create:** It is used to create a database and its objects like (table, index, views, store procedure, function, and triggers).
- **Alter:** It alters or changes the structure of the tables.
- **Drop:** It deletes the objects from a database.
- **Truncate**: It removes all the rows from the table.
- **Rename**: It renames an object in a database.
- **Select**: It retrieve data from a database.
- **Insert**: It insert data into a table.
- **Update**: It update an existing data from a table.
- **Delete**: It delete all records from a database table.
- **DCL:** It is **Data Control Language**; it grants and revokes permissions to the users.
- **Grant:** It set the access privileges to the user.
- **Revoke:** It withdraws the access privileges from the users.
- **TCL:** It is **Transaction Control Language**, these commands deal with a transaction.
- **Commit**: It makes the changes permanent in a database.
- **Rollback**: It revert a transaction which means that changes made will not persist in the database.
- **Savepoint:** To roll back the transaction up to this point (that is Save point).
- **SQL:** SQL stands for Structured Query Language. SQL allows accessing and manipulating databases.
- **DDL:** It stands for Data Definition Language. DDL is used for creating, modifying and deleting the database, tables, views, and indexes.
- **DML:** It stands for Data Manipulation Language. DML is used for inserting, updating, selecting and deleting rows from the table(s).
- **CREATE** TABLE: It is a DDL statement. It is used to create a table.
- **ALTER** TABLE: It is a DDL command. It is used to add, modify and drop columns from a table.
- **DROP** TABLE : It is a DDL command. It is used to drop a table, which means its physical structure is removed.
- **INSERT** INTO: It is a DML command. It is used to insert row(s) into a table.

- **SELECT:** A SELECT command in a relational database is used to retrieve row(s) from one or more tables or views.
- **UPDATE:** The UPDATE command modifies the existing row(s) in a table.
- **DELETE:** It is a DML command. It is used to delete row(s) from a table.
- **DESCRIBE:** It displays the logical structure of the table.
- **PRIMARY KEY:** A primary key in a relational database is unique for each row in a table. It is a unique identifier for a row in a table and it does not contain NULL values. A table in the relational database must only have one primary key.
- **FOREIGN KEY:** A foreign key in a relational database is a column or group of columns in a table. It references the primary key of another table.
- **CANDIDATE KEY:** A candidate key in a relational database is a column, or a group of columns, that are eligible for becoming a primary key of the table that can uniquely identify a row. A table may have one or more candidate keys.
- **CONSTRAINTS:** SQL constraints are used to set rules. They can specify data that can be inserted/ deleted or not. SQL constraints maintain the integrity, accuracy and reliability of the data in the table. In case of violation of the constraint, the action is aborted.
- **NOT NULL:** NOT NULL constraint specifies that the column value is not null, it must contain a value.
- **DEFAULT** CONSTRAINT: The DEFAULT constraint provides value to a column. The default value is inserted to all new records if no other value is provided.
- **UNIQUE CONSTRAINT:** The UNIQUE constraint ensures that there is no same value in any two rows of a column.
- **PRIMARY KEY CONSTRAINT:** The primary key constraints is used to identifying a row uniquely in a table. A PRIMARY constraint is a combination of UNIQUE and NOT NULL.
- **CHECK CONSTRAINT:** The check constraint allows inserting only a set of values in a column.
- **FOREIGN KEY CONSTRAINT:** A foreign key constraint or integrity constraint in a relational database is a column or group of columns in a table that is the primary key of another table, thereby, establishing a link between them.

Very Short Questions and Answers 1 Mark

1. **Define SQL?**

Ans. SQL stands for Structure Query Language (It is pronounced as ess-que-el). It is an **American National Standards Institute (ANSI)**, the standard language for interaction with **Relational Database Management Systems (RDBMS)**.

2. **Define SQL command?**

Ans. SQL commands are instructions, which are used to communicate with the database. It is also used to perform specific tasks, functions, and queries on data.

SQL commands are used to create a database, create a table; insert data into tables; delete data from tables; modifying the table, drop the table set permission for the users.

3. **What are the group functions?**

Ans. Aggregate functions are called group functions. Aggregate Functions perform calculations on single or multiple rows and return a single value.

4. **How to fetch a minimum value of a column?**

Ans. The min() function fetches the minimum value from a column. For example:

```
SELECT min(salary)
FROM employee;
```

5. **How to fetch the maximum value of a column?**

Ans. The max() function fetches the maximum value from a column. For example:

```
SELECT max(salary)
FROM employee;
```

6. How to fetch an average value of a column in a table?

Ans. The avg() function calculates an average value of a column. For example:

```
SELECT avg(salary)
FROM employee;
```

7. How to sum all the values of a column in a table?

Ans. The sum() function sums of all the values of a column. For example:

```
SELECT sum(salary)
FROM employee;
```

8. How to count all the rows in a table?

Ans. The COUNT(*) function returns the number of rows { count(*) } that match the condition specified in the WHERE clause. For example:

```
SELECT count(*)
FROM employee
/* fetch a number of rows in a table */

SELECT count(*) FROM employee where dept_id = 20;
/* fetch a number of rows in a table based on the condition */
```

9. How to select distinct values of a column in a table?

Ans. The SELECT DISTINCT filters out the duplicate values from a column and returns unique values.

Syntax:

```
Select DISTINCT column from table name
```

Example:

```
SELECT DISTINCT (City) FROM customer;
```

10. How to filter rows using a select clause?

Ans. The WHERE clause filters record based on a condition.

Syntax:

```
SELECT col1, col2, ... FROM table-name WHERE condition;
```

Example:

```
SELECT customer_name
FROM customer
where city='Mumbai';
```

Note: The WHERE clause is also used in UPDATE, DELETE statement, etc.

11. Does the aggregate function work on numeric data only?

Ans. No, they work on both numeric and non-numeric data types; however, SUM and AVG functions only work on numeric data.

12. How do aggregate functions treat null values?

Ans. Aggregate functions exclude nulls values while computing on the data.

13. How to select all the columns of a table using a SELECT command?

Ans. The select * command is used to retrieve all the rows from a table. For example:

```
SELECT * FROM table-name Example:
SELECT * FROM customer;
```

14. What is the default sort order of the ORDER BY clause?

Ans. Ascending

Short Questions and Answers 2 Marks

1. Mention the most commonly used RDBMS that uses SQL.

Ans. The commonly used **Relational Database Management Systems (RDBMS)** that uses SQL are:

- MySQL
- Oracle
- Db2
- Microsoft SQL Server
- Access

2. Mention the different types of SQL commands.

Ans. Different types of SQL commands are:

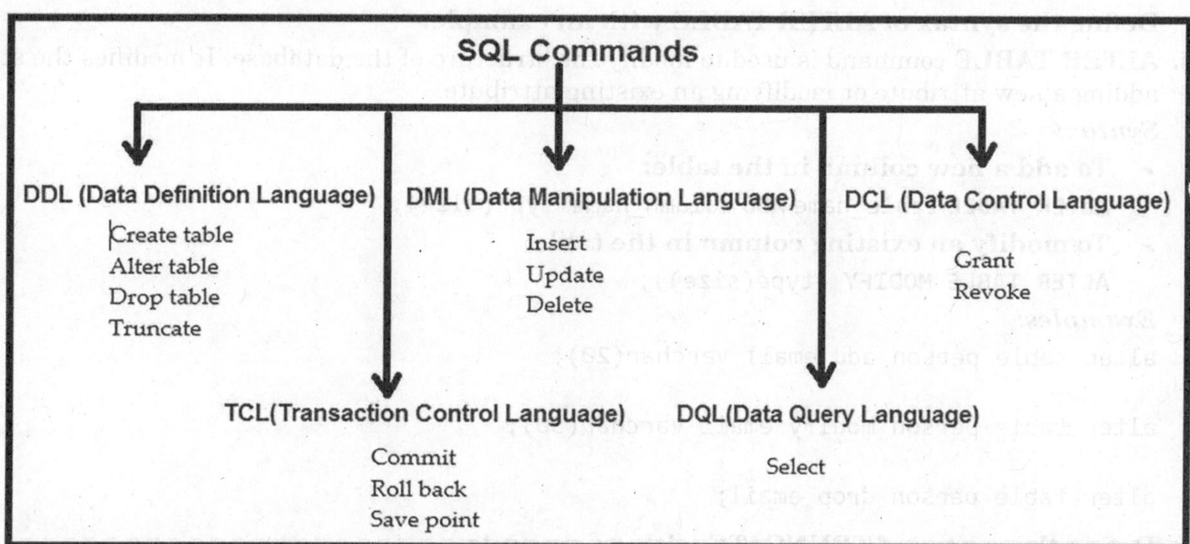

3. Explain the Data Definition Language (DDL).

Ans. DDL creates or changes the structure of the table (creating a table, altering a table, deleting a table). DDL command is auto-committed; it makes the changes permanent in the database.

Some commands that come under DDL:

- CREATE table
- ALTER table
- DROP table
- TRUNCATE

4. Define the syntax of Create command with an example.

Ans. **CREATE** command is used to create a new table in the database.

Syntax:

```
CREATE TABLE TABLE_NAME (
COLUMN_NAME DATATYPES[size]
.
.
.
);
```

Example:

```
CREATE TABLE EMPL(
EMP_ID int(11),
```

```
EMP_NAME varchar(20),
EMP_ADDRESS varchar(100),
.
.
);
```

5. Define the syntax of DROP TABLE with an example.

Ans. **DROP TABLE** command is used to delete the records and the structure of a table.

Syntax:

```
DROP TABLE TABLE_NAME;
```

Example:

```
DROP TABLE EMPL;
```

6. Define the syntax of ALTER TABLE with an example.

Ans. **ALTER TABLE** command is used to modify the structure of the database. It modifies the structure by adding a new attribute or modifying an existing attribute.

Syntax:

- **To add a new column in the table:**
  ```
  ALTER TABLE table_name ADD column_name type(size);
  ```
- **To modify an existing column in the table:**
  ```
  ALTER TABLE MODIFY (type(size));
  ```

Examples:

```
alter table person add email varchar(20);

alter table person modify email varchar(50);

alter table person drop email;
```

7. Define the syntax of TRUNCATE with an example.

Ans. **TRUNCATE** command deletes all the rows from a table and releases the space occupied by the table.

Syntax:

```
TRUNCATE TABLE table_name;
```

Example:

```
TRUNCATE TABLE PERSON;
```

8. Explain Data Manipulation Language.

Ans. The **Data Manipulation Language (DML)** commands modify data in the table(s). The DML commands are not auto-committed which means they can be roll-backed or commit to making changes permanent.

Some DML commands are:

- INSERT
- UPDATE
- DELETE

9. Define the syntax of INSERT with an example.

Ans. **INSERT** command is used to insert a row into a table.

Syntax:

```
INSERT INTO TABLE
(col1, col2, ... col N)
VALUES (val1, val2, .... valN);
```

Example:

INSERT INTO person (pid, pname) VALUES (1, "Suresh Kumar");

10. Define the syntax of UPDATE with an example.

Ans. **UPDATE** command is used to modify the value of a column in a table.

Syntax:

```
UPDATE table SET
[col1= val1,...col2 = val2]
[WHERE CONDITION]
```

Example:

```
UPDATE person
SET pname = 'Suresh Kumar Kant'
WHERE pid = 1
```

11. Define the syntax of DELETE with an example?

Ans. DELETE command is used to remove one or more rows from a table.

Syntax:

```
DELETE FROM table
[WHERE condition];
```

Example:

```
DELETE FROM person
WHERE pid= 2
```

12. Define Data Control Language.

Ans. **Data Control Language (DCL)** commands are used to set permissions for the users. It grants or revokes permissions to / from the users.

DCL commands are:

- **Grant:** It sets the privileges for the users.
- **Revoke:** It is used to take back permissions from the user.

13. Define Transaction Control Language.

Ans. **Transaction Control Language (TCL)** commands are executed after DML commands such as INSERT, DELETE, and UPDATE only.

TCL commands are:

- **Commit:** It is used to make changes permanent to the database.

Syntax:

```
COMMIT;
```

- **Rollback:** It rollbacks all previous commands.

Syntax:

```
ROLLBACK;
```

- **SAVEPOINT:** It rollbacks the transaction back to a certain point (save point) without rolling back the entire transaction.

Syntax:

```
SAVEPOINT SAVEPOINT_NAME;
```

14. Mention the numeric data types and its subtypes

Ans. Commonly used numeric data types in MySQL are:

- **Integer Types** (Exact Value):
  - INT, SMALLINT, TINYINT, MEDIUMINT, BIGINT.
  - **Fixed-Point Types** (Exact Value): DECIMAL.
  - **Floating-Point Types** (Approximate Value): FLOAT, DOUBLE.

15. Name the subtypes of DateTime and date types.

Ans. Commonly used DateTime data types in MySQL are:

- DATE,
- DATETIME
- TIMESTAMP
- TIME

16. Mention the string data type and its subtypes in MySQL

Ans. Commonly used string data types in MySQL are:

- CHAR,
- VARCHAR
- BLOB
- TEXT

17. What is SQL used for?

Ans. SQL is a language that is used to communicate with a relational database management system. SQL is used to perform the following tasks:

- Creating a new table and database
- Creating views
- Accessing data from a table(s)
- Inserting data into a table(s)
- Updating rows in a table(s)
- Deleting table(s)
- Deleting rows from a table
- Sorting and filtering the result-set

18. Name the aggregate functions used in MySQL.

Ans.
- Min
- Max
- Avg
- Sum
- Count

19. Why is the GROUP BY clause used?

Ans. The GROUP BY clause in SQL is used for arranging rows based on similar data values of a column with the help of some functions. For example, GROUP BY arranges results based on each city.

> ***Note:*** If a particular column has the same values in different rows then it will arrange these rows in a group. This clause can be used with the SELECT clause

Syntax of GROUP BY clause:

```
SELECT col1, col2,..., aggregate_function(val)
FROM table-name
WHERE Condition (s)
GROUP BY col1, col2,... ;
```

Example:

Table CUSTOMERS			
Cust ID	**Last Name**	**First Name**	**City**
1.	Chinmay	Baral	Jabalpur
2.	Laveena	Thomas	Bhopal

3.	Nishtha	Das	Indore
4.	Umesh	Deep	Gwalior
5.	Jamshed	Sangha	Allahabad
6.	Raj	Warrior	Pune
7.	Kasturi	Lodi	Kanpur
8.	Jasmin	Badami	Jabalpur
9.	Naresh	Halder	Surat
10.	Bhaagyasree	Dugal	Mumbai
11.	Kusum	Sama	Bhopal
12.	Radhika	Badami	Guwahati
13.	Pooja	Deshpande	Indore
14.	Narendra	Ben	Bhopal
15.	Mahmood	Minhas	Mumbai
16.	Alka	Tara	Kanpur
17.	Baber	Iyer	Mumbai
18.	Prabha	Prasad	Delhi
19.	Tanay	Dutta	Mumbai
20.	Ram	Kumar	Mumbai

select city, count(city) from customers Group by city

Output:

City	count (city)
Allahabad	1
Bhopal	3
Delhi	1
Guwahati	1
Gwalior	1
Indore	2
Jabalpur	2
Kanpur	2
Mumbai	5
Pune	1
Surat	1

20. Why is the HAVING clause used?

Ans. The HAVING clause filters the result-set based on the group of rows. This clause is often used in conjunction with the GROUP BY clause that filters groups based on the specified condition(s). If it is not mentioned (omitted) in the SQL; it just behaves like a WHERE clause.

Syntax:

```
SELECT col1, col2, ... FROM tablename WHERE condition(s)
GROUP BY col1, col2, ...
HAVING condition(s)
```

Example: To fetch records from table customers (given in question 19) where the number of customers is greater than 2 from a city.:

select city, count(city) from customers Group by city having count(city) > 2

Output:

City	Count (city)
Bhopal	3
Mumbai	5

21. Illustrate the scalar and group functions in SQL with examples.

Ans. The single row function is also known as a scalar function. These functions work on every row and return the results for every row. For example:

select firstname ,month(dob) from student

The month(dob) function extract month from the date of birth for each row. For example: The output of the query is as follows:

Fisrt Name	Month (dob)
Krithika	7
Anu	7
Neelam	8
Khushi	8
Vidhya	9
Kavya	9
Jay	9
Pawan	11

➢ Multiple rows or Group function: Group functions work on the multiple rows or groups of rows and return an aggregate value.

```
select max(dob) from student
```

Output:

Month (dob)
11/22/2012

22. Write a query that fetches the number of customers in each city from the table of customers (given in question 19).

Ans. Select city, count(city) from customers group by city;

Output:

City	count (city)
Allahabad	1
Bhopal	3
Delhi	1
Guwahati	1
Gwalior	1
Indore	2
Jabalpur	2
Kanpur	2
Mumbai	5
Pune	1
Surat	1

23. How to use where clause and group by clause in a single query? Using Table customers (given in question 19).

Ans. Below is the query that uses where and group by clause:

```
Select city, count(city) from customers where custid > 10 group by city having count(custid)
> = 2
```

Output:

City	count (city)
Bhopal	2
Mumbai	4

24. Illustrate how 'having clause' filters the results with a query? Using Table customers (given in question 19).

Ans.
```
select custID, city from customers having city in ('Bhopal', 'Indore')
```

Output:

Custmor ID	City
2	Bhopal
3	Indore
11	Bhopal
13	Indore
14	Bhopal

25. Write a query that uses logical operators (and, or) with 'Having' clause. Using Table customers (given in question 19).

Ans. Example 1: Using "and" operator with the "having" clause:

```
SELECT COUNT(CustID), City FROM Customers
GROUP BY City HAVING COUNT(CustID) > 2 and COUNT(CustID) < 5
```

Output:

COUNT (Custmor ID)	City
3	Bhopal

Example 2: Using "or" operator with the "having" clause.

```
SELECT COUNT(CustID), City FROM Customers
GROUP BY City HAVING COUNT(CustID) >= 2or city in('Indore','Mumbai')
```

Output:

COUNT (Custmor ID)	City
3	Bhopal
2	Indore
5	Mumbai

26. How to arrange the result-set in sorted order?

Ans. Results of a query using SELECT statement are not in order, which means that the result-set can be in any order. To sort the results set, the ORDER BY clause is used with the SELECT statement.

Using Table customers (given in question 19).

Syntax of ORDER BY clause:

```
SELECT col1, col2 FROM table-name
ORDER BY col1 [ASC|DESC], col2 [ASC|DESC], ...
```

Example:

```
SELECT * FROM customers ORDER BY lastname;
```

Output:

CustmorID	FirstName	Lastname	City
8	Jasmin	Badami	Jabalpur
12	Radhika	Badami	Guwahati
1	Chinmay	Baral	Jabalpur
14	Narendra	Ben	Bhopal
3	Nishtha	Das	Indore
4	Umesh	Deep	Gwalior
13	Pooja	Deshpande	Indore
10	Bhaagyasree	Dugal	Mumbai
19	Tanay	Dutta	Mumbai
9	Naresh	Halder	Surat
17	Baber	Iyer	Mumbai
20	Ram	Kumar	Mumbai
7	Kasturi	Lodi	Kanpur
15	Mahmood	Minhas	Mumbai
18	Prabha	Prasad	Delhi
11	Kusum	Sama	Bhopal
5	Jamshed	Sangha	Allahabad
16	Alka	Tara	Kanpur
2	Laveena	Thomas	Bhopal
6	Raj	Warrior	Pune

27. Write a query that arranges result-set in descending order of a column.

Ans. The following is a query that arranges the result-set based on the descending order of the last name:

Using Table customers (given in question 19).

```
SELECT * FROM customers ORDER BY lastname DESC;
```

Output:

CustmorID	FirstName	Lastname	City
12	Radhika	Badami	Guwahati
8	Jasmin	Badami	Jabalpur
1	Chinmay	Baral	Jabalpur
14	Narendra	Ben	Bhopal
3	Nishtha	Das	Indore
4	Umesh	Deep	Gwalior
13	Pooja	Deshpande	Indore
10	Bhaagyasree	Dugal	Mumbai
19	Tanay	Dutta	Mumbai
9	Naresh	Halder	Surat
17	Baber	Iyer	Mumbai
20	Ram	Kumar	Mumbai

7	Kasturi	Lodi	Kanpur
15	Mahmood	Minhas	Mumbai
18	Prabha	Prasad	Delhi
11	Kusum	Sama	Bhopal
5	Jamshed	Sangha	Allahabad
16	Alka	Tara	Kanpur
2	Laveena	Thomas	Bhopal
6	Raj	Warrior	Pune

28. Write a query that counts the number of customers in each city. Using Table customers (given in question 19).

Ans. The group by statement arranges the result-set based on each city as shown in the below query.

```
SELECT city, count(*) FROM customers GROUP BY city
```

Output:

City	Count (*)
Allahabad	1
Bhopal	3
Delhi	1
Guwahati	1
Gwalior	1
Indore	2
Jabalpur	2
Kanpur	2
Mumbai	5
Pune	1
Surat	1

29. Write a query that counts customers in each city and arrange them in descending order of the city.

Ans. To count the customers in each city, we have to use the GROUP BY command and then use the ORDER BY command to arrange results in descending order as shown below:

Using Table customers (given in question 19).

```
SELECT city, count(*) FROM customers GROUP BY city ORDER BY city DESC
```

Output:

City	Count (*)
Surat	1
Pune	1
Mumbai	5
Kanpur	2
Jabalpur	2
Indore	2
Gwalior	1
Guwahati	1

Delhi	1
Bhopal	3
Allahabad	1

Table SPORTS

ID	Sports_name	Name	Enrollment Date	Fees	Sex
1	Badminton	Rita Sridhar	2019-01-14	2000	F
2	Basketball	Damini Somani	2019-01-22	1000	M
3	Judo	Labeen Saraf	2019-01-25	1500	F
4	Tennis	Laveena Pandey	2019-04-02	2500	M
5	Table Tennis	Hanuman Sami	2019-07-03	1250	M
6	Tennis	Kamlesh Cherian	2019-03-12	2500	F
7	Tennis	Mukti Bhatt	2019-03-21	2500	M
8	Table Tennis	Qadim Prasadv	2019-01-04	1250	M
9	Badminton	Uday Lodi	2019-04-22	2000	M
10	Basketball	Amir huasain	2019-04-24	1000	M
11	Judo	Aadil Bhatt	2019-04-25	1500	M
12	Tennis	Ram Gopal Sharma	2019-05-17	2500	F
13	Table Tennis	Urvashi Handa	2019-05-20	1250	F
14	Tennis	Ananya Dhingra	2019-05-23	2500	F
15	Badminton	Manish Verma	2019-06-18	1500	M

30. Write a query that sum up the fees for all females enrolled in any sports from the sports table. (Using Table SPORTS)

Ans. To sum up, the fees we have to use the sum() function and filter it where sex= female as shown below:

```
SELECT SEX, SUM(Fees) FROM sports where sex ='F'
```

Output:

Sex	Sum (Fees)
F	12250

31. Write a query that sums up the fees for all the sports. (Using Table SPORTS)

Ans. `SELECT sports_name, SUM(Fees) FROM sports GROUP BY sports_name`

Sports_name	Sum (Fees)
Badminton	5500
Basketball	2000
Judo	3000
Table Tennis	3750
Tennis	12500

32. Write a query that sums the fees for all sports_name and arranges them in increasing order of sports_name. (Use table SPORTS)

Ans. `SELECT sports_name, SUM(Fees) FROM sports GROUP BY sports_name ORDER BY sports_name`

Output:

Sports_name	Sum (Fees)
Badminton	5500
Basketball	2000
Judo	3000
Table Tennis	3750
Tennis	12500

33. Which function is used in ORDER BY clauses to specify sort order?

Ans. There is no function used to define the order of a result-set. We use DESC or ASC clause along with order by clause to sort the results in descending or ascending order.

34. Write a query that sorts a result-set based on two columns.

Table STUDENT						
Enrollment Id	**First name**	**Marks**	**Dob**	**Class**	**Club id**	**Stream id**
111	Ramanan	45	11/6/2012	11	3	3
98	Shekhar	45	10/21/2012	12	2	2
110	Deep	55	11/5/2012	12	2	2
97	Deepro	55	10/18/2012	9	1	4
88	Ajay	56	10/8/2012	10	4	4
42	Kamalika	56	8/9/2012	11	6	6
112	Aniket	58	11/7/2012	11	4	4
99	Anurag	58	10/22/2012	9	3	4
117	Atul	59	11/13/2012	11	3	3
104	Kartik	59	10/29/2012	12	2	2
94	Gokul	65	10/16/2012	11	4	4

Ans. `Select * From Student ORDER BY  marks, firstname`

Output:

Marks	First name
45	Ramanan
45	Shekhar
55	Deep
55	Deepro
56	Ajay
56	Kamalika
58	Anurag
59	Atul
59	Kartik
65	Gokul

35. Write a query for table students (column names are section, project-group, marks) that sorts data on Project-Group (in ascending order), section (in descending order), and Marks (in descending order).

Ans. `Select * From Students ORDER BY projectgroup ASC, section DESC, marks DESC`

36. Differentiate between HAVING and WHERE clauses.

Ans.

Where Clause	Having Clause
WHERE clause allows filtering on each and every row.	HAVING clause allows filtering groups in SQL.
WHERE clause is used before GROUP BY clause.	Having clause is used after the GROUP BY clause.
WHERE clause is applied first on individual rows and only rows which pass the condition are included for creating groups.	Once a group is created, the 'HAVING' clause is used to filter groups based upon the specified condition.

37. What is the use of the GROUP BY clause?

Ans. The GROUP BY clause is used to group rows where the column contains the same values. This is used in the SELECT statement. It can be used in conjunction with aggregate function(s) that produce a summary for the column data.

Table SPORTS					
ID	**Sports_name**	**Name**	**Enrollment Date**	**Fees**	**Sex**
1	Badminton	Rita Sridhar	14/01/2019	2000	F
2	Basketball	Damini Somani	22/01/2019	1000	M
3	Judo	Labeen Saraf	25/01/2019	1500	F
4	Tennis	Laveena Pandey	04/02/2019	2500	M
5	Table Tennis	Hanuman Sami	07/03/2019	1250	M
6	Tennis	Kamlesh Cherian	12/03/2019	2500	F
7	Tennis	Mukti Bhatt	21/03/2019	2500	M
8	Table Tennis	Qadim Prasadv	01/04/2019	1250	M
9	Badminton	Uday Lodi	22/04/2019	2000	M
10	Basketball	Amir huasain	24/04/2019	1000	M
11	Judo	Aadil Bhatt	25/04/2019	1500	M
12	Tennis	Ram Gopal Sharma	17/05/2019	2500	F
13	Table Tennis	Urvashi Handa	20/05/2019	1250	F
14	Tennis	Ananya Dhingra	23/05/2019	2500	F
15	Badminton	Manish Verma	18/06/2019	1500	M

(i) Find the output of the following SQL statement.

Ans. `SELECT DISTINCT( sports_name) FROM Sports;`

Output:

Sports_name
Badminton
Basketball
Judo
Tennis
Table Tennis

(ii) Find the output of the following SQL statement.

Ans. `SELECT COUNT (DISTINCT sports_name) FROM Sports;`

Output:

count (DISTINCT (sports_name))
5

(iii) Find the output of the following SQL statement.

Ans. `SELECT sum(Fees) FROM sports WHERE Sports_name = 'Badminton';`

Output:

Sum (Fees)
5500

(iv) Find the output of the following SQL statement.

Ans. `SELECT SUM( Fees) FROM Sports WHERE EnrollmentDate >= '2019-04-01';`

Output:

Sum (Fees)
16000

(v) Find the output of the following SQL statement.

Ans. `SELECT sports_name, SUM( Fees) FROM Sports GROUP BY sports_name;`

Output:

Sports name	Sum (Fees)
Badminton	5500
Basketball	2000
Judo	3000
Table Tennis	3750
Tennis	12500

(vi) Find the output of the following SQL statement.

Ans. `SELECT sports_name, SUM( Fees) FROM Sports GROUP BY sports_name ORDER BY sports_name;`

Output:

Sports name	Sum (Fees)
Badminton	5500
Basketball	2000
Judo	3000
Table Tennis	3750
Tennis	12500

(vii) Find the output of the following SQL statement.

Ans. `SELECT sports_name, AVG( Fees) FROM Sports GROUP BY sports_name;`

Output:

sports_name	Avg (Fees)
Badminton	1833.3333
Basketball	1000.0000
Judo	1500.0000
Table Tennis	1250.0000
Tennis	2500.0000

(viii) Find the output of the following SQL statement.

Ans. `SELECT sports_name, avg( Fees) FROM Sports GROUP BY sports_name HAVING sports_name='Badminton'`

Output:

sports_name	Avg (Fees)
Badminton	1833.3333

(ix) Find the output of the following SQL statement.

Ans. `SELECT sports_name, avg( Fees) FROM Sports GROUP BY sports_name HAVING sports_name in ('Badminton','Basketball','Judo')`

Output:

sports_name	Avg (Fees)
Badminton	1833.3333
Basketball	1000.0000
Judo	1500.0000

(x) Find the output of the following SQL statement.

Ans. `SELECT sports_name, avg( Fees) FROM Sports GROUP BY sports_name HAVING sports_name in ('Badminton','Basketball','Judo') And avg(fees) > 1000`

Output:

sports_name	Avg (Fees)
Badminton	1833.3333
Judo	1500.0000

(xi) Find the output of the following SQL statement.

Ans. `SELECT sports_name, sum( Fees) FROM Sports GROUP BY sports_name`

Output:

sports_name	Sum (Fees)
Badminton	5500
Basketball	2000
Judo	3000
Table Tennis	3750
Tennis	12500

(xii) Find the output of the following SQL statement.

Ans. `SELECT` sports_name, max(fees) AS MAXFEES FROM Sports

Output:

sports_name	MAXFEES
Badminton	2500

(xiii) Find the output of the following SQL statement.

Ans. `SELECT sports_name, min(fees) AS MINFEES FROM Sports`

Output:

sports_name	MINFEES
Badminton	1000

(xiv) Find the output of the following SQL statement?

Ans. `SELECT sports_name, fees FROM Sports HAVING fees > avg(fees)`

Output:

sports_name	Fees
Badminton	2000

(xv) Find the output of the following SQL statement?

Ans. `SELECT sports_name, avg(fees), fees FROM Sports HAVING fees > avg(fees)`

Output:

sports_name	avg (Fees)	Fees
Badminton	1783.333	2000

Table order_details

orderNo	productCode	quantity	price	orderLineNumber
9900	S18_1749	30	136	3
9900	S18_2248	50	55.09	2
9900	S18_4409	22	75.46	4
9900	S24_3969	49	35.29	1
9901	S18_2325	25	108.06	4
9901	S18_2795	26	167.06	1
9901	S24_1937	45	32.53	3
9901	S24_2022	46	44.35	2
9902	S18_1342	39	95.55	2
9902	S18_1367	41	43.13	1
9903	S10_1949	26	214.3	11
9903	S10_4962	42	119.67	4
9903	S12_1666	27	121.64	8
9903	S18_1097	35	94.5	10
9903	S18_2432	22	58.34	2
9903	S18_2949	27	92.19	12
9903	S18_2957	35	61.84	14
9903	S18_3136	25	86.92	13
9903	S18_3320	46	86.31	16
9903	S18_4600	36	98.07	5
9903	S18_4668	41	40.75	9
9903	S24_2300	36	107.34	1
9903	S24_4258	25	88.62	15
9903	S32_1268	31	92.46	3
9903	S32_3522	45	63.35	7
9903	S700_2824	42	94.07	6
9904	S12_3148	34	131.44	1

(xvi) Find the output of the following SQL statement.

Ans. `SELECT orderno, SUM(quantity) AS itemsCount, SUM(price*quantity) AS total FROM Order_details GROUP BY orderno HAVING total > 1000;`

Output:

orderno	itemscount	total
9900	151	10223.83
9901	142	10549.01
9902	80	5494.78
9903	541	50218.95
9904	34	4468.96

(xvii) Find the output of the following SQL statement.

Ans. `SELECT orderno, SUM(quantity) AS itemsCount, SUM(price *quantity) AS total FROM Order_details GROUP BY orderno HAVING total > 10000 AND itemsCount > 100;`

Output:

orderno	itemscount	total
9900	151	10223.83
9901	142	10549.01
9903	541	50218.95

38. Find the output of the following SQL statement.

Ans. `SELECT productCode, avg(quantity) FROM Order_details GROUP BY productCode`

Output:

ProductCode	Avg (quantity)
S10_1949	26.0000
S10_4962	42.0000
S12_1666	27.0000
S12_3148	34.0000
S18_1097	35.0000
S18_1342	39.0000
S18_1367	41.0000
S18_1749	30.0000
S18_2248	50.0000
S18_2325	25.0000
S18_2432	22.0000
S18_2795	26.0000
S18_2949	27.0000
S18_2957	35.0000
S18_3136	25.0000
S18_3320	46.0000
S18_4409	22.0000
S18_4600	36.0000
S18_4668	41.0000
S24_1937	45.0000
S24_2022	46.0000
S24_2300	36.0000

S24_3969	49.0000
S24_4258	25.0000
S32_1268	31.0000
S32_3522	45.0000
S700_2824	42.0000

(i) Find the output of the following SQL statement.

Ans. `SELECT productCode, avg(quantity) FROM Orderdetails GROUP BY productCode HAVING avg(quantity) > 40.00`

Output:

Product Code	Avg (quantity)
S10_4962	42.0000
S18_1367	41.0000
S18_2248	50.0000
S18_3320	46.0000
S18_4668	41.0000
S24_1937	45.0000
S24_2022	46.0000
S24_3969	49.0000
S32_3522	45.0000
S700_2824	42.0000

(ii) Find the output of the following SQL statement.

Ans. `SELECT productCode, quantity FROM Order_details`
`WHERE quantity > 40 ORDER BY productcode, quantity DESC`

Output:

Product Code	Quantity
S10_4962	42
S18_1367	41
S18_2248	50
S18_3320	46
S18_4668	41
S24_1937	45
S24_2022	46
S24_3969	49
S32_3522	45
S700_2824	42

(iii) Find the output of the following SQL statement.

Ans. `SELECT productCode, quantity FROM Order_details WHERE quantity > 40 ORDER BY quantity`

Output:

Product Code	Quantity
S18_1367	41
S18_4668	41

S10_4962	42
S70_2824	42
S24_1937	45
S32_3522	45
S24_2022	46
S18_3320	46
S24_3969	49
S18_2248	50

39. What will be the output of the following query? (CBSE D 2016)

Table SALES

SID	Sales
S101	20000
S102	10000
S103	NULL
S104	15000

Ans. `Select AVG(Sales) from sales.`

Output: 15000

40. Find the output of the following SQL statement.

Table Doctor

ID	Name	DEPT	SEX	Experience
101	John	ENT	M	12
104	Mukesh	ORTHOPEDIC	M	5
107	Vijay	CARDIOLOGIST	M	10
114	Lata	SKIN	F	3
109	Uma	MEDICINE	F	9
105	Dinesh	ORTHOPEDIC	M	10
117	Manish	ENT	M	3
111	Leena	MEDICINE	F	12
130	Vikas	ORTHOPEDIC	M	15

Table SALARY

ID	Basic	Allowance	Consultation
101	12000	1000	300
104	23000	2300	500
107	32000	4000	500
114	12000	5200	100
109	42000	1700	200
105	18900	1690	300
130	21700	2600	300

1. Display the name of all doctors who are in "MEDICINE" and have more than 10 years of experience from table DOCTOR.

2. Display the average salary of all the doctors working in ENT using tables DOCTORS and SALARY = BASIC + ALLOWANCE.
3. Display the minimum salary of the female doctors.
4. Display the highest consultation fees of male doctors.
5. Find the output of query select count(*) where sex='F'.
6. SELECT name, dept, basic from a doctor, salary Where dept=" ENT" AND DOCTOR.ID = SALARY. ID.

Ans. 1. `Select name from doctor where dept ="ENT" and experience > 10`

2. `Select avg(salary),salary.basic+salary.allowance as salary from doctor, salary where doctor.ID = salary.ID AND doctor.dept='ENT'`
3. `Select min(s.salary) from doctor d salary s where d.sex = 'F' and d.ID = s.ID`
4. `Select max(s.consultation) from doctor d, salary s where s.ID = d.ID and d sex='M'`
5. `3`
6.

```
name   id   salary
john   101  12000
```

41. Find the output of queries using the following tables. (Delhi 2008)

Table GARMENT

GCODE	DESC	PRICE	FCODE	READY_BY
10023	PENCIL SKIRT	1150	F03	19-DEC-08
10001	FORMAL SHIRT	1250	F01	12-JAN-08
10012	INFORMAL SHIRT	1550	F02	06-JAN-08
10024	BABY TOP	750	F03	07-APR-08
10090	TULIP SKIRT	850	F02	31-MAR-07
10019	EVENING GOWN	850	F03	06-JAN-08
10009	INFORMAL PANT	1500	F02	20-OCT-08
10007	FORMAL PANT	1350	F01	09-MAR-08
10020	FROCK	850	F04	09-SEP-08
10089	SLACKS	750	F03	20-OCT-08

Table FABRIC

FCODE	TYPE
F04	POLYESTER
F02	COTTON
F03	SILK
F04	TERELENE

1. To display the GCODE and description of each garment in descending order of GCODE.
2. To display the details of all the garments, which have a ready date between 08-dec-07 and 16-jun-08 (inclusive of both dates).
3. To display the average price of all the garments, which are made up of the fabric with FOCDE as F03.
4. To display FABRIC wise highest and lowest price in the GARMENT table. (Display FCODE of each GARMENT along with the highest and lowest price).
5. Select sum(price) from table garment where fcode='F01'.
6. SELECT Description, type, from garment, fabric where garment.fcode = fabric.focde and garment. price > 1260.

7. Select max(fcode) from fabric.
8. Select count(distinct(price)) from garment.

Ans. 1. select gocde, description from garment order by gcode desc
2. select * from garment where ready_by between ('08-dec-07' and '16-jun-08')
3. select avg(price) from garment where price ='F03'
4. select min(price), max(price) from garment group by FCODE
5. 2600
6. Description type
```
Informal shirt COTTON
Formal pant
Formal pant TERELENE
```
7. F04
8. 7

42. Find the output of the following table. (Delhi 2008)

Table WORKER					
ECODE	**NAME**	**DESIGN**	**PLEVEL**	**DOJ**	**DOB**
11	Radhe Shyam	Supervisor	P001	15-SEP-04	23-AUG-81
12	Chander Nath	Operator	P003	22-FEB-10	12-JUL-87
13	Fizza	Operator	P003	14-JUN-09	14-OCT-83
15	Ameen Ahmed	Mechanic	P002	25-AUG-06	13-MAR-84
18	Sanya	Clerk	P002	19-DEC-05	09-JUN-83

Table PAYLEVEL		
PLEVEL	**PAY**	**ALLOWANCE**
P001	26000	12000
P002	22000	10000
P003	12000	6000

Write the queries for the following.

1. To display the details of all workers in descending order of DOB.
2. To display the name and design of those workers whose plevel is either P001 or P002.
3. To display the content of all the workers whose DOB is between 19-Jan-84 and 11-JUL-84.
4. Add a new row with worker table with the following data:
(19, 'data Kishore', 'operator', 'P003', '19-JUN-08','11-JUN-84')
5. Select count(plevel), plevel from workers group by plevel
6. SELECT MAX(DOB), MIN(DOJ) FROM WORKER
7. SELECT name, pay, from workers w , paylevel p Where w.plevel = p.plevel and w.ecode < 13
8. Select count(PLEVEL) , PAY + ALLOWANCE FROM paylevel WHERE plevel = 'P003'

Ans. 1. Select * from workers order by DOB desc
2. Select name, design from workers where (plevel = 'P001' or plevel='P002')
3. Select * from workers where dob is between '19-Jan-84' and '11-JUL-84'
4. Insert into workers (ECODE,NAME,DESIGN,PLEVEL,DOJ,DOB) values (19, 'data Kishore', 'operator', 'P003', '19-JUN-08','11-JUN-84')
5. Count (plevel) plevel
```
1 P001
2 P001
```

```
   2              P001
6. MAX(DOB),      MIN(DOJ)
   12-jul-87      13-sep-04
7. Radhe Shyam  26000
   Chander Nath 12000
8. PLEVEL    PAY+ALLOWANCE
   P003      18000
```

43. Find the output/queries using the following tables. Delhi 2012

Table CAB

Vcode	Name	Make	Colour	Capacity	Charge
100	Innova	Toyota	White	7	15
102	SX4	Suzuki	Blue	4	14
104	C Class	Mercedes	Red	4	35
105	A-star	Suzuki	White	3	14
108	Indigo	Tata	Silver	3	12

Customer

Ccode	CName	Vcode
100	Innova	101
102	SX4	108
104	C Class	105
105	A-star	104

(A) Write queries for the following:

1. To display the name of the white-colored cars.
2. To display the name of the vehicle, make, and capacity of all the vehicles in ascending order of their seating capacity.
3. To display the highest charge.
4. To display the customer name and vehicle name hired by them.

(B) What will be the output of the following queries?

1. Select Count (distinct(make)) from cab
2. Select max(charges), min(charges) from cab
3. Select count(*), make from cab group by make
4. Select Vehicle from cab where capacity=4

Ans. (A) 1. Select name from cab where color =' White'
2. Select name, make, capacity order by capacity ASC
3. Select max(charges) as Maxprice from the cab
4. Select name, cname from cab c, customer r where c.vcode = r.vcode

(B) 1. 4
2. 35 12
3. 1 Toyota
 2 Suzuki
 1 Mercedes
 1 Tata
4. SX4 Class

44. Find the output/queries using the following tables:

Table EMPLOYEE					
Eno	**NAME**	**Gender**	**DCODE**	**DOJ**	**DOB**
1001	Radhe Shyam	M	D01	15-SEP-04	23-AUG-81
1002	Riya	F	D03	22-FEB-10	12-JUL-87
1003	Ramesh	M	D05	14-JUN-09	14-OCT-83
1007	Ameen Ahmed	M	D04	25-AUG-06	13-MAR-84
1004	Sanya	F	D01	19-DEC-05	09-JUN-83
1005	Anil kumar	M	D02	20-JAN-04	05-MAR-89
1006	Fizza	F	D05	30-NOV-02	07-APR-90

Table DEPT		
DCODE	**DNAME**	**LOCATION**
D01	INFRA	DELHI
D02	MARKETING	DELHI
D03	MEDIA	MUMBAI
D04	FINANCE	KOLKATA
D05	HR	MUMBAI

Write the query for the following:

1. To display Eno, Name, gender from the table employee in ascending order of Eno.
2. To display the names of all employees where the gender is male in the table employee.
3. To display all the employees where dob between 09-JUN-83 and 05-MAR-89.
4. To count female employees who joined after 01-JAN-01.

Find the output of the following:

5. Select count(*), dcode from employee group by dcode having count(*) > 1
6. Select distinct(dname) from dept;
7. Select name, dname, from employee e, dept d where e.dcode = d.dcode and eno < 1003
8. Select Max(doj), Min(doj) from employee

Ans. 1. Select eno, name, gender from employee order by eno ASC;

2. Select name from employee where gender='M'
3. Select * from employee where dob is between 09-JUN-83 and 05-MAR-89
4. Select count(*) from employee where gender ='f' and doj > 01-JAN-01
5. 2 D01
   2 D05
6. MARKETING
   INFRA
   MEDIA
   FINANCE
   HR
7. Name Department
   Radhe Shyam INFRA
   Riya MEDIA
8. 22 - FEB - 10 20 - JAN - 04

45. Find the output/queries using the following tables:

Table ACCOUNT		
ANO	**ANAME**	**ADDRESS**
101	Neeraj Kumar	Bangalore
102	Rohan Sharma	Chennai
103	Abdul Rana	Hyderabad
104	Rishabh Kumar	Chennai
105	Harpreet	Chandigarh

Table TRANSACT				
TRNO	**ANO**	**AMOUNT**	**TYPE**	**DOT**
T001	101	2500	W	2017-02-21
T002	103	3000	D	2017-06-01
T003	102	2000	W	2017-05-12
T004	103	1000	D	2017-03-22
T005	101	12000	D	2017-11-06

Write queries for the following:

1. To display all the transactions of type D from table TRANSACT.
2. To display ano, amount of all deposits, and withdrawals done in the month of October 2017 using table transact.
3. To display the last date of transaction from table TRANSACT where ano is 103.
4. To display the ano, aname, and dot from transact where amount less than or equal to 3000.
5. Select ano, aname from accounts where address not in ('Bangalore', 'Chennai').
6. Select distinct(ano) from transact.
7. Select ano, count(*), min(amount) from transact Group by and having count(*) > 1.
8. Select count(*), sum(amount) form transact where DOT is <='2017-06-01'.

Ans.

1. `Select * from transact where type ='D'`
2. `Select ano, amount from transact where dot is >= '2017-10-1' and dot<='2017-10-31'`
3. `Select max(dot) from transct where ano = 103`
4. `Select a.ano, a.name, a.dot from account a, transact t where a.ano = t.ano and t.amout < =3000`
5. ```
   ANO NAME
   103 Neeraj kumar
   105 Rohan Sharma
   ```
6. ```
   Distinct ANO
   101
   102
   103
   ```
7. ```
   ANO COUNT (*) MIN(AMOUNT)
   10122500      10321000
   ```
8. `COUNT(*) SUM(AMOUNT) 28500`
   ```

Long Questions and Answers 3/4 Marks

1. List the characteristics of the Numeric (Integer) Data Types

Ans. Characteristics of INTEGER data types in MySQL are:

Type	Range	Stores up to
INT	2147483648 to 2147483647 OR 0 to 4294967295.	11 digits
TINYINT	-128 to 127 OR 0 to 255.	4 digits
SMALLINT	-32768 to 32767 OR 0 to 65535.	5 digits
MEDIUMINT	-8388608 to 8388607 OR 0 to 16777215.	9 digits
BIGINT	-9223372036854775808 to 9223372036854775807. OR 0 to 18446744073709551615.	20 digits

Characteristics of FLOAT data types in MySQL are:

FLOAT(M, D)	It displays length (M) and the number of decimals (D). Example: Float (10, 2); here 2 is the number of decimals, and 10 is the total number of digits (including decimals). ***Note:*** Decimal precision can go to 24 places for a FLOAT
DOUBLE(M, D)	It is the same as Float (M, D), whereas decimal precision can go to 53 places DOUBLE. REAL is a synonym for DOUBLE.
DECIMAL(M, D)	It defines the display length (M) and the number of decimals (D) is required. NUMERIC is a synonym for DECIMAL.

2. List the characteristics of Date and Time Data Type.

Ans. Characteristics of Date data types in MySQL are:

Type	Description
DATE	A date in YYYY-MM-DD format, between 1000-01-01 and 9999-12-31.
DATETIME	A date and time combination in YYYY-MM-DD HH:MM:SS format, between 1000-01-01 00:00:00 and 9999-12-31 23:59:59.
TIMESTAMP	Stores the Date and Time in YYYYMMDDHHMMSS format. A timestamp between midnight, January 1st, 1970, and sometime in 2037.
TIME	Stores the time in a HH:MM:SS format.

3. List the characteristics of string Data Type.

Ans. Characteristics of Date data types in MySQL are:

CHAR(M)	A fixed-length string between 1 and 255 characters in length. For example CHAR(5), right-padded with spaces to the specified length when stored). Defining a length is not required, but the default is 1.
VARCHAR(M)	A variable-length string between 1 and 255 characters in length. For example, VARCHAR(25). It is required to define a length for the VARCHAR field.
TEXT	The TEXT can store 65,535 characters. There is no need to specify a length with TEXT. **The MySQL has four types for text type:** TINYTEXT, 255 Bytes (255 characters) **TEXT, 64KB** (65,535 characters) MEDIUMTEXT, 16MB (16,777,215 characters) LONGTEXT, 4GB (4,294,967,295 characters)

Match the following

1.	CREATE DATABASE	(a) removes an index
2.	CREATE TABLE	(b) removes a table
3.	SELECT	(c) creates a new database
4.	UPDATE	(d) delete(s) rows from table(s)
5.	DELETE	(e) update(s) rows in a table(s)
6.	ALTER TABLE	(f) modifies (alters) a table
7.	DROP TABLE	(g) creates a new table
8.	CREATE INDEX	(h) create an index
9.	DROP INDEX	(i) retrieves rows from a table(s)

Ans. **1.** (c) **2.** (g) **3.** (i) **4.** (e) **5.** (d) **6.** (f) **7.** (b) **8.** (h) **9.** (a)

Multiple-Choice Questions and Answers

1. Which of the following is not an aggregate function in SQL?

a. min b. max c. count d. total

Ans. Option d, that is, total.

2. The ___________ aggregation function adds all values of the column.

a. total b. add c. sum d. max

Ans. Option c, that is, sum.

3. State true or false: attributes used in the aggregation function can be renamed.

a. True b. False

Ans. Option a, True.

4. Which of the following keyword is used to rename the resulting attribute using the aggregation function?

a. replace b. as c. rename d. to

Ans. Option b, that is, as.

5. Which of the following values are ignored by the count(*)?

a. duplicate values b. Null values c. date values d. character values

Ans. Option b, that is, Null values.

16 SQL JOINS

LEARNING OBJECTIVES

- Classify the various types of joins in SQL
- Write queries using inner join, left join, right join, full join, natural joins
- Distinguish between inner and outer join, left join, right join, full join

DEFINITION

- **Join:** The JOIN in SQL is used to combine rows from two or more tables and creates a temporary table with the resultant set of rows.
- **Equi-Join:** It is a simple SQL join, which uses the equal sign(=) as the comparison operator for the condition used for combining.
- **Non Equi-** Join: on Equi-Join uses operators like >, <, >=, <= along the condition.

Very Short Questions and Answers — 1 Mark

1. Classify the type of Joins.

Ans. Different types of joins are:

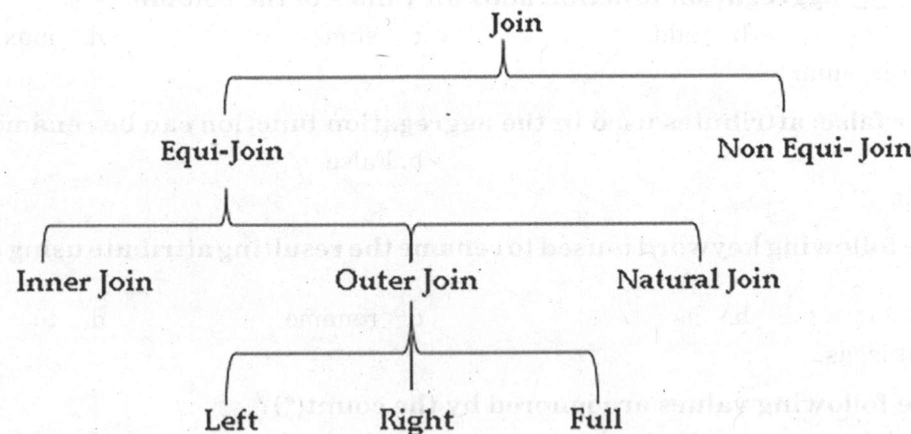

2. Explain how joins works?

Ans. The join specifies how columns from different table are matched. Most of the times the aim is to find equal values among the tables, and include those values in matches. The most common case match is among the foreign key of one table to the primary key of another table.

Inner join does not include rows that do not match rows, whereas outer join does include them.

3. Explain how inner join works.

Ans. An inner join return row(s) from two or more tables which qualifies the match condition mention in the query.

4. Differentiate between Equi-Join and Non Equi-Join.

Ans.

Equi-Join	Non Equi-Join
A join using only the **equals comparison** in a join condition is **Equi-Join.**	A Join that has at least one comparison in the join condition that is **non equals comparison** is **Non Equi-Join.**

5. Differentiate between Inner and Outer Join.

Ans.

Inner Join	Outer Join
Inner joins don't include non-matching rows	Outer joins include the non-matching rows.

Short Questions and Answers 2 Marks

1. Explain the concept of the inner join with the help of the diagram.

Ans. Let's assume there are two tables: Table1 and Table2, these tables has a column that is used for the join, the resultant rows contains rows that have same column values. ***Example:***

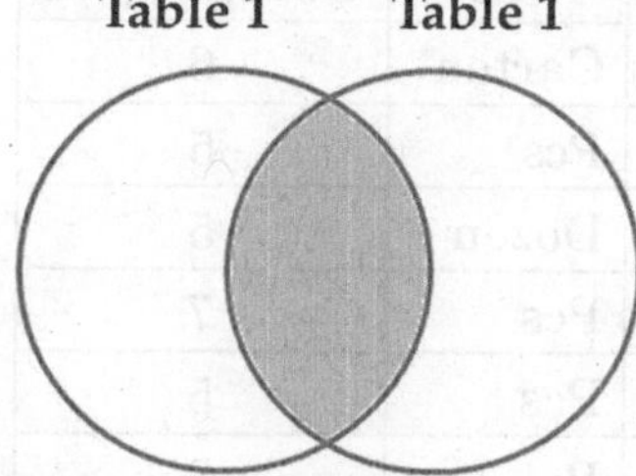

Let's assume there are two tables and we join these tables by using column companyID

Table: FoodItems

ItemId	ItemName	Unit	CompanyId
1	Navratan Namkeen	Carton	6
2	Cheez-It	Pcs	5
2	Parle-G	Dozen	5
3	Banana Chips	Pcs	7
4	Haldiram Pudina Chips	Pcs	5
5	Britannia Cakes	Pcs	8
7	Salt n Shake	Pcs	9
8	Bikaneri Bhujiya	Pcs	10

Table: Company

CompanyID	CompanyName	CompanyCity
4	choco-lates	Jaipur
8	Food All	Mumbai
5	Hill Jack Ltd	chandigarh
6	Akash Foods	Delhi
7	Foodies	Gurgaon
9	Shakes-n-Bite	South Delhi

The final rows in the result of the query from table where companyids in **(5,6,7,8,9)** which are common in both the tables.

2. Write a syntax of the query of INNER JOIN.

Ans. Syntax

```
SELECT
* | values
FROM table1
INNER JOIN table2 ON join_condition1
INNER JOIN table3 ON join_condition2
. . . .;
```

In the above syntax:

The main table (table1) specified in the FROM clause.

The join condition is specified after the ON keyword of the INNER JOIN clause. The join condition specifies matching rows between the main table and the others appeared in the INNER JOIN clause.

3. Write a query for inner join by using table: FoodItems, Company.

Table: FoodItems

ItemId	ItemName	Unit	CompanyId
1	Navratan Namkeen	Carton	6
2	Cheez-It	Pcs	5
2	Parle-G	Dozen	5
3	Banana Chips	Pcs	7
4	Haldiram Pudina Chips	Pcs	5
5	Britannia Cakes	Pcs	8
7	Salt n Shake	Pcs	9
8	Bikaneri Bhujiya	Pcs	10

Table: Company

CompanyID	CompanyName	CompanyCity
4	choco-lates	Jaipur
8	Food All	Mumbai
5	Hill Jack Ltd	chandigarh
6	Akash Foods	Delhi
7	Foodies	Gurgaon
9	Shakes-n-Bite	South Delhi

Ans.

```
select *

FROM fooditems

INNER JOIN company

ON fooditems.companyid = company.companyid;
```

Output:

ItemId	ItemName	Unit	Company Id	Company ID	CompanyName	CompanyCity
1	Navratan Mamkeen	Carton	6	6	Akash Foods	Delhi

2	Cheez-It	Pcs	5	5	Hill Jack Ltd	chandigarh
2	Parle-G	Dozen	5	5	Hill Jack Ltd	chandigarh
3	Banana Chips	Pcs	7	7	Foodies	Gurgaon
4	Haldiram Pudina Chips	Pcs	5	5	Hill Jack Ltd	chandigarh
5	Britannia Cakes	Pcs	8	8	Food All	Mumbai
7	Salt n Shake	Pcs	9	9	Shakes-n-Bite	South Delhi

4. Explain how outer join works.

Ans. An outer return rows even if the join condition fails.In the case where condition fails it may return non-matching rows from a table or from both tables depending on its type.

The type are:

- Left outer join (left join)
- Right outer join (Right join)
- Full outer join

5. Explain how left outer join works.

Ans. A Left outer join is used to return results by combining rows from two (primary and other table). It will return matching rows and rows even if the join condition fails from the main table.

6. Explain the concept of left outer join with the help of the diagram.

Ans. Let's assume there are two tables: Table1 and Table2 , these tables have common column that is used for joining the tables, the resultant table contains rows that have same column values and non-matching rows from the Table1. ***Example:***

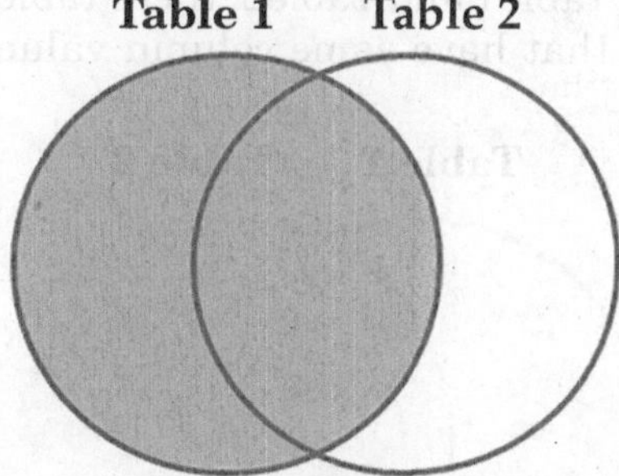

Consider two tables **FoodItems and Company**

The final rows in the result of the left outer join query from table where companyids **(4,5,6,7,8,9)** are common in both the tables and additional row with company id is **10**.

7. Write a syntax of the query of the left outer join.

Ans. Syntax

```
SELECT
    * | values
FROM table1
LEFT OUTER JOIN table2
ON join_condition1
. . . . ;
```

In the above syntax:

The main table (table1) specified in the FROM clause

The join condition is specified after ON clause. The join condition specifies matching rows between the table1 and the table2 and non-matching rows form table1.

8. Write a query for left outer join using below given table.

Ans.
```
SELECT *

FROM fooditems

LEFT OUTER JOIN company

ON fooditems.companyid = company.companyid;
```

Output:

ItemId	ItemName	Unit	Company-Id	Company-ID	Company Name	CompanyCity
5	Britannia Cakes	Pcs	8	8	Food All	Mumbai
2	Cheez-It	Pcs	5	5	Hill Jack Ltd	chandigarh
2	Parle-G	Dozen	5	5	Hill Jack Ltd	chandigarh
4	Haldiram Pudina Chips	Pcs	5	5	Hill Jack Ltd	chandigarh
1	Navratan Namkeen	Carton	6	6	Akash Foods	Delhi
3	Banana Chips	Pcs	7	7	Foodies	Gurgaon
7	Salt n Shake	Pcs	9	9	Shakes-n-Bite	South Delhi
8	Bikaneri Bhujiya	Pcs	10	NULL	NULL	NULL

9. Explain the concept of the right outer join with the help of the diagram.

Ans. Let's assume there are two tables: Table1 and Table2, these tables has a column that is used for the join, the resultant rows contains rows that have same column values and non-matching rows from table2.

Example:

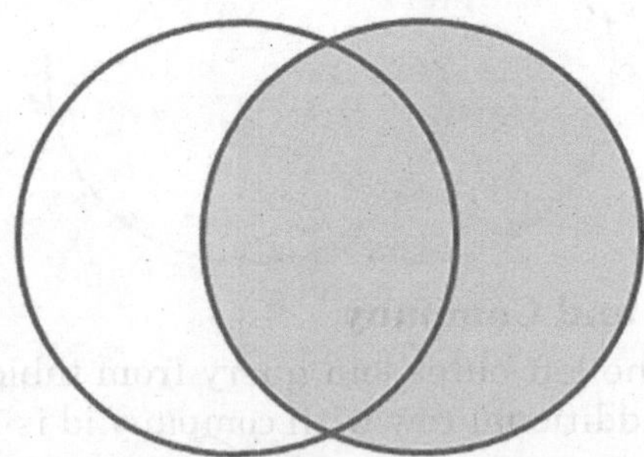

The final rows in the result of the query from table where companyids **(5, 6, 7, 8, 9)** are common in both the tables and additional row with company id **4**.

10. Write a syntax of the query of right outer join.

Ans. Syntax

```
SELECT
    * | values

FROM table1

RIGHT OUTER JOIN table2

ON join_condition1
```

. . . . . ;

In the above syntax:

The main table (table1) specified in the FROM clause

The join condition is specified after ON clause. The join condition specifies matching rows between the table1 and the table2 and non-matching rows form table2.

11. Write a query for the right outer join?

Ans. **SELECT ***
FROM fooditems
RIGHT OUTER JOIN company
ON fooditems.companyid = company.companyid;.
Output:

ItemId	ItemName	Unit	Company Id	Company ID	Company Name	CompanyCity
1	Navratan Nam-keen	Carton	6	6	Akash Foods	Delhi
2	Cheez-It	Pcs	5	5	Hill Jack Ltd	chandigarh
2	Parle-G	Dozen	5	5	Hill Jack Ltd	chandigarh
3	Banana Chips	Pcs	7	7	Foodies	Gurgaon
4	Haldiram Pudina Chips	Pcs	5	5	Hill Jack Ltd	chandigarh
5	Britannia Cakes	Pcs	8	8	Food All	Mumbai
7	Salt n Shake	Pcs	9	9	Shakes-n-Bite	South Delhi
NULL	NULL	NULL	NULL	4	choco-lates	Jaipur

12. Explain the concept of full outer join with the help of the diagram.

Ans. Lets assume there are two tables: Table1 and Table2, these tables has a column that is used for the join, the resultant rows contains rows that have same column values and non-matching rows from the table1 and table2. ***Example:***

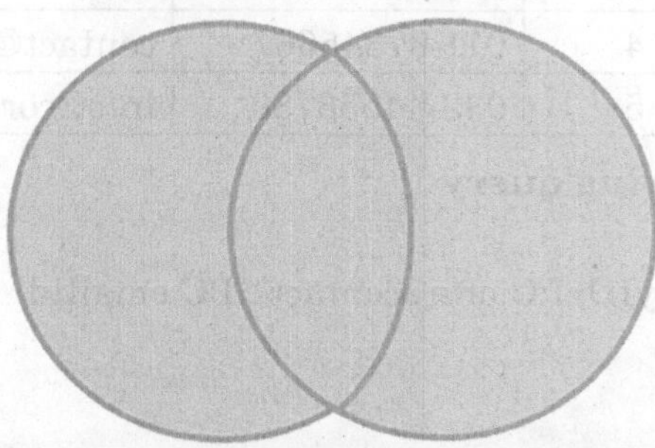

Note: The FULL OUTER JOIN is not supported by MYSQL. But this can be achieved by UNOIN operation on left and right join.

Long Questions and Answers 3/4 Marks

1. Table: Person

EntityId	title	Fname	Lname	Age	incomegroup	areagroup
1	Mr.	Vikas	Sharma	26	C	A
2	Mr.	Mukesh	Verma	21	C	A

3	Mrs.	Ruchi	Sharma	20	B	A
4	Mrs.	Kavita	Sharma	23	B	B
5	Mr.	Pankaj	Goyal	38	E	E
6	Mr.	Navneesh	Garg	36	A	E

Table: PersonContact

EntityId	officecontact	mobile	Altmobile	emailid
1	011-22345678			info@zyus.com
2	022-40056780	+91-7987544332		info@abccrop.com
3	044-65045600			sales@abc.com
4	011-67345667			contact@xyzee.com
5	033-44556789			info@corp.com
8	0141-22305687			admin@parapharma.com
9	011-22987651			info@vedanshinfo.com

a. Find the output of the following query

SELECT
P.EntityID, P.Fname , PC.EntityID, PC.officecontact , PC.emailId
FROM Person AS P
INNER JOIN
PersonContact AS PC
ON
P.EntityID = PC.EntityID

Ans. Output:

EntityID	Fname	EntityID	officecontact	emailId
1	Vikas	1	011-22345678	info@zyus.com
2	Mukesh	2	022-40056780	info@abccrop.com
3	Ruchi	3	044-65045600	sales@abc.com
4	Kavita	4	011-67345667	contact@xyzee.com
5	Pankaj	5	033-44556789	info@corp.com

b. Find the output of the following query

SELECT
P.EntityID, P.Fname , PC.EntityID, PC.officecontact , PC.emailId
FROM Person AS P
LEFT OUTER JOIN
PersonContact AS PC
ON
P.EntityID = PC.EntityID

Ans. Output:

EntityID	Fname	EntityID	officecontact	emailId
1	Vikas	1	011-22345678	info@zyus.com
2	Mukesh	2	022-40056780	info@abccrop.com
3	Ruchi	3	044-65045600	sales@abc.com
4	Kavita	4	011-67345667	contact@xyzee.com

5	Pankaj	5	033-44556789	info@corp.com
6	Navneesh	NULL	NULL	NULL
7	Ajay	NULL	NULL	NULL

c. Find the output of the following query

```
SELECT
P.EntityID, P.Fname , PC.EntityID, PC.officecontact , PC.emailId
FROM  Person AS P
LEFT OUTER JOIN
PersonContact AS PC
ON
P.EntityID = PC.EntityID
```

Ans. Output:

EntityID	Fname	EntityID	officecontact	emailId
1	Vikas	1	011-22345678	info@zyus.com
2	Mukesh	2	022-40056780	info@abccrop.com
3	Ruchi	3	044-65045600	sales@abc.com
4	Kavita	4	011-67345667	contact@xyzee.com
5	Pankaj	5	033-44556789	info@corp.com
NULL	NULL	8	0141-22305687	admin@parapharma.com
NULL	NULL	9	011-22987651	info@vedanshinfo.com
NULL	NULL	10	011-65045010	sales@conf.com

Table: Employee

EmpId	Fname	Lname	Age	EmailId
1	Himani	Kumar	22	himani@abc.com
2	Ajay	Sharma	31	Ajay@abc.com
3	Aayushi	Raj	24	aayushi@abc.com
4	Mukesh	Sharma	25	mukesh@abc.com
5	Swati	Kapoor	21	swati@abc.com

Table: Project

ProjectId	EmpId	ClientId	Pname
110	1	3	Project-1
120	2	1	Project-2
130	3	5	Project-3
140	3	2	Project-4
150	5	4	Project-5
160	9	1	Project-6
170	7	2	Project-7
180	8	3	Project-8
190	10	6	Project-100
200	8	10	Project-101

d. Find the output of the following query

```
select
*
from emp
inner join project
on emp.EmpId = project.EmpId
```

Ans. Output:

EmpId	Fname	Lname	Age	EmailId	ProjectId	EmpId	ClientId	Pname	StartDate
1	Himani	Kumar	22	himani@abc.com	110	1	3	Project-1	2019-04-21
2	Ajay	Sharma	31	Ajay@abc.com	120	2	1	Project-2	2019-02-12
3	Aayushi	Raj	24	aayushi@abc.com	130	3	5	Project-3	2019-01-10
3	Aayushi	Raj	24	aayushi@abc.com	140	3	2	Project-4	2019-04-16
5	Swati	Kapoor	21	swati@abc.com	150	5	4	Project-5	2019-05-23

e. Find the output of the following query

```
select
*
from emp
LEFT OUTER join project
on emp.EmpId = project.EmpId
```

Ans. Output:

EmpId	Fname	Lname	Age	EmailId	ProjectId	EmpId	ClientId	Pname	StartDate
1	Himani	Kumar	22	himani@abc.com	110	1	3	Project-1	2019-04-21
2	Ajay	Sharma	31	Ajay@abc.com	120	2	1	Project-2	2019-02-12
3	Aayushi	Raj	24	aayushi@abc.com	130	3	5	Project-3	2019-01-10
3	Aayushi	Raj	24	aayushi@abc.com	140	3	2	Project-4	2019-04-16
5	Swati	Kapoor	21	swati@abc.com	150	5	4	Project-5	2019-05-23
4	Mukesh	Sharma	25	mukesh@abc.com	NULL	NULL	NULL	NULL	NULL

f. Find the output of the following query

```
select
*
from emp
RIGHT OUTER join project
on emp.EmpId = project.EmpId
```

Ans. Output:

EmpId	Fname	Lname	Age	EmailId	ProjectId	EmpId	ClientId	Pname	StartDate
1	Himani	Kumar	22	himani@abc.com	110	1	3	Project-1	2019-04-21
2	Ajay	Sharma	31	Ajay@abc.com	120	2	1	Project-2	2019-02-12
3	Aayushi	Raj	24	aayushi@abc.com	130	3	5	Project-3	2019-01-10
3	Aayushi	Raj	24	aayushi@abc.com	140	3	2	Project-4	2019-04-16
5	Swati	Kapoor	21	swati@abc.com	150	5	4	Project-5	2019-05-23
NULL	NULL	NULL	NULL	NULL	160	9	1	Project-6	2019-01-12
NULL	NULL	NULL	NULL	NULL	170	7	2	Project-7	2019-07-25
NULL	NULL	NULL	NULL	NULL	180	8	3	Project-8	2019-08-20
NULL	NULL	NULL	NULL	NULL	190	10	6	Project-100	NULL
NULL	NULL	NULL	NULL	NULL	200	8	10	Project-101	NULL

2. What is natural join and how to write query for NATURAL join

Ans. The NATURAL JOIN performs the same task as an INNER or LEFT OUTER JOIN, in a manner that all the columns with the same name of associated tables will appear once only.

Points to remember for Natural Join:

➢ The associated tables should have one or more pairs of identically named columns.

➢ The columns must be of the same data type.

➢ ON clause is not used a NATURAL JOIN.

Syntax of NATURAL JOIN:

```
SELECT
    * | values
FROM table1
NAURAL JOIN table2
. . . . ;
```

Query

```
SELECT
*
FROM fooditems
NATURAL JOIN
company;
```

ItemId	ItemName	Unit	CompanyId
1	Navratan Namkeen	Carton	6
2	Cheez-It	Pcs	5
2	Parle-G	Dozen	5
3	Banana Chips	Pcs	7
4	Haldiram Pudina Chips	Pcs	5
5	Britannia Cakes	Pcs	8
7	Salt n Shake	Pcs	9
8	Bikaneri Bhujiya	Pcs	10

Company ID	Company Name	Company City
4	choco-lates	Jaipur
8	Food All	Mumbai
5	Hill Jack Ltd	chandigarh
6	Akash Foods	Delhi
7	Foodies	Gurgaon
9	Shakes-n-Bite	South Delhi

CompanyId	ItemId	ItemName	Unit	CompanyName	CompanyCity
6	1	Navratan Namkeen	Carton	Akash Foods	Delhi
5	2	Cheez-It	Pcs	Hill Jack Ltd	chandigarh
5	2	Parle-G	Dozen	Hill Jack Ltd	chandigarh
7	3	Banana Chips	Pcs	Foodies	Gurgaon
5	4	Haldiram Pudina Chips	Pcs	Hill Jack Ltd	chandigarh
8	5	Britannia Cakes	Pcs	Food All	Mumbai
9	7	Salt n Shake	Pcs	Shakes-n-Bite	South Delhi

INTERFACING PYTHON WITH MYSQL

LEARNING OBJECTIVES

- Recall the syntax of functions:connect(), cursor(), fetchone(), fetchmany() and fetchall()
- Develop the code that can create a table, insert, delete, and update row(s) in a table
- Write a code that can iterate over a result-set and perform commit and rollback

DEFINITION

- **Database connectivity:** Database connectivity means a script or a code that can connect and access a database management system.
- **Cursor:** The cursor allows executing the SQL commands and queries using Python code.
- **Rollback:** Rollback allows restoring a database to its previously defined state which helps to recover from an error at the end of the transaction.
- **Commit:** A commit makes changes permanent to the database so that it is visible to other users.

Very Short Questions and Answers — 1 Mark

1. Name the package that is imported for connecting to MYSQL using Python.

Ans. The mysql.connector package is used for connecting to MYSQL.

2. Write the import statement to retrieve the connection object.

Ans. The MySQL Connection object returns the connection object, which can be imported by using the below import statement:

```
import mysql.connector as con
```

Here, con is an object of MYSQL Connection.

3. Mention the name of the function that is used to connect database.

Ans. connect() is a constructor that creates a connection to MySQL server and it returns a MySQL Connection object.

4. Describe the parameters used in the connect() function.

Ans. The connect() function accepts four arguments.

1. host, It is the hostname or IP address of the database server.
2. user, It is a user name.
3. password, It is the password of the database user.
4. databasename, It is the name of the database to which the user wants to connect to.

5. Why is function roll back()?

Ans. Rollback ensures that in case of an exception (an error occurs) the changes are revert back and data remains in a stable state.

6. Why is the function commit() used?

Ans. The commit function is used to make changes permanently which are made by query or a transaction.

7. What is the purpose of the function fetchall()?

Ans. The fetchall() method is used to fetch all the rows from the table in a database; It returns a list of tuples. If there are no more rows available, an empty list is returned.

8. How to retrieve specific numbers of rows from the table (s) in a database?

Ans. The fetchmany() method is used to retrieve a set of rows. The number of rows is specified by its size's parameter and it returns a list of a tuple. It will return the empty list in case no more rows are available. Here's the syntax of the fetchmany() method:

```
result_rows = cursor.fetchmany(size=1)
```

The default value of the size is 1. If the size is greater than the total number of rows, all rows are returned

9. How to fetch a single row from the table(s) in a database?

Ans. The fetchone() method is used to fetch the next row from the query result. The fetchone() is used with iterator (that is while loop). Here's the syntax of the fetch one method:

```
result_row = cursor.fetchone()
```

10. When and why is the cursor's close() method used?

Ans. The method close() is used before closing the connection.

This method is used to close the cursor, reset results, and ensure that there is no reference to its associated connection object. The syntax of the close method is as follows:

```
cursor.close()
```

11. How to use the function execute() ?

Ans. The execute() method executes a command or a query. The syntax of the execute() method is as follows:

```
result_iterator = cursor.execute(query, params=None, multi=True)
```

The params (parameters) are passed through tuple or dictionary that is bound to query.

Example:

```
stmt = "SELECT * from employees cursor.execute(stmt)
```

Example:

```
stmt = "SELECT * from employees where empid = %(empid)"
cursor.execute(stmt, { 'empid': 2 })
```

The execute() methods return an iterator in case multi is True.

12. Differentiate between function fetchmany() and fetchall() ?

Ans.

fetchmany()	fetchall()
The fetchmany method fetches multiple records provided as an argument (size).	The fetchall method fetches all the records.

13. How are functions fetchmany() and fetchall() similar?

Ans. Both methods can fetch multiple rows; however, they will not fetch those records which have been already fetched.

14. Write a code that checks if a connection with database is established successfully.

Ans.

```
import mysql.connector as con
mycon = con.connect(host="localhost",user="root",passwd="", database='pythondb')
if( mycon.is_connected()):
    print("Connected to Mysql...!")
mycon.close()
```

Output:

```
connected to Mysql...!
```

15. How to use keyword arguments with the function connect()?

Ans. The following code demonstrates the use of keyword arguments with the execute function:

```
import mysql.connector as connection

dbconfig = {
    'user': 'root',
        'password': '',
        'database': 'pythondb',
        'host': '127.0.0.1',
        'raise_on_warnings': True
}

conn = connection.connect(**dbconfig)
if(conn.is_connected()==True):
    print("Successfully connected to Mysql...!")
else:
    print("There is a problem in connecting to database")

conn.close()
```

Output:

```
Successfully connected to Mysql...!
```

16. Write an algorithm that updates a row(s) of a table.

Ans. Algorithm for updating row:

1. Connect to the MySQL server.
2. Create a cursor object.
3. Execute the update query using the execute method.
4. Perform the commit.
5. Close the connection.

17. Write a program that retrieves the version of MySQL.

Ans.

```
import mysql.connector as con
mycon= con.connect(host="localhost",
user="root",
passwd="",
database='pythondb')

if(mycon.is_connected()==True):
    print("Successfully connected to Mysql...!")
else:
    print("There is a problem in connecting to database")
cursor=mycon.cursor()
cursor.execute("select version()")
data= cursor.fetchone()

if data:
    print('version retrieved:', data)
else:
```

```
    print('version not retrieved')
cursor.close()
```

Output:

```
successfully connected to Mysql...!
version retrieved: ('5.7.21')
```

18. What if a commit statement is written after the connection is closed?

Ans. If the commit statement is written after the connection is closed, the commit state will throw an exception as shown below:

```
mysql.connector.errors.OperationalError: 2055: Lost connection to My
SQL server at 'localhost:3306', system error: 10038 An operation was
 attempted on something that is not a socket
```

Overall, the changes made will not be reflected in the database.

19. Write a program that delete row(s) from a table.

Ans.

```
import mysql.connector as con
mycon=con.connect(host="localhost",\
user="root",\
password="",\
database='pythondb')
if(mycon.is_connected()==True):
    print("successfully connected to Mysql...!")
else:
    print("There is a problem connecting to database")
cursor=mycon.cursor()
query="delete from users where user_id > 10"
cursor.execute(query)
print("Affetced rows: "+ str(cursor.rowcount))
mycon.commit()
cursor.close()
```

Output:

```
successfully connected to Mysql...!
Affected rows: 5
```

20. Identify the missing statements in the below code segment.

Ans.

```
import mysql.connector as con
mycon=con.connect(host="localhost",user="scott",
    passwd="king",
    database="test")
cursor=mycon.cursor()
cursor.execute("SELECT *FROM books")
______________________________ #1

while row is not None:
          ________________ #2

          row=cursor.fetchone()
```

Ans. a. `row=cursor.fetchone()`

b. print(row)

21. Write a program that update row(s) in the table.

Ans.
```
import mysql.connector as con
mycon=con.connect(host="localhost",user="root",passwd="",database='pythondb')
if(mycon.is_connected()==True):
    print("successfully connected to Mysql...!")
else:
    print("There is a problem in connecting to database")

cursor=mycon.cursor()
query="update users set First_Name='Rajesh' where user_id= 2"
cursor.execute(query)
print("Affetced rows: "+ str(cursor.rowcount))
mycon.commit()
cursor.close()
mycon.close()
```

Output:
```
successfully connected to Mysql...!
Affected rows: 1
```

22. Identify the missing statements in the below code segment.

Ans.
```
import mysql.connector as con

mycon=con.connect(host="localhost",user="root",
    passwd="",
    database='pythondb')

______________________#1
query="SELECT * from users"
cursor.execute(query)
data=cursor.fetchall()

#print all rows
______________________ #2
    print(row)
mycon.close()
```

Ans. a. cursor = mycon.cursor()

b. for row in data:

Short Questions and Answers — 2/3 Marks

1. What Python DB API does?

Ans. The Python DB API is designed to access databases. This allows accessing databases using various python modules. This Python code is portable across multiple databases. The Python DB API provides a standard way of working with databases using Python. This API allows doing the following:

- Obtaining a database connection
- Executing SQL and stored procedures

➢ Closing the connection

2. Explain how Python interfaces with MySQL database using MySQL connector.

Ans. MySQL Connector is implemented using pure Python. It implements Python DB APIs which allows accessing the MySQL database from Python. It is a standardized database driver provided by MySQL. The following diagram demonstrates the logical design of the database connector, interfacing with the database management system:

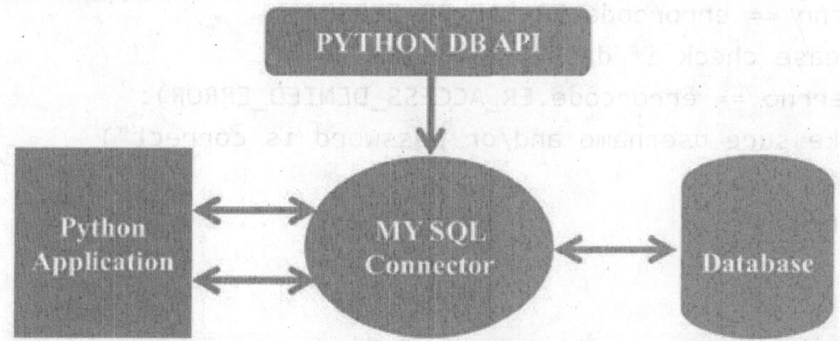

MySQL Connector implements Python DB API. It obtains the connection (can be thought of as a stream between the connector and MySQL DB). Connection returns the cursor object which allows executing the query. Once we are done, the cursor and connection can be closed.

3. Write steps and code that demonstrates how to connect to the MySQL server.

Ans. The following steps are used to connect to the MySQL server:

1. Import mysql.connector
2. Use the connect function object to obtain the connection by providing the user name, password, host, and database.
3. Close the connection.

Let's demonstrate the code:

```
import mysql.connector
conn = mysql.connector.connect(user='root', \
    password='',\
    host='127.0.0.1',\
    database='pythondb')
conn.close()
```

Alternatively,we can create a connection using connection. MySQL Connection() class, for example:

```
from mysql.connector import connection

conn = connection.MySQLConnection(user='root', \
        password='',\
        host='127.0.0.1',\
    database='pythondb')
conn.close()
```

4. Explain how to handle the error during connecting to the database.

Ans. The try and expect block are used to deal with the error. We put connect() method in try block and except block deal with the errors as illustrated below:

```
import mysql.connector
from mysql.connector import errorcode

try:
    conn = mysql.connector.connect(user='root', \
```

```
        password='',\
        host='127.0.0.1',\
    # non existing database
        database='pythondb1')
except mysql.connector.Error as dberr:
    if (dberr.errno == errorcode.ER_BAD_DB_ERROR):
        print("Please check if database exists")
    elif (dberr.errno == errorcode.ER_ACCESS_DENIED_ERROR):
        print("Make sure username and/or password is correct")
    else:
        print(dberr)
else:
    conn.close()
```

Output:

```
Please check if database exists
```

Note: In case user name and password are incorrect, the above message is displayed: Make sure username and/or password is correct.

5. Write a Python program that iterates a result set.

Ans.

```
import mysql.connector
conn = mysql.connector.connect(user='root', \

    password='',\
    host='127.0.0.1',\
    database='pythondb1')

# Using cursor as an iterator
cursor.execute("SELECT * from books")

for result_row in cursor:
    print(result_row)

# Using fetchone with a while loop
cursor.execute("SELECT * from books")

#Fetch the row first
result_row = cursor.fetchone()

while result_row is not None:
    print(result_row)
    result_row = cursor.fetchone()

conn.close()
```

Output:

```
(1, 'let us c', 5, 'BPB', 225,1)
(2, 'Python companion class 12',4,450,1)
```

6. Write a program to insert a record(s) in the below table.

```
+------------+-------------+------+-----+---------+----------------+
| Field      | Type        | Null | Key | Default | Extra          |
+------------+-------------+------+-----+---------+----------------+
| User_ID    | int(11)     | NO   | PRI | NULL    | auto_increment |
| First_Name | varchar(20) | NO   |     |         |                |
| Last_Name  | varchar(20) | NO   |     |         |                |
| Address    | varchar(70) | NO   |     |         |                |
| PhoneNo    | varchar(10) | NO   |     |         |                |
| Email      | varchar(30) | NO   |     | NULL    |                |
+------------+-------------+------+-----+---------+----------------+
```

Ans.

```
import mysql.connector as con
mycon=con.connect(host="localhost",\
    user="root",\passwd="",
    \database='pythondb')
if(mycon.is_connected()==True):
    print("successfully connected to Mysql...!")
else:
    print("There is a problem in connecting to database")

cursor=mycon.cursor()
query="INSERT INTO users(First_Name,Last_Name,Address,PhoneNo,Email)\
    VALUES('{}','{}','{}','{}','{}')".format('Satyam','Kumar',\
    '23 E-Pkt Sadar bazar','7676767676','sk@test.com')
cursor.execute(query)
print("Affetced rows: "+ str(cursor.rowcount))
cursor.close()
mycon.close()
```

Output:

```
successfully connected to Mysql...!
Affected rows: 1
```

User ID is not auto-increment, hence it is not provided in the query.

7. Write a program to count the number of rows in a table.

Ans. Method 1: Retrieve the result using query:

```
select count(*) from users;
import mysql.connector as con
mycon=con.connect(host="localhost",user="root",passwd="",database='pythondb')
if(mycon.is_connected()==True):
    print("successfully connected to Mysql...!")
else:
    print("There is a problem in connecting to database")
cursor=mycon.cursor()

#Retrieves row count from query
query="SELECT count(*) from users"
cursor.execute(query)
row=cursor.fetchone()
print("The number of rows " + str(list(row)) )
```

```
cursor.close()
mycon.close()
```

Output:

```
The number of rows 4
```

Method 2:

- Using select * from users
- Iterate cursor over all rows
- Print row count using cursor.rowcount

```
import mysql.connector as con
mycon=con.connect(host="localhost",user="root",passwd="",database='pythondb')
if(mycon.is_connected()==True):
   print("succesfully connected to Mysql...!")
else:
   print("There is a problem in connecting to database ")

cursor = mycon.cursor()
query="SELECT * from users"
cursor.execute(query)
row=cursor.fetchone()

while row is not None:
    row=cursor.fetchone()
print("The number of rows", end='')

print(cursor.rowcount)
cursor.close()
mycon.close()
```

Output:

```
The number of rows 4
```

8. Write a program to insert multiple rows in a table using a single query.

Ans.

```
import mysql.connector as con

mycon=con.connect(host="localhost",
   user="root",
   passwd="",
   database='pythondb')

if(mycon.is_connected()==True):
   print("successfully connected to Mysql...!")
else:
   print("There is a problem in connecting to database")

cursor = mycon.cursor()

query="INSERT INTO users(First_Name,Last_Name,Address,PhoneNo,Email)\
   VALUES \
```

```
    ('Narayan','Mishra','Shivaji Nagar', '9807654321', 'narayan@test.com'),\
    ('Prateek','Sharma','Bapu Nagar','9999765432','prateek@test.com'),\
    ('Dinesh','vijaykumar','Shastri Nagar','9899654321','dinesh@test.com'),\
    ('Manish','Verma','9807654321','T Nagar','narayan@test.com');"

cursor.execute(query)
mycon.commit()
print("Affected rows: "+str(cursor.rowcount))
cursor.close()
mycon.close()
```

Output:

```
Affected rows: 4
```

9. Write a program that fetches (n) rows from the database and displays them one by one.

Ans.

```
import mysql.connector as con

mycon=con.connect(host="localhost",\
    user="root",\
    passwd="",
    database='pythondb')

if(mycon.is_connected()==True):
    print("successfully connected to Mysql...!")
else:
    print("There is a problem in connecting to database")

cursor=mycon.cursor()
query="SELECT * from users"
cursor.execute(query)
data=cursor.fetchmany(4)

for row in data:
    print(row)
mycon.close()
```

Output:

```
("1","Narayan","Mishra","Shivaji Nagar","9807654321","narayan@test.com")
("2","Prateek","Sharma","Bapu Nagar","9999765432","prateek@test.com")
("3","Dinesh","vijaykumar","Shastri Nagar","9899654321","dinesh@test.com")
("4","Manish","Verma","9807654321","T Nagar","narayan@test.com")
```

10. Write a program that fetches all the rows from a table in a database and displays them one by one.

Ans.

```
import mysql.connector as con

mycon=con.connect(host="localhost",user="root",passwd="",database='pythondb')

if(mycon.is_connected()==True):
    print("successfully connected to Mysql...!")
    else:
```

```
    print("There is a problem in connecting to database")

cursor=mycon.cursor()
query="SELECT * from users"
cursor.execute(query)
data=cursor.fetchall()
for row in data:
    print(row)
mycon.close()
```

Output:

```
successfully connected to  Mysql...!
Narayan,Mishra,Shivaji Nagar,9807654321,narayan@test.com
Prateek,Sharma,Bapu Nagar,9999765432,prateek@test.com
Dinesh,vijaykumar,Shastri Nagar,9899654321,dinesh@test.com
Manish,Verma,9807654321,T Nagar,narayan@test.com
```

11. Write a program that demonstrates the use of commit and rollback.

Ans.

```
import mysql.connector as connection
# Open database connection
dbconn = mysql.connector.connect(user='root', \
    password='',\
    host='localhost',\
    database='pythondb')

# Create a cursor using cursor() method
cursor = dbconn.cursor()

#The SQL query to INSERT records in a table.
sql = "query=SELECT * FROM USERS "

try:
    # Execute the SQL command using execute
    cursor.execute(sql)
    # Commit the changes in database
    dbconn.commit()

except:
    # Rollback in case of an error
    dbconn.rollback()

# disconnect from server
dbconn.close()
```

12. Mention the generic steps to execute a query using Python.

Ans. Steps to execute a query using python:

1. Import the package
2. Open connection by providing credentials
3. Get a connection object
4. Create a cursor

5. Execute query
6. Extract data from the result
7. Close the cursor/connection

13. Draw a flow chart of the steps mentioned in the question 12.

Ans. The steps can be represented with the following flowchart:

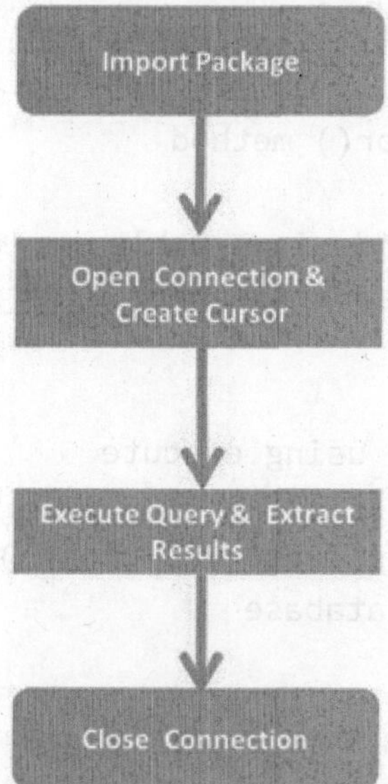

14. Write a program to connect to a MySQL database and fetch all records where the grade is 'A' from the students table.

Ans.
```
import mysql.connector as con

mycon=con.connect(host="localhost",user="root",passwd="",database='pythondb')

if(mycon.is_connected()==True):
    print("successfully connected to Mysql...!")
else:
    print("There is a problem in connecting to database")

cursor=mycon.cursor()
query="SELECT * from students where grade='A' "
cursor.execute(query)
data=cursor.fetchall()

for row in data:
    print(row)

mycon.commit()
cursor.close()
mycon.close()
```

Output:
```
successfully connected to Mysql...!
(5, 'Ashish', 'kishan lal', 8, 'A')
(23, 'Mukesh Kumar', 'Mahesh Sharna', 8, 'A')
(27, 'Naresh', 'Suresh Kumar', 8, 'A')
```

15. Write a function that updates row(s) using a parameterization query.

Ans. A parameterized query allows providing parameters that can be inserted into the query at the time of execution. The following example demonstrates the use of parameterizing a query:

```
import mysql.connector as con
def updatephone(id,PhoneNo):
    # Open database connection
    dbconn = con.connect(user='root',password='',host='localhost',database='pythondb')

    # Create a cursor using cursor() method
    cursor = dbconn.cursor()
    # SQL query to INSERT a records in a table.
    sql = 'update users set phoneno= %s where user_id = %s'
    dtuple = (PhoneNo,id)
    try:
        # Execute the SQL command using execute
        cursor.execute(sql,dtuple)
        print('Affected rows: '+str(cursor.rowcount))
        # Commit the changes in database
        dbconn.commit()
    except:
        # Rollback in case of an error
        dbconn.rollback()
        # disconnect from server
    dbconn.close()

updatephone(1,'1234567891')
```

Output:

```
successfully connected to Mysql...!
Affected rows: 1
```

16. Assume that table users have 15 rows. Find out the output of the following code.

Ans.

```
import mysql.connector as con

mycon=con.connect(host="localhost",\
    user="root",\
    passwd="",\
    database='pythondb')

if(mycon.is_connected()==True):
    print("successfully connected to Mysql...!")
else:
    print("There is a problem in connecting to database")

cursor=mycon.cursor()
query="SELECT * from users"
cursor.execute(query)
data =cursor.fetchone()
count = cursor.rowcount
```

```
print (count)
data =cursor.fetchmany(4)
count = cursor.rowcount

print (count)
data =cursor.fetchall()
count = cursor.rowcount
print (count)
```

Output:

```
Successfully connected to Mysql...!
1
4
10
```

17. Explain database operations.

Ans. Database operations are:

- **Insert:** Insert is a DML statement used to add the record or row in a table.
- **Select:** It fetches rows from table or tables.
- **Update:** It changes the values of the row or rows based on a query.
- **Delete:** It removes the row or rows based on a query.
- **Commit:** It instructs the database to make changes permanent done by a query.
- **Rollback:** It undoes or reverts the changes made by the query.

18. Name the databases that can be accessed using Python.

Ans. The following databases can be accessed using Python:

- MySQL
- Oracle
- Postgre
- SQLite
- Sybase
- SQLServer
- Microsoft Access

19. Write an equivalent query for the following string.

```
query = "insert into users (First_Name,Last_Name,Address,PhoneNo,Email) values
('%s','%s','%s','%s','%s')"  %  ('Ashish','Bhargava','Address  1','9999988888','email@
test.com')
```

Ans. The equivalent query is as follows:

```
insert into users (First_Name,Last_Name,Address,PhoneNo,Email)
values('Ashish','Bhargava','Address 1','9999988888','email@test.com')
```

Multiple-Choice Questions and Answers

1. Which of the following is true?

a. MySQL Connector/Python allows accessing MySQL databases.

b. It is written in pure Python.

c. It does not have any dependencies except for the Python Standard Library.

d. All of the above.

Ans. Option d, that is, All of the above.

2. **Which of the following methods is not used with the cursor?**
   a. fetchone()
   b. fetchmany()
   c. fetchall()
   d. fetchmultiple()

Ans. Option d, that is, fetchmultiple().

3. **Which of the following is not the method of connection object?**
   a. commit
   b. rollback
   c. autocommit
   d. cursor

Ans. Option c, that is, autocommit.

Fill in the blanks

1. **The ___________ method confirms that the modification made by query or transaction is permanent.**

Ans. commit()

2. **The ___________ method undoes the modification made by query or current transaction.**

Ans. rollback()

3. **The cursor object allows running the query using the ___________ method.**

Ans. execute()

4. **The fetchone() method returns the ___________ of a query row or ___________.**

Ans. next row, None

18 MODEL QUESTION PAPER 1

Q1	UNIT-I	
(a)	**Which of the following is a valid logical operator in Python:** (i) // (ii) ? (iii) < (iv) and	1
Ans.	iv	
(b)	**Identify the type of tokens below:** (i) break (ii) _name	1
Ans.	(i) the break is a keyword (ii) _name is an identifier (name of a variable)	
(c)	**Name the Python Library modules which need to be imported to invoke the following functions:** (i) fabs() (ii) rand ()	1
Ans.	(i) Math module (ii) random module	

(d)	**Rewrite the following code in python after removing all syntax error(s). Underline each correction done in the code.**
	`10=Val`
	`If val%2==0:`
	`    print("Even")`
	`Else:`
	`    print("odd")`
		2

Ans.	**Error (mention with underline) — Code with Correction** 10=Val → Val=10 If → if val%2==0: → Val%2==0: Else: → else:	

(e)	**Find the output of the following python code:**
	`def change(s):`
	`    tmp=""`
	`    for char in range(0,len(s)):`
	`        if(s[char].isupper()):`
	`            tmp=tmp+s[char].lower()`
	`        elif s[char].islower():`
	`            tmp=tmp+s[char].upper()`
	`        else:`
	`            tmp=tmp+'xx'`
	`    print(tmp)`
	`change('gmaiL@.com')`
		2

Ans. **Output:**

```
GMAIlxxxxCOM
```

(f) **What will be the output of the following code?** 2

```
def defaultargs(num1 = 10, num2 = 20):
    num1 = num1+num2
    print( str(num1) +"#" + str(num2))

defaultargs(5)
defaultargs(5,10)
```

Ans. **Output:**

```
25#20
15#10
```

(g) **What are the possible outcomes of the following code?** 2

```
String ='CBSEONLINE'
num = random.randint(0,3)
n= 9
 while string[n] != 'L':
   print(string[n]+string[num]+'#', end='')
   num = num -1
   n= n-1
```

a) ES#NE#IO# b) LE#NO#ON# c) NS#IE#LO# d) EC#NB#IS#

Ans. **d**

The loop will execute 3 times. Each iteration print two alphabets followed by #.

The value of variable 'n' will vary from 9 to 7 the first alphabet will be E, N, or I so options 'b' and 'c' are eliminated. The value of variable num ranges from 0 to 3. The second alphabet can be C, B, S or E, so alphabet O cannot be the second character. Hence the option 'a' is also eliminated, so option d is correct.

Q2

(a) **Specify the syntax and explain the utility of the inbuilt function range()?** 1

Ans. ***Syntax:*** range(start, stop, step)

Utility: The in-built function range() generates a sequence of successive numbers between the range specified by the arguments. It accepts three arguments 1) start 2) stop 3) step.

Argument Name	Argument Utility	Argument Status
Start	An integer that specifies from where to start,	Optional, the default value is 0.
Stop	An integer that specifies where to end.	Required.
Step	An integer number that specifies the value of decrement or increment.	Optional, The default value is 1.

(b) **Which is the correct form of declaration of a tuple?** 1

(i) `Month={1:'Jan',2:'Feb',3:'Mar'}`

(ii) `Month=(1,'Jan',2,'Feb',3,'Mar')`

(iii) `Month=[1:'Jan',2:'Feb',3:'Mar']`

(iv) `Month={1'Jan',2'Jan',3'Jan'}`

Ans. (ii)

(c)	**Identify the valid type of the variable _t?** `_t = (2, [2,3], 'list', 3.14159)` (i) list (ii) dictionary (iii) array (iv) tuple	1
Ans.	(iv)	

(d)	**What is the output of the following?**
	`(i)`
	`_vowels = ['a', 'e','i' 'o','u']`
	`vowel = "a"`
	`while (vowel in _vowels):`
	`    print(vowel, end = " ")`
	`(ii)`
	`while (vowel not in _vowels):`
	`    print(vowel, end = " ")`
		2

Ans.	(i) It is an infinite loop; as the condition remains always true. Hence the loop will never terminate. (ii) No output The condition "vowel not in _vowels " is false since 'a' exists in the list. The condition is false, the while loop will not be executed. Hence, there is no output.	

(e)	**What is the output of the following?**
	`def swapgobal():`
	`    global x, y`
	`    x,y = y,x`
	`    print("Swapping the global variable")`
	`    print(x,y)`
	
	`x = 10`
	`y = 20`
	`swapgobal()`
	
	`print("Values after swapping the global variable")`
	`print(x,y)`
		2

Ans.	**Output:**
	`#Swapping the global variable`
	`#20 10`
	`#Values after swapping the global variable`
	`#20 10`	

(f)	**Explain how to access a global variable in a function where a local variable is declared in function with the same name as of global.**
	`def change():`
	`    global var`
	`    print("The global variable")`
	`    print(var)`
	`    # declare a local variable with the same as a global variable`
	`    var = 100`
	`    print("The local variable")`
	`    print(var)`
		2

	`# Global Scope`
	`var = 10`
	`change()`	

Ans.	**Output:**
	`The global variable`
	`10`
	`The local variable`
	`100`	

(g)	**Write a function in python to count the number of vowels in a text file.**	2

Ans.

```
def vcount():
    vowelcount = 0
    _file = open("f:\\examples\\quotes.txt", 'r')
    ch =_file.read(1)
    while True:
        if not ch:
            break
        else:
            if( ch in 'aeiouAEIOU' ):
                vowelcount+=1
        ch =_file.read(1)
    return vowelcount
print("The number of Vowels in file :")
print(vcount())
```

OR

Write a function to read a text file and display those words starting with A or E.

Ans.

```
def wcount():
    _file = open("f:\\files\\exercises.txt", 'r')
    lines = _file.readlines()
    wordcount = 0
    for line in lines:
        words = line.split()
        for word in words:
            if(word[0] == 'A' or word[0] =='E'):
                wordcount += 1
    return wordcount
print("The number of words in a file starts with A or E:")
print(wcount())
```

(h) **Write a recursive function in python that searches an element in a list.** — 3

The lower bound is 0 and the upper bound is len(list).

Ans.

```
def binsearch_rec(_list, ele, start=0, end=None):
    if end is None:
        end = len(_list) - 1
    if start > end:
        return False
```

```
    mid = (start + end) // 2
    if ele == _list[mid]:
        return mid
    if ele < _list[mid]:
        return binsearch_rec(_list, ele, start, mid-1)
    if ele> _list[mid]:
        return binsearch_rec(_list, ele, mid+1, end)
l=[2,3,5,7,9,11,15,20,25]
print(binsearch_rec (l,11,0,len(l)-1))
```

OR

Write a recursive function that returns the sum of all the digits of a number passed as an argument.

Ans.

```
def sumdigit(num):
#base case
   if ( num == 0):
      return 0
   else:
      num = num % 10
      return sum + sumdigit(num//10)
```

(i) **Write the functions push(value) and pop() to perform insertion and deletion operations in a stack using a list as a global variable.** 4

Ans.

```
# create the empty list
stack=[]
def push(val):
    # add element to the end of stack (top)
    stack.append(val)

def pop():
    #if stack is empty returns none
    if(stack == []):
       return None
    else:
       return stack.pop()
```

OR

Write a function, insert(name) and remove() to add and delete names from the queue. Use list as a global variable.

Ans.

```
queue =[]
def enqueue(val):
# add element to the end of queue(rear)
    queue.append(val)

def dequeue():
    #if queue is empty returns none
    if(queue == []):
       return None
    else:
       return queue.pop(0)
```

(j) Ans.	**Explain the difference between a text file and a CSV file.** <table><tr><th>CSV file</th><th>Text file</th></tr><tr><td>The values in CSV files are comma-separated.</td><td>The values in text files are plain text.</td></tr><tr><td>The extension of csv file is .csv.</td><td>The extension of a text file is .txt.</td></tr></table>***Note:*** **All the CSV files are text file but all text files are not CSV files.**	2

Q3(a)
Ans.
	How to write multiple rows using function writerows() **to the CSV file?**
	The Writerows function accepts a list of lists and writes all the rows at once.
	`import csv`
	`with open('F:\\file\\employee2.csv', mode='w', newline='') as _file:`
	`    _writer = csv.writer(_file, delimiter='|', quotechar='"')`
	`    _writer.writerows(`
	`        [`
	`            ['Vijay Shankar', 'Accounting', 'November'] ,`
	`            ['Kiran Kumar', 'IT', 'March']`
	`        ]`
	`        )`
		2

(b) Ans.	**Define what is byte array.** A byte-array is a mutable sequence of integers in the range between 0 to 255. The bytearray() function manipulates its elements as the numbers range between 0-255 or one-char strings.	1
(c) Ans.	**The rb+ and wb+ modes used for reading and writing to a binary file then what is the difference between them?** wb+ creates the file from scratch whereas rb+ does not create the file from scratch.	1
(d) Ans.	**Write an algorithm to write to a binary file?** Algorithm for writing into a binary file: **Step 1:** Open a file in write and binary mode **Step 2:** Write byte-array to the file **Step 3:** Close the file	1

(e)
Ans.
	Write a program that writes and reads a list of integers using a binary file?
	#Example: Write list to a Binary File
	`f=open("F:\files\list.dat","wb")`
	`num=[5, 10, 15, 20, 25]`
	`arr=bytearray(num)`
	`f.write(arr)`
	`f.close()`
	`#The tuple() function converts the bytearray to list`
	`f=open("F:\files\list.dat" ,"rb")`
	`#convert byte array to list`
	`num= list(f.read())`
	`print (num)`
	`f.close()`
		2

(f) Ans.	**Explain the utility of pickle?** Pickling is helpful where applications need to store data persistently on secondary storage devices. The program can use it later from the disk. It is also used to send data over an internet (Transmission Control Protocol/Internet Protocol or a socket connection) to access it remotely or save python objects in a database.	2

Q4	UNIT-II	
(a) Ans.	**Which clause is used to sort the query result?** Order by	1
(b) Ans.	**Which clause is used to sort the query result in descending order?** Order by desc	1
(c) Ans.	**Mention an aggregate function that adds all the value of a column?** Sum	1
(d) Ans.	**Differentiate between foreign key and Primary key**	2

Primary Key	Foreign key
A **Primary Key** uniquely identifies a record in the table.	A **foreign key** is a field in the table that is the **primary key** in another table.
A table can have only one primary key in a table.	A table can have more than one foreign key in a table.

(e) **Table employee.** 2

empid	fname	lname	email	contact	sex	deptid
1	Akash	Jain	ajain@abcinc.com	999087645	M	1
2	Mukesh	Verma	mverma@abcinc.com	789035671	M	2
3	Aparna	Jain	ajain@abcinc.com	991090387	F	1
4	Jay	Arora	jarora@abcinc.com	987549875	M	2
5	Jyoti	Sharma	jsharma@abcinc.com	983456778	F	1

Find out the following from a relation employee.

1. **Cardinality**
2. **Degree**
3. **Domain values for attribute sex**
4. **Identify primary key**

Ans.

1. 5
2. 7
3. M, F
4. Empid

(f) **Write a output for SQL queries (i) to (iii), which are based on the table:**

STUDENT				
Name	**class**	**dob**	**stream**	**marks**
Ankit	12	12-12-2002	science	471
Akash	12	10-11-2002	science	479
Beena	12	11-11-2002	science	451
Brijesh	12	10-09-2001	science	540
Charu	12	09-10-2002	science	502
Dinesh	11	08-10-2002	commerce	491
Manish	11	07-06-2002	commerce	477
Manju	11	01-03-2002	commerce	501
prince	11	06-06-2002	commerce	399
Zeeba	11	02-05-2002	commerce	445

<table>
<tr><td>(i)
Ans.</td><td>SELECT COUNT(*), stream FROM STUDENT GROUP BY stream HAVING COUNT(*) >1;
Count(*) stream
5 science
5 commerce</td><td>1</td></tr>
<tr><td>(ii)
Ans.</td><td>SELECT MIN(DOB), MAX(DOB), FROM STUDENT;
MIN(DOB) MAX(DOB)
10-09-2001 12-12-2002</td><td>1</td></tr>
<tr><td>(iii)
Ans.</td><td>SELECT details FROM STUDENT WHERE stream=' science';
Name class dob stream marks
Ankit 12 12-12-2002 science 471
Akash 12 10-11-2002 science 479
Beena 12 11-11-2002 science 451
Brijesh 12 10-09-2001 science 540
Charu 12 09-10-2002 science 502</td><td>1</td></tr>
<tr><td>(g)</td><td>Write SQL queries for (i) to (iv), which are based on the table: STUDENT given in the question (f).</td><td></td></tr>
<tr><td>(i)
Ans.</td><td>To display details of students in alphabetical order of their name.
Select * from student order by name ASC.</td><td>1</td></tr>
<tr><td>(ii)
Ans.</td><td>To display Class, stream, and where marks are between 400 and 520.
Select class, stream from student where marks >=400 and marks <=520.</td><td>1</td></tr>
<tr><td>(iii)
Ans.</td><td>To display Name, Class and marks obtained are greater than 450 each class
Select name, class, marks from student group by class having marks > 450.</td><td>1</td></tr>
<tr><td>(iv)
Ans.</td><td>To decrease marks by 5 where a stream is commerce.
Update student set marks = marks - 5 where stream ='commerce'.</td><td>1</td></tr>
<tr><td>Q5</td><td>Here are two tables

Table Member
<table><tr><th>member_id</th><th>name</th></tr><tr><td>1</td><td>Akash</td></tr><tr><td>2</td><td>Mahesh</td></tr><tr><td>3</td><td>Mukesh</td></tr><tr><td>4</td><td>Ramesh</td></tr><tr><td>5</td><td>Vinay</td></tr></table>
Table Committee
<table><tr><th>committee_id</th><th>name</th></tr><tr><td>1</td><td>Akash</td></tr><tr><td>2</td><td>Mukesh</td></tr><tr><td>3</td><td>Vinay</td></tr><tr><td>4</td><td>Ajay</td></tr><tr><td>5</td><td>Naresh</td></tr></table></td><td></td></tr>
</table>

(a)	**Write a query that joins these tables based on an inner join.**	

Ans.

```
SELECT
members.member_id,
members.name ,
committees.committee_id,
committees.name
FROM
members
INNER JOIN committees
   ON committees.name = members.name;
```

Output:

member_id	name	committee_id	name
1	Akash	1	Akash
3	Mukesh	2	Mukesh
5	Vinay	3	Vinay

(b)	**Write a query that joins these tables based on left join.**	2

Ans.

```
SELECT
members.member_id,
members.name ,
committees.committee_id,
committees.name
FROM
members
LEFT JOIN committees
   ON committees.name = members.name;
```

Output:

member_id	name	committee_id	name
1	Akash	1	Akash
3	Mukesh	2	Mukesh
5	Vinay	3	Vinay
2	Mahesh	NULL	NULL
4	Ramesh	NULL	NULL

(c)	**Write a query that joins these tables based on a Right join**	2

Ans.

```
SELECT
members.member_id,
members.name ,
committees.committee_id,
committees.name
FROM
members
```

	RIGHT JOIN committees ON committees.name = members.name; **Output:**	

member_id	name	committee_id	name
1	Akash	1	Akash
3	Mukesh	2	Mukesh
5	Vinay	3	Vinay
NULL	NULL	4	Ajay
NULL	NULL	5	Naresh

Q6	**UNIT-III**	
(a) **Ans.**	**Name two protocols that retrieve the email from the server to an email client.** **Two protocols that retrieve the email from the server to** an email client are: IMAP and POP	1
(b) **Ans.**	**Differentiate between domain and web hosting?** Web Hosting is buying a space usually called a server or cloud to store files and serve the request through the Internet. Domain Registration is where an individual or organization buys or leases a name in a human-readable form of an IP address. It is known as a **domain** name. Each domain has a unique IP address on the Internet to access it.	1
(c) **Ans.**	**Define an URL?** **URL** stands for *Uniform Resource Locator*. It is the address of web resources to uniquely identify it on the World Wide Web (WWW). It is also known as the web address of a resource. URL is consist of multiple parts- including a domain name, protocol, resources name including path, it tells a web browser where the resources are located.	1
(d) **Ans.**	**What is XML?** XML stands for eXtensible Markup Language. It is designed to store data in a self-descriptive way and transport the data. It is a markup language and it is used to create the own data type. XML data is self-defining or self-describing. The structure is embedded within the data itself.	1
(e) **Ans.**	**Define web service?** A web service is a set of standards and protocols that are used to exchange data between applications. It includes software, application, or cloud technology that can be accessed through the HTTP or HTTPS (web protocols) to, communicate, interoperate and exchange messages over the internet.	1
(f) **Ans.**	**Give the full forms of the following** **(i) HTTPS** **(ii) TCP** **(iii) SMTP** **(iv)SCP** **HTTPS:** HyperText Transfer Protocol Secure **TCP:** Transmission Control Protocol **SMTP:** Simple Mail Transfer Protocol **SCP:** Secure Copy Protocol	1
(g)	**Explain how the network layout is designed across the building or multi cities?** ABC Corp. has set up its new center at Xyz city for its office. It has 4 blocks in buildings named Block A, Block B, Block C, Block D.	4

Building	Number of Computers
Block A	22
Block B	45
Block C	110
Block D	15

Shortest distances between various Blocks in meters:

Block A to Block B	65 m
Block B to Block C	45 m
Block C to Block A	35 m
Block D to Block C	55 m
Block A to Block B	65 m

Answer the following questions:

(i) What is the most suitable block where a server can be placed?

Ans. A server is a place where most of the computers are installed; hence the server should be placed at block C.

(ii) Suggest the network (topology) to connect all the blocks.

Ans. To connect the network we can use star topology where the central node is connected to every node.

(iii) The company is planning to link all the blocks through a secure and high speed wired medium. Suggest a way to connect all the blocks.

Ans. For a high-speed network, Optic fiber should be laid out although it might be costly as compared to other alternatives.

(iv) Advice the most suitable wired medium for connecting each computer installed in every block out of the following network cables:

Ethernet Cable

Coaxial Cable

Single Pair Telephone Cable.

Ans. i. Ethernet Cable (It is suitable for providing connectivity in a building).

MODEL QUESTION PAPER 2

Q1	UNIT-I	
(a)	**Which of the following is a valid arithmetic operator in Python:** (i) // (ii) ? (iii) < (iv) and	1
Ans.	i	
(b)	**Identify the type of tokens given below:** (i) continue (ii) name_123	1
Ans.	(i) continue is a keyword (ii) name_123 is an identifier(name of a variable)	
(c)	**Name the Python Library modules which need to be imported to invoke the following functions:** (i) ceil() (ii) randint ()	1
Ans.	(i) Math module (ii) random module	

(d)	**Rewrite the following code in python after removing all syntax error(s). Underline each correction done in the code.**
	`1=Val`
	`while( val < 10):`
	`    if(Val = 5):`
	`        break`
		2

Ans.	Error(mention with underline): <u>`1=Val`</u> → Code with Correction: `Val = 1`
	`while(` <u>`val`</u> `< 10):` → `while( Val < 10):`
	<u>`if(Val = 5)`</u> → `if(Val == 5)`
	`break` → `break`
	<u>Increment is missing</u> → `Val+=1`	

(e)	**Find and write the output of the following python code:**	2

```
def counts(s):

    digitcount=0
    alphacount=0

    for char in range(0,len(s)):
        if(s[char].isdigit()):
            digitcount+=1
        elif s[char].isalpha():
            alphacount+=1
        else:
            pass
    #return a tuple
    return (digitcount, alphacount)
```

```
#unpacking tuple
nd, ac =counts('mail@123.com')
print("Number of digits in string is ", nd)
print("Number of the alphabets in a string is ", ac)
```

Ans. Number of digits in string is 3

Number of alphabets in string is 7

(f) **What will be the output of the following code?** 2

```
def defaultargs(num1 , num2 = 0):
    num1 = num1+num2
    print( str(num1) +"#" + str(num2))
defaultargs(5)
defaultargs()
```

Ans. 5#0

#TypeError: defaultargs() missing 1 required positional argument: 'num1'

(g) **What are the possible outcomes of the following code?** 2

```
_list =[100,75,10,125]
rand = random.randint(1) + 2
while(rand < 4):
    print(_list[rand],"*")
    rand+=1
```

i. 100*75

ii. 75*10*125*

iii. 75*10*

iv. 10*125*

Ans. **iv**

The minimum value of rand is 2, when randint(0,1) = 0. In this case, 10*125* will be printed.

The maximum value of rand is 3, when random(0,1) = 1. Only 125* get printed which is not an option. Hence, option iv is a correct option

Q2

(a) **Specify the syntax and explain the utility of the inbuilt function random.randrange()?** 1

Ans. ***Syntax:***

randrange (start, stop, step)

Utility:

The inbuilt function randrange() generates a sequence of successive numbers between the range specified by the arguments. It accepts three arguments

1. start
2. stop
3. step

Argument Name	Argument Utility	Argument Status
Start	An integer that specifies from where to start.	Optional, the default value is 0.
Stop	An integer that specifies where to end.	Required.
Step	An integer number that specifies the value of decrement or increment.	Optional, The default value is 1.

(b)	**Which is the correct form of declaration of a dictionary?** (i) `Month={1:'Jan',2:'Feb',3:'Mar'}` (ii) `Month=(1;'Jan',2;'Feb',3;'Mar')` (iii) `Month=[1:'Jan',2:'Feb',3:'Mar']` (iv) `Month={1'Jan',2'Jan',3'Jan'}`	**1**
Ans.	(i)	
(c)	**Identify the valid type of a variable _t?** `_t = (2, [2,3], 'list', 3.14159)` (i) list (ii) dictionary (iii) array (iv) tuple	**1**
Ans.	iv	

(d)	**What is the output of the following?**
	i) `while True:`
	`        num = int(input("Enter an integer : "))`
	`        print("The double of",num,"is",2 * num)`
	ii) `i =1`
	`    while (True):`
	`        break`
	`        print(i, end = " ")`
		2

Ans.	i) Infinite loop; the condition is always true. Hence, this will never terminate ii) No output The break will terminate the loop. Hence, there is no output	

(e)	**What is the output of the following?**
	`def swap(a , b ):`
	`    a,b = b,a`
	`    print("Values swapped in function ")`
	`    print(a,b)`
	`x = 10`
	`y = 20`
	`swap(x,y)`
	`print("Values after the function call")`
	`print(x,y)`
		2

Ans.	Values swapped in function 20 10 Values after the function call 10 20 Variable 'a' and 'b ' are local to the function swap, swapped in function, the value will not reflect outside the function.	

(f)	**Find the output of the following**
	`def sim_interest (prin,rate=0.07,time=2):`
	`    return prin*rate*time`
	a) `print( sim_interest(rate=0.12,prin=10000,time=4) )`
	b) `print( sim_interest(10000,rate=0.05))`
	c) `print(sim_interest(rate=0.05,10000) )`
	d) `print(sim_interest(time=2,rate=0.05))`
		2

Ans.	4800.0 1000.0 SyntaxError: positional argument follows keyword argument TypeError: sim_interest() missing 1 required positional argument: 'print'	

Q3		
(a)	**Write a program that adds rows to a CSV file?**	2

Ans.

```
import csv
_file =open('F:\\files\\employee1.csv', mode='w',newline='')
with _file:
    employee_writer = csv.writer(_file, delimiter=',', quotechar='"')
    employee_writer.writerow(['Vijay Shankar', 'Accounting', 'November'])
    employee_writer.writerow(['Kiran Kumar', 'IT', 'March'])
```

Output:

```
Vijay Shankar, Accounting, November
Kiran Kumar, IT, March
```

(b) Write a program to display the number of words in the text file, use the read() method to read the content of the file, below is the content of the file is — 2

Dream it. Wish it. Do it.
Success doesn't just find you. You have to go out and get it.
Push yourself, because no one else is going to do it for you.

Ans.

```
wordcount = 0
_file = open("f:\\examples\\quotes.txt", 'r')
wordcount = len( (_file.read()).split())
_file.close()
print("The number of words in a file:")
print(wordcount)
```

Output:

```
The number of words in a file:
32
```

OR

Write a program to display the number of words by reading a file line by line

Ans.

```
wordcount = 0
_file = open("f:\\examples\\quotes.txt", 'r')
lines = _file.readlines()
for line in lines:
    words = line.split()
    wordcount += len(words)
print("The number of words in a file:")
print(wordcount)
```

Output:

```
The number of words in a file:
32
```

(c) How to write the dictionary to a CSV file? — 2

Ans. The DictWriter is used to write the dictionary to the CSV file.
For example:

```
with open('F:\\files\\names.csv',mode='w',newline='') as _f :
#Creating header for the file
fnames = ['first_name', 'last_name']
```

```
writer = csv.DictWriter(_f, fieldnames=fnames)
writer.writeheader()
    writer.writerow({'first_name' : 'Khaniya', 'last_name': 'Kumar'})
    writer.writerow({'first_name' : 'Zoya', 'last_name': 'Khan'})
    writer.writerow({'first_name' : 'Julia', 'last_name': 'Roberts'})
```

Output:

F:\Files\names.csv - Notepad++

```
1 first_name,last_name
2 Khaniya,Kumar
3 Zoya,Khan
4 Julia,Roberts
```

(d) Write a program that pickle and unpickle a string? 2

Ans.

```
string ="this is test string"
with open('F:\\files\\stringdata.dat', 'wb') as _file:
pickle.dump(string,_file)
# Unpickling the string

with open('F:\\files\\stringdata.dat', 'rb') as _file:
_dataretrieve =pickle.load(_file )
print(_dataretrieve)
```

Output:

```
"this is test string"
```

(e) (i) Write a Recursive function in python that search an element in a list. 3

Ans.

```
def bubble_sort(_list,n):
    for i in range(len(_list)-2):
        if _list[i] > _list[i+1]:
            #swap by simultaneous assignment
            _list[i], _list[i+1] = l[i+1], l[i]
        if n>1:
            bubble_sort(_list,n-1)
l = [9,2,6,11,3,8,7,15]
n=len(l)
bubble_sort(l,n)
print(l)
```

Output:

```
[2, 3, 6, 7, 8, 9, 11, 15]
```

OR

Write a Recursive function that returns the multiplication of all digits of a number passed as an argument.

Ans.

```
def muldigit(num):
    global mul
    #base case
    if ( num <10):
```

	``
	        return num
	    else:
	        mul = num % 10
	        num = num//10
	        return mul * muldigit(num)
	num = 1234
	print(muldigit(num))
	``
	Output
	24	

(f) **Ans.**	**Why is complexity used?** The complexity of an algorithm in computer science is a way of classifying how efficient an algorithm is as compared to its alternative ones.	**1**
(g) **Ans.**	**Define Big O notation.** The Big O notation tells how long an algorithm takes to run. It helps in comparing the efficiency of different algorithms. The Big O notation is an expression that tells how quickly it grows relative to the input.	**1**
(h) **Ans.**	**Why is the performance of an algorithm measured?** A problem can be solved by using multiple algorithms. The performance of an algorithm helps to select the most suitable algorithm among multiple algorithms that can solve a problem. The performance of an algorithm is a process of making an evaluative judgment about algorithms. The Big O notation is one way to evaluate the performance of an algorithm.	**1**

(i)
Ans.
	Write the functions push(list, value) and pop(list) to perform insertion and deletion operations in a stack.
	``
	# create the empty list
	def push(stack, val):
	    # add element to the end of stack (top)
	    stack.append(val)
	def pop(stack):
	    #if stack is empty returns none
	    if(stack == []):
	        return None
	    else:
	        return stack.pop()
	_list =[]
	push(_list,5)
	push(_list,10)
	pop(_list)
	pop(_list)
	``
	Output
	10
	5
	OR
	Write a function, insert(name) and remove() to add and delete names from the queue. Use list as a global variable.
	``
	def enqueue(queue,val):
	    # add element to the end of rear (rear)
	``
		4

```
    queue.append(val)

def dequeue(qu):
    #if queue is empty returns none
    if(queue == []):
        return None
    else:
        return queue.pop(0)
q=[]
enqueue(q, 5)
enqueue(q,10)
print(dequeue(q))
print(dequeue(q))
```

Output:

```
5
10
```

Q4		
(a) **Ans.**	**Which clause is used to group results based on column values?** Group By	1
(b) **Ans.**	**Which clause is used to sort the query result in ascending order?** Order by asc or Order by	1
(c) **Ans.**	**Which clause is used to update the records of a table?** Update clause	1
(d) **Ans.**	**An aggregate function that fetches the average value of a column?** Avg() function	1
(e) **Ans.**	**Write the use of GROUP BY clause.** The GROUP BY clause in SQL is used for arranging rows based on the similar data values of a column with the help of some functions. For example, GROUP BY city; arranges results based on each city	2
(f) **Ans.**	**Define the following terms:** ➢ Tuple ➢ Attributes ➢ Cardinality ➢ Primary key ➢ **Tuple:** A record or a row in a relation. ➢ **Attributes:** The column in the relation/ table is called attributes. ➢ **Cardinality:** Cardinality the number of tuples in a relation. ➢ **Primary key:** An attribute or a set of attributes that identify a tuple uniquely.	2
(g)	**Write a output for SQL queries (i) to (iii), which are based on the below table: STUDENT**	

Name	class	dob	stream	marks
Ankit	12	12-12-2002	science	471
Akash	12	10-11-2002	science	479
Beena	12	11-11-2002	science	451
Brijesh	12	10-09-2001	science	540

	Charu 12 09-10-2002 science 502 Dinesh 11 08-10-2002 commerce 491 Manish 11 07-06-2002 commerce 477 Manju 11 01-03-2002 commerce 501 prince 11 06-06-2002 commerce 399 Zeeba 11 02-05-2002 commerce 445	1
Ans.	**(i) SELECT COUNT(*), class FROM STUDENT GROUP BY stream HAVING COUNT(*) >1;** Count(*) class 5 12 5 11	
	(ii) SELECT MAX(DOB), MIN(DOB), FROM STUDENT;	1
Ans.	MIN(DOB) MAX(DOB) 10-09-2001 12-12-2002	
	(iii) **SELECT details FROM STUDENT WHERE class =12;**	1
Ans.	Name class dob stream marks Ankit 12 12-12-2002 science 471 Akash 12 10-11-2002 science 479 Beena 12 11-11-2002 science 451 Brijesh 12 10-09-2001 science 540 Charu 12 09-10-2002 science 502	
(h)	**Write SQL queries for (i) to (iv), which are based on the table: STUDENT given in the above question (g).**	
	(i) **To display details of students in descending order of their name.**	1
Ans.	`Select * from student order by name DESC`	
	(ii) **To display name, marks, and where the marks are between 400 and 520.**	1
Ans.	`Select name, marks from student marks >=400 and marks <=500`	
	(iii) **To display Name, Class, marks, stream and marks obtained > 500 based on each stream**	1
Ans.	`Select name, class, marks, stream from student group by class having marks > 500`	
	(iv) **To increase marks by 5 where a class is 12**	1
Ans.	`Update student set marks = marks + 5 where class = 12`	
Q5		
(a)	**Write a query that joins below tables using an inner join**	2
Ans.	**Table Member**	

member_id	name
1	Akash
2	Mahesh
3	Mukesh
4	Ramesh
5	Vinay

Table Committee

committee_id	name
1	Akash
2	Mukesh
3	Vinay
4	Ajay
5	Naresh

```
SELECT
members.member_id,
members.name ,
committees.committee_id,
committees.name
FROM
committees
INNER JOIN members
   ON committees.name = members.name;
```

Output:

member_id	name	committee_id	name
1	Akash	1	Akash
3	Mukesh	2	Mukesh
5	Vinay	3	Vinay

(b) Write a query that joins tables using left join. 2

Ans.

```
SELECT
members.member_id,
members.name ,
committees.committee_id,
committees.name
FROM committees
LEFT JOIN members
   ON committees.name = members.name;
```

Output:

member_id	name	committee_id	name
1	Akash	1	Akash
3	Mukesh	2	Mukesh
5	Vinay	3	Vinay
NULL	NULL	4	Ajay
NULL	NULL	5	Naresh

(c) Write a query that joins tables using right join. 2

Ans.

```
SELECT
members.member_id,
members.name ,
```

	committees.committee_id, committees.name FROM committees RIGHT JOIN Members ON committees.name = members.name;	

Output:

member_id	name	committee_id	name
1	Akash	1	Akash
3	Mukesh	2	Mukesh
5	Vinay	3	Vinay
2	Mahesh	NULL	NULL
4	Ramesh	NULL	NULL

Q6 **UNTI-III**

(a) **How to secure a system from cyber criminals?** 1

Ans. Here are the steps to safeguard the system from cyber criminals

- Use a Firewall
- Use strong passwords
- Keep the OS and software updated
- Manage social media settings

(b) A ________ reads the hardware addresses of incoming packets to transmit them to the appropriate destination. 1

Ans. Switch

(c) **Differentiate between a Switch and a Router** 1

Ans.

Switch	Router
A switch can only be used with a wired network.	A router can also link wired network or wireless network. A router has additional features, but its cost is higher than a switch.
The switches are designed to connect devices within a network.	The routers are designed to connect multiple networks.

(d) **Give the full forms of the following** 2

i) **HTTP** ii) **IP** iii) **POP** iv) **SSH**

Ans.

i) **HTTP:** HyperText Transfer Protocol

ii) **IP:** Internet Protocol

iii) **POP:** Post Office Protocol

iv) **SSH:** Secure Shell or Secure Socket shell

(e) **Identify the cybercrime form for the following situations:** 2

i) **A person gets a call over the phone that you have to perform KYC to run your Paytm, ask to install an app and allow to access the SMS, etc. and after a few minutes you see the transaction from your bank account this is a case of?**

Ans. This is a case of cyber crime or online fraud.

ii) **Some One downloaded the software from the illegal site and selling it to others.**

Ans. **Piracy**

(h) **A university campus has 4 wings as shown below:** **4**

Wing A

Wing B

Wing C

Wing D

Wing A to Wing B	**100 m**
Wing A to Wing C	**200 m**
Wing A to Wing D	**400 m**
Wing B to Wing C	**300m**
Wing B to Wing D	**100 m**
Wing C to Wing D	**450 m**

Wing A	**150 computers**
Wing B	**10 computers**
Wing C	**5 computers**
Wing D	**50 computers**

Answer the following questions:

a) **Suggest a suitable topology.**

b) **Identify the Wing where the server should install.**

c) **Suggest the placement for HUB and Switches.**

d) **Suggest the possible connection for network and internet.**

Ans. a) Star topology

b) The server should be placed in wing A, Since it has the highest computers.

c) In Wing A, D switches can be placed. In C, B Hubs can be placed. Repeaters can be used between A and D.

d) DSL / Leased line.

CASE STUDY 1: CREATING DATE CONVERSION UTILITY

- The date converter utility accepts the discrete values (day, month, year) and converts these values into a string that represents a date. This utility validates the input and converts it into the desired date format based on the parameter passed.

LEARNING OBJECTIVES

- Create a module that converts and store discrete values into string confirming to pre-specified date format.

Solution

The entire solution is divided into two parts:

a. A module that contains the code to convert values into a string

b. A program that tests the module

To validate input values, is leap Year() and is Valid Date() functions are created. Function dateformat() converts these input values into a string that represents a specified data format.

Code for Module Date format

The following code is from date format.py file:

```
# separators for the date
seperators='/-'

#list of the date formats
formats=['ddmmyy','ddmmmyy','ddmmyyyy','mmddyy','mmmddyy','mmddyyyy','yyyymmdd']

# This dictionary stores month number and their three word abbreviation
threechar_month={1:'Jan',2:'Feb',3:'Mar',4:'Apr',5:'May',6:'Jun',\
7:'Jul',8:'Aug',9:'Sep',10:'Oct',11:'Nov',12:'Dec'}
#  Valid  days  is  a  dictionary  that  contain  maximum  number  of  days  in  a  month
validdays={1:31,2:29,3:31,4:30,5:31,6:30,7:31,8:31,9:30,10:31,11:30,12:31}

# To check if a year is a leap year
# Return value: 1 if a year is a leap year
# Argument int year

def isleapYear(y):
    if( y % 4 == 0):
        if( (y % 100 == 0) and (y % 400 == 0)):
            return 1
```

```
        else:
            return 0
    else:
        return 0

# To check if a date is valid or not
# Return value: 1 if a date is a valid date
# @ Arguments int day, month, year
def isValidDate(d, m ,y):
    if (m >12):
        return 0
    if(d > 31):
        return 0
#if numbers of days are more than specified days in a month
if(d > validdays[m]):
    return 0
if(isleapYear(y) and m ==2 and d > 29):
    return 0

if(not isleapYear(y) and m ==2 and d > 28):
    return 0
return 1

# Converts the day, month, and year as a string in date format
# Returns a string that represents a date based on request format
# Arguments int day, month, year, Separator, format
# Separator and format are default arguments

def dateformat(dval, mval,yval, seperator='-',format='ddmmyy'):
    if( not isValidDate(dval,mval,yval)):
        print("Invalid Date")
        return
    #check if seperator is correct or not
    if( not( seperator in seperators) ):
        print("Not a valid  seperators")
        return
    #check if format in format list
    if( not( format in formats) ):
        print("Not a valid format ")
        return
    #join the day, month   and year
    if(format=='ddmmyy'):
        return str(dval)+seperator+str(mval)+\
        seperator+str(yval)[-2::] #fetch last 2 characters
    elif(format=='ddmmmyy'):
```

```
        return str(dval)+seperator+str(threechar_month[mval])+\
        seperator+str(yval)[-2::]
    elif(format=='ddmmyyyy'):
        return str(dval)+seperator+str(mval)+\
        seperator+str(yval)
    elif(format=='mmddyy'):
        return str(mval)+seperator+\
        str(dval)+seperator+str(yval)[-2::]
    elif(format=='mmmddyy'):
        return str(threechar_month[mval])+str(dval)+seperator+\
        seperator+str(yval)[-2::]
    elif(format=='mmddyyyy'):
        return str(mval)+seperator+str(dval)+\
        seperator+str(yval)
    elif(format=='yyyymmdd'):
        return str(yval)+seperator+str(mval)+\
        seperator+str(dval)
    else:
        return
```

Python program that tests the date format module (Test.py):

```
import dateformat
print(dateformat.dateformat(12,12,2001))
```

Output:

```
12-12-01
```

```
print(dateformat.dateformat(12,12,2001,'/'))
```

Output:

```
12/12/01
```

```
#Print date with separator '/' in various formats
print(dateformat.dateformat(12,12,2001,'/','ddmmyy'))
print(dateformat.dateformat(12,12,2001,'/','ddmmmyy'))
print(dateformat.dateformat(12,12,2001,'/','ddmmyyyy'))
print(dateformat.dateformat(12,12,2001,'/','mmddyy'))
print(dateformat.dateformat(12,12,2001,'/','mmmddyy'))
print(dateformat.dateformat(12,12,2001,'/','mmddyyyy'))
```

Output:

```
12/12/01
12/Dec/01
12/12/2001
12/Dec/01
Dec/12/01
Dec/12/2001
```

```
#Print date with separator '-'in various formats
print(dateformat.dateformat(12,12,2001,'-'))
print(dateformat.dateformat(12,12,2001,'-','ddmmyy'))
```

```
print(dateformat.dateformat(12,12,2001,'-','ddmmmyy'))
print(dateformat.dateformat(12,12,2001,'-','ddmmyyyy'))
print(dateformat.dateformat(12,12,2001,'-','mmddyy'))
print(dateformat.dateformat(12,12,2001,'-','mmmddyy'))
print(dateformat.dateformat(12,12,2001,'-','mmddyyyy'))
print(dateformat.dateformat(12,12,2001,'/','yyyymmdd'))
```

Output:

```
12-12-01
12-dec-01
12-Dec-2001
12-12-01
Dec-12-01
Dec-12-01
12-12-2001
2001/12/12
```

```
#invalid Date format
print(dateformat.dateformat(12,12,2001,'/','yyymmdd'))
```

Output:

```
Not a valid format None
```

```
#invalid separator
print(dateformat.dateformat(12,12,2001,'//'))
```

Output:

```
Not a valid separators
None
```

```
#invalid date month of April cannot have 31 days
print(dateformat.dateformat(31,4,2001,'-'))
```

Output:

```
Invalid Date
None
```

```
#invalid date month > 12
print(dateformat.dateformat(12,13,2001,'-'))
```

Output:

```
Invalid Date
None
```

```
#valid date in a leap year
print(dateformat.dateformat(29,2,2020,'-'))
```

Output:

```
29-2-20
```

```
print(dateformat.dateformat(32,4,2020,'-'))
```

Output:

```
Invalid Date
None
```

CASE STUDY 2: CREATING AND USING PACKAGE

INTRODUCTION

Generally, we do not place all our files in the same location on our computer. For easier access, we use a well organized directory hierarchy.For example, we can keep all the songs in the song folder in the same directory, futher we can divide our songs based on singer's name. Likewise, Python arranges code in has folder (package)and files (modules).

A Python package is directory with a file __init__.py. It may have sub-packages(directory) and modules(file). Packages in python helps large programs to divide in sub-packages and modules. We put similar modules in one package and other modules in different packages. It makes easy to plan a project (program) and makes it transparent conceptually.

A package is a directory that must contain a file called __init__.py; It is required to treat python as a package. This file can be left empty. Generally, the initialization code for that package is placed in this file.

LEARNING OBJECTIVES

- Create a custom package for a word guessing game.

Solution

First, we create a package and module to generate a random word. The steps are:

1. Create a directory Guessing App.
2. Create a directory guessing game.
3. Create __init__.py and paste the below code in __init__.py
   ```
   from .GuessingGame import wordgenerator
   ```
   Note: The '.' represents the current directory.
4. The package guessing game is created. Create the files word generator file and game.py and add it to a directory (package) guessing game. When all the files are created, the below structure is created as shown below:

Name

pycache

init

game

wordgenerator

Directory structure of package guessing game

The following will be the content in the word generator.py:

```
words=['about','above','abuse','actor','acute','admit','adopt','adult','af-
ter','again','agent','agree','ahead','alarm','album','alert','alike','alive','al-
low','alone','along','alter','among','anger','Angle','angry','brand','bread','break',
'breed','brief','bring','broad','broke','brown','build','built','buyer','cable','ca-
lif','carry','catch','cause','chain','chair','chart','chase','cheap','check','chest'
```

```
,'chief','child','civil',dance','dated','dealt','death','debut','delay','empty','en-
emy','enjoy','enter','entry','equal','error','event','every','exact','exist','ex-
tra','faith','false','fault','fiber','field','fifth','fifty','frame','frank','fraud','fresh'
,'front','fruit','fully','funny','giant','given','glass','globe','horse','hotel','house-
','human','ideal','image','index','inner','input','issue','jones','judge','known','la-
bel','large','laser','later','laugh','layer','learn','lease','least','leave','le-
gal','level','lunch','lying','magic','major','maker','march','maria','match','may-
be','mayor','meant','mouth','movie','music','needs','never','newly','occur','prize','
proof','proud','prove','queen','quick','quiet','quite','radio','raise','range','rap-
id','ratio','reach','ready','shall','shape','share','sharp','sheet','shelf','she
ll','shift','shirt','shock','shoot','short','shown','sight','table','taken','tas
te','taxes','teach','teeth','terry','undue','union','unity','until','upper','up-
set','urban','usage','usual','valid','value','video','virus','visit','vi-
tal','voice','waste','watch','water','wheel','where','which','while','white','whole','w
hose','woman','women','world','worry','worse','worst','worth','would','wound','write',
'wrong','wrote','yield','young','youth']

import random
def randomword():
    return random.choice(words)
```

5. Create the file game.py:

```
#import wordgenerator from the package
import wordgenerator

#import the time module
import time
name = input("Enter your name? ")

print("Hello, " + name, " Start playing word guessing game")
print("You have to guess five letters word in 10 guesses")
print (" ")
# Delay for 1 second
time.sleep(1)

print("Start guessing a word game")
time.sleep(0.5)

# Get a 5 letter random word
word = wordgenerator.randomword()
#creates an empty string
guesses = ''
nturns = 10
#check the number turns left
while nturns > 0:

    # a counter for failure
    failed = 0
```

```
    # fetch a character
    for char in word:

    # Check if a character is in  guesses string print it
        if char in guesses:

            print( char, end=' '   )

        else:

        # If no match, print a dash
            print ("_",end=' ')

        # Increase the failed counter by one
            failed += 1

    # if failed is equal to zero

    if failed == 0:
        print( " \nWow You have won the game!!!"  )

    # exit the script
        break

    print('\n')

    # Ask player to guess a letter
    guess = input("Guess a character: ")

    # set the players guess to guesses
    guesses += guess

    if guess not in word:

    # if the guess is not found decrease nturns counter by 1
        nturns -= 1

        print ("Wrong choice"  )

    # Number of terms left
        print( "You have ", + nturns, ' terms left now' )

    # if the nturns are equal to zero
        if nturns == 0:

            print ("You Lost the game")
            print("The correct word is ", word)
```

6. Run a script using the following command:
`E:\Python3x>python f:\guessingapp\guessinggame\game.py`

Note: E:\Python3x is the python installation directory.

7. Python executes the program game.py and produces the following output:

```
Enter your name? Narayan
Hello, Narayan Start playing word guessing game
You have to guess five letters word in 10 guesses
Start guessing a word game
_ _ _ _ _
# Guess a character: i
# _ i _ i _
# Guess a character: s
# Wrong choice
# You have   9  terms left now
# _ i _ i _
# Guess a character: c
# c i _ i _
# Guess a character: v
# c i v i _
# Guess a character: l
# c i v i l
# Wow You have won the game!!!
```

22 PRACTICAL FILE WITH SOLUTION

<table>
<tr><th>Q.No</th><th>Question</th></tr>
<tr><td>1</td><td>Write a program to calculate and displays the floor and block number basis of the customer number.
Assume there are 10 blocks (‘A’ to ‘J’) with 5 floors (0 to 4) each allocated customers sequentially as per their customer number.
For example customer no 1 get [Block A Floor 0], customer number 7 gets [Block B Floor 1]

Use only Arithmetic operator (No relational operator)
Hint: use chr() to convert number to Alphabet</td></tr>
<tr><td>Source Code</td><td><pre>num = int(input("Enter a number between 1 and 50"))

block = (num + 4) // 5
floor = (num - 1) % 5
print("Customer No. ", num,'Block ', chr(block + 64) , "Floor", floor)</pre></td></tr>
<tr><td>Output</td><td>Enter a number between 1 and 50 44
Customer No. 44 Block I Floor 3</td></tr>
<tr><td>2</td><td>Write a program to find the largest number among three numbers.</td></tr>
<tr><td>Source Code</td><td><pre>num1 = int(input("Enter number 1: "))
num2 = int(input("Enter number 2: "))
num3 = int(input("Enter number 3: "))

if(num1 > num2):
    if(num1 > num2):
        print("The largest number among ", num1, num2, num3, " is :", num1)
    else:
        print("The largest number among ", num1, num2, num3, " is :", num2)
else:
    if(num2 > num3):
        print("The largest number among ", num1, num2, num3, " is :", num2)
    else:
        print("The largest number among ", num1, num2, num3, " is :", num3)</pre></td></tr>
<tr><td>Output</td><td>Enter number 1: 1
Enter number 2: 2
Enter number 3: 3
The largest number among 1 2 3 is : 3

Enter number 1: 3
Enter number 2: 2
Enter number 3: 1
The largest number among 3 2 1 is : 3</td></tr>
</table>

<table>
<tr><td></td><td>Enter number 1: 1
Enter number 2: 3
Enter number 3: 2
The largest number among 1 3 2 is : 3</td></tr>
<tr><td>3</td><td>Write a program to input a character and to print whether a given character is an alphabet, digit, or any other character.</td></tr>
<tr><td>Source Code</td><td><pre>char = input("Enter a character ")

if(char.isdigit()):
    print(char, " is a digit")
elif(char.isalpha()):
    print(char, " is as alphabet")
else:
    print(char, " is not a digit or an alphabet")</pre></td></tr>
<tr><td>Output</td><td>Enter a character e
e is as alphabet

Enter a character 4
4 is a digit

Enter a character @
@ is not a digit or an alphabet</td></tr>
<tr><td>4</td><td>Write a program in Python to check whether a number is prime or not.</td></tr>
<tr><td>Source code</td><td><pre>num=int(input("Enter the number: "))
isPrime = True
for i in range(2,num):
    if num%i==0:
        isPrime = False
        break
    else:
        pass #no action is required

if(isPrime):
    print(num, "is a prime number")
else:
    print(num, "is not a prime number")</pre></td></tr>
<tr><td>Output</td><td>Enter a number : 17
17 is a prime number

Enter the number: 21
21 is not a prime number</td></tr>
<tr><td>5</td><td>Write a program that removes vowel from a sentence.</td></tr>
<tr><td>Source code</td><td><pre>string= input("Enter a string: ")
newstring=''
for ch in string:
    if(ch in 'aieouAEIOU'):</pre></td></tr>
</table>

<table>
<tr><td></td><td><pre>
        pass
    else:
        newstring+=ch

print(newstring)
</pre></td></tr>
<tr><td>Output</td><td>Enter a string: The sky is the limit
Th sky s th lmt</td></tr>
<tr><td>6</td><td>Write a program that reverses a number using while loop.</td></tr>
<tr><td>Source code</td><td><pre>
num = int(input("Enter number: "))
revnum= 0

while(num > 0):
    revnum = revnum * 10 + num %10
    num = num // 10

print(revnum)
</pre></td></tr>
<tr><td>Output</td><td>Enter number: 1234
4321</td></tr>
<tr><td>7</td><td>Write a program that reverses a number using for loop.</td></tr>
<tr><td>Source code</td><td><pre>
import math
revnum=0
num = int(input("Enter number : "))
# int(math.ceil(math.log10(num))) compute the number of digits in a number

for i in range(int(math.ceil(math.log10(num)))):
    revnum = revnum* 10 + num %10
    num = num // 10
print(revnum)
</pre></td></tr>
<tr><td>Output</td><td>Enter number: 1234
4321</td></tr>
<tr><td>8</td><td>Write a Python program that prints the following pattern using a while and for loop.
*
* *
* * *
* * * *
* * * * *</td></tr>
<tr><td>Source Code</td><td><pre>
#Print pattern using while loop
rows = 5
i = 1
while(i <= rows):
    j = 1
    while(j <= i):
        print('*',end="\t")
        j+=1
    i+=1
    print()
</pre><pre>
Print pattern using for loop
rows = 5
for i in range(rows):
    for j in range(i+1):
        print('*',end="\t")

    print()
</pre></td></tr>
</table>

Output	* * * * * * * * * * * * * * *
9	**Write a python program that prints the following pattern using a while and for loop.** **5 5 5 5 5** **4 4 4 4** **3 3 3** **2 2** **1**

Source Code	#Print pattern using while loop
	`rows = 5`
	`while( rows >=0):`
	`    j = rows`
	`    while(j >=0):`
	`        print(rows, end='\t')`
	`        j-=1`
	`    rows-=1`
	`    print()`
	
	Print pattern using for loop
	`rows = 5`
	`for i in range(rows,0,-1):`
	`    for j in range(i+1,0,-1):`
	`        print(i, end="\t")`
	`    print()`

Output	5 5 5 5 5 4 4 4 4 3 3 3 2 2 1
10	**Write a program that simulates a dice and generates a random number between 1 to 6.**

Source code	`import random`
	`def rolldice():`
	`        random.seed(random.choice(range(1,101)))`
	`    #Generate random number from 1 to 6`
	`        return random.randint(1,6)`
	
	`print("Value is " ,rolldice())`
	`print("Value is " ,rolldice())`
	`print("Value is " ,rolldice())`
	`print("Value is " ,rolldice())`
	`print("Value is " ,rolldice())`

Output	Value is 3 Value is 6 Value is 2 Value is 1 Value is 5
11	**Write a program to display the ASCII code of a character and vice versa.**

Source Code	`def ascii_ord(val):`
	`    #if input is string character returns its ascii code`
	`    if(isinstance(val, str)):`

	``
	        return ord(val)
	    #if input is ascii values returns the character
	        elif (isinstance(val, int)):
	            return chr(val)
	    else:
	            return
	
	print(ascii_ord('a'))
	print(ascii_ord(65))
	``

Output	97 A
12	**Write a program to remove duplicate elements from the list.**

	``
	_list = [1,2,3,6,5,2,3,4,6,10,12]
	unique=[]
	for element in _list:
	    if(element in unique):
	        pass
	    else:
	        unique.append(element)
	print("The unique list is " , unique)
	``

Output	The unique list is [1, 2, 3, 6, 5, 4, 10, 12]
13	**a) Write a program that converts tuple to a dictionary.** **#Assume that tuple contains values in pair. For example** **_tuple= (('a','b'),('c','d'))** **b) Write a program that converts a dictionary to a tuple**

Source Code	```
	a) def tuple_dict(val):
	        if(isinstance(val, tuple)):
	            return dict(val)
	        else:
	            return
	
	b) def dict_tuple(val):
	        if(isinstance(val, dict)):
	            _tuple = tuple(val.items())
	            return _tuple
	        else:
	            return
	
	    # Printing dictionary
	    print(tuple_dict((('a','b'),('c','d'))))
	    # Printing tuple
	    print(dict_tuple({'a': 'b', 'c': 'd'})
	``

Output	{'a': 'b', 'c': 'd'} (('a', 'b'), ('c', 'd'))
14	**Write a function that converts a list of characters to a string.**

Source Code	```
	def listchar_string(_list):
	    string=''
	``

	``
	    for ch in _list:
	        string+=ch
	    return string
	
	print(listchar_string(['p','y','t','h','o','n']))
	``

Output	Python
15	**Write a function that reverses a string.**

Source Code	```
	#Method 1 reverse using slicing
	def rev_string(string):
	    revstring=''
	    revstring = string[::-1]
	    return revstring
	
	#Method 2 retrieve character by character
	# and append it in the end of the string
	def rev_string_1(string):
	    revstr = ""
	    for ch in string:
	        revstr = ch + revstr
	    return revstr
	
	print(rev_string('nohtyp'))
	print(rev_string_1('nohtyp'))
	``

Output	python python
16	**Write a function that calculates the factorial of a number.**

Source Code	```
	def fact(num):
	    factorial=1
	    while(num > 1):
	        factorial*=num
	        num= num-1
	    return factorial
	
	print(fact(6))
	``

Output	720
17	**Write a function that inserts an element in a stack.**

Source Code	```
	stack=[]
	def push(val):
	    stack.append(val)
	``

18	**Write a function that deletes an element from a stack.**

Source Code	```
	stack=[]
	def pop():
	    if(len(stack) >0):
	        return stack.pop()
	``

19	**Write a function that inserts an element in a queue.**

Source Code	`stack=[]`
	`def enqueue():`
	`    stack.append(val)`

20	**Write a function to remove an element from a queue.**

Source Code	`stack=[]`
	`def dequeue():`
	`    if(len(stack) >0):`
	`        return stack.pop(0)`

21	**Write a program to print the Fibonacci series using recursion.**

Source code	`def fibo_rec(num):`
	`    if num <= 1:`
	`        return num`
	`    else:`
	`        return(fibo_rec(num-1) + fibo_rec(num-2))`
	
	`terms = 10`
	`for i in range(terms):`
	`        print(fibo_rec(i),end=', ')`

Output	0, 1, 1, 2, 3, 5, 8, 13, 21, 34
22	**Write a recursive Python program to test if a string is a palindrome or not.**

Source Code	`def isPalindrome(string, start=0, end=0) :`
	`    # If there is only one character`
	`    if (start == end ):`
	`        return True`
	`    # return false if first and last characters do not match`
	`    if (string[start] != string[end]) :`
	`        return False`
	`    # check if the middle substring is also`
	`    # palindrome or not.`
	`    if(start < end + 1) :`
	`        return isPalindrome(string, start + 1, end - 1);`
	`      return True`
	
	`print(isPalindrome('nitin',0,len('nitin')-1))`
	`print(isPalindrome('ashish',0,len('ashish')-1))`

Output	True False
23	**Write a program to check whether a number is palindrome or not.**

Source Code	#To check if a number is palindrome first convert into string and use the function to check if it palindrome.
	`num = int(input("Enter a number: "))`
	`string = str(num)`
	`print(num, " is a palindrome: "\`
	`isPalindrome(string,0,len(string)-1))`

Output	Enter a number: 121 121 is a palindrome: True
23	**Write a program to calculate the factorial of an integer using recursion.**

Source Code	`def fact_rec(num):`
	`    if (num ==1):`
	`        return 1`
	`    else:`
	`        return num * fact_rec(num-1)`
	`print(fact_rec(7))`

Output	5040
24	**Write a program to create a module in python and import it into a program.**

Source Code	`# Define a function and variable in a file and save it as hello.py`
	
	`def Welcome(string):`
	`    print("Welcome !!! " + string)`
	
	`# Define a variable`
	`msg = "Good Morning"`
	#Here program and hello.py are in the same directory
	
	#To use the module import it
	`import hello`
	
	`print(hello.msg , end =" ")`
	`print( hello.Welcome("Narayan"))`

Output	Good Morning Welcome!!! Narayan
25	**Write a program to copy a line to another text file that contains the word "Artificial Intelligence." Below is the content of the file:** In computer science, the artificial intelligence (AI) is sometimes called machine intelligence. Autonomously operating cars, and military simulations use artificial intelligence. Artificial intelligence was founded as an academic discipline in 1956. AI research has been divided into subfields that often fail to communicate with each other "logic" or deep philosophical differences.

Source code	`_file = open('f:\\examples\\ai.txt','r')`
	`_filecopy = open('f:\\examples\\aicopy.txt',  'w')`
	`# read the line`
	`line = _file.readline()`
	`# keep reading one line at a time, until file is empty`
	`while line:`
	`    if(line.find('artificial intelligence') >=0):`
	`        #copy line that contains artificial intelligence`
	`        _filecopy.write(line)`
	`    # use realine() to read next line`
	`    line = _file.readline()`
	`_file.close()`
	`_filecopy.close()`

<table>
<tr><td>Output</td><td>In computer science, the artificial intelligence (AI) is sometimes called machine intelligence.
Autonomously operating cars, and military simulations use artificial intelligence.
Artificial intelligence was founded as an academic discipline in 1956.</td></tr>
<tr><td>26</td><td>Write a program to count the number of vowels present in a text file. Below is the content of the text file:
Dream it. Wish it. Do it.
Success doesn't just find you. You have to go out and get it.
Push yourself, because no one else is going to do it for you.</td></tr>
<tr><td>Source code</td><td><pre>
vowcount = 0
_file = open("f:\\examples\\quotes.txt", 'r')
ch =_file.read(1)
if ch in 'aeiouAEIOU':
    vowcount+=1
while True:
    if not ch:
        break
    else:
        if ch in 'aeiouAEIOU':
            vowcount+=1
        ch =_file.read(1)

print("The number of vowels in the file :")
print(vowcount)
_file.close()
</pre></td></tr>
<tr><td>Output</td><td>The number of vowels in the file:
48</td></tr>
<tr><td>27</td><td>Write a program to count the number of words and lines in a file.</td></tr>
<tr><td>Source code</td><td><pre>
_file = open("f:\\examples\\quotes.txt", 'r')
#read the entire text and split it into words
text = _file.read().split()
print("The number of words in the file "+ str(len(text)))
#Move the file pointer to the beginning of the file
_file.seek(0, 0)
lines = _file.readlines()
print("The number of lines in the file "+ str(len(lines)))
</pre></td></tr>
<tr><td>Output</td><td>The number of words in the file 32
The number of lines in the file 3</td></tr>
<tr><td>28</td><td>Write a program to find the frequency of the vowels 'a', 'e', 'i 'o 'u' in a file.</td></tr>
<tr><td>Source code</td><td><pre>
.
_dict={'a':0,'e':0,'i':0,'o':0,'u':0}
_file = open("f:\\examples\\quotes.txt", 'r')
ch =_file.read(1)
if ch in 'aeiouAEIOU':
    vowcount+=1
while True:
</pre></td></tr>
</table>

<table>
<tr><td></td><td><pre>
    if not ch:
        break

    else:
        if ch in 'aeiouAEIOU':
            if(ch == 'a'):
                _dict['a']+=1
            elif(ch == 'e'):
                _dict['e']+=1
            elif(ch == 'i'):
                _dict['i']+=1
            elif(ch == 'o'):
                _dict['o']+=1
            else:
                _dict['u']+=1
        ch =_file.read(1)

_file.close()

print("The number of vowels in file :")
print(_dict)
</pre></td></tr>
<tr><td>Output</td><td>{'a': 4, 'e': 11, 'i': 9, 'o': 15, 'u': 9}</td></tr>
<tr><td>29</td><td>Write a program that creates a binary file and copies it to another binary file.</td></tr>
<tr><td>Source Code</td><td><pre>
quote =b'keep away from people who try to belittle your ambitions. Small people always do that, but the really great make you feel that you, too, can become great. Mark Twain'

filepath = "F:\\files\\quotes.dat"
with open(filepath,"wb") as _wfile:
    _wfile.write(quote)

copyfilepath = "F:\\files\\quotescopy.dat"
data=""

_rfile = open(filepath,"rb")
_wfile = open(copyfilepath,"wb")

data = _rfile.readline()
_wfile.write(data)

_rfile.close()
_wfile.close()

data=""
with open(copyfilepath,"rb") as _rfile:
    data = _rfile.read()
print(data.decode('ascii'))
</pre></td></tr>
</table>

<table>
<tr><td>Output</td><td>Keep away from people who try to belittle your ambitions. Small people always do that, but the really great make you feel that you, too, can become great. Mark Twain</td></tr>
<tr><td>30</td><td>How to create a tab-delimited file?</td></tr>
<tr><td>Source Code</td><td>To create the tab-delimited file the TAB {'\t'} is used as a separator. For example:
<pre>
import csv
_file =open('F:\\files\\employeetab.csv', mode='w',newline='')

with _file:
    _writer = csv.writer(_file, delimiter='\t', quotechar='"')
    _writer.writerow(['Vijay Shankar', 'Accounting', 'November'])
    _writer.writerow(['Kiran Kumar', 'IT', 'March'])
</pre></td></tr>
<tr><td>31</td><td>Write a program that converts a data list to a csv file.
data=[
['rollno','name','class','physics','chemistry','maths'] ,
[1,'Ashish',12,98,87,85],
[2,'Dinesh',12,92,87,91],
[3,'Gurpreet',12,98,89,85],
[4,'Mukesh',12,94,78,82],
[5,'Naresh',12,93,81,79],
[6,'suresh',12,93,87,7]
]</td></tr>
<tr><td>Source code</td><td><pre>
import csv
filepath = "f:\\files\\studentsdata.dat"

def list_to_csv(_list):
    retstr=""
    for item in _list:
        retstr= retstr+str(item)+','
        #remove addtional ',' from the last

        return retstr[0:-1]

def write_to_csvfile(filepath, datalist):
    _file =open(filepath,'bw')

    for record in datalist:
        line = list_to_csv(record)+ "\n"
        #convert the string into bytearray using ascii encoding
        bytestream = bytearray(line,'ascii')
        _file.write(bytestream)

    _file.close()
write_to_csvfile(filepath,data)
</pre></td></tr>
</table>

Output	F:\Files\studentsdata.dat - Notepad++ 1 rollno,name,class,physics,chemistry,maths 2 1,Ashish,12,98,87,85 3 2,Dinesh,12,92,87,91 4 3,Gurpreet,12,98,89,85 5 4,Mukesh,12,94,78,82 6 5,Naresh,12,93,81,79 7 6,suresh,12,93,87,7
32	**How to create a tab-separated file?**
Source Code	see code below

```
#To create the tab separated file, the TAB {'\t'} is used as a separator. For example
import csv
_file =open('F:\\files\\employeetab.csv', mode='w',newline='')

with _file:
    _writer = csv.writer(_file, delimiter='\t', quotechar='"')
    _writer.writerow(['Vijay Shankar', 'Accounting', 'November'])
    _writer.writerow(['Kiran Kumar', 'IT', 'March'])

_file =open('F:\\files\\employeetab.csv', mode='r')

with _file:
    _reader = csv.reader(_file,delimiter=',')
    for row in _reader:
        print(''.join(row))
```

Output	Vijay Shankar Accounting November Kiran Kumar IT March
33	**Write a code to find and replace a word in a binary file.**
Source Code	see code below

```
binstr = b"When one door of happiness closes, another opens; but often we look so long at the closed door that we do not see the one which has been opened for us.-Helen Keller"

_file =open("replacetext.dat",'bw')
_file.write(binstr)
_file.close()
#Open file for read and writing
_file =open("replacetext.dat",'rb+')
data = _file.read()
data = data.decode('ascii')
data = data.replace('one','One')

data =data.encode(encoding='ascii')
_file.write(data)
```

	`_file.close()`
	
	`_file = open("replacetext.dat",'br')`
	`content = _file.read()`
	`content = data.decode('ascii')`
	`_file.close()`
	`print(content)`

Output	When One door of happiness closes, another opens; but often we look so long at the closed door that we do not see the One which has been opened for us.-Helen Keller
34	**Write a program that prints the following:** **Pickle and unpickle a float value** **Pickle and unpickle a list** **Pickle and unpickle a tuple** **Pickle and unpickle a dictionary**

Source Code	`import pickle`
	
	`#saving and retrieve float value`
	`pi = 3.14159`
	`_out = open("floatval.dat","wb")`
	`pickle.dump(pi, _out)`
	`_out.close()`
	
	`_out = open("floatval.dat","rb")`
	`pival= pickle.load(_out)`
	`_out.close()`
	`print(pival)`
	
	`#saving and retrieve a list`
	`_listordersize = [100,120,94,200,145,97,105]`
	`_out = open("orders.dat","wb")`
	`pickle.dump(_listordersize, _out)`
	`_out.close()`
	
	`_out = open("orders.dat","rb")`
	`orders= pickle.load(_out)`
	`_out.close()`
	`print(orders)`
	
	`#saving and retrieve a tuple`
	`_tuple = (12,18,23,26)`
	`_out = open("tuple.dat","wb")`
	`pickle.dump(_tuple, _out)`
	`_out.close()`
	
	`_out = open("tuple.dat","rb")`
	`_tuple= pickle.load(_out)`
	`_out.close()`

<table>
<tr><td></td><td>

```
print(_tuple)
#saving and retrieve a dictionary
_covidcases = {"US":2208400,"Brazil": 928834,"Russia":537210,"India":354161}
_out = open("dict.dat","wb")
pickle.dump(_covidcases, _out)
_out.close()

_out = open("dict.dat","rb")
_dict= pickle.load(_out)
_out.close()
print(_dict)
```

</td></tr>
<tr><td>Output</td><td>3.14159
[100, 120, 94, 200, 145, 97, 105]
(12, 18, 23, 26)
{'US': 2208400, 'Brazil': 928834, 'Russia': 537210, 'India': 354161}</td></tr>
<tr><td>35</td><td>Delete a record from database binary file using pickle.</td></tr>
<tr><td>Source code</td><td>

```
import pickle
#  create the database using dictionary
employeedb = {}

def storeData():
    # initializing data to be stored in db
    employee1 = {'name' : 'Sankar Mahadev','desigantion' : \
'SE-II', 'pay-bracket' : 'C'}
    employee2 = {'name' : 'Vishnu Pathak', 'desigantion' : '\
Architect-I', 'pay-bracket' : 'E'}
    employee3 = {'name' : 'Ganesh Shankar','desigantion' : '\
Evangalist', 'pay-bracket' : 'D'}

    employeedb['20111234'] = employee1
    employeedb['20112345'] = employee2
    employeedb['20122356'] = employee3


    dbfile = open('F:\\files\\employee.dbf', 'ab')

    pickle.dump(employeedb, dbfile)
    dbfile.close()

def delrecord(recordkey):
    # for loading open file in binary mode
    dbfile = open('F:\\files\\employee.dbf', 'rb')
    empdb = pickle.load(dbfile)
    dbfile.close()

    dbfile = open('F:\\files\\employee.dbf', 'wb')
    del employeedb[recordkey]
```

</td></tr>
</table>

	`pickle.dump(employeedb, dbfile)`
	`dbfile.close()`
	
	`storeData()`
	`delrecord('20112345')`
	
	`dbfile = open('F:\\files\\employee.dbf', 'rb')`
	`_dict = pickle.load(dbfile)`
	`print(_dict)`
	`dbfile.close()`

Output	`{`
	`'20111234': {'name': 'Sankar Mahadev', 'desigantion': 'SE-II', 'pay-bracket': 'C'},`
	`'20122356': {'name': 'Ganesh Shankar', 'desigantion': 'Evangalist', 'pay-bracket':`
	`'D'}`
	`}`

36	**Create a functions that computes sum of a column from a csv file. (Here column name is passed as an argument in the function).** **rollno,name,physics,chemistry,maths,cs** **1,Akash,98,89,90,95**
	2,Babita,99,89,90,93 **3,Neeraj,87,90,89,76** **4,Mahesh,90,89,91,98** **5,Ramesh,88,89,78,79** **6,Vinay,87,90,87,90**
Source Code	See code below

```
#Method 1
def  sumcol(filepath, column):
    _list = []
    with open(filepath) as f:
        header= f.readline().split(',')
        idx =  header.index(column)
        lines =f.readlines()
        for line in lines:
            values = line.split(',')
            _list.append(int(values[idx]))
    return(sum(_list))

print(sumcol('f:\\files\\student.csv','physics'))

#Method 2
import csv
def sumcol_csv(filepath, colname):
    with open(filepath, 'r') as f:
        _list=[]
        dict_reader = csv.DictReader(f)

        #Retrieves the field names from DictReader and store in the list
        headers = dict_reader.fieldnames
```

<table>
<tr><td></td><td><pre>
        for record in dict_reader:
            #Add marks to list
            _list.append(int(record[colname]))

        print(sum(_list))

sumcol_csv('f:\\files\\student.csv','physics')
</pre></td></tr>
<tr><td>Output</td><td>549
549</td></tr>
<tr><td>37</td><td>Write a program to convert a decimal number to binary number.</td></tr>
<tr><td>Source Code</td><td><pre>
stack=[]
num = 10
while(num > 0):
    q= num % 2
    stack.append(str(q))
    num//=2

print(''.join(stack[::-1]))
</pre></td></tr>
<tr><td>Output</td><td>1010</td></tr>
<tr><td>38</td><td>Write a program that evaluates postfix evaluation.</td></tr>
<tr><td>Source Code</td><td><pre>
exp="2 3 + "

resultstk=[]
res=0
for i in range(len(exp)):
    if(exp[i].isdigit()==True):
        resultstk.append(int(exp[i]))
    elif(exp[i]=='*'):
        operand1=resultstk.pop()
        operand2 =resultstk.pop()
        res = operand2 * operand1
        resultstk.append(res)
    elif(exp[i]=='+'):
        operand1=resultstk.pop()
        operand2=resultstk.pop()
        res = operand2 + operand1
        resultstk.append(res)
    elif(exp[i]=='-'):
        operand1=resultstk.pop()
        operand2=resultstk.pop()
        res = operand2 - operand1
        resultstk.append(res)
    elif(exp[i]=='/'):
        operand1=resultstk.pop()
        operand2=resultstk.pop()
</pre></td></tr>
</table>

	`res=operand2/operand1`
	`resultstk.append(res)`
	
	`print('The  result is',resultstk[0])`

Output	**5**
39	**Write a program that performs bubble sort.**

Source Code	`def bubble_Sort(_list):`
	`    n = len(_list)`
	
	`    # Traverse through list`
	`    for i in range(n):`
	
	`        for j in range(0, n-i-1):`
	
	`            # Swap if the element is greater than the next element`
	`            if _list[j] > _list[j+1] :`
	`                _list[j], _list[j+1] = _list[j+1], _list[j]`
	`    return _list`
	
	`print(bubble_Sort([2,5,6,3,1,9,7,8]))`

Output	[1, 2, 3, 5, 6, 7, 8, 9]
40	**Write a program that performs the linear search.**

Source Code	`def linear_search(_list, searchelement):`
	`    index=0`
	`    while(index < len(_list)):`
	`        if(_list[index] == searchelement):`
	`            return index+1`
	`        index+=1`
	
	`    return -1`
	
	`idx =linear_search([3,9,8,0,5,4,6,2,1],5)`
	
	`if(idx > 0):`
	`    print("The element found at location ", idx)`
	`else:`
	`    print("Element not found in the list")`
	
	`idx =linear_search([3,9,8,0,5,4,6,2,1],7)`
	`if(idx > 0):`
	`    print("The element found at location ", idx)`
	`else:`
	`    print("Element not found in the list")`

Output	The element found at location 5 Element not found in the list

41	**Write a program that performs the binary search.**

Source Code	<pre>def binary_Search(_list, start, end, element):
	
	    while start <= end:
	
	        mid = start + (end - start)//2;
	        # Check if x is present at mid
	        if _list[mid] == element:
	            return mid
	
	        # If x is greater, ignore left half
	        elif _list[mid] < element:
	            start = mid + 1
	
	        # If x is smaller, ignore right half
	        else:
	            end = mid - 1
	
	    # If we reach here, then the element was not present
	
	_list =[1, 2, 3, 5, 6, 7, 8, 9]
	print("The element found at location ",binary_Search(_list, 0, len(_list), 5))
	print("The element found at location ",binary_Search(_list, 0, len(_list), 4))</pre>

Output	The element found at location 3 The element found at location None
42	**Write a program to connect Python with MySQL.**

Source code	<pre>import mysql.connector as con
	mycon = con.connect(host="localhost", \\
	    user="root",\\
	    passwd="", \\
	    database='pythondb')
	if(mycon.is_connected()):
	    print("Connected to Mysql...!")
	mycon.close()</pre>

Output	Connected to Mysql...!

Use the below sample table to answer questions(38-41)

User_ID	First_Name	Last_Name	Address	PhoneNo	Email
1	Saytam	Khan	Sarita Vihar	1234567891	satyam@text.com
2	Rajesh	Kumar	Khajuri Khas	1234567890	ashish@text.com
3	Narayan	Mishra	Shivaji Nagar	9807654321	narayan@test.com
4	Prateek	Sharma	Bapu Nagar	9999765432	prateek@test.com
5	Dinesh	vijaykumar	Shastri Nagar	9899654321	dinesh@test.com
6	Manish	Verma	T Nagar	9807654391	narayan@test.com

<table>
<tr><td>43</td><td>Write a function that inserts a row in a table</td></tr>
<tr><td>Source Code</td><td><pre><code>import mysql.connector as con
mycon=con.connect(host="localhost",\
                     user="root",\passwd="",
                     \database='pythondb')
if(mycon.is_connected()==True):
    print("Successfully connected to Mysql...!")
else:
    print("There is a problem in connecting to database")

cursor=mycon.cursor()
query="INSERT INTO users(First_Name,Last_Name,Address,PhoneNo,Email)\
        VALUES('{}','{}','{}','{}','{}')".format('Satyam','Kumar',\
        '23 E-Pkt Sadar bazar','7676767676','sk@test.com')
cursor.execute(query)
print("Affetced rows: "+ str(cursor.rowcount))
cursor.close()
mycon.close()</code></pre></td></tr>
<tr><td>Output</td><td>Successfully connected to Mysql...!
Affected rows: 1</td></tr>
<tr><td>44</td><td>Write a function that fetches a row from a table.</td></tr>
<tr><td>Source Code</td><td><pre><code>import mysql.connector

conn = mysql.connector.connect(user='root', \
password='',\
    host='127.0.0.1',\
    database='pythondb1')

# Using cursor as an iterator
cursor.execute("SELECT * from books")

for result_row in cursor:
    print(result_row)

# Using fetchone with a while loop
cursor.execute("SELECT * from books")

#Fetch the row first
result_row = cursor.fetchone()

while result_row is not None:
    print(result_row)
    result_row = cursor.fetchone()

conn.close()</code></pre></td></tr>
<tr><td>Output</td><td>(1, 'let us c', 5, 'BPB', 225,1)</td></tr>
</table>

<table>
<tr><td>45</td><td>Write a function that updates a row in a table.</td></tr>
<tr><td>Source Code</td><td><pre>import mysql.connector as con
mycon=con.connect(host="localhost",\
user="root",\
passwd="",\
database='pythondb')
if(mycon.is_connected()==True):
    print("successfully connected to Mysql...!")
else:
    print("There is a problem in connecting to database")

cursor=mycon.cursor()
query="update users set First_Name='Rajesh' where user_id= 2"
cursor.execute(query)
print("Affetced rows: "+ str(cursor.rowcount))
mycon.commit()
cursor.close()
mycon.close()</pre></td></tr>
<tr><td>Output</td><td>Successfully connected to Mysql...!
Affected rows: 1</td></tr>
<tr><td>46</td><td>Write a function that deletes a row from a table.</td></tr>
<tr><td>Source Code</td><td><pre>import mysql.connector as con
mycon=con.connect(host="localhost",\
user="root",\
passwd="",\
database='pythondb')
if(mycon.is_connected()==True):
    print("successfully connected to Mysql...!")
else:
    print("There is a problem connecting to database")
cursor=mycon.cursor()
query="delete from users where user_id > 4"
cursor.execute(query)
print("Affected rows: "+ str(cursor.rowcount))
mycon.commit()
cursor.close()</pre></td></tr>
<tr><td>Output</td><td>Affected rows: 2</td></tr>
<tr><td>47</td><td>Write a query to fetch all distinct department id from employee table</td></tr>
<tr><td>Query</td><td><code>select distinct (deptid) from employee</code></td></tr>
<tr><td>48</td><td>Write a query to fetch the details of all the employees whose salary is greater than 700.</td></tr>
<tr><td>Query</td><td><code>select * from employee where salary > 700</code></td></tr>
<tr><td>49</td><td>Write a query to fetch employee works for department id 10.</td></tr>
<tr><td>Query</td><td><code>select * from employee where deptid = 10</code></td></tr>
</table>

50	**Write a query to fetch all the employees whose first name start with 'j'.**
Query	`select * from employee where first_name like 'j%'`
51	**Write a query to fetch first name, last name from employee's table not assigned to any department.**
Query	`select first_name, last_name from employee where deptid = NULL`
52	**Write a query to fetch all the employees in descending order of employee id.**
Query	`select * from employee order by  id desc`
53	**Write a query to find the average salary of each department id.**
Query	`select  deptid, avg(salary) from group by deptid`
54 a)	**Find the average salary of all the employees in the EMPLOYEE table.**
	select avg(salary) from employee
b)	**Find the minimum salary of a female employee in the EMPLOYEE table.**
Query	`select min(salary) as MIN_SALARY_FEMALE  from employee where gender ='F'`
c)	**Find the maximum salary of a male employee in the EMPLOYEE table.**
Query	`select max(salary) MAX_SALARY_MALE from employee where gender  ='M'`
d)	**Find the total salary of employees for department id is 20**
Query	`select sum(salary) as Total_Salary from employee where deptid = 20`
e)	**Find the number of rows in the EMPLOYEE table.**
Query	`select count(*)   from employee;`
55	**Write a program that writes a dictionary to the .csv file.**

Source code

```
import csv
_extension = {'C' : '.c', 'Python' : '.py', 'Java' : '.java'}
_file = open('data.csv', 'w')
writer = csv.writer(_file, delimiter=',')
for key, val in _extension.items():
#write row by row
    writer.writerow([key, val])
```

Output

```
File  Edit  Format  View  Help
C,.c

Python,.py

Java,.java
```

56

```
Table EMP
+----+--------+-----+-----------+--------+
|ID| NAME     |AGE| ADDRESS    | SALARY   |
+--+----------+---+-----------+----------+
|1 |Chaitali  |32 | Delhi      |2000.00   |
|2 |Hardik    |25 | Ahmedabad  |1500.00   |
|3 |kaushik   |23 | Mumbai     |2000.00   |
|4 |Khilan    |25 | Kota       |6500.00   |
|5 |Komal     |27 | Indore     |8500.00   |
```

<table>
<tr><td></td><td>

```
|6 |'Muffy'   |22 |'Prayagraj'|4500.00  |
|7 |'Ramesh'  |24 |'Bhopal'   |10000.00 |
+--+---------+---+-----------+----------+
```

Table ORD

```
+-----+------------+-----------+------+
|OrdID |ORDDATE     |CUSTOMER_ID|AMOUNT|
+-----+------------+-----------+------+
|102  |'2019-11-20'|3          |3000  |
|100  |'2019-10-08'|3          |1500  |
|101  |'2019-06-20'|2          |1560  |
|103  |'2020-04-20'|4          |2060  |
+-----+------------+-----------+------+
```

Write a query that fetches all the records from the table EMP and the matched records from the table ORD. Display NULL when there is no match from table EMP.</td></tr>
<tr><td>Query</td><td>

```
SELECT  ID, NAME, AMOUNT, orddate
   FROM EMP
   LEFT JOIN ORD
   ON CUST.ID = ORD.CUSTOMER_ID;
```
</td></tr>
<tr><td>Output</td><td>

```
+------+----------+--------+------------+
| ID   | NAME     | AMOUNT | orddate    |
+------+----------+--------+------------+
|    3 | kaushik  |   3000 | 2019-11-20 |
|    3 | kaushik  |   1500 | 2019-10-08 |
|    2 | Hardik   |   1560 | 2019-06-20 |
|    4 | Khilan   |   2060 | 2020-04-20 |
|    1 | Chaitali |   NULL | NULL       |
|    5 | Komal    |   NULL | NULL       |
|    6 | Muffy    |   NULL | NULL       |
|    7 | Ramesh   |   NULL | NULL       |
+------+----------+--------+------------+
SELECT  ID, NAME, AMOUNT, orddate
FROM ord
RIGHT JOIN cust
   ON CUST.ID = ORD.CUSTOMER_ID;
+------+----------+--------+------------+
| ID   | NAME     | AMOUNT | orddate    |
+------+----------+--------+------------+
|    3 | kaushik  |   3000 | 2019-11-20 |
|    3 | kaushik  |   1500 | 2019-10-08 |
|    2 | Hardik   |   1560 | 2019-06-20 |
|    4 | Khilan   |   2060 | 2020-04-20 |
|    1 | Chaitali |   NULL | NULL       |
|    5 | Komal    |   NULL | NULL       |
|    6 | Muffy    |   NULL | NULL       |
|    7 | Ramesh   |   NULL | NULL       |
+------+----------+--------+------------+
```
</td></tr>
</table>

57 **Table company**

CompanyID	CompanyName	CompanyCity
4	chocolates	Jaipur
8	Food All	Mumbai
5	Hill Jack Ltd	Chandigarh
6	Akash Foods	Delhi
7	Foodies	Gurgaon
9	Shakes-n-Bite	South Delhi
11	mango-bites	Delhi

Table item

ItemId	ItemName	Unit	CompanyId
1	Navratan Namkeen	Carton	6
2	Cheez-It	Pcs	5
9	Parle-G	Dozen	5
3	Banana Chips	Pcs	7
4	Haldiram Pudina Chips	Pcs	5
5	Britania Cakes	Pcs	8
7	Salt n Shake	Pcs	9
8	Bikaneri Bhujiya	Pcs	10

Write a query that fetches all the records from the table company that matches records from the table fooditems. Display NULL when there is no match from table fooditems.

Query

```
The right join can fetch the above results, below is the query
select itemid, itemname, company.companyid, company.companyname from fooditems
right join company
on fooditems.companyid = company.companyid
```

Output

itemid	itemname	companyid	companyname
1	Navratan Namkeen	6	Akash Foods
2	Cheez-It	5	Hill Jack Ltd
9	Parle-G	5	Hill Jack Ltd
3	Banana Chips	7	Foodies
4	Haldiram Pudina Chips	5	Hill Jack Ltd
5	Britania Cakes	8	Food All
7	Salt n Shake	9	Shakes-n-Bite
NULL	NULL	4	chocolates
NULL	NULL	11	mango-bites

23 PROJECT

The Abstract

The CBSE board result Analysis of Class X results is an important part of all the CBSE schools as future admissions and reputation of the school depends on these results. CBSE declares the results and hands it over to the individual schools as a text file. It is a difficult task to convert the text file into the desired excel or SQL format for proper analysis and creating visualizations for an easy understanding.

Instead of doing routine analysis, which is easy to perform, like finding the highest and lowest marks of a subject, the number of students scoring above 90%, and more. The following code used EDA to find the answers to the questions which are never analyzed like before:

- What is the best subject combination for a low achiever?
- Which subjects are better and high scoring for an average child?
- Can we generalize that high achievers are always good scorers in the internal assessments also?
- What is the better subject choice out of offered subjects?

Proposed Solution

Exploratory Data Analysis (EDA) helps us analyze the data.

At a high level, the EDA provides the visual and quantitative methods that summarize a dataset without any assumptions about its contents. Libraries like Pandas and numpy are used for EDA, which includes data cleaning, munging, combining, reshaping, and transforming the data for analysis of the Class X Board Results. For visualization, the `matplotliab` and `seaborn` libraries are used.

Why EDA?

EDA is a critical and the first step in analyzing the data and we do this for the following reasons:

- Finding patterns in data
- Determining the relationships in data
- Checking of assumptions
- Detection of mistakes

Know the Data

The dataset comprises of 163 observations of 35 columns. The following table shows the names of all the columns and their description.

Sr.No	Column name	Description
1	Roll No	CBSE Board Roll No
2	CANDIDATE NAME	Name of the Student
3	SUBJECT1	Code of the First Subject
4	FA	FA Marks of the First Subject
5	SA	SA Marks of the First Subject
6	TOT	Total Marks of the First Subject
7	GP	Grade Point of the First Subject
8	SUBJECT2	Code of the Second Subject

9	FA.1	FA Marks of the Second Subject
10	SA.1	SA Marks of the Second Subject
11	TOT.1	Total Marks of the Second Subject
12	GP.1	Grade Point of the Second Subject
13	SUBJCET3	Code of the Third Subject
14	FA.2	FA Marks of the Third Subject
15	SA.2	SA Marks of the Third Subject
16	TOT.2	Total Marks of the Third Subject
17	GP.2	Grade Point of the Third Subject
18	SUBJECT4	Code of the Fourth Subject
19	FA.3	FA Marks of the Fourth Subject
20	SA.3	SA Marks of the Fourth Subject
21	TOT.3	Total Marks of the Fourth Subject
22	GP.3	Grade Point of the Fourth Subject
23	SUBJECT5	Code of the Fifth Subject
24	FA.4	FA Marks of the Fifth Subject
25	SA.4	SA Marks of the Fifth Subject
26	TOT.4	Total Marks of the Fifth Subject
27	GP.4	Grade Point of the Fifth Subject
28	RSLT	Final Result as Pass or Fail or Compartment
29	CGPA	Cumulative Grade Point of all Subjects
30	ASL	Marks of ASL
31	SUBJECT6	Code of the Sixth Subject
32	FA.5	FA Marks of the Sixth Subject
33	SA.5	SA Marks of the Sixth Subject
34	TOT.5	Total Marks of the Sixth Subject
35	GP.5	Grade Point of Sixth Subject

Here,

- FA stands for Formative Assessment.
- SA stands for Summative Assessment.
- ASL stands for Assessment for Speaking and Listening.

Sample Data

Fields in sample data

'ROLL NO', 'CANDIDATE NAME', 'SUBJECT1', 'FA', 'SA', 'TOT', 'GP', 'SUBJECT2', 'FA.1', 'SA.1', 'TOT.1', 'GP.1', 'SUBJECT3', 'FA.2', 'SA.2', 'TOT.2', 'GP.2', 'SUBJECT4', 'FA.3', 'SA.3', 'TOT.3', 'GP.3','SUBJECT5', 'FA.4', 'SA.4', 'TOT.4', 'GP.4', 'RSLT', 'CGPA', 'ASL','SUBJECT6', 'FA.5', 'SA.5', 'TOT.5', 'GP.5'

Below is the sample data. (Note: here student name is not used and roll number has been replacing with serial numbers 0 to 162.)

0	ENGLISH	B1	A2	A2	9	FRENCH	A2	A2	A2	9 ...	A2**	9
1	ENGLISH	B2	B1	B2	7	FRENCH	B1	B1	B1	8 ...	B2	7
2	ENGLISH	B1	A2	A2**	9	FRENCH	A2	A2	A2	9 ...	A2	9

3	ENGLISH	A2	A1	A1	10	FRENCH	A1	A1	A1	10 ...	A1	10
4	ENGLISH	B1	A2	A2	9	FRENCH	A1	A1	A1	10 ...	A1	10
5	ENGLISH	B1	A2	A1**	10	FRENCH	A1	A1	A1	10 ...	A2**	9
6	ENGLISH	B2	A2	A2**	9	FRENCH	B1	A2	A2	9 ...	A2	9
7	ENGLISH	B1	A2	B1	8	SPANISH	B2	B1	A2**	9 ...	B1**	8
8	ENGLISH	B2	B1	B1	8	GERMAN	B1	C2	C1	6 ...	C1	6
9	ENGLISH	A2	A2	A2	9	SPANISH	B2	B2	B2	7 ...	B2	7

Key libraries used for this project

Numpy

NumPy is an array-processing package. It is high-performance multidimensional arrays. It is the fundamental package which is used for scientific computing.

Pandas

Pandas is a library that allows data manipulation in Python. It is built on the top of Numpy that provides an easy way to create, manipulate, and wrangle the data.

Matplotlib

Matplotlib is a plotting library for Python programming language and it's a numerical mathematics extension of NumPy.

seaborn

Seaborn library provides a high-level interface for drawing attractive and informative statistical graphics.

Project's Code

```
import numpy as np
# numpy Implements multi-dimensional array and matrices
import pandas as pd
# matplot library For data manipulation and analysis
import matplotlib.pyplot as plt
# Plotting library for Python programming language and
#it's numerical mathematics extension NumPy
import seaborn as sns
# Seaborn provides a high-level interface for drawing attractive and
#informative statistical graphics
%matplotlib inline
sns.set()
school_data = pd.read_csv("F:\\schooldata.csv")
school_data.shape
# returns the number of rows and columns in the data set
 (163, 35)
# Importing training dataset
school_data.columns
# display all the columns in the data set
Index(['ROLL NO', 'CANDIDATE NAME', 'SUBJECT1', 'FA', 'SA', 'TOT', 'GP', 'SUBJECT2',
'FA.1', 'SA.1', 'TOT.1', 'GP.1', 'SUBJECT3', 'FA.2', 'SA.2', 'TOT.2', 'GP.2', 'SUBJECT4',
'FA.3', 'SA.3', 'TOT.3', 'GP.3','SUBJECT5', 'FA.4', 'SA.4', 'TOT.4', 'GP.4', 'RSLT', 'CGPA',
'ASL','SUBJECT6', 'FA.5', 'SA.5', 'TOT.5', 'GP.5'],
```

```
    dtype='object')

school_data.drop(school_data.columns[[0,1]], axis=1, inplace=True)
#Remove name and roll number as they are not required for computation
school_data.head()
#Print the top 5 rows from school's data
```

	SUBJECT1	FA	SA	TOT	GP	SUBJECT2	FA.1	SA.1	TOT.1	GP.1	...	TOT.4	GP.4	RSLT	CGPA	ASL	SUBJECT6	FA.5	SA.5	TOT.5	GP.5
0	101	B1	A2	A2	9	18	A2	A2	A2	9	...	A2**	9	QUAL	9.2	A2	--	--	--	--	--
1	101	B2	B1	B2	7	18	B1	B1	B1	8	...	B2	7	QUAL	7.0	B1	--	--	--	--	--
2	101	B1	A2	A2**	9	18	A2	A2	A2	9	...	A2	9	QUAL	9.0	A2	--	--	--	--	--
3	101	A2	A1	A1	10	18	A1	A1	A1	10	...	A1	10	QUAL	10.0	A1	--	--	--	--	--
4	101	B1	A2	A2	9	18	A1	A1	A1	10	...	A1	10	QUAL	9.6	A2	--	--	--	--	--

5 rows × 33 columns

```
# Replace subject code with subject name
school_data['SUBJECT1']=school_data['SUBJECT1'].replace(101,'ENGLISH')
replace_values={85:"HINDI",18:"FRENCH", 20:"GERMAN",96:"SPANISH" }
school_data=school_data.replace({"SUBJECT2":replace_values})

replace_values={41:"MATHS",165:"COMPUTER APPLICATIONS"}
school_data=school_data.replace({"SUBJECT3":replace_values})
replace_values={86:"SCIENCE",165:"COMPUTER APPLICATIONS",49:"PAINTING"}
school_data=school_data.replace({"SUBJECT4":replace_values})

replace_values={87:"SOCIAL SCIENCE",165:"COMPUTER APPLICATIONS", 49:"PAINTING"}
school_data=school_data.replace({"SUBJECT5":replace_values})
school_data.info()
# This will give Index, Datatype and Memory information

<class 'pandas.core.frame.DataFrame'>
RangeIndex: 163 entries, 0 to 162
Data columns (total 33 columns):
SUBJECT1        163 non-null object
FA              163 non-null object
SA              163 non-null object
TOT             163 non-null object
GP              163 non-null int64
SUBJECT2        163 non-null object
. . .
SUBJECT6        163 non-null object
FA.5            163 non-null object
SA.5            163 non-null object
TOT.5           163 non-null object
GP.5            163 non-null object
dtypes: float64(1), int64(1), object(31)
memory usage: 42.1+ KB
```

Data Clean-Up

#The following steps are carried out to clean or transform the data set.

- Dealing with the missing values
- Replacing the entries of SUBJECT6, FA.5,SA.5,TOT.5,GP.5
- Replacing all the subject codes with Subject names for easy analysis.

```
school_data['SUBJECT6']=school_data['SUBJECT6'].replace(0,'NA')
school_data['FA.5']=school_data['FA.5'].replace('--','NA')
school_data['SA.5']=school_data['SA.5'].replace('--','NA')
school_data['TOT.5']=school_data['TOT.5'].replace('--','NA')
school_data['GP.5']=school_data['GP.5'].replace('--','NA')
school_data['GP.4']=school_data['GP.4'].replace('--',0)

school_data.head()  #Top 5 rows
```

	SUBJECT1	FA	SA	TOT	GP	SUBJECT2	FA.1	SA.1	TOT.1	GP.1	...	TOT.4	GP.4	RSLT	CGPA	ASL	SUBJECT6	FA.5	SA.5	TOT.5	GP.5
0	ENGLISH	B1	A2	A2	9	FRENCH	A2	A2	A2	9	...	A2**	9	QUAL	9.2	A2	--	--	--	--	--
1	ENGLISH	B2	B1	B2	7	FRENCH	B1	B1	B1	8	...	B2	7	QUAL	7.0	B1	--	--	--	--	--
2	ENGLISH	B1	A2	A2**	9	FRENCH	A2	A2	A2	9	...	A2	9	QUAL	9.0	A2	--	--	--	--	--
3	ENGLISH	A2	A1	A1	10	FRENCH	A1	A1	A1	10	...	A1	10	QUAL	10.0	A1	--	--	--	--	--
4	ENGLISH	B1	A2	A2	9	FRENCH	A1	A1	A1	10	...	A1	10	QUAL	9.6	A2	--	--	--	--	--

```
5 rows × 33 columns
#show the data columns
school_data.columns
Index(['SUBJECT1', 'FA', 'SA', 'TOT', 'GP', 'SUBJECT2', 'FA.1', 'SA.1', 'TOT.1', 'GP.1',
'SUBJECT3', 'FA.2', 'SA.2', 'TOT.2', 'GP.2', 'SUBJECT4', 'FA.3', 'SA.3', 'TOT.3', 'GP.3',
'SUBJECT5', 'FA.4', 'SA.4', 'TOT.4', 'GP.4', 'RSLT', 'CGPA', 'ASL', 'SUBJECT6', 'FA.5',
'SA.5', 'TOT.5', 'GP.5'],
   dtype='object')
```

How many have students have passed the exam?

```
CountPass = school_data.apply(lambda x: True if x['RSLT'] == "QUAL" else False, axis=1)
# Get a boolean value for row in which value of Result column is QUAL
numCountPass = len(CountPass[CountPass == True].index)
# Count number of True in series
print("The total number of student pass " +str(numCountPass))
The total number of student pass 161
```

Show details of the passed students

```
school_data[school_data.RSLT=="QUAL"].count
<bound method DataFrame.count of    SUBJECT1  FA  SA   TOT  GP SUBJECT2 FA.1 SA.1 TOT.1 GP.1
...  TOT.4 GP.4  \
0    ENGLISH  B1  A2    A2   9   FRENCH   A2   A2    A2    9 ...   A2**   9
1    ENGLISH  B2  B1    B2   7   FRENCH   B1   B1    B1    8 ...    B2    7
2    ENGLISH  B1  A2  A2**   9   FRENCH   A2   A2    A2    9 ...    A2    9
3    ENGLISH  A2  A1    A1  10   FRENCH   A1   A1    A1   10 ...    A1   10
4    ENGLISH  B1  A2    A2   9   FRENCH   A1   A1    A1   10 ...    A1   10
..       ...  ..  ..   ...  ..      ...  ...  ...   ...  ... ...   ...  ...
159  ENGLISH  C2   D     D   4    HINDI   B2   E1    C2    5 ...    A2    9
```

```
160  ENGLISH  B2  C1    C1  6    HINDI   B1   C1   B2    7...   C2  5
161  ENGLISH  C1  C2    C1  6    HINDI   B2   C2   C1    6 ...  C2  5
162  ENGLISH  C1  C2    C2  5    HINDI   C1    D   C2    5 ...  A2  9

     RSLT  CGPA ASL SUBJECT6 FA.5 SA.5 TOT.5 GP.5
0    QUAL   9.2  A2       --   --   --    --   --
1    QUAL   7.0  B1       --   --   --    --   --
2    QUAL   9.0  A2       --   --   --    --   --
3    QUAL  10.0  A1       --   --   --    --   --
4    QUAL   9.6  A2       --   --   --    --   --
--   --
160  QUAL   5.6  B1       --   --   --    --   --
161  QUAL   5.6  B2       --   --   --    --   --
162  QUAL   5.8  B1       --   --   --    --   --

[161 rows x 33 columns]>
```

Easy method to know the count the number of pass and fail students

```
school_data.groupby(['RSLT'])['RSLT'].count()
RSLT
EIOP      2 (Number of student failed)
QUAL    161 (Number of student passed)
Name: RSLT, dtype: int64

sns.countplot(x='RSLT', data=school_data).set_title('Count plot for Passed.')
# Calculate count and show count details of all the failed students
Text(0.5,1,'Count plot for Passed.')
```

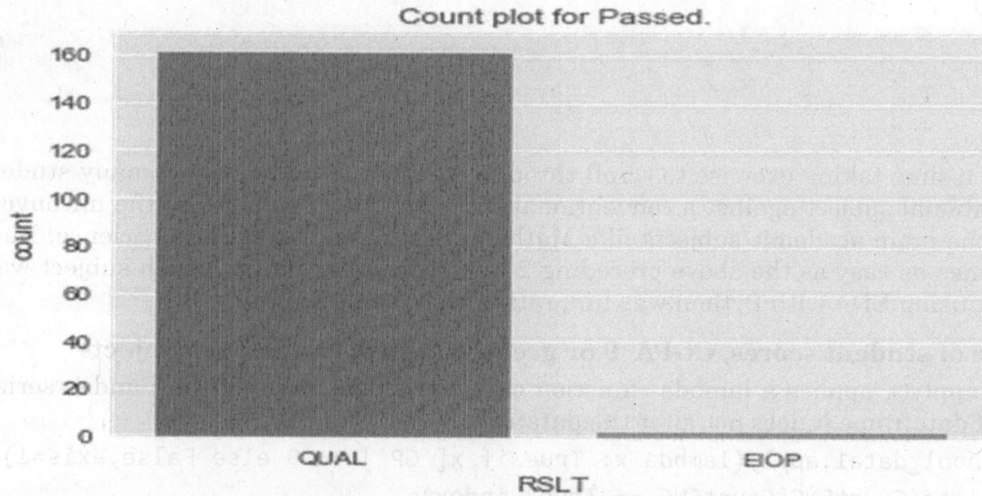


```
CountFail = school_data.apply(lambda x: True if x['RSLT'] == "QUAL" else False,axis=1)
# Get a boolean value for row in which value of Result column is QUAL
numCountFail = len(CountFail[CountFail == False].index)
print("The number of student failed " + str(numCountFail))
```

Output

```
The number of student failed 2
```

```
#Show the details of the failed student
school_data[school_data.RSLT=="EIOP"].count
#details of failed students
<bound method DataFrame.count of      SUBJECT1  FA  SA    TOT  GP SUBJECT2 FA.1 SA.1 TOT.1 GP.1
...  TOT.4 GP.4  \
120  ENGLISH  E1  E1  D **   4     HINDI   E1   E2    E2   -- ...      E2 --
147  ENGLISH   D  E1  C2**   5     HINDI    D   E2    E2   -- ...      E2 --

     RSLT CGPA ASL SUBJECT6 FA.5 SA.5 TOT.5 GP.5
120  EIOP  0.0  B2       --   --   --    --   --
147  EIOP  0.0  B2       --   --   --    --   --
[2 rows x 33 columns]>
```

How many had opted for computer applications?

```
CountCA3 = school_data.apply(lambda x: True if x['SUBJECT3'] == "COMPUTER APPLICATIONS" else
False,axis=1)
# Get a boolean value for row in which value of 'SUBJECT3' column is COMPUTER APLLICATIONS
numCountCA3 = len(CountCA3[CountCA3 == True].index)
CountCA4 = school_data.apply(lambda x: True if x['SUBJECT4'] == "COMPUTER APPLICATIONS" else
False,axis=1)
# Get a boolean value for row in which value of 'SUBJECT4' column is COMPUTER APLLICATIONS
numCountCA4 = len(CountCA4[CountCA4 == True].index)
CountCA5 = school_data.apply(lambda x: True if x['SUBJECT5'] == "COMPUTER APPLICATIONS" else
False, axis=1)
# Get a boolean value for row in which value of 'SUBJECT5' column is COMPUTER APLLICATIONS
numCountCA5 = len(CountCA5[CountCA5 == True].index)
CountCA=numCountCA3+numCountCA4+numCountCA5
print(CountCA)
```

Output

```
13
```

Observation

In general, it is a time taking exercise to scroll through the data to find out how many students have opted for an unconventional subject against a conventional subject, as they can choose the unconventional subject against any of the main academic subjects like Mathematics, Science and Social Science. But using Python for this, it becomes as easy as the above preceding 2-line code. Also, finding which subject was better for an average student using EDA with Python was fun, rather than being painful.

Count number of student scores, CGPA 9 or greater than 9, in various subjects

The function apply(), applies a lambda function on every single value of the Pandas series. It returns a modified copy of dataframe it does not alter the dataframe.

```
CountENG = school_data1.apply(lambda x: True if x['GP'] >= 9 else False,axis=1)
numCountENG = len(CountENG[CountENG == True].index)

CountLAN = school_data1.apply(lambda x: True if x['GP.1'] >= 9 else False,axis=1)
numCountLAN = len(CountLAN[CountLAN == True].index)

CountMAT = school_data1.apply(lambda x: True if x['GP.2'] >= 9 else False,axis=1)
numCountMAT = len(CountMAT[CountMAT == True].index)
```

```
CountSC = school_data1.apply(lambda x: True if x['GP.3'] >= 9 else False,axis=1)
numCountSC = len(CountSC[CountSC == True].index)

CountSST = school_data1.apply(lambda x: True if x['GP.4'] >= 9 else False,axis=1)
numCountSST = len(CountSST[CountSST == True].index)
print(numCountENG)
print(numCountLAN)
print(numCountMAT)
print(numCountSC)
print(numCountSST)
```

Output:

```
74
71
63
58
69
```

Compare the A1 among various subjects

```
from matplotlib import pyplot as plt
Subjects=['English', '2ndLanguage','Maths','Science','Social Science']
No_of_A1=[74,71,63,58,69]
expld=[0.2,0.1,0,0,0.1]
plt.pie(No_of_A1, labels=Subjects,autopct='%0.1f%%',explode=expld)
plt.title("Comparison of A1 between subjects")
plt.show()
```

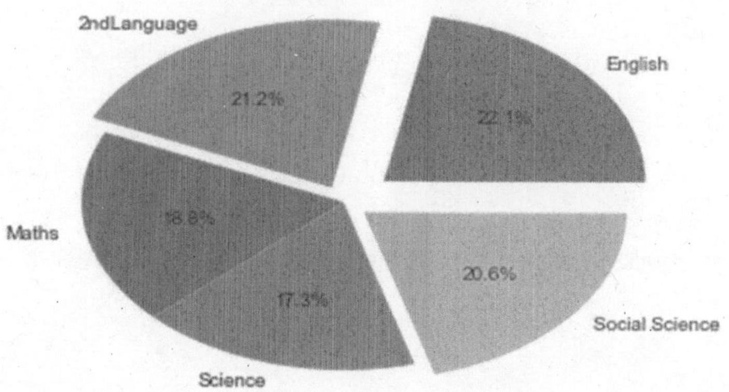

Inference

The maximum number of A1s is in English, followed by the 2nd language, then Social Science, then Maths and the least in Science.

Future prospects

- Extend the functionality to capture the data of different teachers of the same subject and compare the teacher effectiveness ratio.
- Extend the functionality to capture the data of different sexes and compare the gender-wise performance of the students.
- Extend the functionality to capture the data of different years and compare and predict the result for the next year.
- Extend the functionality to split the data of different subjects in different columns, and compare the data between unrelated subjects also.